the greatest dishes!

also by anya von bremzen

Fiesta! A Celebration of Latin Hospitality

Terrific Pacific Cookbook

Please to the Table: The Russian Cookbook

the greatest dishes!

around the world in 80 recipes

anya von bremzen

HarperCollins*Publishers*

FIRST EDITION

Designed by Joel Avirom and Jason Snyder

Printed on acid-free paper

Library of Congress Cataloging-in-Publication Data

Von Bremzen, Anya.
The greatest dishes! around the world in 80 recipes / Anya von Bremzen—1st ed.
p. cm.
Includes bibliographical references and index.
ISBN 0-06-019731-5
1. Cookery, International. I. Title.

TX725.A1V653 2004
641.59—dc21   2003050941
ISBN 0-06-019731-5
04 05 06 07 08 ❖/RRD 10 9 8 7 6 5 4 3 2 1

the
greatest
dishes!
around the world
in 80 recipes

anya von bremzen

HarperCollins*Publishers*

HarperCollins books may be purchased for educational, business, or sales
promotional use. For information, please write: Special Markets Department, HarperCollins
Publishers Inc., 10 East 53rd Street, New York, NY 10022.

FIRST EDITION

Designed by Joel Avirom and Jason Snyder

Printed on acid-free paper

Library of Congress Cataloging-in-Publication Data

Von Bremzen, Anya.
The greatest dishes! around the world in 80 recipes / Anya von Bremzen—1st ed.
p. cm.
Includes bibliographical references and index.
ISBN 0-06-019731-5
1. Cookery, International. I. Title.

TX725.A1V653 2004
641.59—dc21   2003050941
ISBN 0-06-019731-5
04 05 06 07 08 ❖/RRD 10 9 8 7 6 5 4 3 2 1

To my mother and her generous table

a dish is only as great as the people behind it. My profound gratitude to all the people below who shared their meals, their advice, their recipes, and their kindness on the various stages of my journey.

Italy: Massimo Bottura of Osteria Francescana and Signora Luisa; Antonio Pace, Francesco Colonnesi, Pietro Uslengo, Cesare Benelli, and the Ferrari family of Al Bersaglieri restaurant. **Spain:** Clara Maria de Amezua and Gabriela Llamas, Jose Carlos Capel, Juan Carlos Alonso, Pilar Castro of La Riua restaurant, and Pilar Vico of the Tourist Office of Spain. **France:** the Minguella brothers of Le Miramar restaurant, Serge Zarokian of L'Escale, Thierry Huck of Marseilles-Provence Tourism Board, Giles Pudlowski, Francois Simon, Claude, Rigaud of Le Soufflé restaurant, Fatéma Hal of Mansouria restaurant, Dorrie Greenspan, Stephanie Teuwen, Christopher Petkanas, and Adriana Feraru and her mom. **U.K.:** Elisabeth

acknowledgments

Luard and Martine de Geus of the Dorchester Hotel. **Turkey:** Engin Akin. **Greece:** Aglaia Kremezi and Diana Farr Louis. **Korea:** Sung Hee, Dr. Han, and folks at the Suwon Kalbi Factory. **China:** Hwang Xiao Cheng in Chonquing; and in Hong Kong, Stephen Wong, Willie Mark, and the Hong Kong Tourism Board. **Japan:** Robbie Swinnerton of Japan Times, and Moto and Hitomi Shibata. **India:** Rakesh Sethi, the Oberoi Hotels, and Nawab of Loharu Durru Aimaduddin Ahmad and Begum Fauzia Ahmad. **Peru:** Mariano Valderrama and Marisa Giulfo. **Mexico:** the Cervantes family, Irene Acosta, and Soledad Abella. **Singapore:** Mr. and Mrs. Ling. **Thailand:** Maprang Waranthon. **Russia:** my family and friends.

In the United States, I thank Nina Simonds, Stephen Raichlen, Francisco Gutierrez of Le Cirque restaurant, Scott Peacock of Watershed restaurant, Bruce Cost, John Thorne and Matt Lewis Thorne, Terry Zarikian, Sam Hayward of Fore Street restaurant, Christian Delouvrier, Viviana Carballo, Ari Weinzweig of Zingermans, Piedad (aka "arepa lady"), Pia Martinez, Hiroko Shimbo,

Eleanor Bertino and the Rose Pistola restaurant, Fern Berman, Alison Tozzi, Wendy Taylor, and Dun Gifford and Sara Baer-Sinnott of Oldways Preservation and Exchange Trust.

Jane Dystel, my agent, is perfection personified; every author should be so lucky. At HarperCollins, a special thank-you to my editor, Susan Friedland. Where would I be without her enthusiasm for this project—not to mention her brilliant editing and her chicken soup? Thanks also to Califia Suntree for being so helpful and patient, and to Joel Avirom, Jason Snyder, and Roberto de Vicq de Cumptich for the design and cover.

At *Travel+Leisure* magazine, I am dearly indebted to Nancy Novogrod for keeping me on the road all these years. Were it not for her support this book would never have seen the light. At *Food & Wine* magazine I thank Dana Cowin, editor-in-chief extraordinaire, and Tina Ujlaki for so much great food information and a terrific jerk marinade.

Cheers to my food friends, Lauren Deen, Kate Krader, Mitchell Davis, Sam Frier, Steven Hall, and Nancy Jenkins for all their help and advice, and to Melissa Clark whose generosity extended way beyond the incredible ice cream recipe. Without all my pals who came to dinner, critiqued my food, and kept me in stitches until 4 A.M., my kitchen would be lonely and boring. Still, everything I know about hospitality, I learned from my mother, Larisa Frumkin. It is to her and her meals that this book is dedicated.

My final thank-you is to Barry Yourgrau for . . . well, *everything*.

contents

Introduction xii • **apple pie** 2 • **arepas** 6 • **bastilla** 10

biryani 14 • **blini** 20 • **borshch** 24 • **bouillabaisse** 28

caesar salad 34 • **cassoulet** 38 • **ceviche** 44

cheesecake 48 • **chelo** 52 • **chicken soup** 56

chocolate cake 60 • **chowder** 64 • **couscous** 68

crême brulée 74 • **dolma** 78 • **doughnuts** 82

eggs benedict 86 • **feijoada** 90 • **fish & chips** 94

fried chicken 98 • **gazpacho** 102 • **gefilte fish** 106

gnocchi 110 • **hamburger** 114 • **hummus** 118 • **ice cream** 122

imam bayildi 126 • **indian curry** 130 • **jerk pork** 134

korean barbecued short ribs 137 • **laksa** 140

lasagne 144 • **lemon tart** 150 • **lobster rolls** 153

macaroni and cheese 156 • **meatballs** 160

minestrone alla genovese 164 • miso-glazed black cod 167

mole poblano 170 • moussaka 174 • onion soup 178

pad thai 181 • paella 184 • palov 188 • peking duck 192

pesto 196 • pho 200 • pizza 204 • polenta 208 • potato gratin 212

potato salad 216 • pot-au-feu 220 • rice pudding 224

risotto 228 • roast beef with yorkshire pudding 232

roast chicken 236 • roast leg of lamb 240 • sancocho 244

saté 248 • sesame noodles 252 • soba 256 • soufflé 260

spaghetti alle vongole 264 • spanakopita 268 • steak 272

stir-fried greens 276 • summer rolls 280 • sushi 284

tacos 289 • tamales 294 • tandoori chicken 299

tarte tatin 303 • thai red curry 306 • tom yum kung 311

tortilla de patata 314 • trifle 318 • wiener schnitzel 322

appendix: anya's address book 326 • bibliography 330 • index 338

i embarked on this project for one simple reason.

This was the cookbook I was dying to have on my shelf, at my bedside, in my kitchen—but somehow never found in a bookstore.

I wanted a book filled only with recipes we know, love, and want to cook time and time again. A Gold List of the world's greatest hits, featuring authentic recipes and mouthwatering stories.

I wasn't thinking chefs' food, trendy food, great-but-obscure food, or even my own personal favorites. No, what I craved was a collection of classics that kept their grip on our taste buds through changing fashions and fleeting fads.

A pure and crunchy-cool Caesar salad, as might have been tossed by Caesar Cardini himself in Tijuana back in the twenties. A soul-warming onion soup and a glistening-brown tarte Tatin, such as you find at certain burnished Parisian bistros. A *mole* they'd applaud back in Puebla.

introduction

I envisioned vast earthenware crocks of cassoulet baking away in my oven, a pesto as green and fragrant as those in Liguria, a Vietnamese *pho* that would transport me to the clamorous backstreets of Hanoi.

When prepared with love and respect, these classics are a revelation even to the most jaded palate. Like a Cole Porter tune, Chanel No. 5, or a venerable steakhouse they are timeless and irresistible.

My idea seemed wonderfully compelling and simple. Many of these recipes were certainly all out there—somewhere. But what if I wanted easy access to authentic versions of all these treasured classics? How many cookbooks would it take? How many hours spent leafing through back issues of food magazines? And where exactly was that lavishly illustrated bouillabaisse article, or that step-by-step guide to a real paella, or that handwritten recipe for moussaka passed on to me by a Greek colleague? Where were they when I wanted them?

After a while it was obvious that to have all these treats collected neatly between two covers, I'd have to write the book myself.

And so I did.

getting started From the start, *The Greatest Dishes!* seemed an ambitious undertaking. But deep down, I felt strangely unfazed by the challenge.

Having been born and raised in a Communist Moscow of dire food shortages and severe restrictions on travel, I feel particularly blessed to be traveling and writing about food for a living. For the last fifteen years, I've been roaming the globe in pursuit of authentic flavors. For my previous books, *Please to the Table: The Russian Cookbook; Terrific Pacific;* and *Fiesta: A Celebration of Latin Hospitality,* I trekked all over Asia, South America, Europe, and the former Soviet Union and its neighbors, from Turkey to near the Arctic Circle.

These days, I continue my quest for culinary greatness as a food columnist for *Travel+Leisure* magazine, often traveling for five months of the year. I lead my readers to the ultimate Shanghainese dumplings, the sprightliest gazpacho in Andalusia (Le Escudera in Ronda), or New Delhi's smokiest tandoori chicken (at Dastarkhwan-e-Karim). If perfect versions of these great dishes exist, I'm pretty sure I know where to find them.

To research this book, I prowled even farther afield. I schlepped to the drab town of Suwon, Korea, to find the best barbecued short ribs. I discussed the fine points of France's greatest fish soup with the president of Marseilles' Bouillabaisse Charter. I smacked my lips through a dozen paellas in the Levante region of Spain, and spent a week around Venice eating *only* risottos.

I've collected recipes and tips from professional chefs and wizened old ladies, as well as from renowned restaurant critics and complete strangers all over the world. Back home, I've compared notes with fellow cookbook writers, and food magazine editors whose job it is to keep an eye peeled for the best recipes.

I am lucky enough to live in New York with its wealth of great restaurants and fabulous chefs, and specifically in Jackson Heights, Queens, the most ethnically diverse chunk of metropolis in the country. Here, discoveries awaited me right on my doorstep: a heart-melting *carnitas* recipe courtesy of my neighborhood Mexican grocery store, a *sancocho* (a pan-Latin stew) to die for shared with me by my former cleaning lady.

The exhilaration and adventure of finding great food never wane. I'm thrilled to share with you the delicious fruits of my quests.

around the world in 80 dishes   This could be one *veee-ry* long book, containing many more recipes and still more variants of each dish. But with so many good things to eat and so little time, deciding what to cook shouldn't induce a panic attack. The less-is-more approach seemed especially welcome: a perfect number of edible masterpieces cooks would want to revisit time and time again.

I considered structuring the book geographically, or more conventionally, by courses—appetizers, salads, and so on. But that seemed to obscure the focus. Each of these dishes is a world unto itself, and deserves to be treated as such. So the recipes are organized alphabetically. Big one-pot dishes make up the largest proportion—and that's exactly the way I think it should be.

True, the enterprise of reducing the world's wealth of food to eighty recipes seemed impossible at times. But I was always convinced there was a method to my madness. How did I choose the recipes? Well, read on.

choosing the dishes   Roast chicken? No *way*—it's way too plain. Fish and chips a great dish? You gotta be kidding! What's so hot about hummus, anyway? You *must* include *mechouie*, artichokes *barigoule*, madeleines, brownies, chili con carne. . . . C'mon, moussaka is so *over*. At least thirty of your dishes should be desserts, absolutely. No American will ever cook *feijoada*.

And what the hell is *palov*, anyway?

These were only a few of the e-mails and comments from colleagues and friends. I'm sure you, too, will have something to add to the chorus. Each of these remarks caused me sleepless nights.

In selecting the dishes, I was always intensely aware of how relative and problematic the very notion of a canon can be—especially a canon centered on American, French, and Italian masterpieces. But this, you see, was the point of the book. At the end of the day, a classic is a classic is a classic, and a great dish is a great dish.

I began by making a list of dishes whose greatness would not be contested: cassoulet, paella, bouillabaisse, hamburgers, potato salad, apple pie, tandoori chicken, and the like. It wasn't enough for a dish to be plain delicious: it had to answer to adjectives like *classic, archetypal, iconic, mythical, legendary,* or just *wildly popular.*

This took me to about forty recipes. The next twenty were trickier. And with the last twenty, the nightmares started for real. Should I lose an Indian dish to make room for a Turkish one? Would lobster stew or lobster roll better represent a great New England tradition? How to make rice pudding exciting all over again?

I've done my best to come up with a great list of great dishes. For every raised eyebrow I can offer ten reasons this or that item had to be included. For every omission, I feel the deepest regret. But even with just eighty recipes, the book offers a treasure trove of great food.

seeking the perfect recipe
With the recipe lineup finally finished, I moved now to the equally challenging task of choosing the ultimate version of each. My first impulse was to seek out the most inconic rendering: macaroni and cheese with elbow macaroni and Cheddar, as opposed to Gorgonzola and penne. A simple traditional couscous with seven vegetables. A quintessentially Valencian paella with rabbit and chicken.

But while striving for objectivity, somehow I ended up with an extremely personal book, with its flavors dictated by my passion, taste, and experiences traveling and eating. I know that moment well by now: you taste and taste, then you eat, you swoon, you put down your fork. "Search no further," your taste buds inform you.

Once a version of a particular dish was settled, I parked myself by the stove and rolled up my sleeves. Some recipes worked like a dream the first time around. Others, which looked good on paper or tasted incredible in a restaurant, never delivered. Sometimes I nixed a dish just because the homemade version never lived up to the Platonic ideal. Friends and colleagues came by. They ate, they criticized, they licked their fingers, they frowned. I listened. For every flop, there was a triumph. When all was said and done, I'd never eaten so well in my life as I did at my own house during recipe-testing days.

what you will find in this book The bulk of recipes here represent beloved golden oldies, from apple pie to Wiener schnitzel. But there are also surprises: *arepas,* the celestial griddled corncakes from Colombia; the intriguing Malaysian *laksa,* a baroque coconut noodle soup with myriad garnishes; Turkey's melting *imam bayildi,* or eggplant braised in olive oil—as well as Korean barbecued short ribs, Brazil's famed *feijoada,* and one incredible pilaf from far-flung Uzbekistan.

You might or might not know these dishes from travels or menus of ethnic restaurants. But in their respective homelands, they enjoy cultlike devotion and deserve a firm place in any great-dish pantheon—and in every cook's repertoire. I wish I had room for more exotica. But that would mean missing out on stalwarts like chowder and chocolate cake.

Recipes, however, are always only part of the story.

Behind each great dish there is a place, a history, a portrait of a cook, the evolution of a technique. And invariably, endless debates. For me, recipes come alive only in context. So along with the dishes you will find their "biographies": essays on their histories and the origins of their names, quotes from authorities on their preparations, all garnished with my own travel impressions and recollections. Meanwhile, the Cook's Notes will offer hands-on info on ordering special ingredients, techniques, utensils, substitutions, advanced preparation tips, variations, and serving suggestions.

are the recipes easy? I firmly believe that cooking should be a pleasure, and I'll embrace a shortcut whenever I can. Not for me are heroics like home-curing bacon or making tortillas from scratch. If I can buy decent canned chicken broth, I won't bother making my own. By testing and re-testing I have made the recipes as simple and clear as possible. However, maintaining integrity and authenticity always comes first. While you can make a very fine— if not exalted—polenta without any stirring, instant couscous is a sorry substitute for the real thing. A cassoulet is a week-long affair and this is how most people like it.

The same goes for ingredients. Nothing matches a risotto made with a boutique northern Italian rice or a crème brûlée scented with the finest vanilla beans from Madagascar. With so many excellent mail-order sources, getting authentic ingredients is as easy as logging onto the net. And what a difference great raw ingredients make.

At the end of the day, the recipes here are as easy or as hard as they need to be great. Once you master a dish and find the ingredients, you will turn to it again and again.

Fame has its price. Many great classics have spurred countless versions that often bear little resemblance to the original. Others have turned into sad takeout clichés or landed in a can or a package mix. Discovering their true taste is nothing short of a revelation. This book's mission is to restore their joyous uniqueness—with a few shortcuts here and there.

the greatest dishes!

never mind that the English cherish it as more Britannic than the Beatles or Westminster Abbey. Never mind that every French, Dutch, and Russian woman has an heirloom recipe for it up her sleeve somewhere. Or that the fruit that gives it flavor isn't indigenous to any state in the Union.

America is the world's biggest producer of apples, and apple pie is so often invoked as its star-spangled essence, one begins to wonder if it really exists in regular, nonmetaphoric form. Oh, but it does.

We eat our apple pies with a wedge of sharp Cheddar and lick our fingers. We stir cream into the filling and call it Dutch. We bake pies under a crumbly blanket of streusel, beneath a pastry lid, or a cute lattice screen. And for almost a century we've been savoring our apple pie à la mode, with a dollop of vanilla ice cream. There's even such thing as a fried apple pie.

apple pie

Pie, not necessarily made of fruit, figures prominently in history's banquet. The ancient Romans, who likely got the idea from the Greeks, baked whole birds between layers of dough. Medieval European cooks forged "coffyn" pies of towering raised pastry to hold chunks of game, for instance, in a thick armature of dough—a mode of preserving the filling ingredients. This pastry was often not intended for eating, it should be noted. And "coffyn" here meant "container," predating its usage by the undertaker.

Mince pies that mixed meat, dried fruits, and fat also arrived in this age. They point the way to the term "pie" itself, first recorded in the 1300s in England, inspired by the magpie bird with its messy nest of bits and pieces. Daintier fruit pies—also called pasties—appeared in Elizabethan times, as sugar became less pricey. A line from the poet Robert Greene to his lover—"Thy breath is like a steame of apple-pyes"—suggests that they were probably enjoyed warm, and that the apple already held a special place of regard in the English eater's eye. And his stomach.

The double-crust pie, however, really belongs to America, where the apple tale began with the Pilgrims, who brought recipes and seeds with them in 1620. According to historian Evan Jones, however, prototypical American-style pie seems to have been the handiwork of the Pennsylvania Dutch, who refined the art of enveloping fruit in pastry.

Then, in the early 1800s, a buttermilk-loving vegetarian named Johnny Chapman more or less single-handedly made the apple America's fruit, and thereby America's pie. As "Johnny Appleseed" of every third-grader's lore, Chapman in his tin-pot hat went along planting seedlings (his seed scattering of legend appears to be just that) from the Allegheny to Indiana, where he died. Seeds from these orchards then spread west with the wives of the Oregon trail—who also took along dried apples to go into pie crusts they rolled out on wagon seats.

By mid-century, apple pie was the all-American dessert. Mark Twain pined for it from Europe in the 1870s (despite his occasional sneers about "bullet-proof dough"). Americans ate it round-the-clock and grew so pie-mad in general that health reformers started bringing out the knives for the dish's crusty excesses. "All forms of so-called pie are to be condemned," sniffed diet authority Sara Rorer in 1902.

Well, no one listened. The apple is wholesome and refreshing, and apple pie transforms the fruit's best qualities into something unbearably aromatic and plush, all wrapped in a flaky heft of crust. And it keeps. And its warm smell reminds you of home.

apple pie

cook's notes It took me quite some time to come up with the apple pie of my dreams: one that's scrumptious, elegant in its simplicity, and all about apples. Unconventionally, I bake my apples first, which intensifies their flavor and solves most of the notorious apple pie problems: apple shrinkage, a collapsed top crust, the need to rely on cornstarch or flour as thickener. The result is a wonderful brown mass of fruit packed into a buttery crust.

crust

2 cups all-purpose flour

Large pinch of salt

1 tablespoon granulated sugar

½ cup (1 stick) unsalted butter, chilled and cut into small pieces

7 tablespoons good-quality lard or solid vegetable shortening, chilled and cut into small pieces

1 teaspoon distilled white vinegar or cider vinegar

3 tablespoons full-fat sour cream

2 to 4 tablespoons ice water

filling

4 large Granny Smith apples, peeled, cored, and halved

5 large Golden Delicious apples, peeled, cored, and halved

½ cup packed dark brown sugar, plus more to taste

½ cup granulated sugar, plus more to taste

1½ teaspoons ground cinnamon

1½ teaspoons pure vanilla extract

4 tablespoons unsalted butter, melted

2 tablespoons fresh lemon juice

2 to 3 tablespoons Calvados or brandy

Best Vanilla Ice Cream (page 124) or Cheddar cheese, for serving

1 Make the crust: Place the flour, salt, and sugar in the bowl of a food processor and pulse to combine. Add the butter and pulse six times. Add the shortening and pulse until the mixture resembles coarse crumbs but there are still lumps the size of a pea. Add the vinegar and the sour cream and pulse a few more times. Do not overprocess.

2 Transfer the dough to a large mixing bowl and sprinkle in 2 tablespoons of the water, stirring with a fork to distribute the moisture. Squeeze a piece of dough between your fingers; if it doesn't come together, add more water, 1 tablespoon at a time. Divide the dough in half and quickly press each half into a ball. On a lightly floured surface, smear each ball with the heels of your hands to flatten. Using only your fingertips, and working quickly, press each ball into a 6-inch disk. Wrap the disks in plastic and refrigerate for at least 1 hour and up to 24 hours.

anya von bremzen

3 Make the filling: Preheat the oven to 425°F. and line two rimmed baking sheets with foil. Cut each apple half into four wedges, transferring the wedges to a large mixing bowl. Toss the apples to mix them up, then toss with ½ cup each of the brown and granulated sugars, the cinnamon, vanilla, melted butter, and lemon juice. Arrange half of the apples in one layer on each baking sheet and bake until the juices thrown off by the apples are slightly thickened, about 25 minutes. With a spatula, transfer the apple slices and the accumulated juices to a large bowl and let cool completely. (The filling can be prepared up to one day ahead.) Before filling the pie, taste the apples and add more white or brown sugar if you'd like it sweeter. Toss the filling gently with the Calvados.

4 Take the crust out of the refrigerator and let stand at room temperature for 10 minutes. Roll out one of the disks between two sheets of waxed paper to a 13-inch circle. Fit the circle into a 9-inch pie pan and, using scissors, trim off all but ½ inch of overhang. Roll out the second disk to an 11-inch circle.

5 Transfer the filling into the pie shell, mounting it slightly toward the middle. Brush the outside rim of the bottom crust with water. Cover with the top crust, center it over the filling, and trim to fit. Fold in the overhang and press the tines of a fork dipped in flour around the edges to seal. Make four or five vent slits in the top crust and refrigerate the pie for 20 minutes. Preheat the oven to 425°F.

6 Set the pie on a large baking sheet and bake until the top crust is golden brown and crisp, about 40 minutes. Cool the pie on a rack until warm. Serve with vanilla ice cream or cheese, if desired.

Makes one 9-inch pie to serve 8

there are certain foods—starches mainly—that power entire cultures. How could Mexico endure without tortillas? Where would France be *sans* baguettes? Wouldn't life in northern India come to a halt without chapatis? Likewise, Colombians and Venezuelans couldn't survive for a second without *arepas,* the moonlike griddled corn cakes referred to as *el pan nuestro* (our daily bread), or the "bread of the Andes."

Eaten by indigenous Indians "long before Christ handed out communion breads," as one Colombian food critic put it to me, arepas are one of South America's many tributes to maize. Some believe that the word derives from *erepe,* which means maize in the Cariban language of Cumanagoto Indians. Others point to *aripe,* the clay griddle originally used for cooking the cakes. In

arepas

pre-industrial days, when the corn masa was prepared in a hollowed-out tree trunk called a *pilon,* arepa making was a mythically arduous process. Degerming and hulling required the Sisyphian labor

of hitting the kernels against the *pilon* with a double-headed wooden mallet. The corn was then boiled, ground on a large concave stone, mixed with water, shaped into patties, and grilled over charcoal. Whoever invented the *trillador,* a commercial thrasher that hulls corn en masse, brought liberation to millions of arm-weary arepa makers. And while purists might insist on grinding their own masa, most cooks today resort to the perfectly delicious *masarepa,* or precooked arepa flour.

I suspect that between them, Colombia and Venezuela have an arepa variation for every day of the year. There are plate-size arepas and arepas the shape of a Ping-Pong ball. Thick arepas and arepas as thin as tortillas called *arepas de pela,* or sheet arepas. You can choose among sweet arepas, cheesy arepas, arepas flavored with pork crackling, and arepas that are even blander than grits. Venezuelans like to split them and stuff them with minced sausage, ground beef, or the national chicken-avocado salad called *reina pepiada.* Colombians might enjoy them for breakfast simply slathered with butter and cheese or topped with a fried egg.

Not all arepas are created equal. Some are as appealing as Styrofoam while others shoot for the stars. I live in a Hispanic neighborhood where arepa stalls outnumber hot-dog carts three to one, but the arepas made by Piedad were in a league of their own. Piedad—aka "arepa lady"—was a tiny woman with an angelic smile who hawked arepas at night on one seedy streetcorner in Jackson Heights, New York.

When it comes to arepas, Colombians firmly believe in that *toque magico*—the magic touch. Piedad had the touch, but the true magic of her corn cakes proved to be lots of milk—instead of the usual water—plus extra doses of butter, cheese, eggs, and sugar. The resulting arepas are truly celestial: crusty and sizzled on the outside, creamy, fragrant, and cheesy within. Once fried, the cakes are smeared with butter and lashings of grated white cheese that melts into the surface. It's a breakfast of angels.

arepas

cook's notes **cook's notes** Arepas are easy to make provided you can locate the precooked arepa flour, available at most Hispanic markets. It can be called *masarepa, harina de maiz precocida,* or *areparina;* the Goya brand is excellent. Arepa flour looks like very fine cornmeal (*masa harina*), with which it *shouldn't* be confused.

2 cups milk

4 tablespoons unsalted butter, chopped, plus 1½ tablespoons in one piece

1½ cups precooked white arepa flour (see Cook's Notes)

1 teaspoon salt

1½ tablespoons sugar

1 cup grated processed mozzarella (not fresh Italian mozzarella)

Vegetable oil, for brushing the griddle

1¼ cups finely grated Hispanic white cheese (*queso blanco*) or mozzarella

1 In a small saucepan, bring 1½ cups of the milk to a boil, reserving the rest of the cold milk for kneading the arepas. Strain the milk into a bowl and add the 4 tablespoons butter. Let stand while preparing the next step.

2 In a large bowl, stir together the arepa flour, salt, sugar, and mozzarella. Make a well in the middle and pour in the hot milk. Stir the masa and milk together until there are no lumps. Knead the mixture, sprinkling in the remaining ½ cup milk, until you have a smooth, sticky dough. This should take about 5 minutes.

3 Roll the dough out to a ½-inch-thick rectangle between two sheets of waxed paper. With a cookie cutter or rim of a bowl, cut out 3-inch circles. Re-roll the scraps and cut out more circles. You should have eight cakes.

4 Brush a griddle or a large cast-iron skillet lightly with oil and preheat over medium heat. Cook as many arepas as will fit, until they are deep-golden and slightly crusty on the outside, about 4 minutes per side. Keep separating the arepas from the skillet with a metal spatula, or they will stick. Keep the finished arepas warm in a low oven while making the rest.

5 To serve, place the remaining 1½ tablespoons of butter on a fork and brush the hot arepas with the butter. Immediately sprinkle with a generous coating of grated cheese, and serve.

Makes 8 arepas to serve 8 as breakfast or snack

galician empanada, brimming with seafood and melting onion. Greek village pies, bulging with cheese and wild greens. Russian kulebiaka, magnificent with salmon. These are just some of the world's grandest pies. None, however, is as extravagant or indulgent as the Moroccan bastilla.

The name transliterated in a dozen ways, the dish featured at the bounteous Moroccan *difas* (banquets) and eaten authentically with one's hands, bastilla can be as big as a table and as ornate as a Moorish garden pavilion. The pastry defies gravity. The top is lavishly frosted with confectioners' sugar and cinnamon. The filling combination of gamy pigeon meat, sugar, sweet spices, and a great many eggs is truly unforgettable. Perhaps more even than couscous, bastilla embodies the essence of Moroccan cuisine.

bastilla

Though phyllo is normally used outside Morocco, the traditional dough for bastilla is called *warka*. Producing what might be the world's lightest and crunchiest pastry is so complex that even self-respecting Moroccan matriarchs don't normally tackle it. Warka is something better left to the specialty shops—or to the *dadas,* women descended from Sudanese slaves often employed as domestic help and regarded as guardians of Morocco's culinary secrets. "Unless as a little girl you have thrown, like a ball held back by an elastic band, the dab of dough into the hot metal tray, you will never achieve perfection of pastry as white, fine and light as tissue paper," writes Zette Guinaudeau in *Traditional Moroccan Cooking*.

Historian Clifford Wright traces the term *bastilla*—aka *bisteeya, bastella, pestilla*—to the Spanish *pastilla*, or "pastry," itself derived from Latin *pastilum*, or "bread." For Wright, this Moroccan pie appears to be a relic from the endlessly rich and varied Hispano-Muslim repertoire. Without the opulence of the medieval courtly cooking of the Andaluz caliphates, says Wright, Berber cuisine might have remained nothing more than subsistence cooking. (I have a feeling that nationalist Moroccan historians would contest this point.) Bastilla, in turn, counts among its cousins the *pasteles* of the Turkish Jews, the Syrian *pastilla* (fried spiced meat pies), and the Corsican pies called *bastella*.

Today in Morocco, the filling for the bastilla varies slightly from region to region and from cook to cook—looser and chunkier in Fez, sweeter in Marrakech, denser in Tangier, and gamier in Oujda. But the effect remains the same: the world's grandest pie and the pinnacle of North African gastronomy.

warka art While you probably won't be making warka at home any time soon, you might want to know that it starts with small globes of soft dough deftly stretched into near-transparent large round leaves. Held by one end, these leaves are briefly flung onto a device known as a *tobsil*, a griddle-like metal sheet propped on a low charcoal burner. When turned over, the tobsil becomes a receptacle for baking bastilla. Before getting a chance to brown, the finished warka leaves are removed and laid between towels. An average bastilla takes at least 40 leaves!

duck bastilla

cook's notes   An authentic bastilla is so incredibly rich, sweet, and time-consuming to make, one is inevitably forced to compromise. The filling has always posed a problem for me: squab or wild pigeon is the real deal, but expensive and hard to get. Chicken is a rather bland second-best. A solution came to mind during dinner at an excellent Moroccan restaurant in New York called Zitoune, where the chef uses dark duck meat to exquisite effect. (If you'd still prefer chicken, use skinless thighs.)

duck and almond filling

6 duck legs (about 3 pounds total), skinned, trimmed of all fat, and separated into drumsticks and thighs, or 3 pounds skinned chicken thighs

Salt and freshly ground black pepper to taste

5 to 8 tablespoons unsalted butter

3 medium onions, finely chopped

4 large garlic cloves, crushed through a press

2 teaspoons granulated sugar

1¾ teaspoons ground cinnamon, plus more, for decorating the bastilla

1 teaspoon ground ginger

¼ teaspoon freshly grated nutmeg

Large pinch of saffron threads pulverized in a mortar

1½ cups water

2½ teaspoons honey

¼ cup fresh orange juice

2 tablespoons fresh lemon juice

4 tablespoons finely chopped parsley

4 large eggs, beaten until frothy

2 cups blanched almonds, very lightly toasted and coarsely ground in a food processor

½ cup confectioners' sugar, plus more, for decorating the bastilla

pastry

14 sheets phyllo dough, thawed for about 10 minutes

Mild olive oil, for brushing the phyllo

The filling can be prepared ahead, refrigerated overnight, and brought to room temperature before using. For crispest results, the bastilla should be baked right before serving or at least warmed up in a very hot oven. Lots of butter in the filling makes it rich and moist; use as much as you dare.

1 Prepare the duck filling: Rub the legs with salt and pepper. In a large, heavy casserole, preferably nonstick, melt at least 3 tablespoons of butter over medium heat. Add the onions and garlic and sauté for 5 minutes without letting them brown. Add the duck pieces and cook for 3 minutes, turning once. Add the sugar, 1 teaspoon cinnamon, ginger, nutmeg, saffron, and water, and bring to a simmer. Cover and simmer over low heat until the duck is fall-off-the-bone tender, about 1½ hours. (If using chicken, cook for about 45 minutes.) Turn the duck periodically and make sure the onions don't stick to the pan.

2 With a slotted spoon, remove the duck to a bowl and let cool until manageable. Shred the duck meat finely, discarding the bones and set aside. To the cooking liquid, add the honey and the orange and lemon juices and reduce over medium-high heat to about 1 cup, about 6 minutes.

3 Keeping the cooking liquid at a simmer, whisk in the eggs. Cook over medium-low heat, stirring constantly, until the eggs are well scrambled and have absorbed most of the liquid, 3 to 4 minutes. Stir in the duck, then add the parsley, and season to taste with salt and pepper. Cool the mixture to room temperature or better refrigerate to firm.

4 In a bowl, stir together the almonds, ½ cup confectioners' sugar, and ¾ teaspoon cinnamon. Preheat the oven to 425°F. and generously oil a 12-inch tart or pizza pan.

5 On a flat, clean work surface, brush two sheets of phyllo with the olive oil on both sides. Carefully stack them together and lay them, centered, across the pan, letting the edges hang over. Brush another two sheets with the oil and place them on top of the first sheets at a 45° angle, letting the edges hang over. Repeat with four more pairs of phyllo sheets, laying them on in the same fashion. You should have six overlapping sections covering the entire pan, plus two sheets of phyllo remaining. As you work, keep the un-oiled phyllo sheets covered with damp towels to prevent drying.

6 Spread half of the almond mixture on top of the phyllo, spread the duck mixture on top of that, and cover with the remaining almonds. Neatly fold the overhang over the filling. Brush the remaining two phyllo sheets with the oil, and lay them on top of the pie, tucking in the ends neatly under the pie. Bake the bastilla until the top is crisp and golden, about 15 minutes. Remove from the pan and, using oven mitts, invert it onto a plate, then carefully slide it back into the pan. Brush the top again with oil and bake until the top is golden, about 12 more minutes.

7 Through a fine sieve, sprinkle the top generously with remaining confectioners' sugar. Sprinkle cinnamon "stripes" in a diamond pattern on top of the sugar. (Or use a doily as template for decoration.) Cut into wedges and serve immediately.

Serves 6

Imagine a heap of aristocratic basmati rice sending whiffs of Guerlain-worthy fragrance into the air. Rice layered with morsels of meat coated in a tangy marinade rich with the scent of a dozen spices. Rice embellished with splashes of saffron-bright milk and golden rings of fried onions, laced with dried fruit or nuts, decorated with edible silver leaf. This is biryani, an Indian rice masterpiece that once graced the extravagant banquet tables of Moghul nobility and today is often reserved for weddings and special occasions.

Indians have been cultivating and eating rice for at least four millennia, but their rice cuisine owes much of its present-day sophistication to the imperial Persian cooking that reached its zenith at the Savafid courts of the sixteenth century—precisely the time when Moghuls claimed the Indian throne. These Moghul emperors—Muslims of Central Asian origin who would rule India for more than two centuries—adopted many aspects of Persia's culture and food mores. And that meant their armies of cooks paid special attention to rice.

biryani
Indian Layered Rice

Abul Fazal, the Moghul gourmet and courtier who personally oversaw the kitchen of Emperor Akbar, lovingly recounts Akbar's absurdly splendid banquets. And he devotes memorable passages to descriptions of pilaus—such as the "nine-jewel" rice dedicated to Akbar's nine favorite courtiers—and festive biryanis (the name is from the Persian word for "fried"). By the eighteenth century, in the lavish Muslim court of Lucknow, with its six kitchens, rice evolved into a dazzling fetish. Pilau cooks were paid fortunes to invent rice dishes with poetic names like "pearl" or "jasmine," to mold them into fanciful shapes after spending hours applying gold leaf or dyes to each grain until the rice resembled piles of jewels. Today, though pilaus and biryanis are relished throughout India and savored by many religions, they are still associated with Muslim culinary traditions of the former Moghul strongholds of Delhi, Hyderabad in the south, and Lucknow in the Uttar Pradesh province.

I tasted my life-defining biryani at Loharu House, the white Art Deco residence of Durru and Fauzia Ahmad Khan in a leafy diplomatic suburb of Jaipur in the northwestern Indian state of Rajasthan. A charismatic politician, Durru comes from a long line of Nawabs and maharajas. Fauzia, a Montessori teacher and spectacular cook, hails from a food-obsessed family of Hyderabad, India's great Epicurean center. Fauzia is a kitchen wiz who makes dal a hundred different ways and grows her own guavas and mangoes for chutneys. Her exalted rice preparations would have sent Lucknow courtiers into swoons.

Fauzia's Hyderabadi biryani was monumental in its complexity: chicken and mutton were cooked in a rich broth that was reduced to a single cup to flavor the rice. A nut paste and several masalas each composed of a dozen spices enhanced the seasoning. Finally, layers of rice and meats were placed in a deep vessel, which was sealed with dough. Covered with a flat lid, it cooked all night on the grill with a few coals placed on top—a method known as *dum pukht,* for which Hyderabad is famed. This kind of extravagance isn't anything one would attempt without servants, but I hope that my recipe is at least a small tribute to the Moghul grandeur and hospitality that reign at the Loharu House.

hyderabadi lamb biryani

cook's notes This recipe might look long but is no more difficult than making a curry and boiling a pot of rice. Logistically, biryani is best prepared in two stages: make the lamb stew with its spice mixes a day or two in advance, then cook the rice and assemble the biryani about 1½ hours before serving, making the garnishes as the biryani steams.

stew

1 small onion, chopped, plus 2 medium onions, thinly sliced

1 tablespoon chopped fresh ginger

1 tablespoon chopped garlic

2 tablespoons chopped long green chile, such as Anaheim

14 mint leaves, chopped

½ cup chopped cilantro

¾ cup plain yogurt

2 pound boneless lamb shoulder, cut into 1½-inch chunks

Salt

2 tablespoons ghee, clarified butter, or peanut oil

1½ tablespoons garam masala (see Cook's Notes)

½ cup raw cashews, ground in a food processor

½ cup canned coconut milk, well stirred

3 ripe medium tomatoes, peeled and chopped

Peanut or canola oil, for deep-frying the onions

Garam masala is an Indian spice blend sold at Indian groceries and some specialty markets and supermarkets. *Basmati* is an Urdu word meaning "fragrant," and a good basmati rice is central to any biryani. Many Indian chefs I know favor the Lalqilla, Elephant, and Pari brands (see Resources). I do not recommend making this dish with American basmati.

1 Make the stew: In a mini food processor or a blender, process the chopped onion, ginger, garlic, chile, mint, and cilantro to a paste with the yogurt. With a rubber spatula, scrape the mixture into a large bowl. Rub the lamb with salt, add to the yogurt mixture, and toss to coat with the marinade. Marinate the lamb at room temperature for 2 hours or for up to 6 hours in the refrigerator.

2 In a heavy pot, heat the ghee over medium heat. Add the garam masala and stir until fragrant, about 30 seconds. Add the lamb and marinade and bring to a simmer. Stir in the ground cashews, coconut milk, tomatoes, and salt to taste. Turn the heat down to low, cover, and cook until the lamb is tender, about 1¼ hours. If the stew seems too soupy, reduce the sauce, uncovered, over medium heat, stirring, until there is just enough liquid to coat the lamb generously.

3 While the lamb is cooking, heat 1 inch of oil over medium-high heat until almost smoking. In batches, deep-fry the sliced onions until lightly crisp and deep-golden. With a slotted spoon, transfer the onions to drain on paper towels. When the lamb is ready, crumble one-third of the onion slices into it. Reserve the rest of the onions.

rice

2 cinnamon sticks

6 cardamom pods, preferably green

2 imported bay leaves

2½ cups imported basmati rice (see Cook's Notes)

to assemble and decorate

4 to 8 tablespoons ghee or melted clarified butter, plus 1 tablespoon for frying the garnishes

2 tablespoons water

¼ teaspoon saffron threads, toasted, pulverized in a mortar and steeped in ⅓ cup hot milk

1 cup chicken stock or canned broth

12 small mint leaves

½ cup split cashew nuts

½ cup golden or dark raisins

1 hard-cooked egg, sliced (optional)

4 Cook the rice: Bring a large pot with 6 quarts of salted water to a boil over high heat with the cinnamon sticks, cardamom, and bay leaves. Place the rice in a fine sieve and set it over a large bowl. Fill the bowl with cold water and swish the rice with your fingers to rinse. Change the water and keep repeating this process until the water in the bowl is no longer milky, about five or six times. Rinse the rice again under cold running water.

5 When the water boils, add the rice and let the water return to a boil, stirring several times. Cook until the rice is just al dente, 5 to 6 minutes. Be very careful not to overcook. Transfer to a colander and drain. Either discard the cinnamon, bay leaves, and cardamom or add them when assembling the biryani.

6 Assemble the biryani: Preheat the oven to 350°F. Choose a large ovenproof casserole with a tight-fitting lid that can accommodate the rice and stew without overcrowding. Sprinkle the bottom of the casserole with 1 tablespoon of the melted ghee and the water. Arrange one-third of the rice on the bottom and sprinkle with 2 tablespoons of the saffron milk, 2 to 3 tablespoons of stock, and 1 to 2 tablespoons of the ghee, to taste. Scatter with a few mint leaves and some of the reserved fried onions, and spread half of the lamb on top. Top with another third of the rice, then with the rest of the lamb, and then the rice. As you layer, sprinkle each layer of rice with saffron milk, broth, and ghee, scattering it with mint and fried onions, and seasoning the rice lightly with salt. You should have three layers of rice and two layers of lamb.

7 Pour the remaining stock over the rice. Wrap the lid of the pot in a clean kitchen towel, tying the ends together over the top of the lid. Cook the biryani over medium heat for 5 minutes to get the steam going, then transfer the casserole to the oven. Bake until the grains are plump and separate, 35 to 45 minutes. Check the rice midway to make sure there's enough steam in the pot and sprinkle with a little water if dry.

8 While the rice is baking, in a small skillet, heat the remaining 1 tablespoon of ghee over medium heat. Sauté the cashews and raisins until the nuts are lightly browned and the raisins plump up, about 1 minute.

9 Remove the casserole from the oven and let stand, covered, for 15 minutes. To serve, arrange the rice and meat on a large decorative platter, fluffing the rice very gently with a fork. Scatter with fried raisins and cashews. Arrange the egg slices decoratively on top.

Serves 6 as a main course, 8 to 10 with other dishes

variation This recipe is also delicious with chicken instead of lamb: use about 2 pounds of dark thigh meat, cut into chunks, and cook just until done, about 45 minutes. Or, if pressed for time, try it with take-out curry (such as lamb or chicken korma), instead of making your own. Just layer the curry with the rice as directed in the recipe, not forgetting the crisp fried onions and the traditional garnishes.

resources An excellent mail-order source for exotic rices is Altaibat (tel: 877-225-4410 or *www.Altaibat.com*). Otherwise, try Indian markets or gourmet groceries.

*f*inally the kitchen maid appeared with the blini. . . . Risking a severe burn, Semyon Petrovich grabbed at the two topmost (and hottest) blini, and deposited them, plop, in his plate. The blini were deep golden, airy, and plump—just like the shoulder of a merchant's daughter. . . . He reflected a moment and then piled onto the blini the fattest piece of salmon, a smelt, and a sardine, and only then, panting and delirious, he rolled up the blini, downed a shot of vodka, and opened his mouth. . . .

But at this very moment he was struck by an apoplectic fit. . . .

—ANTON CHEKHOV, "ON HUMAN FRAILTY: AN OBJECT LESSON FOR THE BUTTER FESTIVAL"

Habitues of Champagne receptions who know blini only as dainty placeholders for caviar might puzzle at the erotic delirium of Chekhov's unfortunate hero. Not the Russians. For us, blini hold an almost talismanic appeal; they are the stuff of wakes, carnivals, and divinations, of sun worship and ancestral rites. "Blin is the

blini

symbol of sun, good harvest, harmonious marriages and healthy children," wrote another Russian literary great, Aleksandr Kuprin.

In the past, the Russian life cycle pretty much began and ended with these pancakes, from the blini fed to women after childbirth to those served after funerals. But the real blini binge took place during Maslenitsa, or Butterweek, the Slavic answer to Mardi Gras. The Maslenitsa of Old Russia was a sight to behold. Both great cities and tiny hamlets were transformed into amusement parks replete with mime shows, street fairs, wrestling matches, and sleigh rides. While the gentry attended masked balls and afternoon parties, the peasants staged fistfights, sang lewd ditties, and careened down specially constructed ice slopes. One S. Collins, a doctor who attended Czar Aleksei in the seventeenth century, wrote: "Russians indulged themselves to an unbridled extent. They drank as if they thought it was their last chance." With horror, he observed how many fell insensible into the snowdrifts and froze to death. Those who survived ate blini— and more blini still.

The first blini of Maslenitsa honored ancestors; later in the week they were the centerpiece of a ritual exchange of visits between in-laws. And every *traktir* (tavern) and street stall dispensed them by the thousands. "How many blini were consumed in Moscow during Maslenitsa, no one could estimate," Kuprin marveled. "You could have started with hundredweight's, progressed to tons, and wound up with six-masted cargo ships."

Symbolically, the eggs in the blini represented the fertility of Mother Earth; their round shape and the heat of the skillet might have been a tribute to the pagan sun god Yerilo. In traditional households, blini baking was regarded as nothing less than a sacrament. Recipes were guarded as if they were family jewels, while the *opara* (yeast sponge) was taken to a lake or a well late at night to be chanted over in hopes that the moon would breathe on it. Even today, I've seen many a *babushka* make the cross over the batter before pouring the first blin into the skillet.

Though Easter celebrations were pretty much banned by the Soviet regime, Maslenitsa was at least tolerated. We didn't always have *kulich* and *paskha,* the symbolic Easter delicacies, but February always meant blini. And vodka (not that Russians ever needed a special occasion to drink). Caviar and smoked sturgeon were for apparatchiks with access to Party stores, but smothering our blini with sour cream, herring, or even plain jam, we couldn't have been happier.

blini

cook's notes Porous, golden, and springy, real Russian blini are both ethereal and substantial, and utterly unforgettable. In the West, buckwheat blini are perceived as authentic. That much is true, but during Soviet times buckwheat flour completely disappeared from stores. I've never had buckwheat blini in Russia and when I tasted them in the West, I've found them dry and odd—a flavor anachronism.

Russian blini are the diameter of a saucer, never cocktail size (that's not blini, but *oladyi*). They are best fried in a well-seasoned cast-iron skillet (though some Russian émigrés swear by Teflon). "The first blin is always lumpy" the Russian saying goes, but you'll get the knack after three or four. (*Blin,* by the way, is the singular of *blini.*)

sponge

1 envelope active dry yeast (2¼ teaspoons)

1 cup warm water (115°F.)

2 teaspoons sugar

½ cup all-purpose flour

blini

2 cups warm milk, or a little more as needed

4 tablespoons unsalted butter, melted, plus
    4 tablespoons for brushing the blini

2¼ to 2½ cups all-purpose flour

2 large eggs, separated, yolks beaten

4 tablespoons sugar, or more to taste

2 teaspoons salt, or more to taste

Peanut oil, for frying

1 small potato, halved

for serving

Melted butter, sour cream, at least two kinds
    of smoked fish, caviar if you wish, and
    strawberry jam

1 Make the sponge: In a large mixing bowl, stir together the yeast, water, and sugar and let stand until foamy, about 5 minutes. Whisk in the flour until smooth. Place the sponge, covered, in a warm place until bubbly and almost doubled in bulk, about 1 hour.

2 Make the blini batter: Beat the milk, butter, 2¼ cups of the flour, egg yolks, sugar, and salt into the sponge. Whisk the batter until completely smooth and set to rise, covered loosely with plastic, until bubbly and doubled in bulk, about 1½ hours.

3 Sir the batter well, and let rise, once more in a warm place, covered, for 45 minutes.

4 Beat the egg whites until they form soft peaks and fold them into the batter. Let the batter stand for another 10 minutes.

5 Pour some oil into a small, shallow bowl and have it ready by the stove. Skewer a potato half on a fork and dip it into the oil. Rub the bottom of a 7-inch cast-iron skillet, or a heavy nonstick pan with a long handle, liberally with the oil. Heat the pan over medium heat for 1½ minutes. Using a potholder, grip the skillet by the handle, lift it slightly off the heat, and tilt it toward you at a 45-degree angle. Using a ladle, pour enough batter into the skillet to cover the bottom in one thin layer (about ¼ cup). Let the batter run down the skillet, quickly tilting and rotating it until the batter covers the entire surface. Put the skillet back on the burner and cook until the top of the blin is bubbly and the underside is golden, about 1 minute. Turn the blin and cook for 30 seconds more, brushing the cooked side with a little melted butter. If the skillet looks dry when you are turning the blin, rub with some more oil. The first blin will probably be a flop.

6 Make another blin in the same fashion, turn off the heat and taste it. Adjust the amount of salt or sugar, if necessary. The texture of the blin should be light, spongy, and a touch chewy; it should be very thin but a little puffy. If the blin breaks easily when baked, the consistency is too thin: whisk in ¼ cup more flour into the batter. If the blin is too thick, add a little milk.

7 Repeat with the rest of the batter, greasing the pan before making each blin. Slide the blini into a deep bowl, keeping them covered with a lid or foil. Serve the blini hot, with the suggested garnishes. (Blini should really be made fresh. If making them slightly ahead of time, keep them warm in a 275°F. oven. If you must reheat them, place them, covered with foil, in a bain-marie in the oven.) To eat, brush the blin with butter and/or sour cream, place one or more garnishes on top, roll it up, and plop in your mouth.

Makes about 24 blini to serve 8 as an appetizer, 4 as an entree

growing up in Brezhnevian Moscow at the height of "stagnation," I thought borshch was less a dish than a state of affairs, a metaphor for our meatless, sunless existence. Nothing was wrong with the actual soup. My mother's brick-red version, for instance, was a delicious miracle coaxed from a few beets, cabbage, potatoes, and a can of tomato paste. Still, borshch, like Moscow tap water, was something I longed to escape.

Our borshch came in various forms: there was private borshch, comforting and benign, if more than a little monotonous; and the reviled greasy institutional Soviet borshch we endured at schools, hospitals, and workers' canteens. There was cold-weather borshch that sustained us in winter, and there was *svekolnik,* the cold, thin version of the soup popularized in this

borshch

country by Eastern European Jews. Cold borshch symbolized our move to the dacha, the first sighting of cucumbers and scallions, and the endless aromas of just-picked dill sold by gruff kerchiefed women near the metro station.

Parallel to our everyday borshch there was another borshch, the mythical "real" Ukrainian borshch we knew from descriptions in propaganda-filled recipe books about the cooking of the Soviet Republics. Apparently *that* borshch was everything that our frugal vegetarian Moscow version was not. A meal-in-a-bowl, Ukrainian borshch was supposedly hearty and rich, thick enough to stand a spoon in. It came in myriad regional permutations, and it brimmed with all sorts of meats—pork, beef, sausages, even goose. A symbol of abundance, that borshch represented a wholesome, folkloric Ukraine, the country's breadbasket and sugar bowl that didn't know the horrors of state-induced famines and collectivization. In all my years in the former USSR I never tasted anything like a real Ukrainian borshch. Nor was I particularly eager to try.

Emigration, I hoped, would bring liberation from borshch, but the American food deliverance soured with our first visits to Pathmark and McDonald's. Hamburgers, we decided, were inferior to our *kotleti,* American chicken was bland, and the strawberries had no aroma. We longed for the tart crunch of Antonovka apples and moaned collectively about being served Triscuits and

Cheez Whiz at American parties when what we really wanted was black bread and borshch. A steaming bowlful of it with a big dollop of sour cream. Though she now had access to all manner of meats, my mother stubbornly stuck to her frugal vegetarian recipe; and as years went by, her borshch tasted better and better, each spoonful now laced with memories and nostalgia.

And the real Ukrainian borshch? I hadn't encountered it until I set off on a recipe-testing marathon for my Russian cookbook, *Please to the Table*. My very first and most elaborate effort was a goose borshch from the Ukrainian city of Poltava. After that came meatless Christmas borshch with tiny mushroom-filled dumplings, borshch with frankfurters, and a really delicious one with mushrooms and prunes. Yet, strangely, no matter what I did to the soup, each new creation tasted like my mother's borshch, perhaps a little rounder and meatier. And that was more than okay.

I didn't emerge with one ultimate favorite version, either—though I prefer a strong meat borshch to a vegetarian soup (sorry, Mom), I'm not too fond of adding sausage or goose, and insist that the beautiful beet color not be marred by too many tomatoes (my mother, again, disagrees).

If you don't have to endure it seven days a week for dozens of years, borshch is a pretty incredible soup.

russian winter borshch with beef and pork

cook's notes Borshch, like most peasant soups, improves tremendously as it stands and is usually made in huge quantities. It will happily keep for four to five days. Baking the beet in its skin is the secret to a beautiful ruby color. A thick slice of sourdough pumpernickel or rye (rubbed with a little garlic) is a must, and borshch without sour cream is simply unthinkable.

stock

1 pound beef chuck or shin, trimmed of excess fat

1 pound meaty pork spareribs

14 cups water

2 medium onions

2 medium carrots, peeled

1 bay leaf

6 peppercorns

Salt and freshly ground black pepper to taste

soup

2 medium beets (about 1 pound), washed and stemmed

1 slice good smoky bacon, chopped

3 tablespoons unsalted butter

1 medium onion, chopped

1 large carrot, peeled and grated

1 large green bell pepper, cored, seeded, and diced

2 cups chopped green cabbage

3 medium boiling potatoes, peeled and cut into 1½-inch chunks

1 (16-ounce) can plum tomatoes, drained and chopped

1 Make the stock: Combine the beef, pork, and water in a large stockpot and bring to a boil over high heat. Skim thoroughly and reduce the heat to low. Add the rest of the stock ingredients, and season with salt and pepper to taste. Simmer partially covered until the meat is tender, about 1½ hours. Strain the stock; you should have 10 to 11 cups. Discard the marrow bones. Cut the beef and the pork into 1½-inch chunks, discarding the pork bones. Set the meat aside.

2 While the stock is cooking, preheat the oven to 375°F.

3 Make the soup: Wrap the beets individually in aluminum foil and bake until the tip of a small knife slides in easily, about 45 minutes. Unwrap the beets, plunge them into a bowl of cold water, then slip off the skins. Grate the beets on a four-sided box grater or shred in a food processor, and set aside.

4 In a large, heavy soup pot, cook the bacon in the butter over medium heat until it renders its fat. Add the onion, carrot, and green pepper, and sauté until softened, about 7 minutes. Add the cabbage and sauté, stirring, for another 7 minutes. Add the stock, the potatoes, tomatoes, apple, and the reserved meats. Season with salt and simmer until the potatoes are almost tender, about 15 minutes. Stir in the reserved beets and cook the soup over medium-low heat until all the vegetables are soft and the flavors have melded, about 25 minutes more.

Salt

1 small Granny Smith apple, peeled, cored, and diced

3 medium garlic cloves, minced

1 teaspoon freshly ground black pepper

2 tablespoons minced parsley

1½ to 2 tablespoons distilled white vinegar

1½ to 2 tablespoons sugar

Sour cream

Chopped fresh dill and scallions, for garnish

5 With a mortar and pestle, pound the garlic, pepper, and parsley to a paste and add it to the soup. (If you don't have a mortar and pestle, just use ground pepper, crushed garlic and minced parsley.) Stir in the vinegar and the sugar, adjusting the balance of sweet and sour to taste. Let the borshch stand for 10 minutes before serving (or better, serve the next day). To serve, add a teaspoon of sour cream to each bowl and sprinkle liberally with dill and scallions. Instruct the diners to mix the sour cream well into the soup.

Serves 10 to 12

Somewhere between the chunk of conger eel and the ninth crouton slathered with rouille, Pierre Minguella, co-owner of Le Miramar, a mecca for *bouillabaisse Marseillaise,* came to my table, swung his arm around my shoulder, and said: *"Courage, courage!"*

I needed it. Exhausted from my first attack on the gigantic pile of poached fish set in front of me, I was bracing myself for the second round, moistening the contents of my plate with a little broth. This bouillon was the color of mud after a rain and reduced beyond reason—more sea floor than soup. The marine taste was so dense you could cut it with a knife. As I picked at my fish, I reflected, not without horror, that four more bouillabaisse meals awaited me on my Marseilles tasting tour. But, as Minguella said, bouillabaisse reveals itself only to those willing to savor it slowly, *bouche pour bouche.*

bouillabaisse

A true bouillabaisse, I was quickly learning, simmers oceans away from our idyllic, gentrified visions of the Provençal seaside. Like the gritty, swaggering city it represents, this iconic Marseillaise fish stew is pungent and brash, operatically picturesque, and profoundly bound to the sea.

Along the Provençal Coast, bouillabaisse has achieved such a mythical status, legends of its creation involve Phoenicians, Greeks, and Romans; goddesses, angels, and nuns. Its real roots, however, may lie in poverty and improvisation. Bouillabaisse scholars Misette Godard and Jacques Dupuy had little success finding written descriptions of it before 1768. This could be, they concluded, because a soup concocted on the spur of the moment by fishermen from throwaway catch was simply too lowly and unremarkable to merit special attention in records. In 1785, a Provençal dictionary defined *Bouilhe baisso* ("boil low") as "a term used by fishermen to indicate a type of ragout prepared by boiling fish in sea water. It is called *bouilhe baisso* because as soon as the soup is boiling, they turn down the heat."

Subsequent mentions are more frequent, but only with the 1830s—when Marseilles, flush from its new transatlantic port, turned into a requisite stop on the Romantic travelers' circuit—did bouillabaisse become one of the city's most famous tourist attractions, a ritual treat savored at fancy establishments in the Old Port. Its real place, however, claim scholars Godard and Dupuy, remained in the *cabanons,* those beachside sheds "erected . . . by local people who used them for fishing and gatherings with family and close friends."

These days, the *cabanons* mainly function as exclusive seaside retreats for moneyed families. As for Marseilles's poor fishermen's stew—a way of salvaging small bony rockfish that couldn't be sold—it has metamorphosed into a showy and expensive production. The hefty prices charged by good restaurants are in fact justified: indispensable bouillabaisse fish such as rascasse and chapon are becoming as rare as ortolans.

Bouillabaisse authentique—at least as served at restaurants adhering to the rules of the Bouillabaisse Charter, a document created by Marseilles restaurateurs dedicated to preserving traditions—is a two-act drama. First, the broth. Scorpion fish and small cheap rockfish known simply as *soupe* are boiled vigorously with olive oil, onions, tomatoes, garlic, fennel, and saffron until the oil and the fish's natural gelatin begin to emulsify. Most chefs pass the cooked fish, bones and all, through a food mill so that the broth just screams "Sea!" But the broth wouldn't be half as pleasurable without the croutons slathered with that garlicky terracotta-hued mayonnaise, called *rouille* (which means "rust"). Slurping away, one can see why Curnonsky, France's most prominent epicure, called it *soupe d'or,* "soup of gold."

Myself, I could have just the broth and run, but no: the liquid is a mere prelude to a monumental mound of poached fish. A proper bouillabaisse must contain at least four different kinds of Mediterranean fish—better six, including John Dory (*Sainte-Pierre*), spotted weever (*vive*), monkfish (*lotte*), and conger eel (*congre*). The most essential, however, is the scary-looking *rascasse.* Translated as "scorpion fish," it has a slightly iodine flavor, a gelatinous texture that contributes oomph, and a huge flat head full of menacing teeth.

For my last Marseilles dinner I drove out to Le Goudes, a village perched on a hauntingly barren, white-rock creek a short drive from Marseilles. Here, restaurant L'Escale delivered my most memorable bouillabaisse. Perhaps it was the perfect balance of the broth, the potency of the rouille, and the glowingly fresh fish delivered just hours ago by the village fishermen. Or maybe it was the sight of the Mediterranean seething and splashing in the Mistral against the vast window. But it was the only platter of fish that I truly and honestly finished— reflecting, not without sadness, that it might be a long time before I could brave bouillabaisse madness all over again.

bouillabaisse marseillaise

cook's notes It's been said many times that bouillabaisse can't exist away from the Mediterranean and its indigenous fish. Perhaps. But frankly these are not among the world's loveliest fish, and while your bouillabaisse will lack that brash marine essence, this recipe makes an awesome Provençal fish soup. The main thing is for the fish to be impeccably fresh.

For a strong broth you'll need frames, heads, tails, and trimmings from larger fish such as red snapper, sea bass, striped or black bass, grouper, rock cod, or halibut; I also love the gelatinous monkfish tails. Call your fishmonger ahead and ask to reserve these. If you can find them, add smaller fish such as mullet, porgy, ocean perch, or whiting (Chinatown fish markets are a good source for small cheap rockfish.) Feel free to throw in a dozen mussels or a couple of blue crabs for extra flavor, but avoid oily fish such as salmon or bluefish. Though these are not always used in Marseilles, you can enhance the broth with a little white wine, diced carrots, sliced leeks, a bay leaf, and a few sprigs of thyme.

The fish is cooked in the strong bouillon, which is then served as a first course. For a more informal meal, you can serve the fish and the broth together in big soup bowls. The day before, make the bouillon, the rouille, and the croutons. Two to 4 hours before serving, marinate the fish. When guests arrive, gently reheat the bouillon and poach the fish, keeping a watchful eye on it while it cooks.

bouillon

6 to 7 pounds fish carcasses, heads and tails, and/or small bony rockfish (see Cook's Notes), gutted, and scaled

¾ cup mild extra-virgin olive oil

8 garlic cloves, crushed

2 large onions, chopped

1 small fennel bulb and 2 tablespoons of the fronds, chopped

2 pounds very ripe plum tomatoes, seeded and chopped

4 dried fennel stalks (available at some specialty groceries), or 1 tablespoon fennel seeds

15 cups water

2 tablespoons tomato paste, diluted in 3 tablespoons hot water, plus additional as needed

1 tablespoon pastis, such as Pernod or Ricard

½ teaspoon saffron, toasted and pulverized in a mortar, plus additional as needed

1 thin strip of orange rind, white pith removed

Salt and freshly ground black pepper

1 Make the bouillon: Wash the fish carcasses thoroughly and remove all traces of blood and viscera. Cut out all the gills.

2 In a very large stockpot, heat the oil over medium heat and add the garlic, onions, and fennel bulb and fronds. Sauté the vegetables until softened, about 7 minutes. Add the fish, cover, and cook until it just turns opaque, about 10 minutes, shaking the pot and turning the fish. Add the tomatoes and the dried fennel and cook, stirring, for another 5 to 7 minutes. Add the water and bring to a boil over high heat. Let it boil vigorously for 10 minutes, skimming. Steep the saffron for 5 minutes in ¼ cup of the hot liquid and add to the broth along with the tomato paste, pastis, orange zest, and salt and pepper to taste. Reduce the heat to medium-low and cook, uncovered, until the fish begins to disintegrate, about 30 minutes. Skim thoroughly from time to time. Taste the broth: if it doesn't seem powerful enough, reduce it over medium-high heat until the taste is more concentrated.

rouille and croutons

26 baguette slices, ¾-inch thick

6 medium garlic cloves, chopped

3 large egg yolks

1 small roasted pimiento pepper, chopped

1 cup fruity, mild, extra-virgin olive oil

½ teaspoon salt

¼ teaspoon saffron, toasted and pulverized in a mortar, and steeped in 3 tablespoons of hot fish broth

½ teaspoon mild paprika, preferably Spanish

Large pinch of hot paprika or cayenne, or more to taste

fish, marinade, and potatoes

4 pounds mixed fish fillets (such as John Dory, sea bass, striped bass, monkfish, halibut, grouper, red snapper, or tilefish), cut into 3-inch chunks

Sea salt and freshly ground black pepper

¼ cup fruity extra-virgin olive oil

1 tablespoon fennel seeds

4 garlic cloves, crushed

1 tablespoon pastis, such as Pernod or Ricard

5 medium boiling potatoes, such as Yukon Gold, peeled and cut into wedges

12 to 15 mussels, scrubbed and debearded

¼ cup finely minced flat-leaf parsley

3 Strain the liquid into another large pot, leaving the solids in a colander (you will have to do this in several batches). When the fish is cool enough to handle, pick through the solids, discarding the larger pieces of vegetables and the heads, tails, and larger bones that are too tough to puree. Also discard the fennel stalks and the orange zest. Puree about 4 cups of the soft solids through a food mill, then strain through a fine sieve back into the liquid. (If you don't have a food mill, puree the solids in a blender with a little liquid, then strain.) Place the pot over medium-high heat and reduce by one-third, about 15 minutes. The bouillon should be beautifully concentrated. If it loses its reddish hue as it cooks, add a little extra saffron and tomato paste, diluted in water. (The bouillon can be made ahead of time and refrigerated.)

4 Make the rouille: Remove the crusts from two baguette slices and soak them in a little fish broth for 5 minutes. Squeeze and crumble with your fingers.

5 In a blender, puree the bread, garlic, egg yolks, and roasted pepper until completely smooth. With the motor running, drizzle in the oil, a little at a time, until the sauce is emulsified. It should be the consistency of a thick mayonnaise. With a rubber spatula, scrape the rouille into a bowl. Add the salt, saffron, and paprikas, and stir to combine. Refrigerate, covered with plastic, for at least 1 hour for the garlic flavors to develop.

6 Make the croutons: Preheat the oven to 375°F. Arrange the remaining baguette slices on two large cookie sheets. Bake until light golden and crispy, 10 to 12 minutes or less if you like your croutons slightly chewy. Remove the croutons from the oven and leave to dry, uncovered, for a few hours. (Both the croutons and the rouille can be prepared a day ahead.)

7 Prepare the fish: Rub the fish with sea salt and pepper and place in a large glass bowl. Add the olive oil, fennel seeds, garlic, and pastis; stir to coat the fish, cover, and refrigerate for 1 hour. Bring the fish to room temperature before poaching.

8 About 40 minutes before serving, bring the bouillon to a simmer over medium heat, add the potatoes, and cook until tender, about 20 minutes. With a slotted spoon, remove the potatoes to a bowl and keep warm.

9 Bring the bouillon to a simmer. Add the firmer fish, such as monkfish or tilefish, bring the liquid back to a simmer, and cook for 5 to 6 minutes. Gently lower the rest of the fish into the liquid, turn the heat up to high, then reduce to low when the liquid comes back to a simmer. Poach the fish until opaque and just cooked through. Closely watch the fish as it cooks, removing the pieces that are done to a platter with a slotted spoon. Add the mussels and cook until they open. When all the fish and mussels are done, remove to a platter with a slotted spoon, ladle a few tablespoons of hot broth over them, and keep covered with foil while serving the soup course.

10 Ladle the bouillon into bowls and garnish with some parsley. Keep the remaining bouillon at a simmer for the next course. Serve the croutons and the rouille with the bouillon. To eat, slather some rouille on a crouton and set afloat in the soup, letting it soften a little before eating.

11 For the second course, ladle a little of the remaining hot bouillon over the fish. Arrange the potatoes and mussels around it, and garnish with parsley. Serve the fish with additional bouillon in a serving bowl on the side. To eat, spoon some bouillon over the fish, put a dab of rouille on the side of the plate, and gently stir it into the liquid to make a sauce for the fish.

Serves 8 to 10

"t he invention of a new dish," Brillat-Savarin famously wrote, "does more for the happiness of humanity than the discovery of a new star." And what other culinary invention has made humanity happier than Caesar salad, that great Italo-American-Mexican contribution to gastronomy?

For those fuzzy on its history, I telescope rapidly.

Fourth of July, 1924. Prohibition. A coterie of Hollywood honchos sets off across the border to Tijuana for some food, gambling, and booze (not necessarily in that order). They pick a joint called Caesar's Palace, owned by a Sicilian immigrant named Caesar Cardini. They demand salads with their entrees and Cardini panics: it's the holiday weekend, the place is packed, and supplies are dwindling. Heroically, Cardini dashes back to the kitchen and grabs some hearts

caesar salad

of romaine, a couple of eggs, and a garlic clove. He then gets hold of a chunk of good Parmesan and a handful of croutons, plus lemons, olive oil, and a bottle of Worcestershire sauce. He carts it all out to the dining room. He drizzles. He tosses. He conquers! His guests are ecstatic, the word spreads, and the salad becomes a Tijuana sensation, soon copied by fancy Los Angeles steakhouses and later hailed by the International Society of Epicures in Paris as "the greatest recipe to originate from the Americas in the last fifty years."

The last bit is fairly certain, but the rest of the tale is open to dispute: Could it be Caesar's brother Alex who created the recipe? Or was it Cardini's partner, Paul Maggiora, a veteran of the Italian airforce, who tossed the very first Caesar? In the latter version, it was '27, not '24, and instead of Hollywood stars, the guests were a group of American pilots stationed in San Diego. The original name of that dish, it's been ungloriously suggested, was "Aviator's Salad."

From Julia Child who actually sampled the Caesar salad *chez* Cardini in Tijuana in the mid-1920s—and subsequently interviewed Cardini's daughter Rosa—we learn that the early Caesar was: (A) finger food consisting of whole inner leaves of romaine arranged on fancy chilled dinner plates and eaten held by their stems; (B) anchovy-less, containing only Worcestershire sauce (which is flavored with anchovies); (C) always tossed tableside in a huge wooden bowl with great pomp; (D) flavored only ever so subtly with garlic and dressed with barely cooked eggs for that extra-creamy effect. At the same time, the Mexican food authority Diana Kennedy, who got *her* scoop from brother Alex, insists that this being Mexico, the dressing contained lime instead of lemon, and that, yes, it *did* include anchovy paste.

While the true taste will forever remain a mystery, both Kennedy's and Child's "original" versions show that the ur-Caesar was much subtler and a lot more Italian-tasting compared to what we know today. I'm not a fan of skyscraper restaurant–style Caesars, and I abhor Caesars with shrimp, chicken, blue cheese, jalapeños, or croutons from outer space. But I do crave a little oomph, loads of anchovies, and slightly chewy sourdough croutons. Hail Caesar!

caesar salad

cook's notes While you don't need a fancy olive oil for the dressing, good Parmesan cheese is crucial: only a true Parmigiano-Reggiano has the sweetness and depth to counter the acidity of the lemons and the saltiness of the anchovies. If worried about using a barely cooked egg, substitute mayonnaise.

garlic croutons

⅓ cup virgin olive oil

2 garlic cloves, crushed through a press

Four 1-inch-thick slices sourdough bread from a round loaf, cut into 1-inch cubes

salad

2 medium heads romaine lettuce (about 2 pounds in all)

1 large egg (or 1 tablespoon mayonnaise)

2 anchovies (preferably salt-packed) for the dressing, plus more for serving

1 large garlic clove, crushed through a press

¼ teaspoon salt

½ teaspoon Dijon mustard

2 teaspoons red or white wine vinegar

¼ cup fresh lemon juice

⅓ cup extra-virgin olive oil

½ cup freshly grated Parmesan cheese, preferably Parmigiano-Reggiano

3 or 4 drops Tabasco sauce

Dash of Worcestershire sauce

¼ teaspoon freshly ground black pepper, or more to taste

1 Make the garlic croutons: Preheat the oven to 350°F. In a large bowl, whisk together the olive oil and garlic. Add the bread cubes and toss to coat evenly. Arrange cubes on a large baking tray and bake until crisp on the outside and still slightly chewy inside, about 10 minutes. Turn the croutons halfway through baking. Remove from the oven and let stand for at least 1 hour to crisp further. (The croutons can be made a day ahead and stored in an airtight container.)

2 Make the salad: Core the lettuce and discard the shaggy outer leaves so that you are left with tender pale-green inner spears. With a knife, trim about 1 inch from the top. Separate the lettuce into individual spears, wash under cold running water, and drain thoroughly. Unroll five lengths of paper towels on a work surface. Place a few drained leaves on each paper towel and roll up loosely. Chill on the lowest shelf of a refrigerator for about 2 hours.

anya von bremzen

3 Bring a small pot of water to a rolling simmer over medium-low heat. Gently lower the egg into the water and cook for exactly 1½ minutes. Transfer to bowl of ice water to cool.

4 In a mortar, pound the anchovies with the garlic and salt until a paste. (You can also mash them with a fork in a small bowl.) Transfer to a small bowl and add the mustard, vinegar, and lemon juice. Break the egg into the bowl, spooning out the uncooked bits from the shell. (If not using the egg, add the mayonnaise before the lemon juice and whisk until smooth.) Slowly whisk in the oil until the dressing is emulsified. Stir in 3 tablespoons of the Parmigiano, the Tabasco and Worcestershire sauce, and pepper. Taste the dressing and adjust the seasonings.

5 Either leave the romaine leaves whole or tear them into bite-size pieces. In a large salad bowl, gently toss the leaves with about half the dressing and then with the remaining Parmigiano. Add more dressing to taste, taking care not to bruise the leaves. Don't overdress.

6 Serve the salad in chilled bowls or plates, topped with as many anchovies as you like, and with the garlic croutons.

Serves 6

the medieval *esprit* of its birthplace—Castelnaudary. The symbolic seven breakings of the crust as it bakes. The sectarian strife regarding its composition. Cassoulet, France's most epic casserole, is the kind of dish that resonates with legends, with myths.

In case you slept through French Classics 101, cassoulet is a heart-stoppingly rich affair of white haricot beans flavored with plush gelatinous pig bits, layered with duck or goose confit and other meats, and slowly baked until the flavors are gorgeously melded. Cassoulet isn't just a dish but a fortress of food built around traditional southwestern French techniques of preserving pork, duck, and goose for the winter.

A legend places cassoulet's birth in the Languedoc town of Castelnaudary during the Hundred Year's War (1336–1352). With the town under siege, local womenfolk gathered up everything in their larders for a dish vast and fortifying enough to lead their soldiers to victory. While this tale suits cassoulet like bacon fits white beans, serious scholars hint that the dish actually might owe a dept to Arabic bean and lamb casseroles. The name is from *cassole,* a glazed earthenware vessel still produced in the hamlet of d'Issel.

cassoulet

As everyone knows, the great epicenter of cassoulet culture is the Languedoc region of southwestern France. The dish's paternity is fiercely disputed here by three ancient towns along Canal du Midi: Toulouse, Carcassonne, and, *naturelment,* Castelnaudary. An oft-repeated quote by Prosper Montagné, author of *Larousse Gastronomique,* describes cassoulet as "*Dieu de la cuisine Occitane,*" the God of Occitane (southern French) cuisine, split into three incarnations.

God the father is cassoulet from Castelnaudary, the casserole's official cradle and seat of the mighty Cassoulet Brotherhood. This version, considered to be the purest (and porkiest), involves salt pork, fresh bacon—sometimes slightly rancid for that piquant effect—and possibly, but not always, a confit. Cassoulet the son can be sampled in the ravishing walled town of Carcassonne, where the formula is augmented by mutton, plus partridge in season. As for the Holy Ghost, it's the cassoulet from Toulouse which includes lots of confit—duck or goose—and those lusty, garlicky *saucisses de Toulouse.* Some ghost.

Today these strict regional distinctions tend to blur. That isn't to say that any form of truce has been achieved in the cassoulet wars. So should one add wine or tomatoes? Cap the casserole with bread crumbs or let a natural *croûte* form as it bakes? And what's with the business of baking the cassoulet for seven long hours, breaking the crust seven times, a practice religiously followed by cassoulet temples like Chez Emile in Toulouse?

While dried beans are classic, for some contemporary French cassoulet specialists, the legumes of choice are fresh Tarbais, creamy flat kidney-shaped specimens whose vines curl around cornstalks. Fresh beans render cassoulet light—well, almost—and make perfect historical sense. After all, before the South American *Phaseolus vulgaris* reached Europe in the 1500s, cassoulet most likely centered on fresh fava beans. While Tarbais are de rigueur in Toulouse, other regions might swear by the smaller and sturdier Lingot beans, or Soisson or some other heirloom legumes.

Cassoulet may have started life as a ruggedly folkloric Sunday affair, but today it's discussed with the hushed reverence reserved for dusty bottles of old Margaux. "Cassoulet is a *monument historique*," one famous French food critic pronounced to me. Indeed. But what never fails to astonish me is how many American friends—regular nonfoodie folk—have actually tackled the thing. They mail-order Tarbais beans, they seek out the best sausages, they make their own duck confit! Cassoulet, you understand, is *the ultimate kitchen project,* not just a masterpiece to admire from afar.

cassoulet

cook's notes With a little planning and ingredient-scouting, cassoulet isn't hard to make, and the cultlike status you'll achieve among your friends makes it all worthwhile. Beans are the heart of the cassoulet and this is where you should concentrate your resourcefulness. Imported French beans like Tarbais or Lingot appear sporadically at gourmet groceries. Otherwise, try mail order (see Resources) both for beans and duck confit. Unless you find great meaty butcher's salt pork, use pancetta.

If you can't find confit, here is a great, easy stand-by from food writer Regina Schrambling. Place six duck legs in a glass dish and rub generously with cracked pepper, crumbled bay leaf and thyme, plus a little ground nutmeg and cloves. Cover with ¼ cup coarse salt and marinate for 24 hours covered with plastic. Wipe off all the salt, place the duck pieces in single layer in a snug, deep baking dish, and scatter with some smashed garlic cloves and 2 bay leaves. Cover with foil and bake for 3 hours at 300°F., spooning off the fat midway and reserving it for the cassoulet. Remove the foil and pass the duck under a broiler to crisp.

For the cassoulet, use the following game plan: Two days before, make the recipe through Step 4. One day before, prepare Steps 5 through 8 and make fresh bread crumbs. Three hours before serving: prepare the flavor base and assemble the cassoulet. Sit back and relax while it bakes. This recipe was inspired by the great French chef Christian Delouvrier.

beans and broth

4 cups white beans, preferably Tarbais, navy, or great northern, rinsed and picked over

1½ pounds fresh lean (unsmoked, unsalted) bacon, with rind on

1 pound lean salt pork or pancetta, in one piece (see Cook's Notes)

14 cups chicken stock or canned broth

1 head garlic, outer layer of skin peeled, halved crosswise

2 large onions, peeled and halved crosswise

2 large carrots, cut into chunks

2 leeks, white part only, well rinsed

2 bay leaves, 6 whole cloves, 4 sprigs thyme, and 4 sprigs parsley tied in a cheesecloth bag

Salt

1 Make the beans: Bring about 3 quarts of water to a boil over high heat. Add the beans and let boil for 2 to 3 minutes. Take the beans off the heat and let stand for 1 hour. Drain.

2 While the beans are soaking, place the fresh bacon and salt pork in a small pot, bring to a boil over low heat, and blanch for 10 minutes. Drain.

3 In a 6-quart pot, combine the beans, bacon, salt pork, stock, garlic, onions, carrots, leeks, and the bouquet garni, and bring to a boil. Reduce the heat to low, cover, and cook, skimming occasionally, until the beans are tender but still a little resilient, about 1 hour. Add salt, if necessary.

4 Cool the liquid a little. With a slotted spoon, remove the vegetables and bouquet garni and discard. Remove the bacon, leaving the salt pork in the pot. Cut off the bacon rind with a ¼-inch layer of fat attached. Dry the rind well with paper towel, wrap it in some clean paper towel, and refrigerate; it must be completely dry when you're ready to fry it later. Return the bacon to the pot. If making the beans a day ahead of the lamb stew, refrigerate and degrease the liquid before using.

lamb stew

2 to 3 tablespoons duck or bacon fat or mild olive oil

2 pounds lamb shoulder, cut into 1½-inch chunks

2 medium onions, finely chopped

1 large carrot, peeled and cut into large chunks

2 large garlic cloves, chopped

1 tablespoon chopped fresh thyme or 2 teaspoons dried

1½ cups dry white wine

1 cup chopped canned tomatoes with about ⅓ cup of their liquid

1½ tablespoons tomato paste

confit and sausages

6 purchased duck confit legs (about 1½ pounds) or see Cook's Notes

½ cup duck or bacon fat

1 pound fresh garlic pork sausages, preferably not Italian

for seasoning and assembly

4 ounces pancetta, diced

2 medium onions, finely chopped

16 garlic cloves (2 heads), minced in a food processor, divided in half

1 cup dry white wine

Salt and freshly ground black pepper

1½ cups fresh parsley, minced in a food processor

2½ cups coarsely ground bread crumbs made with stale French bread

5 Make the lamb stew: Preheat the oven to 325°F. In a large Dutch oven or heavy casserole, heat the duck fat over high heat. Cook the lamb, in batches, until well browned on all sides, removing the browned pieces to a bowl. Add the onions and carrot and brown well. Replace the lamb in the casserole, add the garlic and thyme, stir for 1 minute, then add the wine, tomatoes, tomato paste, and 3½ cups of the bean cooking liquid. Bring the liquid to a simmer, then carefully transfer the casserole to the oven. Bake, tightly covered, until the lamb is tender, about 1¼ hours.

6 If using duck confit, place the duck with its fat in a baking pan and bake alongside the stewing lamb until the meat is warmed through and the fat has melted, about 15 minutes. Remove from the oven and pat the confit dry lightly with paper towels to remove excess fat. Reserve the duck meat and the rendered fat separately.

7 Also while the lamb bakes, prick the sausages all over with the tip of a small knife. In a large skillet, heat 1 tablespoon of the duck fat over medium heat and sear the sausages on all sides for about 5 minutes. Remove from the skillet and drain on paper towels.

8 When the lamb is ready, remove it from the oven and let cool a little. Drain off the cooking liquid and reserve, discarding the carrot. To the pot with the beans add the lamb pieces, the sausages, and the duck confit. Bring everything to a simmer, and cook over very low heat for 1 hour to meld the flavors. Refrigerate the pot overnight.

9 Assemble the cassoulet: About 3 hours before you are ready to serve, remove the reserved bacon rind from the refrigerator. Using scissors, cut it into ⅓-inch diamond-shaped lardons.

10 Heat 2 tablespoons of the duck fat in a heavy 3-quart stew pot. Add the diced pancetta and cook over medium heat for 5 minutes, stirring, to render the fat. Add the lardons and cover the pot *immediately*, or the lardons will pop out and fly all over the kitchen. Cook, shaking the pot constantly, until the lardons stop popping against the lid, 6 to 7 minutes. Add the onions and half of the minced garlic and sauté, stirring, until soft, about 10 minutes. Add the wine and reduce by half, then add the reserved lamb cooking liquid and bring to a boil. Turn off the heat.

11 Preheat the oven to 325°F. Remove the bean pot from the refrigerator and heat gently to loosen the ingredients. Try to stir as little as possible so as not to squash the beans. Using tongs or a large slotted spoon, remove all the meats from the pot into a large bowl. Drain the beans, reserving their cooking liquid. Add 5 cups of the cooking liquid to the pot with the pancetta and the lamb braising juices, and season, if needed, with salt and pepper. Reserve the rest of the bean cooking liquid in case you need it for baking the cassoulet.

12 Remove the duck confit from the bones, discard the bones, and tear the meat into medium-large pieces. Cut the sausages into ¾-inch slices. Cut the bacon and salt pork into thick slices, removing as much fat as you'd like (I wouldn't!).

13 Stir together the parsley and remaining minced garlic. Stir half of the parsley mixture into the bread crumbs and reserve the rest for sprinkling the cassoulet.

14 Layer one-third of the beans on the bottom of a wide 7-quart earthenware or enameled cast-iron ovenproof casserole (such as Le Creuset) that is at least 6 inches tall. Layer half the duck, lamb, sausages, and bacon and salt pork slices on top. Sprinkle everything with some of the parsley-garlic mixture. Add another third of the beans, top with the rest of the meats and the parsley-garlic mixture, then top with the last layer of beans. As you layer the cassoulet, add salt and pepper to taste. Add enough of the pancetta and lamb braising mixture to come up just ½ inch under the beans. If there isn't enough, add a little bean cooking liquid.

15 Place the casserole in the oven and bake for 1½ hours. If a crust forms on top, push it down gently, adding a little more liquid. Increase the heat to 400°F. Check the amount of liquid and top up if necessary. Sprinkle the top of the cassoulet evenly with the bread crumbs and drizzle the remaining 5 tablespoons duck fat over the top. Bake until the crumbs form a solid, golden crust on top, about 25 minutes. Remove the cassoulet from the oven and let stand for about 10 minutes. Triumphantly carry your cassoulet to the table, stand back, and accept the compliments.

Serves 12 to 14

resources D'Artagnan (tel: 800-D-A-R-T-A-G-N-A-N or *www.dartagnan.com*) is your best source for duck confit. For Tarbais beans, try French Feast (tel: 212-860-7716 or *www.frenchfeast.com*) or Formaggio Kitchen (tel: 888-212-3224 or *www.formaggiokitchen.com*). But call first, as supplies seem sporadic.

judging by the current craze for zestful Latino raw-fish concoctions "cooked" in citrus juice and sparked with chiles and herbs, ceviche is on its way to becoming the sushi of the new millennium.

In Peru, where ceviche is worshiped and believed to have been born—unless you ask Ecuadorians—I was treated to a veritable cocktail of theories about the origins of both the dish and its name. Some were for rationalists, others for romantics. A popular hypothesis among the latter involves reckless seamen who crossed the Pacific on flimsy balsa rafts carrying a recipe for lime-bathed raw fish from Polynesia to Peru. (It's a tale as pretty as it is improbable, given that citrus wasn't known in Polynesia until the 1700s.) Rationalist (and nationalist) food historians insist on the pre-Columbian roots of ceviche, claiming that long before

ceviche

Spaniards set foot in Peru, indigenous peoples along the coast were preserving raw fish by marinating it with chiles and tart passionfruit juice, or *chicha,* the Andean corn beer. Others, meanwhile, propose an Arab-Iberian genesis for the dish, opining that this national treasure was a relatively late addition to the Peruvian table. As for the name, prevailing opinion traces it to the Latin *cibus* (alimentation) that is the etymological source of the Spanish word *cebo,* or "fish bait."

The cold Humboldt current of Peru's northern coast is responsible for some of the world's loveliest catch: delicate corvina (white sea bass), sweet scallops from the Bay of Nazca, pearlescent fluke, black clams, giant crab. To do it justice, contemporary ceviche masters favor preparations so pristine they veer into sashimi territory. To Peruvian purists, ceviche should be nothing more than fresh-off-the boat fish, marinated *briefly* in aromatic northern Peruvian lime juice and enhanced only by onion and *aji amarillo* (fragrant yellow chiles). The final flavor depends on the quality and the cut of the fish; even the most popular garnishes—cilantro, celery, seaweed—are often dismissed as decorative froufrou. But if this minimalist aesthetic owes much to the influence of Peru's Japanese immigrant cooks, the accompaniments are nothing if not Andean: thick slices of boiled sweet potato to soften the pucker of lime, chunks of large-kerneled white corn, and wisps of red onion—all making for a truly spectacular light seafood lunch.

In contrast to Peru's purist ceviches, the raw-fish concoctions of Ecuador have a decidedly Technicolor flair. This is a country of beaches densely lined with *cebicherías*, each offering a dozen varieties. Ecuadorian ceviches are soupier than Peru's. The seafood swims in a tangy puddle of marinade, often presented in a deep plastic bowl or a glass and eaten with a spoon; the garnishes may include popcorn. And while the flavorings come as outlandish as Thousand Island dressing, squid ink, or dry mustard, most emblematic is a spicy tomato marinade that tastes like cocktail sauce from the fourth dimension.

peruvian fish ceviche Classic Peruvian ceviche is so simple, it hardly requires a recipe. For 1½ pounds top-quality, freshest fluke, sole, or sea bass fillets, skinned and cut into ¾-inch dice or very thin slices, use 1 cup of strained lime juice, a small pinch of sugar, and 1 tablespoon finely sliced Peruvian *aji amarillo* (yellow chiles), or thinly sliced red or green serranos, or jalapeños. Marinate until the fish just turns opaque, about 15 minutes, drain, and serve on Boston lettuce leaves garnished with thinly sliced red onion and cilantro leaves, and surrounded by thick slices of boiled sweet potatoes and chunks of corn on the cob. *¡Delicioso!*

spiced orange
shrimp ceviche

cook's notes This ceviche recipe, from my Miami-based Greek-Armenian-Venezuelan friend Terry Zarikian, is zesty, citrusy, spicy, and everything else a great ceviche should be. Make sure not to overcook the shrimp and don't frown on the ketchup—it's an authentic ceviche ingredient in Ecuador. To the marinade you can add a handful of diced jicama for crunch or diced mangoes for sweetness. Try to use oranges that are slightly tart; if they are too sweet, adjust the amount of lime juice.

1 pound extra-large or jumbo shrimp in their shells

½ cup ketchup

¾ cup fresh orange juice

3 tablespoons fresh lemon juice

4 tablespoons fresh lime juice, or more to taste

2 large garlic cloves, crushed through a press

1 small jalapeño chile, cored, seeded to taste, and thinly sliced

½ teaspoon dried oregano

½ teaspoon freshly ground black pepper

Large pinch of ground cumin

Small pinch of ground cinnamon

Small pinch of ground cloves

Salt

Dash of Tabasco sauce

1 In a large saucepan, bring about 3 quarts of salted water to a simmer. Have a large bowl of ice water ready. Add the shrimp, remove from the heat immediately, and let stand for exactly 1½ minutes. Do not overcook. Drain the shrimp and dump them into the ice water to cool. Drain the shrimp again, pat them dry with paper towels; peel and devein.

2 Place the ketchup in a large bowl and gradually whisk in the orange juice until the mixture is completely homogenous. Whisk in the lemon and lime juices, and add the garlic, jalapeño, oregano, pepper, cumin, cinnamon, cloves, and salt and Tabasco to taste. Taste the mixture and adjust lime juice to taste: the marinade should be sweet, tart, and spicy.

1 medium red onion, quartered and thinly sliced

1 medium tomato, seeded and diced

½ cup chopped cilantro leaves, plus a handful of leaves for garnish

2 tablespoons extra-virgin olive oil

1 Belgian endive, for garnish

3 In a large nonreactive bowl, toss the shrimp with the onion, tomato, and cilantro. Pour the marinade over the shrimp, toss, then toss in the oil. Cover with plastic and refrigerate for at least 8 hours or overnight, tossing the mixture once or twice as it marinates.

4 Serve the ceviche in martini glasses, garnished with cilantro and endive spears.

Serves 5 or 6 as an appetizer

ever hear New Yorkers boast that theirs is the world's greatest cheesecake? That's chauvinism. Ever hear New Yorkers claim they *invented* cheesecake? That's sheer chutzpah.

Back in 200 B.C.—long before NY, NY—the Romans were already offering sacrificial cheesecakes called *libum* to their numerous household gods. The blueprint for *libum* offered by the Roman consul Cato in his "On Agriculture" could be the world's first written cheesecake recipe: fresh cheese, rye flour, eggs. Four centuries later—still pre–New York—Athaenaeus, a Greek-Egyptian grammarian-gourmand living in Rome, recorded his own cheesecake formula: "take some cheese and pound it, put in a brazen sieve and strain it, then add

cheesecake

honey and flour made from spring wheat and heat the whole together into one mass."

Athenaeus fondly noted other cheesecakes as well: cheesecakes boiled in oil, cheesecakes devoted to Olympian goddesses, wedding cheesecakes drenched in honey and baked in an open fire.

When the cheesecake paradise that was the Roman Empire went into decline, the cheesecake art evidently declined with it. At least you don't hear much about it until an intriguing recipe surfaces for a sweet curd flavored with rose water and elderflower and baked in a tart crust. This recipe is in the *Forme of Cury*, a landmark fourteenth-century collection compiled by the cook for Richard II. (Did he know from New York? No, he didn't.)

I won't bore you with the subsequent cheesecake lore through the ages, though you might be interested to know that rose water, nutmeg, and cinnamon were a common seasoning well into the eighteenth century. But suffice it to say that fancy cheesecakes were making humanity happy long before 1872, which is when an American dairyman trying to replicate a French cheese, Neufchâtel, accidentally created cream cheese.

In New York City, the first upscale deli to make waves with its cheesecake was probably Reuben's. (Its celebrity-seeking proprietor Arthur Reuben might or might not have created the original Reuben sandwich.) Reuben's triumph was quickly upstaged by Lindy's, the late-night hangout for actors, comedians, and song-pushers; and by Brooklyn's Junior's, whose owner was determined to outdo his rivals with a tall, triple-rich, tire-sized whopper.

The dense but smooth New York cream-cheesecake from Junior's and the creamier but still hefty version from Lindy's had set the gold standards against which all other cheesecakes in the country were measured (at least until Sara Lee came along).

But the New York cheesecake has stiff competition. Think of the rustic ricotta cakes Italians eat every Easter. And the ethereal French *coeur à la crème*. And the soulful pot cheese creations of Poland and Russia, the cultures from which the Jewish New York–style cheesecake tradition was born.

In my own Soviet childhood, every day was cheesecake day. *Paskha* was our "big-event" cheesecake, a mind-bogglingly rich Easter mold. *Paskha* served with *kulich*, the tall Easter cake, was fine for a few bites, then one collapsed into a cholesterol-induced stupor. For the rest of the year we had *syrniki*—the fried pancake-like cheesecakes served at breakfast. And I never stop reminiscing about saving my kopeks for the lemony chocolate-dipped cheese confections sold at Soviet dairy shops.

All this goes a long way toward explaining why I have strong ideas about what a great cheesecake should be. In the following recipe I combine the cream cheese tang of a New York cheesecake with the richness of paskha and the chocolate glaze of my childhood after-school indulgences. To me, this is as good as a cheesecake gets. Even the most chauvinistic New Yorkers might have to agree.

chocolate-glazed lemon cheesecake

cook's notes This is a rich but ethereal lemony cheesecake encased in a bitter chocolate shell. For the glaze, use the best bittersweet chocolate you can find, such as Valrhona. You can also add slivers of candied citron or ginger to the batter or flavor it with orange or Key lime juice, or with mango or banana puree. For a straightforward New York version, simply omit the chocolate glaze and add a crumb crust of your choice. The cake needs to chill for at least six hours, so plan accordingly.

cheesecake

2 pounds (four 8-ounce packages) cream cheese, preferably Philadelphia brand, at room temperature

¾ cup sour cream

1 cup plus 2 tablespoons sugar

3 large eggs plus 2 large egg yolks

Juice and finely grated zest from 3 lemons

1½ teaspoons pure vanilla extract

glaze

6 ounces best-quality bittersweet chocolate, such as Valrhona, finely chopped

⅓ cup heavy cream

1 tablespoon unsalted butter, cut into small pieces

1 Make the cheesecake: Preheat the oven to 325°F. Butter the sides of a 9-inch springform pan, and bring a kettle of water to a boil.

2 In a large bowl, beat together the cream cheese, sour cream, and sugar at medium speed for 2 to 3 minutes. Gradually add the eggs and yolks, beating well after each addition and scraping down the sides of the bowl. Add the lemon juice and zest and the vanilla and beat to incorporate. (The mixture can also be blended in a food processor, with the eggs added gradually through the feed tube.)

3 Line the bottom of the pan with foil, tuck the edges underneath, and assemble the pan. Scrape the batter into the pan, set the pan into a larger pan, and pour enough boiling water to come halfway up the sides. Bake the cake for 55 minutes until the top looks set but the cake still jiggles when you tap the pan. Leave the cake in the oven for 1 hour with the heat turned off and the oven door ajar. Remove the cake to a rack and let cool for another hour. Drape the top of the cake with plastic and refrigerate for at least 6 hours or overnight.

4 To unmold, carefully remove the sides of the pan and invert the cake onto a large plate lined with plastic wrap. Run a long, thin knife between the cake and the foil that lines the pan bottom and remove the pan bottom and foil. Carefully reinvert the cake onto a large serving plate and smooth the sides with a knife, if necessary. Refrigerate the cake while making the glaze.

5 Make the glaze: Place the chocolate and the cream in the top of a double boiler set over simmering water. Heat, stirring, until the chocolate is completely melted, about 5 minutes. Whisk in the butter and stir until the chocolate is glossy.

6 With a rubber spatula, spread the glaze evenly over the top and sides of the cake and wipe the sides of the plate clean with a small piece of damp paper towel. Refrigerate the cake until the glaze is set, about 2 hours. Freeze the cake for 20 to 30 minutes before serving. To serve, cut the cake into slices with a knife dipped in cold water.

Serves 8 to 10

Persian *chelo* is the world's loveliest way of cooking rice—no contest. A big pot of it is enough to make me almost weep with happiness, and I don't need anything else to go with it.

Persia (present-day Iran), in whose sixteenth-century courts some of the world's most sophisticated pilafs were born and perfected, today boasts three main methods of cooking rice. The most basic is *katteh,* a comforting if somewhat frumpy Caspian rice dish cooked by absorption. The grandest is *polo,* a pilaf studded with cubes of meat, legumes, berries, nuts, and dried fruit. And in between sits chelo, which produces a simple and simply spectacular plate of rice.

chelo

Persian Steamed Rice with a Crust

The essence of chelo is the incomparably aromatic slinky-grained rice that perfumes everything in its orbit with elegant nutty aromas. Darbari and domsiah varieties, similar to basmati, are the ones most prized in Iran. The aim in cooking is to tease every bit of fragrance from the grains while keeping them as separate and bouncy as pearls. To achieve this, the rice is first scrupulously rinsed and soaked to remove excess starch, then parboiled and steamed in its own moisture in a pot covered with a towel, which helps condense the vapors.

Before cooking, the pot is lined with a layer of rice whisked with egg and yogurt, or with potatoes or bread, which cling to the bottom and turn golden and crunchy as the rice steams. This is the all-important *tah dig* ("the bottom of the pot"). The Iranian passion for *tah dig* is satirized in a hilarious article I came across in the expatriate online magazine, *The Iranian*. Entitled "The Life and Times of Tah Dig," the piece examines *tah dig* and crime, *tah dig* in the military, *tah dig* and health. ("*Tah dig* has been shown to shatter teeth, break jawbones, jar brains, cause turfwars at dinner table over the last piece of the crispy substance.") Not all that much of an exaggeration, perhaps.

Once the rice is mounded on a platter and scattered with crunchy bits of *tah dig,* it's eaten with grilled meat (chelo kebab) or with one of the many aromatic soupy stews called *khoresht*. Truth be told, however, it's almost a crime to pour a stew over something so fine and so exquisite.

chelo

cook's notes As Persian rice is extremely hard to find in the United States, expatriate Iranians use basmati. The most sought-after brands are Pari, Elephant, and Lalqilla (I prefer Pari). These can be found at Indian or specialty groceries and some health food stores. (See Resources) Once you've sampled the yogurt-egg *tah dig,* try lining the pot with thinly sliced potatoes or split pita bread rounds. The instructions might look involved, but once you've actually cooked the recipe, they make perfect sense and you won't need to look at the recipe again.

2 cups imported basmati rice

Salt

1 large egg, beaten

¼ cup plain yogurt

½ cup (1 stick) unsalted butter, melted

2 tablespoons light vegetable oil

2 tablespoons water

¼ teaspoon saffron threads, toasted and pulverized in a mortar

Pomegranate seeds or mint leaves, for garnish

1 Place the rice in a fine sieve and set it over a bowl. Fill the bowl with cold water and swish the rice with your fingers to rinse. Change the water and keep repeating this procedure until the water is no longer milky, 3 or 4 times. Rinse the rice again under cold running water, place it in a large bowl, and add enough lukewarm water to cover by 2 inches. Add 1 teaspoon of salt and let the rice soak for as long as it takes for the cooking water to come to a boil. (Iranians insist on long soaking, but I noticed that it causes the grains to break.)

2 While the rice is soaking, bring a 6-quart pot of salted water to a boil and let boil, uncovered, for 2 minutes over high heat. Drain the rice and rinse again under cold running water until the water runs clear. Add the rice to the boiling water and stir once to prevent it from sticking to the bottom. After the water returns to the boil, cook the rice, stirring once or twice, for 4 minutes. Taste the rice: it is ready when the outside of the grain is soft and the center is still slightly hard to the bite. This should take 5 to 8 minutes. Take care not to overcook the rice. Drain it thoroughly, and rinse under lukewarm running water to stop the cooking.

3 Put about ½ cup of the cooked rice into a bowl, whisk in the egg and the yogurt, and mix well.

4 Choose a large, heavy, preferably nonstick pot with a tight-fitting lid. Combine 2 tablespoons of the butter with the oil over medium heat, add the water, and cook until steam begins to rise from the pot. Add the yogurt-rice mixture and, using a spatula, spread it in an even layer on the bottom of the pot. Turn the heat up to high and cook for 3 minutes to let enough steam build up. Place half of the rice in the pot, sprinkle with 2 tablespoons of the butter, top with the remaining rice, and sprinkle with the other 2 tablespoons of the butter. Gather the rice into a loose mound and poke four or five holes in the mound with the handle of a long wooden spoon. Pour about 2 teaspoons of water into each hole. Wrap the lid of the pot in a clean kitchen towel, tying the ends together over the top of the lid. Cover the pot tightly, making sure that no steam can escape. Reduce the heat to very low and steam the rice for about 35 minutes. Check the rice midway through cooking and sprinkle in a few tablespoons of water if there doesn't seem to be enough steam. Remove the rice from the heat and let stand, covered, for 10 minutes.

5 While the rice is standing, heat the remaining 2 tablespoons of butter in a small pot, add the saffron, and let steep for 5 minutes. Place a ladleful of cooked rice in the saffron pot and stir until the rice turns bright yellow.

6 Arrange the rest of the rice on a large serving platter and scatter with the saffron rice. Loosen the *tah dig* from the pot with a sturdy spatula. (If the *tah dig* doesn't want to come off, place the bottom of the pot into a sink filled with cold water for 1 minute or place the pot on a wet towel.) Break the *tah dig* into pieces and scatter on top of the rice. Decorate the rice with pomegranate seeds or mint leaves.

Serves 5 or 6

resources Kalustyans (tel: 212-685-3451 or *www.Kalustyans.com*) is a good general mail-order source for imported basmati, as is Altaibat (tel: 877-225-4410 or *www.altaibat.com*). They might require ordering a 10-pound bag, but you'll go through it quicker than you think.

during my childhood, the curative powers of chicken soup eluded me—penicillin, now *that* did the job. Nor will I ever rhapsodize about the taste of my grandmother's soup.

Like most frail Jewish kids reared in subzero Moscow winters, I suffered from chronic tonsillitis. My two grandmothers took turns tending to me. Baba Liza was Jewish, selfless, and nurturing; Baba Alla, an extravagant Slavic chain-smoking blond with a passion for billiards. Which of them was entrusted with preparing my chicken soup? The gentile. This was because Alla's high-powered job as a "federal planner"—God knows of what—gained her access to privileged grocery stores laden with chickens and cream puffs. (For normal Soviets procuring poultry meant unspeakable food queues.) Whenever my illness struck, Baba Alla rushed to my side, bird in hand. For hours she hunched

chicken soup

over the stove until it was time to triumphantly carry the bowl to my sickbed and pour the scorching-hot liquid loaded with dreaded dill down my inflamed throat. Oy . . . the agony. And this is my inspirational soup tale.

Well, inspirational shminspirational. I finally got cured of my ailments, moved to America, and tasted the genuine article at a Jewish-American seder. Whoa, what soup. Deeply chickeny and resonant with root vegetables, it had that prescribed sunny hue and was afloat with two airy matzo balls. This elixir was the *goldene oychet* (golden broth) of Yiddish lore, the liquid form of Bubbie's devotion, an emblem of Ahskenazic Jewish identity, a prelude to wedding, seder, and Sabbath meals—a panacea for the world's ills.

Yes, but can it really cure a cold?

Ancient Romans swore by chicken soup's health-giving properties. So did the Talmudic Rabbi Abba and generations of Chinese herbalists. The great Persian medic Avicenna insisted that chicken soup could rectify corrupted humors, while the twelfth-century Jewish-Egyptian physician Maimonides prescribed it for everything from hemorrhoids to leprosy. One Renaissance

anya von bremzen

Catalan cookbook even attributes chicken soup with the power to return a man from the dead. (As a curious aside, according to historian Barbara Santich, some Renaissance chicken soups would include spices like sandalwood, cloves, and cinnamon and precious stones whose virtues were meant to enrich the broth.)

None of this meant anything to modern medics; they just kept on scoffing at this mother of all remedies. But no longer. The first breakthrough came in 1978, when physicians at Mount Sinai Medical Center in Miami established through controlled experiments that chicken soup does a better job than plain old hot water at clearing sinuses. Recent findings published in *Chest*—not a girlie magazine but a respected journal of American chest physicians—were even more reassuring. After laboratory experiments with one doc's family recipe, pulmonary specialists discovered that our Jewish penicillin does indeed contain compounds that inhibit the movement of inflammation-causing white blood cells.

I guess that settles it. Especially if the said soup comes with a dollop of grandmotherly love, dill or no dill.

susan friedland's double-strength chicken soup

cook's notes When it comes to chicken soup, all arguments stop. Pretty much everyone, be her roots in Vilna or Bialystock, agrees that perfection equals a nice golden color and a massive depth of flavor achieved by simmering a tough old hen for a long time with lots of root vegetables. To get extra oomph, some cooks add extra chicken backs, wings, or feet. Susan Friedland, editor of this book and author of *Shabbat Shalom,* goes a step further. Her double-strength broth involves not one but two hens, poached consecutively in the same broth over two days. As Susan says, the recipe requires not much work but a lot of time. And it wouldn't be nearly as good without Susan's light-as-air matzo balls. As generations of thrifty *shtetl* cooks did before her, Susan uses the chicken fat to render into schmaltz for the matzo balls.

1 Rinse the hens well. Remove the fat from the cavities and reserve for rendering (see box). Refrigerate one of the hens to cook the next day.

2 Place one hen in a stockpot with the water and half the onions and carrots. The ingredients should be barely covered. Bring the water to a boil and lower the heat immediately. Thoroughly skim all the foam that rises to the surface and adjust the heat so that only a bubble or two appears on the surface. Add the parsley and peppercorns, partially cover the pot, and simmer for about 2 hours, skimming occasionally. The hen should be tender but not completely falling apart. Let the hen cool in the soup.

Two 6- to 8-pound stewing hens, including
    neck and giblets but not livers

5 to 6 quarts water

4 large onions, peeled and halved

6 carrots, scraped and cut into large chunks

15 sprigs parsley

10 peppercorns, crushed

Salt

Finely chopped parsley or dill, for serving

Matzo balls, if desired (recipe follows)

3 Place the hen on a board and remove the meat from the bones. Put the skin and the bones back in the broth and bring back to a simmer. Cook for another hour or so. Reserve the meat for another use.

4 Strain the soup into a large bowl or a clean pot and discard everything in the strainer. Cool the soup and refrigerate overnight. Remove the fat that has solidified on the surface. Start again from step 1, using the defatted broth, other hen, remaining vegetables, and enough additional water to barely cover the ingredients.

5 Serve the soup with chopped parsley or dill and the matzo balls, if desired.

Serves 8 to 10

susan's matzo balls

Plural of the Yiddish word *kneydl*, which derives from the German *knodel* (dumplings), *kneidlach* are what most of us know as matzo balls. Or you can just call them delicious. What makes them tasty, however, is a matter of dispute: Small or huge? Water or seltzer? Sinkers or floaters? Katz's versus Carnegie Deli? (I'll take Katz's any day.) Susan's wisdom: Whatever camp you belong to, make sure to give them a rest in the refrigerator because that's what makes them light. The balls can be made a few hours ahead of time and kept on a platter covered loosely with paper towels. The heat of the soup will warm them through.

4 large eggs

½ cup cold water or seltzer

6 tablespoons melted schmaltz, purchased or homemade (see Box)

Salt

1 cup matzo meal

1 In a large bowl, lightly stir the eggs with a fork. Stir in the water or seltzer, the schmaltz, and salt to taste. Gradually add the matzo meal, stirring all the while to eliminate lumps. Refrigerate the batter for at least 1 hour.

2 Bring a large pot of water to a boil. With moistened hands, form the matzo balls using about 2 tablespoons of the batter for each ball. Drop the balls into boiling water. When the water returns to a boil, reduce the heat so that the water simmers, cover the pot, and cook for 30 minutes. Taste one ball to make sure it is cooked through. If done, remove the balls with a slotted spoon, placing one (or better two!) into the bottom of each soup plate. Immediately pour the hot soup over the balls.

Makes about 16 matzo balls

schmaltz

To render chicken fat for schmaltz (and get those delicious *gribenes*, or cracklings, in the process), combine 6 ounces of chicken fat with 1 cup of chopped onion and 4 tablespoons shredded chicken skin in a large, heavy skillet and cook over low heat until the onion is lightly colored and floating in bubbling fat. Strain through a fine sieve. Use the fat for the matzo balls and the cracklings for mashed potatoes or kugel.

"I wish for a chocolate cake so dense," the perpetually incarcerated Marquis de Sade wrote to his wife, "that it is black, like the devil's ass is blackened by smoke." Over the course of his life the Marquis had some rather, er, *peculiar* desires. But in his dark lust for a sublime chocolate cake, he seems like just one of the legion of chocoholics.

Anyone interested in a rich sampler of chocolate history should turn to Sophie Coe's immensely entertaining *The True Story of Chocolate,* and to my friend Maricel Presilla's erudite *The New Taste of Chocolate.* Suffice it to say that the credit for marrying chocolate and sugar goes to the Spaniards. The first chocolate cake was baked sometime in the seventeenth century. The Mercedes-Benz of chocolate cakes—the Viennese Sacher Torte—was invented in 1832 by

chocolate cake

Metternich's chef, Franz Sacher, and was the subject of a grand culinary copyright lawsuit between Sacher's descendants and the Austrian pastry emperor, Demmel, over use of the name.

Perhaps you're already clued in to the fact that the term Baker's chocolate has nothing to do with what you do in the oven and everything with Dr. James Baker, who financed our country's first chocolate factory in 1780. As for our German chocolate cake, it's not a Teutonic but a Texan creation—named after German's Sweet Chocolate, developed by a fellow called Samuel German.

From here on, we can happily drown in the bittersweet lava of chocolate lore and spend lifetimes savoring black glossy desserts that run the gamut from sky-high fudge layer cakes to dense bombes to ephemeral mousses.

Now a confession: far from being a chocoholic, I'd happily trade all the world's tortes, brownies, mud cakes, and dacquises for a good crunchy pickle. But there have been moments. My first-ever taste of Jean-George Vongerichten's much-copied chocolate cake with a molten center left me speechless. Joël Robuchon's elegant, austere bitter chocolate tart was another cocoa bean–induced epiphany. And how can I ever forget Pierre Herme's stunning milk chocolate cake—as texturally complex and multidimensional as the Guggenheim in Bilbao—bought at Herme's eponymous Parisian patisserie?

Recently, I was blown away by still another chocolate cake. This happened not at some posh Parisian haunt but at Rose Pistola, a New Wave Ligurian café in North Beach, San Francisco. There, Reed Heron's chocolate *budino* cake—further perfected by his pastry chef, Galan Warner—arrived before me as a rich but light chocolate-espresso cake poised on a hazelnut Florentine and enrobed in layers of ganache. The dessert rates as something of a legend among San Francisco foodies, and it's the only chocolate cake that ever prompted me to order seconds.

Here, I offer a simplified but still magnificent version of Heron's recipe.

rose pistola chocolate budino cake

cook's notes The original recipe, published in Heron's *Rose Pistola Cookbook,* comprises several elements and requires not insignificant baking skills. Realizing that this might be daunting for some, Heron invites less ambitious cooks to make the cake part alone (he calls it *budino,* or pudding, but it's more like a flourless cake). Even in this simplified form, the cake is a thing of beauty.

Not wanting to lose the lovely nut flavor of the original, I added some hazelnuts and hazelnut liqueur to the cake batter. I love the hazelnuts but if you like your chocolate cakes silky-smooth, omit them. The cake is gigantic, easily enough for sixteen. For a more intimate occasion, halve the recipe and bake in a smaller mixing bowl. For optimum results, use Sharffen Berger dark chocolate. Valrhona or Callebaut are good, too, though the latter tends to be smoky. Lindt "75% Cacao" bars are a fine inexpensive option.

1 Make the cake: Preheat the oven to 325°F. Line a 3-quart metal or stainless mixing bowl with foil. The bowl should be completely covered, with a couple of inches overhang. Make the foil as smooth as possible.

cake

10 large eggs

1 pound best-quality bittersweet chocolate, chopped into small pieces

1 pound unsalted butter, cut into pieces

1½ cups sugar

¼ cup strong brewed espresso

¼ cup hazelnut liqueur, such as Frangelico

1 cup skinned, lightly toasted ground hazelnuts (optional)

glaze

5 to 6 ounces bittersweet chocolate (same as for cake), grated

⅓ cup heavy cream

1½ tablespoons unsalted butter, at room temperature

Unsweetened cocoa powder, for dusting

Unsweetened whipped cream

anya von bremzen

62

2 Break the eggs into a large bowl and whisk until frothy.

3 In a large double boiler or a stainless bowl set over barely simmering water, melt the chocolate with the butter until smooth, stirring, about 8 minutes. Stir in the sugar, espresso, and liqueur and continue to cook, stirring, until the sugar dissolves, about 5 minutes.

4 Gradually, whisk the chocolate into the beaten eggs, whisking constantly, until the mixture is homogenous. Fold in the hazelnuts, if using.

5 Scrape the batter into the prepared bowl. Bake the cake in the middle of the oven until the top is slightly puffy and crisp but the center is still moist, 1¼ to 1½ hours. A cake tester inserted in the center won't come out clean, but it shouldn't have visible liquid on it. Let the cake cool on a rack, then refrigerate, covered loosely with plastic, for at least 6 hours or preferably overnight. (It will continue to firm as it chills.) The cake can be made up to two days ahead.

6 Make the glaze: In the top of a double boiler set over barely simmering water, melt the chocolate in the cream until completely smooth, about 6 minutes. Whisk in the butter until glossy.

7 Invert the cake onto a large cake plate and carefully peel off the foil. With a rubber spatula, coat the cake with the chocolate glaze, wiping the sides of the plate clean with a piece of damp paper towel. Let stand until the glaze is set, about 10 minutes, then refrigerate for another hour. Before serving, dust the cake lightly with cocoa powder using a sifter. Cut into slices and serve with whipped cream and an acidic sorbet or fruit salad, if desired.

Serves 14 to 16

jasper White, the dean of American chowderhounds, pauses for a moment, searching for words. "A great chowder," he finally utters, "is like love—you can't exactly describe it, but there's no mistaking it when it hits."

It's when the fish falls apart in big silky flakes. When the potatoes just melt. When you feel as if you're inhaling sea air as you eat—that's great chowder. And a great chowder, White maintains, is a dish; don't annoy him by calling it soup. He also gets irked when people assume it's a floury paste loaded with "pathetic bits of rubber-like clams." The missionary zeal for setting the story straight is what propelled Jasper White to write the wonderful *50 Chowders*.

chowder

Flour, as it happens, crept into the recipe in the 1820s, the original thickener being hardtack. With salt pork and onion—plus whatever the sea delivered—it constituted standard shipboard provision. Potatoes were added around 1830, milk a decade later; and while clam chowder is now considered iconic, the original main ingredient was in all likelihood cod. "Chowder was the inevitable outcome of a sea cook's confrontation with salt pork, ship's biscuit and a freshly caught cod," writes John Thorne in his "Down East Chowder" chapter of *Serious Pig*.

Opinions diverge about how chowder got its name. But anyone who accepts the French *chaudière* (cauldron) as the etymology, and the Breton communal fish stew, *faire la chaudière,* as the direct ancestor, would be in safe waters. The Bretons might have carried their stew to Newfoundland, Nova Scotia, and then New England sometime in the late seventeenth century. That's the canonical version. Stray from it, and you're in an open sea of suggestions and versions. Some of these involve American Indians; others conjecture that the Cornish word *jowter*—a female fishmonger who presumably made fish stews—offers the real etymology.

The exact composition of chowder produces similarly little consensus. Even the earliest chowder recipes varied wildly, containing such oddities as claret (the very first published chowder recipe from the *Boston Evening Post*); morels or truffles (from the eighteenth-century British food maven Hannah

Glasse); applesauce or mangoes to be served on the side (according to Amelia Simmons's *American Cookery,* 1800); even ketchup (that's where things get really weird!). Surprisingly, the only common and defining ingredient was salt pork. Chowder as we know it today—milk, flour, seafood, potatoes—had fully formed only in the mid-1880s. Manhattan clam chowder, heretically tomato-red, was born at the turn of the twentieth century.

Chowder might be as difficult as love to define, but its true spirit isn't all that elusive. Chowder just isn't chowder without salt pork. The dish should be thick, creamy, and chunky with each ingredient recognizable as itself—a bisque it resoundingly is not. At the same time it should blend into a homogenous whole—textural contrasts, last-minute flashes of flavor, that's *not* chowder, either. And finally, chowder must be sturdy, honest, direct—great American chow. "Chowder for breakfast, and chowder for dinner, and chowder for supper," Melville writes. Lucky Ishmael and Queequeg.

new england fish chowder

cook's notes This recipe, inspired by Jasper White, is for classic fish chowder. Though there's probably no place for it in the purist conception of fish chowder, I couldn't resist adding a handful of fresh corn kernels to the pot. For a nineteenth-century flavor, try a dash of Madeira. The fish stock can be made ahead and frozen or refrigerated for up to 1 day. If not making your own, use best-quality frozen fish fumet. The best accompaniment are old-fashioned New England common crackers—those fat round crackers that are split in two and toasted.

1 Make the fish stock: Rinse the fish frames of all traces of blood and viscera. In a heavy stockpot, melt the butter over medium heat. Add the onion, carrots, leeks, and celery and sweat them, covered, for 5 minutes. Add the fish trimmings, parsley, bay leaf, and peppercorns and stir for another 3 minutes. Cover the pot and cook, shaking it occasionally, for 7 minutes. The vegetables should be soft but not browned.

2 Add the water and wine, and bring to a boil over high heat. Skim thoroughly, reduce the heat to medium-low, and simmer, partially covered, until the liquid is reduced to 6 cups, about 1 hour. Strain through a fine sieve into a clean pot and season to taste with salt and pepper. Reserve 4½ cups of the stock for the chowder and save the rest for another use. (The stock will keep in the refrigerator for a couple of days. Otherwise, it can be frozen and thawed before using.)

fish stock

5 pounds fish carcasses, heads and tails and trimmings from white-fleshed nonoily fish (cod, haddock, pollack, grouper, tilefish, or sea bass), thoroughly rinsed

2 tablespoons unsalted butter

1 large onion, coarsely chopped

2 carrots, coarsely chopped

2 leeks (white part only), rinsed well and coarsely chopped

2 medium celery ribs and leaves, chopped

6 sprigs parsley

1 bay leaf

10 peppercorns

2 quarts water

½ cup dry white wine

Salt and freshly ground black pepper

or

4½ cups fish fumet

3 Make the chowder: In a large, heavy pot, cook the salt pork in 1 tablespoon of the butter over medium heat until it has rendered its fat and begins to brown lightly, about 5 minutes. Add the other 2 tablespoons of butter, the onion, celery, and leek, and cook, stirring, until the vegetables begin to soften, about 4 minutes. Add the bay leaf and the savory, cover, and sweat the vegetables over low heat for another 5 minutes without letting them brown.

4 Add the potatoes and the reserved 4½ cups stock, and bring to a boil over medium-high heat. Reduce the heat to low and cook, partially covered, until the potatoes begin to break apart, about 20 minutes. With a large slotted spoon, remove about ½ cup of the potatoes to a bowl and mash them with a fork. Whisk them back into the broth.

5 Add the milk, cream, and corn, bring to a simmer over low heat and cook for 5 minutes. Season with salt and pepper to taste. Take the chowder off the heat and let stand for 1 hour or refrigerate overnight for the flavor to develop. Right before serving, bring the chowder to a simmer, add the fish, and cook until it just begins to flake, about 4 minutes. Ladle into large bowls, sprinkle with chives and float the crackers on top.

Serves 6 as a main course

chowder

⅓ cup (about 2 ounces) finely diced lean salt pork or meaty bacon

3 tablespoons unsalted butter

1 medium onion, diced

1 celery rib, diced

1 leek (white part only), washed well and diced

1 bay leaf

1 teaspoon chopped savory or thyme, or ½ teaspoon dried

4 large yellow-fleshed boiling potatoes, such as Yukon Gold, halved lengthwise and sliced crosswise ¼ inch thick

1 cup milk

1¼ cups heavy cream

2 pounds skinless cod, haddock, or hake fillets, cut into 1¼-inch chunks

2 cups shucked fresh corn kernels

Salt and freshly ground black pepper

Minced chives, for garnish

6 common crackers, split, buttered and toasted

the kitchen of Mansouria, Paris's most celebrated Moroccan restaurant, is a blur of commotion, frenzied as any souk. Fatéma Hal, the reigning queen of Maghrebi cooking in France, is whirling around in her chic suit, shouting, imploring, pacifying on her cell phone. Fatéma has a headache; later today she's due at a food festival in Lausanne—to cook for hundreds. And she's just realized that the enormous load of her prized hand-rolled couscous hadn't made it onto the truck with the other provisions.

In the midst of this madness I'm getting a couscous class from Hajja and Habiba, Fatéma's trusted elderly cooks. A huge platter of golden semolina granules moistened with water is set on a counter. With the precise studied motion of keyboard virtuosi, meditative and oblivious to the commotion around

COUSCOUS

them, the women are rubbing and raking, their dark fingers scooping, circling, massaging the grains. Suddenly, Fatéma stops panicking and joins in.

Within minutes, she's sweet as pie. No matter. She will personally drag the twenty-pound couscous sack to Switzerland on the train.

"Like a Berber horseman," Habiba chuckles.

When I finally get to taste it, Hajja's and Habiba's couscous isn't just light; it has the ethereal fragility of just-fallen snow. When couscous is this good, it isn't the most famous dish of Morocco. It might be *the* best treat on the planet.

While it resembles a grain, couscous is a form of pasta: tiny pellets of semolina, which itself is produced from the floury core of durum wheat. North African couscous, however, can be made of cracked maize, barley, sorghum (Fatéma's favorite), or such exotica as acorn flour or black seeds of the goosefoot weed. In Morocco, couscous describes several things: the dried granules of semolina; the dish itself, a vast platter of airy grain moistened with a spiced brothy stew; and more broadly, a cooking technique by which a gluten-less grain is steamed repeatedly until it swells up light as a whisper.

A lyrical explanation for the word *couscous* is that it's onomatopoeic for the clatter of grains as they're rubbed in one's hand; or perhaps for the kss-kss-kss of the steam rising in the pot. More scholarly theories trace the word to the Arabic *kaskasa* (to grind or pound small). Western Arabists place the first printed couscous recipe around the thirteenth century, with the actual dish dating back one or two centuries earlier. However, archaeological findings of what might be primitive couscous pots inspire some North African scholars to place origins much further back.

To the Western imagination, couscous is the extravagant centerpiece of a Moroccan feast. But its function, in the culture and at the table, can be both more humble and resonant: an offering served before the end of a meal to assure that no one leaves hungry. Embedded as it is in North Africa's social and religious life, couscous is eaten by families for a Friday lunch (a Muslim day of rest), offered to pilgrims returning from Mecca, given away by mosques to the poor.

"In the Maghreb, couscous accompanied people from birth to death. It united Muslims, Christians, and Jews," Fatéma pronounces.

To produce a mound of uniform little granules by the traditional method, fine and coarse flours are moistened with water, then rubbed and rolled together until they form crumbs. These are sieved and rolled and sieved again and finally dried in the sun. Today, however, Moroccan city sophisticates buy couscous from shops, while rural families might send their grain to the mill.

But when it comes to cooking couscous, all shortcuts must end.

Habiba and Hajja show me the way—the only way, they insist—to get feathery grains swollen to their full fluffy potential. First, Hajja rubs a little oil into the couscous, rolling and raking in circles until there are a million little separate granules. "Here, here, a lump!" points Habiba. Hajja rolls her eyes. "Don't listen," I'm told. "She's just jealous."

Most Moroccan cooks steam couscous twice—often over a soupy stew that infuses the grains with its redolent vapors. H & H shake their heads, no. Only three steamings can render couscous practically weightless. Steamed thrice and drizzled with *smen* (preserved butter), the couscous is fit to eat.

On her way out Fatéma recites her favorites. Ah, how she adores the lyrical couscous with tiny wild green kuran figs, from the southern town of Taraudants. The cornmeal couscous (*baddaz*) from the area around Essaouira. Couscous musky with preserved lamb. Couscous peppery with wild turnip fronds. And, of course, the proverbial seven-vegetable couscous.

And now she must run. She and her twenty-pound couscous sack.

couscous with seven vegetables

Kasksou seb 'khadari

cook's notes When I returned home and applied Hajja and Habiba's lesson to steaming couscous the traditional way, I discovered that the method wasn't just simple and pleasant, but actually calming and therapeutic. And instant couscous seemed leaden in comparison.

Try to get the loose "long-cooking" semolina couscous from Middle Eastern, health food, or gourmet grocery stores. If quick-cooking (instant) couscous is the only option, follow the instructions on the package, soaking it in the broth from the vegetables with a nice pat of butter.

Though the authentic two-tiered *couscousière* is a romantic piece of kitchenware, a Chinese dumpling steamer works just as well. Or improvise with a large pot and a metal sieve, sealing the seam with foil. For the couscous, three steamings are optimum but two will do; everything up to the final steaming can be done ahead of time and leftovers reheat nicely in the microwave. The seven-vegetable couscous broth is among the most traditional, seven being a lucky number. But to the mandatory zucchini, chick peas, and carrots, you can add chunks of slender eggplants, fresh fava beans, green beans, red pepper, or chunks of fruit, such as green apples or quince. For the meat, you can use chunks of boneless lamb or beef if you prefer.

broth

2 tablespoons unsalted butter

1 tablespoon mild olive oil

2 large onions, quartered and sliced

2 pounds skinless chicken thighs

2 pounds veal shanks or lamb shanks, hacked into sections, or meaty lamb neck

2½ quarts water

2 large tomatoes, peeled, seeded, and quartered

1½ teaspoons ground ginger

2 cinnamon sticks

1 teaspoon mild paprika

Large pinch of cayenne, or more to taste

Large pinch of saffron threads, toasted and pulverized in a mortar

10 sprigs each parsley and cilantro, tied into a cheesecloth bag

Salt and freshly ground black pepper

1 Make the broth: In a heavy stockpot, heat the butter with the oil over medium heat and sauté the onions, stirring, for 5 minutes. Add the chicken and the veal and cook, turning the meats, until they turn completely opaque, about 5 minutes per side. Add the rest of the broth ingredients, bring to a boil, skim off the foam, cover, and simmer over low heat until the chicken is tender, 45 to 50 minutes. With a slotted spoon, remove the chicken to a bowl so that it doesn't overcook. Continue cooking the broth until the veal or the lamb is tender, about 1 hour longer. (While the meat is cooking, you can start preparing the couscous in step 3.)

2 Cook the vegetables: Add the carrots, turnips, and celery to the broth; raise the heat until it comes back to a simmer, lower the heat again, and cook for 15 minutes. Add the zucchini, squash and chickpeas, raise the heat again until the liquid returns to a simmer, lower the heat, and cook until the vegetables are soft and tender but not mushy, about 20 minutes more. Keep an eye on the vegetables, removing those that are looking too soft, especially the squash, to a bowl. Put the chicken back in the pot until warmed through, and adjust the seasonings to taste. Remove the cheesecloth bag. The broth and vegetables can be prepared a day ahead.

vegetables

2 fat carrots, scraped, quartered, and cut into 2-inch lengths

3 medium turnips or boiling potatoes, peeled and quartered

3 fat celery ribs, cut into 2-inch sections, or 1 medium fennel bulb with a little of the stalk, cut into large chunks (scrape the outer layer of the fennel bulb with a vegetable peeler if it's tough)

2 large zucchini, halved and cut into 2-inch sections

1 pound butternut squash or calabaza pumpkin, seeded, cored, and cut into 3-inch chunks

2 cups canned chickpeas, drained

couscous

4 cups (1½ pounds) fine or medium couscous (not instant)

Mild olive oil, for rubbing the couscous

2 to 3 cups water

1 teaspoon salt

2 to 3 tablespoons unsalted butter, cut into small pieces

Store-bought harissa or another pure chile paste, for serving

3 Make the couscous: Place the couscous in a sieve fine enough to hold all the grains. Place the sieve under cold running water and wet the couscous thoroughly. Spread it out in a thick layer on a large rimmed baking sheet (ideally 16 to 18 inches wide) or a huge wooden salad bowl. Let it stand for 10 to 15 minutes to absorb the moisture.

4 Sprinkle the couscous evenly with about 2 tablespoons of oil and work the oil into the grains with your fingers. Take a small handful of grains and rub them between your thumb and your two middle fingers to get rid of all the little lumps. As you work, lift the grains up, letting them drop back into the pan. Alternatively work over another large bowl to keep track of what's been worked over. Repeat with all the couscous.

5 Oil the perforated top of a *couscousière* or large wide steamer (see Cook's Notes). In the bottom part, bring 4 to 5 inches of water to a rolling boil. If there is a lot of steam escaping through the seam between the two parts, seal it with foil. When you see a good deal of steam rising up, transfer the couscous to the top part and steam uncovered for 15 to 18 minutes.

6 Return the couscous to the baking pan and spread it out again, breaking the lumps with a fork, and let cool until just manageable. In a measuring cup, combine 2 cups water and salt, and sprinkle evenly and gradually over the couscous, working the water in with your fingers. Spread it out again and let stand for another 10 to 15 minutes. Oil your hands and repeat the procedure in step 2 but without adding more oil. Steam again as in previous step for about 15 minutes. By now, the grains will be fluffy and separate and slightly al dente. (If not planning to steam couscous for a third time, steam it now for about 20 to 25 minutes total, until tender.)

7 If steaming for a third time, return the couscous to the baking pan, work in 1 more cup of water, spread it out, and let stand until ready for the final steaming. Before steaming, rub it again to remove lumps and steam one final time, 12 to 15 minutes.

8 Turn off the heat, leaving the couscous in the steamer, and carefully stir in the butter, breaking up any lumps that might have formed with a fork. Set aside.

9 To serve, reheat the broth and vegetables. Mound the steamed couscous on a large platter. Make a big well in the middle and pile some of the vegetables into this mound. Arrange the veal and chicken around the mound and scatter some chickpeas around it also. Moisten with about 1 cup of the broth. If you like, mix 1 cup of broth with 1½ to 2 tablespoons harissa to serve on the side. Serve the rest of the vegetables and broth in a large deep bowl, accompanied by harissa.

Serves 8

Couscous, of course, isn't confined to Morocco. Algerian couscous, which you might have tasted in Paris, is larger grained, denser, more rugged, with the broth, vegetables, and meats (like the spiced *merguez* sausage) all served separately, accompanied by fiery harissa paste. In Tunis, on the other hand, it is served and often steamed, mixed with other ingredients. Here you'll taste couscous sparked with various chiles and redolent of native spice blends like the famed *tabil* flavored with caraway. Couscous also exists beyond North Africa. You'll find it in the Sicilian city of Traponi, in Egypt and Yugoslavia, even in Senegal (with millet) and Brazil (cornmeal), where it was brought by West African slaves.

ot and cold, rich but light, creamy and crunchy, homey and haute, crème brûlée finished first in the race for the title "most crowd-pleasing dessert" of the late twentieth century—beating out tiramisù, panna cotta, even the sexy chocolate cake with a molten center.

By now, everyone knows what it takes to make crème brûlée: cream, vanilla, sugar, and egg yolks combined into a silky loose custard and baked in a water bath. The top is sprinkled with a thin, even layer of sugar, caramelized briefly with a salamander or blowtorch, or under a broiler, and voilà, you have that signature sheer crust of brown ice. Seductive and simple.

For the creators of crème brûlée, most look to England where the dessert has been a hit since the seventeenth century under various names: grilled cream, crackling cream, or burnt cream (French translation, *crème brûlée*). It also

crème brûlée

earned the monikers Trinity cream or Cambridge burnt cream, after the university where the custard achieved notoriety in the 1860s. (In Trinity College, Cambridge, the sugar came branded with the college crest and a small gold hammer was passed around to break the caramel ice.) Jane Grigson, the doyenne of British food writers for whom crème brûlée was "the best of all English puddings," argues that the Gallic title came into vogue in the 1800s thanks to French cuisiniers who came to Britain seeking fame and fortune.

Jolly good, so it is English, you say? Not so fast. France-bashers might be disappointed by the crème brûlée entry in the indisputably authoritative *Oxford Companion,* which reinstates the dessert's Gallic origins by claiming that the French term was applied as early as 1691 (to a *French* dessert), but fell into disuse in the nineteenth century. And we shouldn't overlook *crema catalana,* an ancient Catalan custard that is almost identical to crème brûlée, only a little runnier, thickened with cornstarch, and flavored with lemon peel.

Brûlée or burnt, custard or crème, British or Gallic, in this country crème brûlée was a nonentity until just recently—1982 to be exact. Enter Sirio Maccioni, the worldly ringmaster of Le Cirque restaurant in New York City, and his then-pastry chef Dieter Schorner. Together, they turned crème brûlée into the copycat dessert of the decade.

By the year 2000, crème brûlée had conquered the world, boasting a rainbow of flavors from jasmine to kaffir lime, and spawning savory spinoffs like lobster or corn brûlée. My prize for most extravagant crème brûlée presentation goes to the French six-Michelin-starred chef Marc Veyrat, who serves up a hollowed-out tree trunk filled with a half-dozen ramekins holding brûlées in flavors like carrot or lavender. Still. Nothing beats the smooth-crunchy effect of the vanilla classic still served at Le Cirque. Especially if the man making it is Francisco Gutierrez. Here is his recipe.

classic crème brûlée

cook's notes Since vanilla is the only flavoring here, I strongly recommend Madagascar or Tahitian beans (see Resources). While regular ramekins will do, shallow 1-cup porcelain dishes are ideal. And if you are a dedicated crème brûlée maker and love playing with fire, invest in a mini-blowtorch (see Resources). The custard needs sufficient time to chill and the dark brown sugar has to be really dry.

1 good-quality vanilla bean, split lengthwise

4 cups heavy cream

7 large egg yolks

¾ cup granulated sugar

1 cup dark brown sugar

1 With the tip of a small knife, scrape out the seeds from the vanilla bean, break the shell into pieces, and place the seeds and the shell in a medium heavy saucepan together with the cream. Heat the cream until bubbles just begin to form around the edges. Do no overheat. Remove from the heat and let steep for 30 minutes.

2 Preheat the oven to 325°F. and bring a kettle of water to a boil. In a large mixing bowl, whisk together the egg yolks and granulated sugar just until well combined; do not overwhisk. In a steady stream, whisk in the warm cream just until blended. Strain the mixture into a large pitcher or into two large measuring cups with spouts.

3 Place eight shallow, wide 1-cup ramekins into a large baking dish and transfer the baking dish to a rack in the oven. Pull the rack out of the oven as much as it will go without losing balance and carefully pour the custard into the ramekins. They should be as full as possible. Carefully pour enough hot water into the pan to come halfway up the sides of the ramekins. Push the oven rack in and bake the custards until they are just set in the middle but tremble slightly when you wiggle the ramekins, about 30 minutes. Test one with a skewer; if there's too much visible liquid oozing out from under the surface, bake for another 5 to 7 minutes. Wearing oven mitts, carefully remove the ramekins from the baking dish and let them cool completely. Cover loosely with plastic and refrigerate for at least 2 hours or overnight.

4 About 2 hours before serving, sift the dark brown sugar onto a large baking sheet. Let it dry until serving time.

5 Preheat the broiler, if using. Immediately before serving, place about 2 tablespoons of the sugar into a small sieve. Holding it directly over one ramekin, sprinkle the sugar over the top of the custard, pushing the sugar down with the back of a spoon or with your fingers. You should have a thin, even layer of sugar that covers the custard completely. Repeat with the rest of the custards. Place the ramekins on a baking sheet. Place the sheet about 4 inches under the broiler and broil until the top is hard and caramelized, about 1½ minutes. Watch it closely, lest the sugar burn, and move the baking sheet around if the custards are not caramelizing evenly. To use a blowtorch, light it and holding it 2 to 3 inches above the surface, depending on the intensity, caramelize the sugar, working in circles from the edges to the center. Serve immediately.

Serves 8

resources For vanilla beans, try The Spice House (tel: 847-328-3711 or *www.thespicehouse.com*); for a blowtorch, try Williams-Sonoma (tel: 800-541-2233 or *www.williams-sonoma.com*).

the greatest dishes!

n some parts of the world, vegetables—even some fruit—exist to be stuffed. After all, what could be more practical, festive, delicious?

The vast stuffed-vegetable empire encompasses the entire Turkic and Arabic-speaking world, stretching from the Middle East to the eastern Mediterranean to the Balkans into Eastern Europe. The nomenclature varies from language to language and often from dish to dish, with the most common term being a variant of dolma. Derived, appropriately, from the Turkish word for "stuffed," *dolma* can denote a specific dish of filled grape leaves (such as the Greek *dolmathes*) or refer to stuffed vegetables in general, as in Iranian *dolmeh* or Armenian *tolma*.

dolma

Stuffed Vegetables

As a vessel for stuffing, cooks can choose anything from apples to zucchini. The repertoire of fillings ranges from grains to meat. Vegetarian dolma is often braised in olive oil and eaten cold. Meat dolma is either stuffed with uncooked meat and poached, or baked with a filling of sautéed spiced lamb. If one were to collect all the world's dolma recipes, it would be one plump tome.

For me, Armenian dolma was the subject of my earliest and most intense gastronomic longing. My family and I sampled it during our trips to the Armenian capital, Yerevan, to visit friends called Nune (she) and Edik (he). Nune was a dentist whose passion for stuffing vegetables was equaled only by Edik's love of *hashi,* the garlic-laden hangover soup. I now think of Nune as a culinary taxidermist of sorts: potatoes, apricots, apples—nothing escaped her coring knife. Had bean sprouts been known in Yerevan, Nune would find a way of stuffing these, too.

There was Nune's theatrical hollowed-out pumpkin filled with rice, dried *kizil* (a sour plum), and ground walnuts. There were onions brimming with sautéed lamb, chestnuts, and prunes. Eggplants sported an interior of cracked wheat and chickpeas; grape leaves were rolled around yellow peas, raisins, and slivered dried apricots. Vine-leaf dolma, Nune insisted, was born in the ancient vineyards of the Caucasus, a reasonable claim given that Caucasus is the probable birthplace of viniculture.

Nune's coup de grâce was Echmiadzin dolma, a bright mélange of stuffed vegetables formally named after the city that houses the seat of the Orthodox Armenian church, but usually is just called "summer dolma." Being Christian, Armenians often stuff dolma with pork or beef. Nune, however, preferred lamb, procured from a sheep farmer in exchange for an occasional gold tooth. Tarragon, opal basil, and furry bunches of dill were spread out on her red oilcloth to be minced into the stuffing so that the kitchen swooned with their perfume. Once stuffed, the vegetables were gently poached in a pot as vast as the universe, in a liquid fortified with some lamb bones, chickpeas, and chopped quince.

We ate these with a cinnamon-spiked yogurt and tried hard not to moan with pleasure. Here's Nune's recipe.

armenian summer dolma

cook's notes Make sure that the tomatoes and apples don't fall apart during cooking: choose ones that are ripe but extremely firm. You can serve the poaching liquid as a soup course, topped with thinly sliced red onion and sprinkled with chopped mint. Feel free to substitute pork for ground lamb, which is typically Armenian. The scooped-out insides of the vegetables can be used for a quick vegetable caviar or ratatouille. If preparing in advance, reheat the dolma very gently in the poaching liquid.

1 Make the stuffing: Combine the beef, lamb, rice, canned tomatoes, onion, ice water, paprika, herbs, and salt and pepper in a large mixing bowl. Stir the mixture together until just uniform. Do not overhandle.

2 Stuff the vegetables: Cut off the tops from the tomatoes and reserve. Using a grapefruit spoon, scoop out the pulp, leaving at least a ¼-inch shell; reserve the pulp for another use. Stem the eggplants and zucchini; cut crosswise into 2½-inch-long sections. With an apple corer, hollow out the eggplants and zucchini, leaving a ¼-inch-thick shell. Reserve the vegetable flesh for another use. Cut off the tops from the peppers and reserve. Seed and de-rib the peppers. Cut the tops from the apples and reserve. With an apple corer, core the insides of each apple, then, using a paring knife, hollow the apples, leaving about a 1-inch-thick shell. Sprinkle the insides of the vegetables and apples generously with salt.

3 Wet your hands in cold water and stuff each vegetable loosely with the meat filling; they should be about three-fourths full as the rice will expand during the cooking. Close the tomatoes, peppers, and apples with the reserved tops and secure each of the lids with one or more toothpicks.

stuffing and vegetables

1 pound lean ground beef

¾ pound lean ground lamb

⅔ cup medium-grain rice

4 canned tomatoes, drained and finely chopped

1 small onion, grated on a four-sided box grater

3 tablespoons ice water

1 teaspoon sweet paprika

½ cup each of finely chopped basil, mint, and parsley

Salt and freshly ground black pepper

6 medium, ripe but very firm tomatoes

3 long, slender Japanese eggplants (approximately 8 by 1½ inches)

3 long, slender zucchini

6 small Italian (frying) peppers

4 Granny Smith apples, the smallest you can find

If you have any filling leftover, shape it into balls and add to the pot once the liquid comes to a boil.

4 Arrange the eggplants, zucchini, and apples (lid side up) side by side on the bottom of a squat 6-quart pot. Arrange the peppers on top and tuck in the tomatoes between the other vegetables, lid side up. The vegetables should sit as snugly as possible. Scatter the chickpeas and apricots over the top. Place a lid from another pot (slightly smaller than your poaching pot) or a heavy heatproof plate over the vegetables to keep them in place during cooking. Add enough cold water to cover the vegetables by 1½ inches. Bring the liquid to a boil over high heat.

broth and yogurt sauce

2 cups canned chickpeas, drained

½ cup slivered dried apricots, preferably Californian

2 heaping tablespoons tomato paste diluted in hot water

3 to 5 tablespoons fresh lemon juice

2 teaspoons dried mint

1 teaspoon sweet paprika

Salt

2 cups plain yogurt

1 large garlic clove, crushed through a press

Large pinch of cinnamon

Pomegranate seeds (if available), for garnish

Fresh chopped parsley and mint, for garnish

As soon as the liquid boils, reduce the heat to low so that the liquid barely bubbles. Gently press down on the lid so that it is completely submerged in the liquid and skim off all the foam. Using tongs, remove the lid and skim off more foam. Very carefully, stir in the tomato paste, lemon juice, mint, paprika, and salt into the liquid that covers the vegetables. Recover the vegetables with a lid to keep them submerged, cover, and simmer over very low heat until the rice in the filling is tender, about 20 minutes.

5 While the dolma is cooking, make the yogurt sauce: In a serving bowl stir the yogurt with the garlic and add salt to taste. Let stand for 15 to 20 minutes for the flavors to develop. Sprinkle the top evenly with the cinnamon and decorate with pomegranate seeds.

6 Once the vegetables are cooked, allow them to sit in the broth for about 15 minutes; this will plump up the rice. With a slotted spoon, carefully remove the vegetables along with the chickpeas and dried apricots and place on a serving platter. Skim the fat from the poaching liquid if needed. Sprinkle the vegetables with 5 to 6 tablespoons of the poaching liquid and then with the parsley and mint. Serve with additional poaching liquid for sprinkling and with yogurt sauce on the side. If you'd like, you can serve the poaching liquid as a soup course (see Cook's Notes).

Serves 6

Setting: a trim old diner, sitting modestly by a local highway somewhere in small-town New England. Time: a nippy fall morning, crimson and yellow leaves underfoot. You take a stool at the worn but spotless Formica counter, smile good morning to the waitress—and slowly take that first bite of what you drove all the way here for.

Fresh doughnuts.

Brown, warm, and crunchy-just-so on the outside, cake-moist and butter-sweet within. It's a doughnut purist's paradise. There might be a dash of cinnamon or cider or buttermilk in the batter. But that's it for variety here: plain aromatic classics, with a hole, of course—light but hefty enough to dunk, leaving no grease on the fingertips.

doughnuts

The origins of deep-fried leavened pastry—which is what a doughnut is—go back to ancient China, Pompeii, and Greek Marseilles. In the Middle Ages, northern Europeans would fry cakes pre-Lent for Shrove Tuesday or Mardi Gras (*Fastnacht,* in German—which is the name for the doughnuts traditionally served by the Pennsylvania Dutch on the day).

By the nineteenth century, baking soda had come along and made for a cakier batter than did yeast. More momentously, the all-important hole was established, likely again by the Pennsylvania Dutch. A Mark Twain-ish piece of Americana gives the credit to a Maine sea captain, Hanson Gregory, who claimed to have had the bright idea for a central hole in 1847 so he could stack doughnuts on the spokes of his wheel for snacking and steering.

Like a few other things so American (Hemingway, for instance), the popular taste for doughnuts was launched by Yanks over in France—when Salvation Army girls during World War I started frying them up on the spot for U.S. soldiers. Then, in 1920, a Russian-born immigrant named Adolph Levitt became the Henry Ford of this new taste, not just by helping invent the first doughnut-making machine but also by having the savvy to operate it in the window of his Harlem bakery. Within a year Levitt had sold 123 of these "Wonderful Almost Human Automatic" devices. The doughnut boom was on.

The Depression drew doughnuts even closer to Main Street, USA. Cheap and sweet, they offered a fatty caloric bang (250 to 300 calories plain) for pennies. And by the 1950s, the fresh-baked franchises had loomed onto the scene: southern-based Krispy Kreme pumping out its signature vanilla-rich sugar-glazeds, behemoth-to-be Dunkin Donuts from Massachusetts ever expanding its varieties.

These days enough doughnuts are produced annually to feed three dozen to every American. Sugar-glazed are the number-one style adored by millions. But I'll take the plain New England classic any morning.

doughnut lore The Dutch settlers of New Amsterdam draw the first possible mention of the word "doughnuts," by Washington Irving, in his account of New York life in 1809. These were hole-less fried balls of dough cooked in hog's fat and were also known as *oly koeks* (oil cakes). Irving calls them "delicious." Aside from that, "doughnut" doesn't seem to have a clear etymological history. Speculation has it deriving from a colonial fritter shaped like a "lover's knot"—later "Love Knot" and "Dough Knot." But this is just one *maybe* among a number. And doughnuts aren't just classic dunkers, of course. Broadly speaking, they can come long and narrow, round and bunlike, cream-and-jelly-filled, glazed, and frosted. And they answer to monikers like Bismarks, Long Johns, Chicagos, and twisters.

As for dunking, the fashion was supposedly launched when actress Mae Murray, "The Girl with the Bee-Stung Lips," accidentally dropped her doughnut into her coffee at Lindy's Deli in the 1920s. "Hey, where'd you learn to dunk?" Clark Gable's offended regular joe demanded of Claudette Colbert's heiress in *It Happened One Night*, in 1934. "Dunkin's an art," Gable indignantly informed her. "Aw, I oughta write a book about it." (He never did.)

buttermilk doughnuts

cook's notes   Because I like lighter, airier doughnuts, I use slightly less flour than in most recipes, making a very moist batter that barely holds together. For denser doughnuts, add ⅓ cup more flour. Refrigerating the batter also yields lighter results.

The key to just-right frying is keeping the oil between 350° and 375°F. but not higher, lest your doughnuts burn. An instant-read deep-fat thermometer is indispensable and the frying pan should be heavy. If you must glaze, use a simple glaze made with 3 to 4 tablespoons boiling dark apple cider mixed with 1½ cups sifted confectioners' sugar and dip the doughnuts directly into a saucepan of glaze.

1   In a large mixing bowl, sift together the flour, salt, baking powder, baking soda, nutmeg, ginger, and allspice. Gather the dry ingredients into a mound and make a big well in the middle.

3 cups plus 2 tablespoons cake or all-purpose flour, plus more as needed

1 teaspoon salt

2 teaspoons double-acting baking powder

1 teaspoon baking soda

¾ teaspoon freshly grated nutmeg

½ teaspoon ground ginger

¼ teaspoon ground allspice

2 large eggs, beaten

½ cup sugar

3 tablespoons vegetable shortening or unsalted butter, softened

¾ cup buttermilk, preferably full-fat

3 tablespoons plain yogurt, preferably full-fat

Peanut or canola oil, for deep-frying

1 cup sugar mixed with 1 tablespoon cinnamon, for dusting

2   In another bowl, whisk the eggs with the sugar, shortening, buttermilk, and yogurt until fluffy and smooth. You can use a hand-held electric mixer for this, beating everything at low speed.

3   Add the egg mixture to the well in the dry ingredients. Using your hands or a rubber spatula, work in the dry ingredients, incorporating all the stray crumbs from the sides, until you have a moist, very soft dough. If it feels overly wet and sticky, add about 2 extra tablespoons of flour. Turn the dough out onto a lightly floured surface and knead four to six times just to combine. Do not overwork the dough; it will firm up in the refrigerator. Wrap the dough in plastic and refrigerate for 2 to 6 hours or overnight.

4 On a lightly floured surface, with a floured rolling pin, roll the dough out between ¼ and ⅓ inch thick. Dip a doughnut cutter in flour and stamp out the doughnuts in one firm motion (if you twist, they may not rise properly), saving the holes. Alternatively, use a 3-inch cookie cutter and a ¾-inch pastry tip for the holes. Transfer the finished doughnuts to a baking sheet lined with waxed paper. Let the doughnuts dry for about 10 minutes.

5 Line a cookie sheet with a double thickness of paper towels. In a deep, heavy pot about 12 inches in diameter, heat 3 inches of oil to 360°F. Fry the doughnuts, four at a time, until golden brown, 2 to 4 minutes total, turning each doughnut twice. Regulate the heat to maintain oil temperature, turning the heat down a notch if the doughnuts brown too fast. Transfer the finished batch to drain on paper towels and repeat with the rest of the doughnuts. Once all the doughnuts are finished, fry the holes, which will take about 1½ minutes per batch.

6 While the doughnuts are still warm, combine the sugar and the cinnamon in a large paper bag. Add the doughnuts to the bag a few at a time, and shake. Serve as fresh as possible.

Makes 12 to 14 doughnuts, plus holes

in 1894, a Wall Street broker named Lemuel Benedict sauntered over for breakfast at the Waldorf-Astoria, nursing a mean hangover. Hungover Benedict summoned a waiter and called for poached eggs, bacon, and buttered toast. Plus a "hooker of hollandaise sauce." Lemuel piled everything on his toast and drowned his breakfast in hollandaise. Oscar Tschirky, Waldorf's mythical maître d' and greeter of presidents and celebrities, heard of Benedict's inspiration and liked it enough to include it on his regular menus, upgrading the idea with muffins and Canadian bacon (truffles and *glace viande* also feature in some accounts).

However, there is a conflicting scenario, which shifts the scene to the fabled Delmonico's (of Lobster Newburg and Baked Alaska fame) and stars a wealthy dame called LeGrande Benedict. Ms. Benedict,

eggs benedict

so it seems, was bored with eggs, bored with toast—bored with everything on Delmonico's menu. "Chef, darling, make me something extra-special for breakfast," she cooed (or maybe barked). And got the first eggs Benedict, too.

Delmonico's, the Waldorf, hangover, boredom, maître d's to the Belle Epoque *beau monde*. . . . What's it matter really as long as we can mount a crisp porous muffin with Canadian bacon and a perfect poached egg, and drown it in luxurious swaths of hollandaise sauce? Admittedly, Benedict isn't a wildly original concept. Think of eggs florentine on their bed of spinach, of *oeufs à la Benedictine* (no relation) perched on creamed salt cod. Think, too, of eggs sardou, that New Orleans icon with spinach plus artichoke bottoms invented in 1908 at Antoine's for a French playwright. But of all the poached egg and sauce combos with fancy names, Benedict is iconic.

Magnificent as eggs Benedict are, this breakfast masterpiece gives even the bravest of home cooks pause. Do you want to spend *your* morning negotiating between the Scylla of perfect poached egg and the Charybdis of treacherous emulsified sauces?

Yes, you do.

Poached eggs couldn't be simpler if you retire your fancy poachers and follow my simple recipe. As for hollandaise, that most temperamental of sauces, the solution came to me in the book *The Curious Cook* by the brilliant kitchen scientist Harold McGee. For certain chemical reasons, which a science flunkout like me can't relay lucidly, the most foolproof way with hollandaise also happens to be idiot proof. You just start the sauce in a cold pan and heat everything together, whisking. In four minutes, perfect hollandaise. Hollandaise the McGee way is no harder than white sauce or mayonnaise, and I have no idea why people still bother doing it any other way.

Between easy hollandaise and even simpler poached eggs, there's no excuse now for not greeting each morning with luscious voluptuous eggs Benedict (calories be damned). Who knows? Maybe it can even cure a hangover.

the fickle sauce Mentioned in print as early as 1758 (when it was made without eggs), hollandaise ranks as the most capricious of sauces. Here's why. Water—which accounts for 50 percent of the yolk's content—and fat don't take well to each other; that much we know. Fortunately for hollandaise lovers, a natural chemical stabilizer called lecithin contained in the eggs makes emulsifying and thickening possible. But only barely. When egg yolk and butter meet each other under precisely regulated conditions, a fragile bind takes place.

Classically, to make hollandaise you first melted the butter, preferably clarifying it for extra stability. Then you warmed beaten yolks in a bowl set over simmering water, and started introducing the butter—bit by small bit, whisking *vigorously*! The road to a smooth hollandaise was fraught with dangers. Under which circumstances could the sauce thin and break? A) Butter added too quickly. B) Butter too hot or too cold. C) Too much butter added at once. D) Yolks scramble over too high a heat. The answer? All of the above. That is, until Harold McGee came along and introduced his incredible simplified method.

perfect, simple eggs benedict

cook's notes The eggs can be made ahead of time and reheated by sliding them into simmering water for 30 seconds. If you're not a huge fan of Canadian bacon, consider using smoked salmon, cooked spinach, good ham, or crab cakes. And since this recipe will leave you with a bit of extra hollandaise, poach a few fat spears of asparagus.

hollandaise sauce

3 large egg yolks, at room temperature

1 to 2 tablespoons fresh lemon juice,
 or to taste

1 teaspoon Dijon mustard

12 tablespoons unsalted butter, cut into
 ½-inch pieces

Salt

Pinch of cayenne pepper

4 large very fresh eggs, at room temperature

1 tablespoon vinegar, such as apple cider,
 tarragon, or white wine

4 English muffins, split

4 slices Canadian bacon

1 tablespoon butter, plus more for buttering
 the muffins

1 Make the hollandaise sauce: In a small bowl, whisk together the yolks, lemon juice, and mustard until frothy and smooth. Transfer the mixture to a medium pan with a heavy bottom. Have an instant-read thermometer handy. Add all the butter to the pan and set it over medium heat. As soon as the butter begins to melt, start whisking, first gently, then more vigorously. Regulate the heat as you whisk so that the butter melts gently and evenly into the yolks. When all of the butter has melted, about 1½ minutes, turn the heat down to low (don't stop whisking while you do this). Keep on whisking until the sauce is smooth and well thickened. Take the sauce off the heat as soon as it is thickened. The entire procedure should take 4 to 5 minutes. Do not let the temperature of the mixture exceed 170°F. If your sauce gets too hot and breaks, add one ice cube and re-whisk. It will be thinner than it was originally but still fine.

2 Remove the hollandaise from heat and season with salt to taste and cayenne. Add more lemon juice to taste and thin out the sauce, if you wish, with 2 to 3 tablespoons warm water. Set aside and keep warm, in a bowl placed over barely simmering water or on top of a double boiler, while making the eggs.

3 Preheat the oven to 425°F. Carefully break the eggs into four small egg cups, measuring cups, or coffee cups. Fill a medium skillet with 2 to 3 inches of water, add the vinegar, and bring to a steady simmer over low heat.

4 Place the muffins on a baking sheet and bake until toasty and golden, 7 to 8 minutes. While the muffins are baking, lower a cup with the egg sideways into the simmering water so that the lip of the cup is slightly submerged in the water. Slide the egg carefully into the water and repeat with the rest of the eggs. When the water goes back to a simmer, cover the skillet, turn off the heat, and let the eggs sit for exactly 3½ minutes for medium-runny eggs.

5 While the eggs are cooking, heat a buttered griddle or heavy skillet over high heat and brown the bacon lightly, about 45 seconds per side. Do not overcook or it will turn rubbery.

6 Remove the muffins from the oven, butter them, place on plates, and top with the bacon. With a slotted spoon, remove the poached eggs from the water in the order you put them in, gently shaking off the excess liquid. Place them on the bacon. Pour some hollandaise (the more the better) on each portion and serve at once.

Serves 4

orkier than Alsatian choucroute, beanier than all the cassoulets of Languedoc, the *feijoada*, with its carnival of trimmings, is a feast of black beans and pig parts, as extravagant as any samba parade.

Feijoada is like a cauldron bubbling with three cultures, Brazilians like to repeat. African slaves on the sugar plantations created the dish from the cheapest common denominator, *feijoas*, or black beans (an import from Africa), which they cooked up with scraps of dried and cured meats from the master's table. The indigenous Indians provided their staple, fried manioc flour (*farofa*), as an accompaniment. And the Portuguese contributed the mandatory side dish of shredded kale—not to mention the smoky meats that give the feijoada its flavor.

Traditionally, Brazilians eat feijoada on Wednesdays and Saturdays, the weekend affair being more full and elaborate. For Cariocas (inhabitants of Rio), Saturday begins with a morning on the beach (where else?), followed by a *very* long feijoada meal, then a late siesta. Life resumes after ten with supper, samba, and arguments over soccer (what else?).

feijoada

Brazilian Black Bean and Mixed Meats Casserole

At fancy establishments, such as the Caesar Park Hotel in Rio, the Saturday feijoada is an affair to remember. Even before you enter the restaurant, a lady in a ruffled Bahian outfit sways around you at the entrance with glasses of *batida* (cocktails of tropical fruit juice and *cachaça*, Brazil's "white lightning"), and a plate of *toresmos*, the dangerously addictive pork cracklings. You finally settle in, drink some more, then leisurely start helping yourself to the meal. Cariocas say that feijoada should be eaten like it cooks, slowly and languidly, a little at a time. You're in for a lunch that inevitably morphs into dinner.

At home the beans and the meats are cooked and served together. But at better restaurants, they are laid out separately buffet style: a black cauldron of beans and heaping plates of dried beef, Portuguese sausages called *linguiça*, and *paio*, smoked bacon, pig's tongue, ears, and feet of pig, perhaps a roast pork of some kind. The thick dark bean liquid might be drunk as a soup and the traditional feijoada trimmings are strictly mandated: crunchy *farofa* (buttered fried manioc flour), white rice, stir-fried shredded kale or collard greens, palate-cleansing sliced oranges, and pickled chiles of varying degrees of heat, the hottest ones being the tiny *malaguetas*.

While Brazilian restaurants tend to serve feijoada with everything, what meats are meant for a home-style feijoada is a matter of heated debate. While the Southerners swear by a hefty chunk of beef, Northern purists adhere to the "pork only" rule. Some like pig's ears, others adore tail. Things get even more complicated in the United States, where one is forced to make substitutions. American corned beef has its defenders and its detractors. So do Polish kielbasa and Italian sausage. "We didn't emigrate to America to eat pig's ears and snout," you'll hear someone scoff. "Pig's ears are the very soul of the feijoada," others counter.

Everyone, however, agrees that without *carne seca* (dried beef) and pig's feet, no feijoada deserves the name. The other item of consensus is the cooking time: long and slow, to allow the smoky flavors of the meat to permeate the beans. It's the ultimate party dish.

caiperinhas No feijoada bash is complete without *caiperinhas*, the national cocktail of Brazil made with *cachaça* (Brazilian *aguardiente*), sugar, and crushed lime. If you don't have *cachaça*, don't despair: mix up an authentic *caiperoska*—that's the same libation made with vodka. For 10 to 12 drinks, you will need 14 large limes, halved crosswise; 10 to 12 tablespoons granulated sugar, or to taste; 3 cups *cachaça* or vodka; and plenty of ice cubes. Squeeze some juice from the lime halves into a pitcher, but not so they are completely dry. Cut the limes, with the skin, into 1½-inch chunks. Add the limes to the pitcher, and crush them with the sugar, using a large wooden spoon. Add the *cachaça* or vodka, and stir to blend. Pour into glasses (with the crushed limes) and add ice cubes to taste.
Makes 10 to 12 drinks

feijoada completa

cook's notes The version below features a slightly abridged but still authentic roster of meats. Most of them can be found at a good Hispanic butcher shop, though a German or Polish butcher is also a good bet for smoked meats. If you can't find dried beef or beef jerky, use corned beef, soaked in cold water for 2 hours and drained. I include a kale recipe but omit the *farofa* since mandioc meal is too difficult to find in this country.

3 cups (1½ pounds) dried black turtle beans

1 pound dried beef, such as *carne seca, tasajo, charqui,* or unflavored beef jerky

2 pounds smoked tongue (optional)

2 pig's feet, split lengthwise

½ pound best-quality smoked slab bacon or meaty salt pork, in one piece

4 tablespoons mild olive oil

One 3-pound beef brisket or boneless pork loin

Salt and freshly ground black pepper

1 pound sweet Italian sausage, without fennel, pricked in several places with a fork

2 pounds smoked pork chops, loin, or butt

6 smashed garlic cloves, 2 bay leaves, and 12 bruised cilantro sprigs, tied into a cheesecloth bag

1 pound *linguiça* or kielbasa sausage

1 large onion, finely chopped

6 garlic cloves, crushed through a press

⅓ cup fresh orange juice

accompaniments

Stir-Fried Shredded Kale (recipe follows)

Cooked white rice

6 juicy, tart oranges, cut into slices or wedges

Several kinds of pickled chiles

1 Soak the beans in cold water to cover for at least 6 hours or overnight. In separate bowls, soak the dried beef and the smoked tongue (if using) in cold water to cover for at least 4 hours or overnight. Drain and rinse before cooking.

2 In a large pot of boiling water, blanch the pig's feet for 5 minutes. Add the bacon and cook for another 5 minutes. Drain.

3 In a large skillet, heat 2 tablespoons of the oil over high heat. Rub the beef or pork generously with salt and pepper, and brown well on all sides, about 7 minutes. Remove the beef to a bowl, add the Italian sausage to the skillet, and brown on all sides for about 5 minutes. Pat dry the beef and the sausage with paper towels to remove grease.

4 In a 7-quart stockpot, combine the beans, reserved dried beef and tongue (if using), pig's feet, bacon, brisket or pork loin, and smoked pork chops, loin, or butt. (Reserve the Italian sausage.) Add the cheesecloth bag and enough water to cover the beans and the meats by 2½ inches and bring to a boil, skimming. Reduce the heat to low, cover, and simmer for 1½ hours. Skim from time to time and keep checking the level of liquid, adding more cold water to keep it at the same level. Add the kielbasa and continue cooking over very low heat until the beans and all the meats are very tender, about 1 hour longer, checking and replenishing the liquid periodically. (While the feijoada is cooking, make the kale recipe below; the kale can be reheated at serving time.)

5 In a large skillet, heat the remaining 2 tablespoons of the oil over medium heat. Add the onion and garlic and cook, stirring, until the onion is soft, about 7 minutes. With a slotted spoon, remove about 2 cups of beans from the liquid and add them to the skillet. Mash the beans right in the skillet with a fork. Add the orange juice and cook this mixture, stirring, for about 5 minutes, then pour the contents of the skillet back into the bean pot. Add the reserved Italian sausage, season with salt and pepper to taste, and cook over low heat for another 15 minutes.

6 To serve, remove the cheesecloth bag. With a slotted spoon, transfer the meats to a large bowl or cutting board. When just cool enough to handle, cut the sausages into thick slices. Cut all the other meats into slices. If you like bacon, slice it, too; otherwise discard. You can either arrange all the meats on a large serving platter or, for a more casual presentation, stir them back into the beans. Transfer the beans to a large serving bowl. Serve the beans and meats accompanied by rice, stir-fried shredded kale, orange wedges, and pickled chiles.

Serves 10

stir-fried shredded kale

1 Roll up a few kale leaves and shred them into thin ribbons. Repeat with the rest of the kale.

2 In a large skillet or wok, heat 2 tablespoons of the oil over high heat. Add half of the garlic and stir for 1 minute. Add half of the kale and stir-fry for 3 to 4 minutes, until it turns bright-green. Transfer to a large bowl and repeat with the rest of the oil, garlic, and kale. Taste the kale: if it doesn't seem tender enough, replace all the kale in the skillet, add 3 to 4 tablespoons water, cover, and steam for a few minutes.

2 pounds kale, rinsed and thoroughly dried

4 tablespoons mild olive oil, or more as needed

1 tablespoon finely minced garlic

Salt

Serves 10 as an accompaniment

On a gray British day no other food ritual is more gratifying than a jaunt to a proper fish 'n chips shop, preferably a battered old storefront squeezed in among row houses. It's about to start drizzling. You jostle your way in, soaking up the urban vernacular and the funky odor of sizzling oil. You call out your fish—cod, haddock, plaice—shouting no to ketchup and yes to salt, vinegar, red pickled onions, or mushy peas. Then you tote your hot paper-swaddled booty somewhere sheltered and dive in. If your chippie is a good honest chippie, the batter fairly shatters under your teeth, giving way to moist milky fish flesh. The chips are nice and limp, as they should be, brought to life by a dash of salt and generous squirts of malt vinegar.

fish and chips

Eating lacy fried fish at a beach shack in Andalusia might be a culinary experience of a much higher order, but there's something inevitable and addictive about Brit fish and chips.

Of course, the British can't lay claim to having invented batter-fried fish; most likely the method arrived in England with Portuguese Morano Jews who fled north in the sixteenth century to escape the Inquisition. As it happens, Jewish fishmongers also controlled the all-important fish trade of London's East End. This is where a newly arrived Eastern European Jew named Joseph Malin first started selling fish and potatoes in 1860. Malin's could well be the world's first official chippie—though Northerners hold that this distinction belongs to Mrs. Lee's Fish and Chip Hut in Mossley Market, Lancastershire. And credit is due to subsequent immigrants—Italian, Cypriot, Chinese—for maintaining the trade.

Still, the fish and chips shop was and remains a quintessentially British and decidedly urban institution. A child of the industrial revolution, it flourished in the clamorous back alleys of Yorkshire and Lancashire towns to offer cheap nourishment to employees of factories and cotton mills. The child came into its own with the late nineteenth-century development of the steam trawler, supported by the extensive network of trains that rushed fresh fish from big ports to every corner of Britain.

Very well, but what of the chips (British for french fries)? The original accompaniment to fried fish, historians say, was a slice of bread, subsequently replaced by a baked potato. It wasn't until the 1860s that the baked spud morphed into thinly cut oil-fried potatoes. By the early twentieth century, the fish and chip were inseparable, wrapped in yesterday's paper—the flavor of newsprint being as essential as salt and malt vinegar. (To the great chagrin of traditionalists, the newspaper wrapping was outlawed by the hygiene police in the 1990s.) Sir Winston Churchill famously dubbed fish and chips "the good companions," and by the onset of World War II, the staple was so essential to British life that the nation's minister of food not only flatly refused to ration fish and chips but even dispatched chippie carts to feed starving evacuees.

Today, nudged aside by pizza parlors, curry joints, and doner kebab dives, British relics such as eel and pie shops are going the way of the dodo. The fish and chips trade, however, goes swimmingly. How swimmingly? According to the National Federation of Fish Fryers (a Leeds-based organization founded in 1913), by the start of the twenty-first century there were eight chippies in Britain for every McDonald's, turning over a whopping annual profit of $1 billion, and going through 60,000 tons of fish and 500,000 tons of spuds per year. That's a lot of happy gray days.

fish and chips

cook's notes Three issues should concern an aspiring fish fryer. First, the choice of fish. Here, cod is Britain's number one and my own preference, followed by haddock (even if Northerners do maintain that "haddock is for heroes and cod is for zeroes"). Halibut is also delicious; as is the humble whiting. For the fat, beef drippings might be authentic, but contemporary British chefs go for clean-tasting oils, such as peanut or canola. The correct oil temperature—hot enough to puff a piece of batter on contact—is the key to light, greaseless results. For frying the chips (British for french fries), I've come to swear by a simple method attributed to Joël Robuchon and relayed by Jeffrey Steingarten in *The Man Who Ate Everything*, which involves starting the potatoes in cold oil. The fish is also wonderful just on its own, with lemon wedges and a green salad.

3 russet (Idaho) potatoes (about 1½ pounds total), peeled

1½ pounds 1-inch-thick white fish fillets (cod, haddock, halibut, or whiting), cut crosswise into 2½-inch pieces

Salt

¾ cup self-rising flour

¾ cup ice water

3 tablespoons beer

1 egg yolk

2 egg whites

All-purpose flour for dusting the fish

Peanut or canola oil, for deep-frying

Malt vinegar and/or ketchup, pickled onions, and gherkins, for serving

1 Rinse the potatoes under cold running water and pat dry with paper towels. Trim the potatoes to 3½-inch lengths and trim off the curved sides so that you have neat rectangles. Slice the potatoes lengthwise into ¼-inch slices. Stack a few slices together and cut them lengthwise into ¼-inch-wide strips. In batches, rinse the potatoes well under cold running water and dry as thoroughly as you can with paper towels. Spread them on a baking sheet and let them dry a bit more. Meanwhile, rub the fish pieces generously with salt and let stand until ready to fry.

2 Make the batter: In a large bowl toss the flour with ¾ teaspoon salt. Whisk in the water, beer, and egg yolk until the batter is completely smooth. Let the batter stand while preparing the potatoes.

anya von bremzen

3 Line a cookie sheet with a double thickness of paper towels and preheat the oven to 300°F. Place all the potatoes in one layer in a very large, deep, heavy skillet or wok and cover with cold oil by 2 inches. Turn the heat on to high and let the oil come to 250°F. on an instant-read thermometer. Cover the pan with a screen as the oil will splatter. Continue cooking the potatoes until the oil comes to 350°F., then turn the heat down to very low and cook for another 2 minutes. Turn the heat off under the oil. With a slotted spoon, transfer the potatoes to drain on paper towels. Once drained, sprinkle them with salt and keep warm in the oven while frying the fish.

4 To fry the fish: Whisk the egg whites until frothy and whisk into the batter. Spread a thin layer of flour on a large plate and dredge the fish lightly with the flour.

5 Reheat the oil over high heat to 360°F. (A piece of batter dropped in the oil should puff on contact.) Using a fork, dip a piece of fish in batter until well coated, quickly shake off the excess, and drop into the oil. Dip 3 to 4 more pieces of fish into the batter and drop into the oil. Fry until golden-brown and cooked through, about 2 minutes per side. With a slotted spoon, transfer the fish to drain on a brown bag or paper towels. Fry the rest of the fish in the same fashion. Serve at once, with the chips, malt vinegar or ketchup, onions, and gherkins.

Serves 4

fried chicken

the arguments over perfect fried chicken are fierce enough to start sectarian wars. Flour-dusting versus batter versus bread crumbs— debates bubble and spatter like seething cauldrons of oil, or shortening, unless, of course, you insist on frying in bacon fat, lard, or clarified butter. If you're one to give the bird a bath before cooking, are you of the milk, buttermilk or plain water camp? Pan-fried or deep-fried? Turned continuously or once only? Small pieces or large? Seasoned or plain? Gravy, lemon, Tabasco?

To resolve these disputes once and for all and deliver the "ultimate crispy fried chicken," a team from *Cooks Illustrated* magazine—aka America's test kitchen—approached the subject as if it were rocket science. Every coating, from panko (Japanese bread crumbs) to cornflakes, was given a test-run. Such arcana as brining and air-drying were tried. Gallons of Crisco and thirteen soaking methods later, *Cooks Illustrated* came up with the verdict: perfection equaled a Bell and Evans bird, soaked in "buttermilk brine," coated with a double veneer of flour, and fried in shortening at 375°F.

Could anyone argue with such conclusive empirical data? Well, this is what Camille Glenn, the grande dame of Southern cooking, has to say on the subject: "Correctly fried Southern Chicken is simplicity itself," she opines, "it is not dipped in milk, crumbs, or batter—just a generous coating of flour." *De gustibus non est disputandum.* Or put plainly, the beauty of a fried chicken is in the eye of the beholder.

The identity issues surrounding fried chicken are no less controversial. In the *Dictionary of American Food and Drink,* John Mariani credits Scottish immigrants with bringing this gift to the American table. James Beard invokes Austria, claiming that "at its best it [fried chicken] resembles a Viennese dish called Wiener Backhendl." Beard even introduces the heretical notion that Austrians do it better!

anya von bremzen

98

Many Americans' sentiments on fried chicken are summed up by James Villas: "When it comes to fried chicken," he writes, "let's not beat around the bush for one second. To know about fried chicken you have to have been weaned and reared in the South. Period."

Well, Mr. Villas, the best fried chicken I know does come from Georgia. But the chicken is neither battered nor floured nor crumbed. And the Georgia in question has its capital in Tbilisi, the heart of the Caucasus, oceans away from Atlanta. This dream chicken is called *tapaka*—after *tapa,* or "lid"—which weighs down the chicken as it fries, producing a gorgeously tan, crispy skin. When my family left Russia as stateless refugees, we were confronted with draconian restrictions on luggage imposed by the Soviet government. Most of the poundage in my mother's suitcase was taken up by a ten-pound lid whose sole purpose was to weigh down *tapaka.* Need I say more?

As much as I'd like to include the *tapaka* recipe as the best-ever fried chicken, I suspect that readers expecting the proper Southern batter-fried bird will never forgive me. So here's an extraordinary recipe from American Georgia. It comes from the southern chef Scott Peacock, of Watershed restaurant in Decatur, co-author, with Edna Lewis, of *The Gift of Southern Cooking.* Brined in salt, soaked in buttermilk, fried in pure lard, and accompanied by a rich pink gravy, this chicken is crispy, moist, and good enough to end all fried chicken arguments once and for all.

scott peacock's fried chicken with tomato gravy

cook's notes Organic chicken produces especially scrumptious results. Note that the chicken has to soak in the brine for at least 8 hours, so plan accordingly. The gravy makes the recipe that much more special, but you can omit.

½ cup coarse kosher salt

2 quarts cold water

One 3½-pound chicken, cut into 8 pieces, rinsed well

3 cups buttermilk

1½ cups all-purpose flour

¼ cup cornstarch

2 tablespoons potato starch (optional)

Fine salt and freshly ground black pepper

1 pound lard or solid vegetable shortening, for frying

8 tablespoons unsalted butter

4 ounces sliced bacon

½ cup finely chopped onion

1 garlic clove, minced

4 cups diced, drained, canned tomatoes (from three 14-ounce cans)

2 teaspoons dried thyme

2 cups heavy cream

1½ cups milk

1 In a large bowl, dissolve the kosher salt in the cold water. Add the chicken, cover, and refrigerate for 4 hours. Pour off the salt water, rinse the chicken, and drain. Put the chicken in a bowl, add the buttermilk, and turn the pieces to coat. Cover and refrigerate for 4 hours or overnight.

2 In a large, sturdy plastic bag, put the flour, cornstarch, potato starch if using, 1½ teaspoons fine salt, and ½ teaspoon pepper and shake to combine. Set aside ½ cup of the flour mixture for the gravy. Lift the chicken from the buttermilk, wiping off any excess liquid. Arrange the pieces on a wire rack and let dry for 5 minutes. Add the chicken to the bag, a few pieces at a time, and shake to coat. Shake off any excess flour and return the chicken to the rack.

3 Meanwhile, in a large cast-iron skillet, melt the lard and butter. Add the bacon and cook over medium heat until crisp, 5 to 6 minutes. Reserve the bacon for another use. Add the chicken, in batches if necessary, and cook over medium heat, turning, until golden, crisp, and cooked through, about 30 minutes. Lower the heat if necessary. Transfer to a wire rack to drain.

4 Transfer ¼ cup of the cooking fat to a large saucepan and add the onion and garlic. Cook over moderate heat, stirring occasionally, until golden, 5 to 6 minutes. Add the reserved ½ cup seasoned flour and cook, whisking, for 2 minutes. Add the tomatoes and thyme, and stir constantly until blended. Whisk in the cream and milk until the sauce is smooth. Season with salt and pepper to taste and cook over moderate heat, stirring occasionally, until thickened, about 10 minutes.

5 Transfer the fried chicken to a platter. Serve the tomato gravy with the chicken.

Serves 4 to 6

'd rather stun myself with gazpacho than to be subjected to the misery of an impertinent doctor who will make me starve.

—SANCHO PANZA

After the first ineffable gazpacho was served to us in Malaga and an entirely different but equally exquisite one was presented in Seville, the recipes for them unquestionably became of greater importance than Grecos and Zurbarans, than cathedrals and museums.

—ALICE TOKLAS

More than the gory spectacle of bull-ring *corrida* or the singular gypsy cry of the *cante jondo*, a pitcher of ice-cold gazpacho is the defining symbol of Andalusia.

gazpacho

"In Andalusia, every man has his gazpacho, like every man has his truth," pronounces Juan Carlos Alonso, a friend and a renowned chronicler of Sevilian food mores. Today, it's scorchingly hot outside, and we're not sipping but guzzling gazpacho straight from water glasses at an anonymous tapas bar near Seville's Calle Sierpes. Early gazpacho, Alonso explains as he takes another gulp, had none of the post-Columbian flourishes we associate with it today: no tomatoes, no peppers. Even as late as the mid-eighteenth century, Juan de la Mata, author of *Arte de Reposteria*, describes a gazpacho commonly called *capon de Galera* as an austere mixture of crustless bread, garlic, vinegar, oil, and anchovy bones.

The word *gazpacho* derives from *caspa*, which means "fragments" (referring to the broken-up bread) in Mozarabic, a Medieval Ibero-Romance language. Some also cite Hebrew *gazaz* ("break into pieces") as a possible etymology. In the past, the main source of both nourishment and refreshment for Andalusian day laborers, gazpacho consisted of a loaf of yesterday's bread wrapped in damp cloth, a handful of vegetables, a jug of oil and vinegar, and a paper packet of salt—all tossed into a shoulder bag before workers headed out to their wheat fields and their olive plantations. Each farm had its own gazpachero, whose unenviable task was to painstakingly pound the ingredients in a huge mortar.

Not until the nineteenth century, when Eugenia de Montijo, wife of Napoleon III, introduced gazpacho to France and Romantic travelers started roaming Andalusia, did gazpacho acquire status and fame.

The map of Andalusia today is a veritable quilt of gazpachos: a Málaga white gazpacho called *ajo blanco* (literally, "white garlic") made with pounded almonds and olives and the cooling accent of grapes; the *gazpacho tostado* (with grilled bread and juice of Sevillian oranges) of Cañete la Real in the region of Ronda; the aromatic green herb and lettuce-based gazpachos of Huelva; *gazpachuelo* of Costa del Sol, which is really a hot fish soup. And in La Mancha in central Spain, shepherd gazpachos, which are hot wintry porridges of stale bread and wild game.

Yet when most Americans call for "gazpacho," they mean coral-colored tomato soup from Seville, the city where tomatoes and peppers made their European debut in the 1500s.

I can't remember ever having a bad gazpacho in Andalusia, but my favorite version comes from Sergio Lopez. Co-owner of the avant-garde restaurant Tragabuche in the bull-fighting citadel of Ronda, Lopez is guru of the nouvelle gazpacho—say, an *ajo blanco* dolled up with caviar ravioli and candied squash. But at his more traditional Ronda restaurant, Escudera, he presents an exalted but simple rendition of the pink classic. Lopez insists he has no secrets: just add as little water as possible, choose the best vegetables at the height of their season, and allow them to speak for themselves. ¡Olé!

classic andalusian gazpacho

cook's notes A fruity Spanish olive oil, preferably from Andalusia, is important, as is a good sherry vinegar, preferably aged. Both can be found at specialty groceries or mail-ordered (see Resources). If you can spare the time, garnish the gazpacho with tiny bread croutons fried in olive oil.

Four 1-inch-thick slices day-old coarse country bread from a round loaf, crusts removed, torn into small pieces

3 pounds ripest, most flavorful tomatoes possible, washed and quartered (do not use Beefsteak tomatoes)

4 tablespoons good-quality sherry vinegar, preferably aged

3 medium garlic cloves

Small pinch of cumin seeds or ground cumin

Coarse sea salt

2 firm medium-sized Kirby (pickling) cucumbers, peeled

1 medium green bell pepper, cored and seeded

1 medium red bell pepper, cored and seeded

One quarter of a medium red onion, peeled

½ cup fragrant, fruity extra-virgin Spanish olive oil, preferably from Andalusia

½ cup bottled spring water, or more to taste

garnish

2 to 3 tablespoons each finely diced cucumbers, peeled green apples, slightly underripe tomatoes, and green bell peppers

Slivered young basil leaves

1 Place the bread in a large bowl, and squeeze out the seeds and some of the juice from the tomatoes over it. Crumble and massage the bread with your fingers. Add 1 tablespoon of the vinegar and let it soak for 5 to 10 minutes.

2 Using a mortar and pestle, pound the garlic to a paste with the cumin and ½ teaspoon of salt.

3 Transfer the bread mixture to a food processor along with the garlic paste, and process until completely smooth. Leave this mixture in the food processor while preparing the next step.

4 Chop the tomatoes, cucumbers, red and green peppers, and onion into medium dice. Place the vegetables in a bowl, stir in three large pinches of salt, and let stand for 15 minutes so that the tomatoes throw off some liquid.

anya von bremzen

5 Working in three batches, process the vegetable mixture in a food processor until as smooth as possible, adding a third of the olive oil to each batch. (The first batch will be processed with the bread mixture.) Transfer each finished batch to a sieve set over a large bowl.

6 Pass the gazpacho through a sieve, pressing on it with the back of a wooden spoon. Whisk in the remaining 3 tablespoons vinegar and the water. Adjust salt to taste. Chill the gazpacho for at least 3 hours before serving. (If making the gazpacho a day ahead, add the garlic 2 to 3 hours before serving, lest it overwhelm the other flavors.) Serve in glass bowls or wine glasses, with the suggested garnishes.

Serves 6

resources Tienda carries excellent Spanish olive oils and vinegars (tel: 888-472-1022 or *www.tienda.com*).

in most Ashkenazi Jewish households, serious food talk usually begins and ends with gefilte fish, the Yiddish term for "filled fish," which once described a regal cold stuffed fish served at the start of the Sabbath.

Eating fish on Friday night as prescribed by the Talmud had been a tradition of Jews East to West for millennia. This mystical symbol of fertility and abundance—Joseph blessed his children to multiply like fish in the sea—can be served at both dairy and meat meals, doesn't require kosher ritual slaughtering, and tastes good cold, just right for the strictly no-cooking Sabbath. Sephardic Jews mainly enjoy their Friday fish fried, but Ashkenazi concocted a recipe for fish flesh mixed with matzo and eggs, stuffed back into its skin and baked. These days, however, the dish is often simplified to fish balls.

gefilte fish

For my family, Jews living under Communist persecution, identity had nothing to do with matzo or fish balls. We were deprived of Sabbaths or seders and knew nothing about the laws of kashrut. My grandmother, who's from Odessa, did boast occasionally about her gefilte fish, but never made it. But her Odessa gave me my first contact with gefilte fish—there in that gaudy piratical port on the Black Sea, with its boulevards shaded by chestnut trees and its riot of faded French Empire architecture. Odessa was the cradle of Russian Jewish culture, and it was here that I was dispatched on an errand to the house of distant relations in the Jewish ghetto of Moldovanka. They lived in a shabby communal apartment crowded with the objects and dust of many generations. In the kitchen I was greeted by three garrulous sisters with fire-engine red hair. They were whacking a pike against the table—"to loosen its skin, so it comes off like a stocking." The sisters smothered me with blustery kisses and plied me with candy and buttermilk. I was instructed to sit and watch "true Jewish food" being prepared.

As one sister filleted the fish, another chopped the flesh with a dull-bladed knife, complaining about her withered arm. The third sister grated onions, wiping off tears. Reduced to a coarse oily paste and blended with onion, carrots, and bread—no matzo was to be found that year in Odessa—the fish was stuffed back into the skin and sewn up with a thick red thread.

It was to be boiled for three hours. Of course, I must stay! Could I grate horseradish? More candy, more buttermilk?

Suffocating from fish fumes and the sisters' entreaties, I made some sorry excuse and ran off gasping for air. The sisters looked hurt. Then I realized: *I had run out on my Jewishness.* For years afterward, consumed by shame, I kept wondering about the taste of their fish.

Many years later, on a cold pre-Passover day, I was flashing back to that scene while buying carp at a fish store in Rego Park, Queens, where hundreds of ex-Soviet Jews make their home. I'd come here to catch up on gefilte-fish lore. The women around me were from Odessa and Minsk, from Tbilisi and Tashkent.

"Make sure you buy lady-carp!"

This was the first piece of wisdom I learned from my fellow carp-buyers, who all deemed female carp sweeter and juicier than the males. And it went without saying that the carp must be live. And that it had to be mixed with some whitefish or pike, though the issue of exact proportions nearly started a fight. And real cooks, naturally, chopped it by hand. And Muscovites like me wouldn't know gefilte fish from a pork chop!

Suddenly I was in possession of a dozen gefilte fish recipes, most of them for stuffed fish steaks and whole stuffed fish, since most Russian Jews regard Polish-style sweetened fish balls with suspicion.

In my book *Please to the Table: The Russian Cookbook,* I include such an authentic whole stuffed fish recipe. Though not simple, it's utterly wonderful, borrowed from an old man from Kishinev, Bessarabia. In the Balkan-Romanian tradition, he poached the fish in a liquid flavored with tomatoes, sugar, and vinegar, which imparted a wonderful savor. For years, my mother and I have been schlepping our stuffed fish to various seders, always to raves. True, we could always make simplified fish balls. But this Passover chore is my way of atoning for running out on my Jewishness that day in Odessa.

traditional russian jewish gefilte fish

cook's notes If you can find a fishmonger who's willing to remove the fish skin in one piece—like a stocking with the tail attached—this is by far the most dramatic and authentic Russian-Jewish way to present gefilte fish. If not serving in the fish skin, form a loaf, lay a strip of skin on top for decoration, and attach the tail and the head at serving time.

The loaf is oven-poached in a sweet-tangy mixture flavored with V-8, an unorthodox touch, indeed, but common among immigrants from Moldova (Besserabia). Russians normally prefer a high proportion of carp, yielding a darker, more gutsy gefilte fish. If you like more whitefish, make the recipe with a whole whitefish and carp fillets.

1 Rinse the carcass and set fish aside.

2 Make the poaching liquid: Combine the fish bones (but not the head and tail) with the water, carrots, and celery in a large pot and bring to a boil. Skim carefully, add the V-8 and the bouquet garni, and bring to a simmer. Add the vinegar and sugar, and keep the liquid at a very low simmer, covered.

1 whole carp, preferably live, about 5 pounds, skinned (see Cook's Notes) and filleted; skin, head, tail, and carcass reserved

poaching liquid

6 cups water

3 whole medium carrots, peeled

1 small celery rib, sliced

1½ cups V-8 or tomato juice

6 sprigs fresh parsley, 6 sprigs fresh dill, 2 bay leaves, 3 allspice berries, and 10 black peppercorns tied in a cheesecloth bag

4 teaspoons red wine vinegar, or more to taste

2 teaspoons sugar, or more to taste

3 Prepare the fish stuffing: Finely chop the 3 large onions. In a large skillet, heat the oil over low heat and sauté the onions, stirring frequently, until very soft but not browned, about 15 minutes.

4 Break the matzo into pieces and soak in cold water to cover for 10 minutes. Squeeze out the liquid, crumbling the matzo into a paste with your hands.

5 Cut the carp fillet into pieces. Working in batches, combine the carp, whitefish fillets, and the carrot and process in a food processor until ground but not pureed. Add the sautéed onions and the matzo to the last two batches.

6 Grate the remaining onion. In a large bowl, combine the ground fish, grated onion, and eggs. Add the water, sugar, salt, and pepper, and mix until the mixture is homogenous. To taste for seasoning, poach or sauté a small fish ball.

7 Preheat the oven to 375°F. Stuff the reserved fish head with some of the fish mixture. If using a whole fish skin with the tail attached, lay it out on a large piece of foil and stuff the fish mixture into the skin. If using only a strip of skin, shape the fish mixture into a loaf approximately 18 by 4 inches on a piece of foil.

fish stuffing

3 large onions and 1 medium onion

4 to 5 tablespoons peanut oil

2 sheets matzo

2 pounds whitefish or pike fillets, cut into pieces

1 large carrot, peeled and cut into small pieces

2 large eggs, beaten

1 large egg white beaten

¼ cup ice water

1 teaspoon sugar, or more to taste

Salt and freshly ground white pepper to taste

Fresh watercress for decoration, if desired

Horseradish, for serving

8 Carefully transfer the whole stuffed fish or the loaf with the foil to a large ovenproof fish poacher or to a large roasting pan. Slide the fish off the foil into the bottom of the pan and remove the foil. (If making loaf, now cover the top of the loaf with a long strip of skin.) Brush the top with a little oil. Add the stuffed fish head and the reserved tail to the pan. Bake until the top of the fish just begins to brown, about 15 minutes.

9 Strain the hot poaching liquid, discarding the fish bones, bouquet garni, and the celery but reserving the carrots. Taste and add more vinegar and sugar if you wish. Carefully, add enough of it to the pan to come three quarters of the way up the fish. If there is not enough liquid, add a little water. Add the carrots. Reduce the oven temperature to 325°F., cover the top of the pan loosely with foil, and continue baking the fish until set and cooked through, about 1 hour. Baste it with the poaching liquid every 10 minutes or so.

10 Allow the fish to cool in the poaching liquid for at least 2 hours. Carefully transfer it to a long serving platter, lined with watercress if desired. Attach the head and tail to the fish. Remove the carrots from the poaching liquid and rinse. Cut them into slices and use to decorate the top of the fish. Spoon a little poaching liquid around the fish and refrigerate for at least 3 hours or overnight. Cut into slices and serve with horseradish.

Serves 10 to 12 as a first course

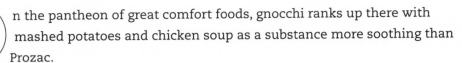

I n the pantheon of great comfort foods, gnocchi ranks up there with mashed potatoes and chicken soup as a substance more soothing than Prozac.

"Every time I eat gnocchi," says my Roman friend Anna Bini, "I feel like a child again. Like my mamma kissed me and everything is suddenly fine."

A great dumpling will do that to you.

Just like pasta, to which they are closely related, gnocchi (which means "little lumps") assume different names and characteristics as you travel through Italy. In the Ligurian Riviera di Levante, they might appear as *troffie*—worm-like mini-dumplings fashioned from chestnut flour and veiled in pesto. In Campania they become *strangoloprieti,* or "strangle the priest," peeking deliciously from a cap of crimson tomato sauce. In Rome you'll eat baked semolina gnocchi; in Brescia, bread crumb gnocchi; zaftig plum gnocchi in Trieste; and pumpkin gnocchi under a thin Gorgonzola cream in Mantua.

However, in their most universal form, gnocchi mean small dumplings made of potato and flour, even though potatoes didn't appear in Italy until the late sixteenth century and the original gnocchi were simply small lumps fashioned from regular pasta dough.

Potato gnocchi are one of those dishes that are exceedingly basic and tricky at the same time. When good, they defy gravity, floating off the plate like tiny clouds. Bad gnocchi, on the other hand, go down like soggy billiard balls. The difference between terrific and terrible might lie in a couple tablespoons of flour.

Gnocchi should melt in the mouth, not in the pot, Italian cooks often repeat. Hence the attention paid to the proportion of potatoes to flour: too little flour and the gnocchi will dissolve in boiling water; overdo it and they come out leaden. Some add an egg to the dough, others claim it toughens the gnocchi. And there's similarly little consensus on the best kind of potato. But everyone agrees that it is important not to overhandle the dough, which renders it gummy, and to let the gnocchi dough rest for a while to "relax" the starches.

Most gnocchi I've had in Italy were pretty good; some were sublime. But nothing ever wowed me more than the dumplings at an obscure Tuscan trattoria called Locanda del Borgo in the hills above Pistoia. The place—more social club than restaurant, replete with an inebriated resident balladeer—didn't promise great food. And when the gnocchi arrived, cloaked in a white, bland-looking sauce, I was skeptical. Then, as I bit into the soft pillowy dough, the gnocco oozed a sharp, creamy filling of Gorgonzola. The sauce tasted both earthy and refined: sautéed garlic and cauliflower, with a touch of Gorgonzola and cream accented with the gentle kick of red chile. I asked Michele Langhella, the demure chef by what magic did melted Gorgonzola get inside the gnocchi. *Sac-a-poche*, he replied: a pastry bag with a very small tip. From such creative lengths does great gnocchi grow.

okey-gnocchi

It has been suggested that gnocchi could have been one of the earliest and most primitive forms of Italian pasta: simply bits of unrolled dough boiled in water. In fact, the words *gnocchi* and *macaroni* were used interchangeably in old Italian texts. And it is perfectly possible that when the 14th century writer Boccaccio describes pasta rolling down a mountain of Parmesan in his *Decameron*, he's talking about gnocchi. Gnocchi made with potatoes are relatively new to Italy, dating back no further than the mid-19th century.

As for the word, *gnocco* (singular of *gnocchi*) derives from Venetian *"gnoco"* (a block), which might in turn stem from the Old Lombardian *"knohha"* (knot or knuckle). Hence, in Venetian dialect, *gnocco* means something like knucklehead. Meanwhile, in modern Northern Italian slang, *gnocca* describes a beautiful babe. In Florence, they call gnocchi *topini* (field mice), in Apulia *cavatelli*, in Sardinia *malloreddus*. Another popular term—*strangulaprievete* or *srangoloprieti* or *strozzaprete* (all meaning "strangle the priest")—owes its existance to an unfortunate Neapolitan priest called Galiani who in his greed choked on a plateful of dumplings. Then again, you can just say *yum*.

potato gnocchi with cauliflower-gorgonzola sauce

cook's notes Per Michele Langhella's instructions, I tried stuffing gnocchi with Gorgonzola cream but soon had to abandon the idea (too complicated). Instead, I gratinee the gnocchi for a few minutes under the luscious Gorgonzola and Cauliflower Sauce. Celestial.

To make gnocchi ahead of time, spread them out on a tray and freeze for a couple of hours, then transfer to a plastic bag and freeze. Frozen gnocchi will take longer to boil. The recipe can be easily doubled for a larger crowd. The gnocchi are also delicious with Ragu Bolognese (page 146) or Pesto (page 198) instead of the cauliflower sauce.

gnocchi

1 pound russet (Idaho) potatoes, unpeeled and well washed

1 large egg yolk, beaten

⅔ to 1 cup all-purpose flour, as needed

4 to 5 tablespoons grated Parmesan cheese, preferably Parmigiano-Reggiano

2 teaspoons salt

cauliflower-gorgonzola sauce

1½ tablespoons good-quality virgin olive oil

2 large garlic cloves, smashed

Small pinch of red pepper flakes

1¾ cups small cooked cauliflower florets

⅔ cup heavy cream

3 ounces Gorgonzola cheese, crumbled

1 Make the gnocchi: Preheat the oven to 400°F. Wrap the potatoes in foil individually and bake until a skewer goes in easily, 45 minutes to 1 hour depending on size. As soon as the potatoes are cool enough to handle, peel them, cut into large pieces, and pass them, one by one, through a ricer. (This has to be done while the potatoes are still warm.)

2 Heap the mashed potatoes in a work bowl. Make a well in the middle and add the egg yolk. Using two forks, stir the egg yolk into the potatoes, then sprinkle in ⅔ cup flour, 2 tablespoons of the Parmigiano, and the salt. Work the mixture quickly with one or two forks or the tips of your fingers until the flour is just incorporated. Turn the dough out onto a large wooden board or a wooden kitchen counter dusted with flour. Knead the mixture briefly and *extremely gently* just until it is homogenous and still slightly sticky (but not loose). The mixture should feel like dough rather than mashed potatoes. Do not overwork the dough or the gnocchi will turn out gummy. If the dough feels too loose and sticky, add more flour, 1 to 2 tablespoons at a time.

3 Bring a small pot of water to a boil. To test the gnocchi, take a small piece of dough and roll it into a ¾-inch-thick rope. Cut it into a couple of ¾-inch lengths and drop them into the boiling water. If the gnocchi start dissolving in the water, mix more flour into the potato mixture. If they float to the surface, you're fine. Cover the dough with plastic and let stand for 30 minutes.

4 Lightly flour a large tray or a baking sheet. Divide the dough into six parts. On a lightly floured surface, gently shape each into a long rope between ¾ and 1 inch thick. Cut the ropes on the diagonal into ¾-inch lengths and flatten lightly. Press each gnocco lightly against the tines of a dessert fork. Place the finished gnocchi on the floured tray, and keep them covered with plastic while you prepare the rest. (The gnocchi can be made up to a few hours ahead and refrigerated, covered with plastic. In fact, they taste lighter when done ahead of time.)

5 Make the cauliflower-gorgonzola sauce: In a heavy skillet, heat the oil over low heat and add the garlic. Sauté until the garlic is very fragrant but not brown, about 2 minutes, then remove and discard. Add the red pepper flakes and sauté for 30 seconds. Add the cauliflower and cook for 2 minutes, gently breaking it up into small pieces with a fork. Add the cream and the Gorgonzola, raise the heat to medium, and cook until the cheese is melted and the cream is thickened and reduced, 4 to 6 minutes.

6 Preheat the broiler. To cook the gnocchi, bring 4 quarts of salted water to a gentle boil in a large pot. Using a large spatula, carefully slide the gnocchi into the water. After about 30 seconds, stir gently to prevent them from sticking to the bottom of the pot. They are ready when they float to the surface, 2 to 3 minutes. With a slotted spoon, carefully transfer the gnocchi to an ovenproof serving platter, shaking off the excess water.

7 Top the gnocchi with the sauce in one even layer, and sprinkle with the remaining 2 to 3 tablespoons Parmigiano. Place the platter under a broiler until the top is lightly brown and bubbly, 2 to 3 minutes. Serve immediately.

Serves 4 as a first course

here's America on a plate: *huge* (who serves a petite burger, except the White Castle with its sackful?), *robust* ("subtle burger" is an oxymoron), *democratic* (from a Dixie dinette's plastic baskets to poolside porcelain at The Four Seasons), and *ingeniously eclectic* (golden arches aside).

Americans eat many of their more than 30 billion burgers a year as Slyders, Whoppers, or Big Macs. They like 'em broiled (sometimes broiled both sides at once), grilled, barbecued, or fried—even, in south-central Connecticut, steamed. They'll call for them draped with fried onions, spooned with melted butter, glopped with chili, bundled with a split hotdog or Polish sausage or a crab cake.

hamburger

Even capped with a fried egg, not to forget the odd crumble of crushed Fritos or the higher tones of foie gras or mango chutney.

It's a lifetime thing. That *gee-I'd-love-a-burger* feeling comes over Americans from first grade right through the rest of their blessed days.

The tale—apocryphal as it might be—of this big bite of USA in fact begins in Russia. Medieval Tartar hordes galloped in with a taste for raw red meat, which they had tenderized under their saddles. German sea traders in the fourteenth century took the taste home, where they called their chopped raw beef dish Steak Tartare. When Germans fried up a wad of it, with onions, they named it Hamburg Steak, after the great seaport. (Northern Germans remained strong aficionados of the raw form as well.) In the early nineteenth century, German immigrants brought this chopped steak to America. By 1834, grand Delmonico's near Wall Street had Hamburg Steak on its menu. By the end of the century so did restaurants in Walla Walla.

Pretty much everybody agrees that the meat-and-bread hamburger was launched at the 1904 World's Fair in St. Louis. A Texan named Fletcher "Old Dave" Davis caused a food sensation with "Old Dave's Hamburger Stand," where he served up his cooked patties between bread slices, with hot mustard and Bermuda onion.

The Hamburger Hall of Fame, however, is in Seymour, Wisconsin. That's where "Hamburger" Charlie Nagreen supposedly first sandwiched a beef circle (here a flattened meatball) at the 1885 Outagamie County Fair. He was fifteen at the time, which would make him a burger prodigy.

A short-order chef named J. Walter Anderson gets general credit for the debut of the bun in 1916. Five years later he co-founded White Castle, in Wichita, Kansas, which was to become the first of the chains. In 1924, a grill chef at The Rite Spot in Pasadena, California, Lionel Sternburger, had the inspiration to add cheese, and thereby hit the third note of the splendid chord with his "Cheese Hamburger." The next thirty years saw burgers become the country's A-1 favorite.

And then in 1954, the world shifted. A middle-aged Illinois milkshake salesman named Ray Kroc called on the burger restaurant of some customers, the McDonald brothers of San Bernardino, California. Of course, with McDonald's and its big brethren, we're in the Fast Food zone, where burgers, or a burger-fries-and-Coke platter, sinks to a kind of base cartridge calibrated to blast saturated fat, sodium, and sugar down its consumer's maw, from Miami to Moscow. Having said this, let's admit McDonald's fries have real appeal; and White Castle's particular steamy minced-onion savor keeps folks like Liz Taylor ordering them.

Even if the golden arches are better recognized in the world than the Christian cross, the burger I crave at home is a classy gold standard: a generous patty of fresh-ground chuck, crusty on the outside and juicy-pink within, glossed with melted aged Cheddar and mounted on a toasted bun along with a lettuce leaf and a slice of red-ripe tomato. No more, no less. A prime vision of the primal.

hamburger

cook's notes The best meat for the job is chuck, preferably from a good butcher, at least 18 percent fat, and coarsely ground to order. As over-handling the meat means losing precious air pockets, be gentle when shaping the patty—and resist all temptation to pick, prod, or tamper while it's cooking. Grill marks never fail to trigger a hungry response but unless your grill is *really* hot, you'll probably get a crustier, juicier burger by pan-frying it in a red-hot cast-iron skillet in its own fat. Broiler? Fuggedaboutit.

24 ounces best-quality chuck, preferably freshly ground twice

Kosher salt and freshly ground black pepper

2 to 3 teaspoons oil, for brushing the burgers

4 slices good aged Cheddar cheese (if making cheeseburgers)

4 high-quality hamburger buns, lightly toasted

4 large slices tomato

4 thick slices Maui or Vidalia onion

4 iceberg lettuce leaves

Pickle slices

Ketchup, mustard, relish

French fries or "chips" (page 96)

1 Divide the meat into four parts. Using your fingertips, gently shape each part into a patty about 1 inch thick and 3 inches in diameter. If it doesn't quite hold together, throw it gently between two cupped hands. Sprinkle each patty generously with salt and pepper.

2 Heat a large cast-iron skillet over medium-low heat for 5 minutes. Brush the burgers very lightly with oil. Increase the heat to high, add two patties, and cook for 4 to 4½ minutes per side for medium-rare, flipping once. Do not fiddle with the burgers while they cook. Remove the cooked burgers to a platter and keep loosely covered with foil while cooking the other two burgers. (Even if your skillet can accommodate all four burgers, do not cook more than two at a time, as they'll throw too much fat into the skillet.) To make cheeseburgers, replace all the burgers in the skillet, top each with a slice of cheese, cover, and cook for 30 seconds more. Serve on the buns with all the suggested trimmings.

Makes 4 burgers

anya von bremzen

burger goes global While nothing beats the simple classic with Cheddar cheese, lettuce, tomato, and ketchup, if you stray away from the iconic version, the sky's the limit. Here are six fabulous global serving ideas to jazz up your next burger bash.

ITALIAN: Top with a few spears of crisp-fried pancetta, arugula, and Gorgonzola; serve on split, toasted foccacia.

MOROCCAN: Make it with lamb, mixing in some hot pepper, cumin, and allspice, smear it with harissa, top with roasted red pepper strips and mint sprigs; serve on grilled pita bread with a drizzle of yogurt.

FRENCH: Top with a slice of Gruyère, and slowly caramelized onions fortified with a little bacon and red wine; serve on a grilled baguette with mustard and/or aioli.

MEXICAN: Make it with ground pork (well-done) spiking the meat with cilantro, and top with Tomatillo Salsa (page 292), crumbled Cotijo cheese, and black beans, if you wish.

CHINESE: Make it with turkey, glaze with a mixture of hoisin, Chinese mustard, and a little chili paste, and top with grilled or sizzled scallions.

RUSSIAN: Make it with veal, top it with mushrooms cooked with a little bacon and sour cream, and thin slices of Kosher pickle; serve on toasted sourdough rye with horseradish and hot mustard.

until I went to the Middle East, I was ho-hum about hummus. To me, the region's ubiquitous chickpea dip was the dull guy of the *mezze* spread—you hustled past it to get to the *kibbeh,* the *dolma,* and the *fattoush.*

I came to understand hummus at the Aleppo souk in Syria, the region's grandest bazaar, which stretches for miles in a dense grid of dim vaulted passageways. A gaggle of Bedouin traders were crowded into a pocket-size hummus shop near a section devoted to saddles, nomadic tent gear, and Bedouin wedding paraphernalia. Their *kaffiyeh* headscarves flung over their heads, they tore off huge rags of flatbread and scooped up bowlfuls of the warm soothing chickpea puree with such abandon you'd think they'd been starving for days. Their hummus wasn't a dip, it was sustenance.

hummus

I came to understand hummus at Café des Orient, a posh Beirut restaurant favored by the BCBG, the *bon chic bon genre* set. The chef talked about hummus as if it were caviar, relating how the excellence of *his* hummus was owed to prized small young chickpeas shuttled in from across the border in eastern Anatolia. In a Mercedes taxi.

I came to understand hummus when my friend Rafik, a food-obsessed Beiruti Armenian, ferried me two hours to Tripoli to one legendary hummus dive on the edge of the souk there. It was noon by the time we arrived, and the place had run out of hummus (in the Middle East, it's breakfast). Rafik sulked for days.

I understood hummus, for real, from an article in the *Arabic News,* which solemnly placed it "at the very center of the Arab-Israeli conflict." While Arabs insist hummus is theirs, "Israelis," the article noted bemusedly, "claim that it dates to the time of the Old Testament and present it worldwide as Israeli food."

Hummus, you see, in this part of the world is as basic as bread, as essential as water.

In Arabic, the word *hummus*—sometimes spelled *hummous*—means chickpeas; the proper name of the dish being *hummus bi tahini,* or "chickpeas with sesame paste." Cultivated probably since Neolithic times, chickpeas were equally loved by the Babylonians, the Egyptians, Greeks, and the Romans, who munched on roasted chickpeas just as we do on popcorn. And what's not to love? Not only are chickpeas easily stored, cheap, versatile, nutty, and tasty, they're also a nutritional powerhouse, containing a rich cocktail of antioxidants, proteins, and minerals.

A silken blend of that miraculous chickpea and the equally potent sesame paste, hummus is the cement that binds Middle Eastern cuisines, prepared with slight variations throughout the region. In Turkey, olive oil is mixed into the puree, while in Lebanon oil is used only as garnish. Syrians might spice theirs with cumin and allspice and scatter it with pomegranate seeds, while Yemenites sprinkle on some za'tar. Throughout the region one samples hummus served by itself or topped with sautéed pine nuts or cooked lamb. Accompaniments range from pickles, olives, or tomato and cucumber salad, to French fries.

Whoever's making it, a good hummus demands smoothness and creaminess. And smooth hummus doesn't come from a can. Anissa Helou, an authority on Middle Eastern cooking and author of *Mediterranean Street Food,* told me that she'd sooner not make hummus at all than use canned chickpeas, which yield grainy results. She also suggests that the secret to perfect texture is the age of the chickpeas—the younger, the creamier. Removing the skin from the cooked legumes—a practice followed religiously by Middle Eastern matriarchs—makes the dish even silkier. I find this chore immensely pleasurable: tactile and calming.

Make this recipe and you, too, will truly understand hummus.

perfect hummus

cook's notes While hummus can be served warm, cold, or at room temperature, I definitely prefer it slightly warm. Great as it is as a party dip, to fully appreciate its soothing subtle goodness try it for breakfast, for a light lunch, or as a substantial snack. Garnishes can include a dusting of paprika, cayenne, or tart sumac; a sprinkling of parsley, mint, or pomegranate seeds, or pine nuts browned in oil or butter, such as here.

1 In a large bowl, cover the chickpeas with water and soak for 4 hours or overnight.

1½ cups dried chickpeas

2 medium garlic cloves, crushed through a garlic press

½ cup tahini, at room temperature, well stirred

¼ cup fresh lemon juice, or more to taste

1 tablespoon unsalted butter

3 tablespoons pine nuts

Large pinch of cayenne pepper

1 to 2 tablespoons fruity extra-virgin olive oil

Finely chopped flat-leaf parsley or shredded mint, for garnish

Good quality flatbread

2 Drain the chickpeas and place in a saucepan with water to cover by at least 3 inches. Bring to a boil, skim, then simmer over medium-low heat, partially covered, until the chickpeas are very tender and creamy to the bite and their skin begin to separate. This should take 2½ hours or more. Periodically check and replenish the liquid. Drain the chickpeas, reserving the cooking liquid. Skin the chickpeas by placing them in a colander and rubbing them between your fingers under cold running water; the skins should slip off easily. Measure about 3 tablespoons of whole chickpeas and reserve.

3 In a food processor, process the remaining chickpeas with ¾ cup of their cooking liquid, the garlic, tahini, and lemon juice until completely smooth, 3 to 4 minutes. Taste and check the consistency: it should be that of whipped cream. If it is too thick, add another ¼ cup of the cooking liquid and process for a few seconds more. Add a little more lemon juice, if desired.

4 Melt the butter in a small saucepan and sauté the pine nuts until golden. Stir in the cayenne.

5 To serve, place the hummus in a shallow bowl and run a spoon around the edge to make a moat. Pour the olive oil into the moat. With the back of a spoon, make a hollow in the center of the hummus and top with the reserved whole chickpeas. Scatter the pine nuts over the hummus, pour the spiced butter over the chickpeas, and sprinkle with parsley. Serve with good-quality warm flatbread or pita wedges.

Serves 6 as an appetizer, breakfast, or snack

is there anything in the food lexicon that expresses the idea of a treat more than ice cream?

"My tongue is smiling," writer Calvin Trillin's four-year-old daughter was moved to declare after a taste. A more worldly grown-up Frenchman, Stendhal, shared the sentiment almost two centuries earlier over spoonfuls in Italy.

"What a pity," he mused famously, "that ice cream isn't a sin."

So don't call it a sin. Call it *gelato* or *sorbetto* in Sicily, *sorbet* or *glace* in Paris, *kulfi* in Calcutta, *sahlab* (from ground orchid roots) in Turkey, *ais kachang* in Malaysia. Call it a mouthful of holiday. A party trick you can eat.

As history, ice cream brings a smile, too. The idea of flavoring ice or snow

ice cream

goes back millennia, to ancients sweltering in China, Mesopotamia, Greece, and Rome. Alexander the Great had snow hauled from the Alps to mix with his wine and fruit in fourth century B.C., and Nero would have slaves haul it for him from the Appenines. That Marco Polo later carried the secret of sherbet making from China to Italy is a very old tale, and a tall one. Credit for Italy's longstanding *amore* with frozen sweets goes rather to the Arabs and their refreshing *sharbats* (probable origin of *sherbet*). These were snow-chilled sweetened slushes the recipe for which they brought to Sicily. Likely they got their idea from the Persians, who got it from the Indians, who got it from the Chinese.

In 1565, when a Spanish physician (a true Dr. Feelgood) invented the first home ice cream freezer—a bone-wearying bowl-within-a-bowl device with ice and saltpeter—the sweet finally made the leap from frozen slush to what *we* know as ice cream. This very same year in Florence, a Medici court architect concocted the very first gelato by means of an ice-and-salt method. Buontalenti ("good talent"), this male midwife of delight was aptly named.

By 1674, when arguably the earliest recipe for ice cream appears in Paris, over 250 shops offered the stuff in the ice-mad French capital, where chefs became adept at adding cream, milk, and butter to a repertoire of extravaganzas like molded *bombes glacés*. The happy phrase "ice cream" had by then surfaced in English. Across the Atlantic it debuted when a guest of Maryland's colonial governor Thomas Bladen wrote (in 1744) of being treated at table to "some fine ice Cream, which, with Strawberries and Milk, eat most Deliciously." Deliciously, but for most folks, still very rarely.

American ice cream finally got to the people in the 1840s, with the patent of a handle-cranked—sweet mercy!—paddle-bladed ice-cream maker. It was a pal of Abe Lincoln who launched the first large-scale ice-cream business, in Baltimore, in the 1850s. By the mid-nineteenth century, a party without ice cream was, well, uncool. Flavor favorites included lemon, almond, strawberry, and, of course, vanilla. Not to forget vegetable ices, such as spinach, celery, or even asparagus with truffles, a repertoire that would make a Barcelona culinary whiz of today give a thumbs-up. The cone made its debut at the ice cream-happy 1904 St. Louis World's Fair (though there's ongoing debate over this issue). And on the American story rolls, through the advent of soft-iced Dairy Queen and the first Baskin-Robbins in 1946, to our boutique, artisanally crafted millennial favorites.

So what tastes best? What a question. But in America, vanilla still leads the way. Hardly a surprise. It's the epitome of cooled comfort food.

best vanilla ice cream

cook's notes Few vanilla ice cream recipes are richer, creamier, and more sinful than this one, from my friend Melissa Clark, a New York food writer and author of the *Ice Cream Machine Cookbook*. With twice the egg yolks of regular ice cream, this recipe, Melissa says, makes a scandalously luscious custard.

Best-quality vanilla beans, such as Madagascar or Tahitian, will make all the difference. (See Resources on page 77.)

2 to 4 best-quality plump vanilla beans, split in half lengthwise

2 cups heavy cream

2 cups whole milk

14 large egg yolks

1¼ cups sugar

Pinch of salt

1 With the tip of a small knife, scrape the seeds from the vanilla bean into a large saucepan. Add the bean, cream, and milk to the saucepan until bubbles just begin to form around the edges. Turn off the heat and let the mixture steep for 30 minutes.

2 Fish the vanilla bean out of the cream mixture and discard. Bring the cream back to a boil, and turn off the heat.

3   In a medium bowl, use a wooden spoon to stir together the egg yolks, sugar, and salt until very smooth. Pour about ¾ cup hot cream into the eggs, stirring constantly and vigorously. Stir in about ¾ cup more hot cream, then return the egg-cream mixture to the saucepan.

4   Set the saucepan over medium-low heat and gently cook the custard, stirring constantly (make sure to stir around the bottom and sides of the pan), until it thickens enough to coat the back of the spoon, about 5 minutes. Never let the custard boil, or the eggs will curdle.

5   Set a fine sieve over a bowl. When the custard has thickened, immediately pour it through the sieve into the bowl.

6   Cover the bowl, and refrigerate the ice cream base until cold, at least 4 hours and up to 2 days.

7   Freeze the ice cream according to the directions included with your ice cream maker.

Makes about 1½ quarts

eggplant is the little black dress of Middle Eastern cooking: so indispensable, so deftly versatile, that in the past no girl was considered marriage material until she learned to cook it at least a thousand ways.

The eggplant—botanically a fruit that migrated west from India along the trade routes—achieved a particularly exalted and privileged status in the hands of Turkish Ottoman cooks. Now, it needs to be said that the Ottoman cult of the kitchen bordered on mania. When Sultan Mehmet Fatih built the Topkapi Palace some twenty years after plundering Christian Constantinople in 1453, he ordered a four-domed kitchen so vast you'd mistake it for the imperial mosque. (And this from a man famous for dining solo!) At the height of his reign, separate battalions of cooks were assigned to kebabs and pilafs, to pancakes, candies, and drinks—plus a small legion for each of the six varieties of halvah. Dishes were plotted as if they were conquests, imperial chefs rose to become viziers, and the Janissaries—the sultan's elite troops—debated state matters around a stew pot, the *kazgan*.

imam bayildi

Turkish Braised Eggplant

The Ottoman Empire collapsed, but Turkish dedication to its cuisine lives on. And wherever you dine you encounter the eggplant: fried to a crispy edible lace, or mashed with tomatoes and peppers into a refreshing dip; pureed and blended with warm milk and cheese to a velvety smoky concoction called *hünkâr beğendi* (sultan's delight); stuffed with rice or spiced lamb; dried for the winter; preserved as a spicy pickle; or even turned into a syrupy sweet.

"In Turkey, we have two million eggplant dishes!" a famous Istanbul chef once boasted to me. That's probably true, but of these multitudes, the best-known creation of the Ottoman kitchen is *imam bayildi*: whole small eggplants braised in olive oil with copious amounts of tomatoes and onions until it becomes sweet and luscious like pudding.

Imam bayildi belongs to a genre of Turkish dishes with the unpronounceable name *zeytinyağli* (*zey-tun-yah-lee*). These are mild vegetables (either solo or stuffed with rice) eaten at room temperature and braised very slowly in a mixture of water and olive oil until they are glistening and impossibly melting and sweet (sugar is usually added to coax out the natural sweetness).

The name of this particular masterpiece translates as "the imam fainted." Why did the Muslim cleric swoon? Most likely from the sheer pleasure of the dish. Or, as some cheekily suggest, it could be his shock at the lavish amount of costly olive oil used in the recipe (imams were a famously parsimonious lot). After tasting this version from my friend Engin Akin, an Istanbul food writer, one certainly believes the first version.

engin's imam bayildi

cook's notes Imam can be served as a luncheon entree with a green salad and warm bread, or as part of a *mezze* spread. If making ahead of time and refrigerating, bring it to room temperature, or warm it very slightly in the oven before serving, as the oil tends to congeal on standing.

6 slender, firm Japanese eggplants, about 7 inches long (about 2 pounds)

Salt

4 medium ripe tomatoes

⅔ cup good-quality mild virgin olive oil

3 medium white onions, halved and sliced medium-thin

12 large garlic cloves, peeled

½ cup lukewarm water

2 heaping teaspoons sugar

⅓ cup finely chopped flat-leaf parsley

2 tablespoons lightly toasted pine nuts, for garnish

Lemon wedges

1 Using a vegetable peeler, slice off strips of eggplant skin in 1-inch intervals so that you have a "zebra" effect, leaving the stems intact. With a small knife, pierce the eggplants in several places and place in a large bowl in one layer. Add water to cover and 1 tablespoon of salt. Weigh the eggplants down with a plate so that they don't float. Soak the eggplants for 30 minutes. Drain, squeeze them, and pat dry thoroughly with a paper towel. (If you are pressed for time and if the eggplants are young and firm, the soaking can be omitted.)

2 Preheat the oven to 350°F. Halve two of the tomatoes, squeeze out the seeds, and grate them on the large holes of a box grater, discarding the skins. Reserve. Remove the seeds from the other two tomatoes and cut them into medium dice.

3 Heat 3 tablespoons of the oil in a large, shallow ovenproof casserole or Dutch oven. Sauté the onions over medium-low heat, stirring, until soft but not brown, about 10 minutes. Stir in the garlic and tomatoes, both grated and diced, and arrange the eggplants among the onions so that they touch the bottom of the casserole. Pour in the rest of the olive oil. Cover and cook over medium-low heat for 10 minutes, turning the eggplants once.

4 Mix the water with the sugar, pour over the eggplants, add salt to taste and transfer the casserole, covered, to the oven. Bake for 35 minutes, turning the eggplants every 10 minutes or so. At the end of cooking, all the water should be absorbed and the cooking liquid (oil and tomato juices) should be glossy and caramelized.

5 Cool the eggplant to a slightly warm or room temperature. Before serving, make a long lengthwise slit in each eggplant and push about 1½ tablespoons of the onion-garlic mixture into the slits, draining it on a fork as you stuff. With a spatula, carefully transfer the eggplants to a serving platter, spoon the sauce around them, and sprinkle with parsley and pine nuts. Squeeze some of the lemon juice on top, to taste. Serve garnished with additional lemon wedges.

Serves 6

indian curry

the word *curry*, used in the West as an umbrella term for almost any spicy South Asian stew, doesn't begin to describe the wealth and intoxicating complexity of Indian cooking. In use in the English language for centuries, the term itself originates, most scholars believe, from the South Indian Tamil *kaari* (spiced sauce), exported by Dutch and British traders (a Dutch account from 1598 refers to a dish called "carriel"). One of the first published spicy curry recipes in the West appears in Britain in 1747, in Hannah Glasse's *Art of Cookery,* with the first commercial curry powder hitting the scene some thirty years later. During the Raj (1858–1947), the British further embraced both the term and the cooking style, and curries have been entrenched in the Western culinary vocabulary ever since. Still, as one travels through India encountering the dizzying diversity of the spicy stews to be spooned over rice or chapatis, the term becomes almost meaningless.

While Indians do occasionally use the word *curry,* in one of those postcolonial linguistic ironies they prefer to describe what we'd call curry sauces with the British word *gravy.* That these gravy dishes, be they from Punjab or Pondicherry, are lavishly spiced goes without saying. India's "curry" styles include the creamy regal Mughlai stews enriched with ground nuts and cream; the lamb-centered rugged northern curries from Kashmir, such as the ever-popular *roganjosh;* the complex dishes of Hyderabad to the south, with their characteristic blending of sour and sweet and their reliance on exotica like opium seeds; the tangy but milder vegetarian curries of Gujarat in the west; and the hot, vividly spiced South Indian gravies lush with coconut milk. Within each region or state there are a million nuances dictated by culture, cast, and religion.

While the West is more familiar with northern-style Indian dishes popularized by Bangladeshi restaurateurs in Britain and the United States, it is only fitting that the one Indian curry recipe featured here should hail from the original South, specifically the lush Malabar Coast where spices define not just the cooking but also the history of the region.

anya von bremzen

Stretching over 500 miles from Goa in the north to Kerala's southernmost tip, the Malabar Coast (known as India's Spice Coast) has been an epicenter of spice trade since antiquity. This is where Columbus was headed in 1492 when he accidentally discovered America, and where his rival, Vasco da Gama, finally landed six years later, establishing the first water trade route between Europe and India. The Portuguese were followed by the Dutch and the British, all looking to establish control over the trade in black gold (aka pepper), cloves, ginger, and cinnamon, and contributing layers of cultures and cooking styles to the region in the meantime.

Malabar curry is less a specific dish, like Mughlai *korma* or Goan *vindaloo*, and more of a manner of cooking seafood—one that captures the region's lushness and its reliance on fish and shellfish, spices, and coconut. I've had many different prawn curries on my trips to South India, but most included a touch of tamarind, tomatoes (or underripe mango) to provide a tart note, fresh grated coconut or/and coconut milk, a host of aromatics like fennel seeds, ginger, and curry (*kari*) leaves—and green and red chiles, those American natives introduced to India in the sixteenth century by Portuguese traders. This is one of my favorite ways to cook seafood.

malabar shrimp curry

cook's notes This simple, wonderful curry is equally delicious with chunks of white-fleshed fish, such as halibut, or other seafood, especially lobster. If you can't find grated fresh coconut, use unsweetened dried shredded coconut soaked in water for 15 minutes and drained. The tamarind pulp gives this curry an authentic tart edge; if you find it too sour, you can balance the acidity with a little extra sugar.

2 teaspoons tamarind pulp (do not use concentrate) or fresh lemon juice

⅓ cup grated fresh coconut, thawed if frozen (see Cook's Notes)

1 tablespoon chopped fresh ginger

2 large garlic cloves, chopped

1 large green serrano chile, chopped, or more to taste

¼ cup chopped white onion

1 teaspoon fennel seeds

¾ cup canned coconut milk, well stirred

8 to 10 fresh or dried curry (*kari*) leaves, bruised, or 2 California bay leaves

4 tablespoons peanut or canola oil

½ teaspoon mustard seeds

1 tablespoon ground coriander

½ to ¾ teaspoon ground chile, preferably Indian

1 Soak the tamarind pulp in about ¼ cup boiling water for 15 minutes. Stir well to dissolve and strain if the pulp has seeds.

2 In a mini food processor, puree the grated coconut, ginger, garlic, chile, onion, and fennel seeds with 2 tablespoons of the coconut milk to a medium-fine paste.

3 In a medium-size heavy saucepan, heat 3 tablespoons of the oil over medium-low heat. Add the curry leaves and mustard seeds and sauté until the mustard seeds pop, about 30 seconds. Add the coconut mixture and cook over low heat, stirring, until the mixture is fragrant and no longer tastes raw, about 5 minutes. (Add a little coconut milk if the mixture begins to stick.) Add the remaining 1 tablespoon of the oil, the coriander, ground chile, turmeric, cardamom, and fenugreek and stir until the spices are fragrant, about 30 seconds. Add the water, the remaining coconut milk, the reserved tamarind pulp, and the tomatoes. Bring to a simmer and cook over low heat for 15 minutes. Taste and add a little sugar, if desired. (The sauce can be prepared ahead up to this point.)

4   Turn the heat up to medium, add the shrimp, and cook until pink and just cooked through, 3 to 5 minutes. Garnish with cilantro and serve with rice.

Serves 4 to 6

¼ teaspoon ground turmeric

¼ teaspoon ground cardamom or cloves

¼ to ½ teaspoon ground fenugreek, if available

1⅔ cups water

2 large, ripe plum tomatoes, chopped

Sugar, to taste (optional)

1¼ pounds large shrimp, shelled and deveined

A handful of cilantro leaves, for garnish

Cooked basmati rice, for serving

there's another smoky Jamaican joy besides the one Bob Marley celebrated with "Rastaman Vibration." It's the fiery haze you'll savor on a Kingston weekend, billowing up from the ranks of steel drums converted into zinc-hatted grills—the smoke of jerk cooking.

Jerk is Jamaican-style barbecue, slow-slow-cooked, marinated, oily-spicy, lascivious, and oh-so-profoundly smoky. Here is a prime pungent example of Jamaica's blended mix of heritages: African and Arawak Indian with currents of Spanish, English, and Asian Indian. Rustic and humble for centuries, it started to go big time in the mid-1970s, as did the reggae beat, you might note.

Jerk, please, refers both to the method of covered grilling and to its saucy seasoning. The word's origin is a hazy thing itself, invoking perhaps the constant turning (jerking) of meat on the grill; or the Jamaica patois *juk,* meaning "to stab," or perhaps a reworking of a Spanish term for dried meat.

jerk pork

Credit for jerk goes to Jamaica's Maroons, the former African slaves originally freed by the Spanish occupiers to harass the triumphant English when they invaded in the mid-seventeenth century. Cuisine followed warfare. The guerilla Maroons lived off wild pig, which they had to preserve between hunts. So the carcass was lathered in a salty hot-peppery paste, bundled up in leaves, and either slowly steamed over heated rocks in the ground—or barbecued over greenwood coals. Barbecuing came from the island's native Arawak Indians, who spit-roasted using wooden grills—*barbacoas*—propped over a slow fire.

Jamaican pimento (the allspice tree) over time became the chosen wood for flavorsome low-heat smoky cooking, with a grid of it underneath and another layer on top. Jerk sauce evolved into a thing of spicy secretive pride. Modern-day Maroon descendants still wave vaguely at the terrain when you inquire about the source of their spices. For that matter, every cook these days has his or her recipe, be it for runny marinades, thicker pastes, or dry rubs.

The spicy heart of jerk sauce is the blistering-hot Scotch Bonnet chile. Along with it, you'll doubtless find lots of black pepper in the seasoning, plus ginger, allspice, nutmeg, cinnamon, escallions (Caribbean chives), and soy sauce—more than twenty ingredients sometimes, a spice chest drawn from Asia, Europe, and Africa.

In the past couple decades, jerk has been modified from its rootsy roots so that chicken outdraws pork, and sausage and fish, even lobster, come jerk style. Bottled sauces with names like Busha Brown's Spicy and Papa Sparrow's gleam on market shelves. But for jerk in all its traditional glory, the place is still down from the Blue Mountains near Port Antonio, seaside capital of the Leeward Maroon parish of Portland, Jamaica. Boston Bay is where you'll find the scruffy little temples of jerk, the earthen pits filled with green pimento-wood fires. Rice and peas and roasted breadfruit are the traditional trimmings, plus plenty of cold Red Stripe beer. Bathing suits optional. But do turn up that backbeat bass.

jerk pork

cook's notes "This is the best ever meat marinade," assured Tina Ujlaki, handing me the jerk recipe that I adapt here. A longtime executive food editor at *Food & Wine* magazine, Tina sees more recipes in a week than most of us do in a lifetime; coming from her, "best" means just that. Grilled pork loin makes a delicious, albeit gentrified alternative to whole boned hog. Pork chops, chicken quarters, flank steak, lamb chops, sausages, and even fish are also wonderful with this marinade. The meat needs to marinate overnight so plan accordingly.

marinade

1 medium onion, coarsely chopped

3 scallions, trimmed and coarsely chopped

2 to 6 Scotch bonnet chiles, coarsely chopped

2 garlic cloves, chopped

1 tablespoon five-spice powder

1 tablespoon allspice berries, coarsely ground

1 tablespoon coarsely ground pepper

1 teaspoon dried thyme, crumbled

1 teaspoon freshly grated nutmeg

1½ teaspoons salt

2 to 3 tablespoons distilled wine vinegar

1 tablespoon dark brown sugar

3 tablespoons soy sauce

2 tablespoons vegetable oil, plus more for brushing the meat

3 pork tenderloins, 14 to 16 ounces each, preferably with some fat

1 Make the marinade: In a food processor or a blender, combine the ingredients and process to a coarse paste. Spoon the marinade into a shallow dish, add the pork tenderloins, and turn to coat. Cover and refrigerate overnight. Bring the pork to room temperature before grilling.

2 Preheat the grill to medium-high. Set an oiled rack 4 to 6 inches over glowing coals. Grill the pork, covered, turning it every 5 minutes, until a meat thermometer inserted diagonally into the center of a tenderloin, registers 155°F., 25 to 30 minutes. Using tongs, transfer the pork to a cutting board, cut into thick slices, and serve.

Serves 6 to 7

nce a year I get desperate for a Memphis barbecue fix. Ditto for Texas brisket and Argentinean *asado*. But when I lie in bed dreaming of meat on the grill, my thoughts turn to Korean *kalbi*: ribbons of butterflied beef short ribs soaked in an aromatic dark marinade that makes the meat sing with spicy caramelized sweetness. Sit at a Korean restaurant, sizzling a morsel of meat on the tabletop grill. Wrap it in a crisp lettuce leaf, dab on some sweet-spicy chile paste, then pop the parcel into your mouth. A shot of *soju*, Korea's mellow and sweet potato vodka, a bite of sinus-clearing kimchi. Repeat the procedure several times, and life suddenly seems worth living.

In Korea, where the barbecue culture is incredibly specialized, entire streets—even neighborhoods—are devoted to a particular item, from pig's ears

korean barbecued short ribs

Kalbi Kui

or chitterlings and other innards, to respectable eel, baby octopus, pork ribs, and all manner of beef. Of the latter, *bulgogi* (paper-thin strips of beef round) might be the most famous, but in Seoul the fanciest cars and most discerning gourmets gravitate toward the enormous multi-storied kabli houses. If Korea is one of this planet's barbecue meccas, then kalbi is its religion.

A few years ago I got to visit the Korean town of Suwon, a little south of Seoul. Other than an eighteenth-century fortress and legends of a king famous for having been buried in a rice crate (a foodie, obviously), Suwon has little to recommend itself to a traveler. No matter. Pilgrims of the beef faith flock here for Korea's very best kalbi butchered from a special breed of young cows that graze in the surrounding lush countryside. The ribs, cut by hand and beautifully marbled, combine the chewy resilience of a great hanger steak with the buttery richness of foie gras.

To eat this miracle meat you have to fly to Suwon—unless you stock up on vacuum-packed Suwon ribs at Seoul International Airport. But the marinade is a different matter. The following recipe—my favorite marinade of all times—is a trophy from the Suwon Kalbi Factory, a gleaming theme park devoted to kalbi, replete with a grotto and a sensational restaurant. Besides the usual soy sauce, sesame seeds, scallions, and ginger, the ingredients include things like nashi pear, pineapple juice, coffee, and *soju*. Someone could get *really* rich bottling this stuff.

korean barbecued short ribs

cook's notes Korean groceries sell specially butchered butterflied short ribs for kalbi, both on and off the bone. Otherwise, look for flanken-style ribs, which are short ribs cut across three bones. The marinade will also work wonders with skirt or flank steak.

marinade

½ cup mild dark soy sauce

¼ cup *soju* (Korean spirit), Korean rice wine, or sake

¼ cup pineapple juice

3 tablespoons strong coffee

2 tablespoons sugar

2 tablespoons toasted sesame seeds

3 tablespoons chopped garlic

¼ cup chopped scallions

¼ cup grated onion

1 tablespoon grated fresh ginger

1 small Asian pear, cored, peeled, and cut into small chunks

3 tablespoons Asian (toasted) sesame oil

2 teaspoons Korean red chili powder (*gocho karu*), or 1 teaspoon regular chili powder

2 teaspoons freshly ground black pepper

4 pounds Korean *kalbi* or flanken-style short ribs

1 Make the marinade: Combine the ingredients in a food processor and process to a puree; transfer to a large bowl. Toss with the ribs and marinate at room temperature for at least 3 hours, or refrigerate, covered, overnight.

2 Make the scallion salad: Trim 1 inch of the white part from the scallions. Cut each scallion into 4-inch lengths, then shred lengthwise. Place the scallions in a bowl filled with ice water until curled, about 1 hour. Drain well just before serving. Transfer the scallions to a bowl and toss in the remaining ingredients, massaging them very gently into the scallions.

anya von bremzen

138

3 Light the grill or preheat the broiler. Remove the ribs from the marinade and shake off the excess. Grill or broil the ribs until cooked through, about 5 minutes per side (less for thinly butterflied short ribs).

4 Grill the pork, covered, turning it every 5 minutes, until a meat thermometer inserted diagonally into the center of a tenderloin, registers 155°F., 25 to 30 minutes. Using tongs, transfer the pork to a cutting board, cut into thick slices, and serve.

5 Serve the ribs with the salad and instruct the diners to wrap a morsel of meat in a lettuce leaf dabbed with Korean chili paste.

Serves 6

scallion salad

1 large bunch scallions

2 tablespoons rice vinegar

2 teaspoons sugar

1 tablespoon Asian (toasted) sesame oil

½ teaspoon Korean red chili powder (*gocho karu*)

Coarse salt to taste

for serving

1 head red-leaf lettuce, separated into leaves

Korean sweet-spicy chili paste (*kochujang*), if available

h ad any *laksa* lately? Probably not. But in parts of Asia eating it is a ritual of near-religious importance. More satisfying than any Chinese noodle dish, richer than all the pastas of Emilia-Romagna, as intricately flavored as a great Oaxacan mole, laksa is a rococo Malaysian-Singaporean slurpfest of noodles and seafood afloat in a chile-sparked coconut broth showered with garnishes.

Laksa also happens to be a history class in a bowl.

If you thought "fusion" was the brainchild of some California superchef, think again. Centuries ago the vicissitudes of colonial history had already achieved many of the same postmodern culinary effects. The Nonya cuisine of Malaysia and Singapore, of which laksa is one of the proudest creations, is a case in point: an inspired blend of Chinese traditions and folklore with the tropical produce of the Malay Peninsula.

laksa

Malaysian Noodles, Chicken, and Shrimp in Spiced Coconut Broth

The "marriage" of flavors here isn't a metaphor. One popular legend traces the Nonya lineage to the union of a Ming Dynasty Chinese princess with the Muslim Sultan of Melaka, sometime in the mid 1400s. Legend aside, male traders from southern China settled along the Strait of Melaka beginning in the 1500s, taking Malay women as wives. These men were referred to as *Babas* (an Indian-originated word, denoting respect) and the women as *Nonyas* (from the Portuguese word for "grandmother"). While most aspects of the culture are known as Baba, the cuisine was named for the female side of the union.

Baba men introduced their wives to the foods of their native China, such as stir-fried, steamed, and double-cooked dishes, and, of course, noodles. But the women, used to lush, multilayered flavors, found Chinese cooking unbearably monochromatic. So they grafted on bright new tastes: the heady flavors of lemongrass, ginger and kaffir lime; hot and sweet spices borrowed from Indian traders; *asam* (tamarind) and *lemak* (creamy coconut) curries.

And so laksa was born.

Laksa is said to be a Baba corruption of *luak sua,* which means something like "spicy hot sand" in Hainanese, presumably because of the slightly gritty spice paste used as a flavor base. More likely the word derives from *lakhsha,* an old Persian term for noodles exported by Muslim traders. As the dish traveled around Malaysia and Singapore it acquired a rainbow of regional accents. In Penang I marveled at the local *asam laksa,* based on tamarind rather than coconut, and uniquely scented with fresh ginger flower. In the state of Johor, there was the famous "spaghetti laksa" made with fresh fish and dried Italian pasta. And in Katong, Singapore's Peranakan suburb, I counted four different stalls claiming to serve *the* "original" Katong *laksa,* which is enriched with condensed milk and dried shrimp and heaped with minced cockles, shrimp, fish cakes, and minty *daun keson* (aka *laksa* leaves).

Depending on where you eat your laksa, garnishes can include seafood, deep-fried tofu, chicken and bean sprouts, crab legs and quail eggs—the possibilities are almost endless. There's even a rumor that a Hokkien version exists using brine-pickled sea worms.

kari laksa lemak

cook's notes A good laksa starts with good *rempeh,* the pounded mixture of aromatics that is the sine qua non of Nonya and Malay food. If the spice paste is made ahead of time, laksa becomes an almost instant affair. The ideal laksa noodles are the fat, round, fresh rice noodles called *chor bee hoon;* otherwise, use dried rice sticks, soaked in warm water for 30 minutes. A combination of rice sticks and Chinese egg noodles is also good, or give spaghetti a try.

1 Make the *rempeh:* Stem the chiles and shake out the seeds. Using scissors, cut the chiles into pieces. Soak in boiling water to cover for 10 minutes. Drain, reserving 3 tablespoons of the soaking liquid. Chop the chiles. Flatten the shrimp paste, wrap it in a double layer of foil, and toast in a small hot skillet until fragrant, about 2 minutes per side. In a mini food processor or small blender, puree the chiles, shrimp paste, and the rest of the spice paste ingredients, adding a little of the reserved chile soaking liquid to form a smooth paste. (The spice paste can be prepared ahead and refrigerated.)

rempeh (spice paste)

12 large dried red chiles, about 3 inches long

½ tablespoon Malaysian shrimp paste (*blacan*) or Thai shrimp paste (*kapi*)

6 candlenuts or macadamia nuts, chopped (do not eat the candlenuts raw)

7 large garlic cloves, chopped

A 2-inch piece fresh ginger, peeled and chopped, if available

A 2-inch piece fresh or frozen galangal, chopped, if available

A 2-inch piece fresh or frozen turmeric root, or 1 teaspoon ground turmeric

3 lemongrass stalks (3 inches of the lower stalk, tough outer leaves discarded), chopped

3 medium shallots, preferably red, chopped

2 Make the chicken: Combine the chicken and stock in a snug saucepan (if there's not enough stock to cover the chicken, add some water). Bring to a boil, skim thoroughly, then turn the heat down to very low and simmer until the chicken is just cooked through, about 15 minutes. Let it cool, covered, in the broth. (The chicken can be prepared one day ahead and refrigerated in the broth.) Remove the chicken from the broth, and shred into bite-size pieces, discarding the bones. Reserve the chicken and the broth.

3   Make the coconut liquid: In a large, heavy saucepan heat the oil over low heat. Add the curry powder and cook, stirring for 1 minute. Add the *rempeh* and cook over the lowest possible heat, stirring often, until the flavor mellows and the oil begins to separate. This should take about 8 minutes. Add the coconut milk, a little at a time, if the mixture begins to stick. Stir in the rest of the coconut milk and 3 cups of the reserved broth and bring to a simmer. Simmer for 10 minutes. Turn off the heat and let the liquid infuse for about 30 minutes. Strain through a fine sieve into a clean pot. Season the liquid with salt and sugar. (The coconut liquid can be prepared one day ahead.)

4   Bring a pot of salted water to a boil. Cook the rice noodles for 1 minute, drain, rinse, and reserve. (If using dry rice vermicelli, soften them first in warm water for 20 minutes and drain. Cook in boiling water for 30 seconds, drain, and rinse under cold running water.)

soup

One 1½-pound bone-in skinless chicken breast, rinsed and patted dry

3 cups chicken stock or canned broth

3 tablespoons peanut oil, or more as needed

2 teaspoons good-quality curry powder

3 cups canned unsweetened coconut milk, well stirred

Salt to taste

½ tablespoon sugar, or more to taste

1 pound fresh round rice noodles, or 10 ounces dried rice vermicelli (see Cook's Notes)

12 large shrimp, peeled and deveined, with tails left on

garnishes

2 cups bean sprouts, blanched for 15 seconds and rinsed under cold running water

4 tablespoons thinly sliced scallions

½ cup torn cilantro leaves

Lime wedges

4 small hot red chiles, seeded and thinly sliced

Diced or julienned cucumber

Sambal oelek (Indonesian chile paste)

5   Bring the coconut liquid to a simmer and add the reserved chicken. Add the shrimp and cook until they just turn pink, about 1½ minutes.

6   To serve, divide the noodles among six bowls and ladle some liquid over the noodles along with some shrimp and chicken. You can either garnish individual portions with bean sprouts, scallions, cilantro, lime wedges, chiles, cucumbers, and sambal oelek, or pass the garnishes separately in small bowls.

Serves 6 as a light main course

Ligurian lasagne, laced with bits of ricotta and slathered with pesto, is pretty great stuff. So is the baroque Neapolitan version overflowing with ragu, cheese, and meatballs. But when I want to eat lasagne in all its classic glory, I head to the northern Italian region of Emilia-Romagna.

Synonymous with Italy's other holy trinity—Parmigiano-Reggiano, prosciutto, and balsamic vinegar—the cuisine of this dairy and grain-rich region shares little with the ascetic lyricism of Liguria or Tuscany's deluxe minimalism. Here the Italian middle-class table is at its richest and most indulgent. Think golden egg pastas and dumplings floating in strong capon broth, lavished with butter and cream, or served *al ragu*. Think *salumi* (prosciutto, culatello, mortadella), the pig's proudest moments. And, of course, think lasagne.

lasagne

Lasagne actually started life in Ancient Rome as *laganum,* mentioned by the poet Horace in the first century B.C. and featured in Apicius' *De re coquinaria* as a dish loaded with meat, fish, and sauce and symbolic of rich people's fare. Scholars still fiercely debate whether ancient Roman laganum was a boiled pasta dish or whether the word denoted bits of fried dough used to thicken a stew. Historian Clifford Wright—whose monumental *A Mediterranean Feast* is a brilliant revisionist effort to demonstrate the Arabic origins of much of that region's cuisine—even proposes that lasagne, both dish and name, could relate to the Arabic *lawzinaj,* a thin cake made with crushed almonds.

Whether or not Horace's *lagani* truly resembled the version we love, we know that lasagne—along with maccheroni and vermicelli—was the earliest and most ubiquitous pasta shape, mentioned repeatedly in medieval manuscripts. By the fourteenth century, in a cookbook compiled at the court of Naples, we find lasagne layered with spices and grated cheese. And over the next century it's described sprinkled with ground walnuts and sugar; or cooked in fatty broth and flavored with cheese, pepper, and cinnamon. Today the emblematic lasagne of Emilia-Romagna is constructed from layers of flat pasta, ragu, and *balsamella* or *besciamella* (béchamel).

Whenever I'm in Bologna, Emilia's well-fed capital, I regard a lasagne lunch at Diana as something of a sacrament. Properly weathered, with a window display dominated by a giant dangling mortadella, Diana is an *establishment*. Here, *piatti della tradizione*—tagliolini in broth, tortellini with cream, bollito misto—are dispensed by white-jacketed waiters amid a stately pantomime of carving, stirring, joking, and meddling. Everything at Diana is reliable and traditional, but the *lasagne al forno,* presented in individual gratin pans, feels particularly like a souvenir from another, gentler era. It's not as flamboyant as some *cucina creativa* renditions, but it's everything an old-fashioned lasagne should be. The pasta sheets are thin and eggy, soft but not overcooked. The ragu is rich without being greasy, infused with the sweetness of onion and carrots; the béchamel has the texture of velvet, acting as a gentle binder rather than industrial-grade plaster. A savory layer cake is how I think of Diana's lasagne: indulgent, for sure, but supremely dignified. This is my best approximation of Diana's recipe.

classic bolognese lasagne al forno

cook's notes While there's no ricotta, tomato sauce, or oozing cheese here, the results are unbelievably luscious. "This is too good to be called lasagne!" some of my guests exclaimed after tasting this recipe. For the noodles, the simplest option is to purchase sheets of fresh pasta available at some gourmet or Italian groceries; or you can make the pasta yourself. If using dried commercial lasagne noodles, look for an imported brand, such as De Cecco; I do not recommend the no-boil dried lasagne noodles. Exactly how much pasta you'll need will depend on the size of the pasta sheets and the exact size of your pan. Figure on 1½ pounds fresh or dried pasta, but you might end up using less.

The classic, long-simmered Ragu Bolognese in this recipe is also fabulous tossed with other pastas, such as fresh fettuccine, tagliatelle, or spaghetti. And it's delicious over polenta or gnocchi.

ragu bolognese

2 tablespoons olive oil

3 tablespoons unsalted butter

4 ounces pancetta, finely chopped

1 large carrot, peeled and finely diced

1 medium celery rib, finely diced

2 medium onions, finely chopped

1 pound ground veal or pork

¾ cup ground beef chuck

⅓ cup dry white wine

Salt and freshly ground black pepper to taste

3 cups chicken stock or canned broth

1 bay leaf

2½ tablespoons tomato paste

½ cup whole milk

1 Make the ragu: In a large heavy pot, heat the oil with the butter over medium heat. Add the pancetta and cook, stirring, for 2 minutes. Add the carrot, celery, and onions and cook for 5 minutes, stirring. Cover and cook, shaking the pot occasionally, until the vegetables begin to soften, about 6 minutes. Raise the heat to high and add the veal and beef. Cook, breaking the meat thoroughly with a fork, until it just loses its pinkness, about 5 minutes. Add the wine and cook until it almost evaporates. Season the meat with salt and pepper.

2 Add 1½ cups of the broth and the bay leaf, and heat to boiling. Partially cover the pot, reduce the heat to low, and cook until almost all of the liquid has been absorbed, about 1 hour. Pour ¼ cup of the broth into a small bowl and whisk in the tomato paste until smooth. Add the diluted tomato paste, the remaining 1¼ cups broth, and the milk to the ragu and continue simmering, partially covered, until most of the liquid has been absorbed, about 1½ hours, stirring from time to time. The ragu should be tender and very juicy but not too liquidy. Remove the bay leaf and adjust the amounts of salt and pepper to taste. (The ragu can be prepared up to a day ahead and reheated gently to warm before using if the meat clumps.)

pasta and béchamel

1½ pounds store-bought fresh pasta sheets, or 1 recipe Basic Egg Pasta Dough (recipe follows), or 1½ pounds dried lasagne noodles

Salt

4½ tablespoons unsalted butter, plus more for buttering the pan

3½ tablespoons flour

2½ cups hot milk

Several gratings of nutmeg

2¼ cups freshly grated Parmesan cheese, preferably Parmigiano-Reggiano, plus more for serving

3 Cook the pasta: If making and rolling your own pasta, see recipe. If using store-bought fresh pasta sheets, bring 6 quarts of water to a boil and add salt. Keep a large bowl of iced water next to the pot. Lower four or five pasta strips into the water and cook until al dente, anywhere from 30 seconds to 2 minutes depending on the pasta. Take care not to overcook the pasta. With a slotted spoon or tongs, transfer the cooked pasta to the bowl of iced water to cool. Drain and rinse the pasta strips under cold running water and arrange without overlapping on a sheet of paper towels. Pat dry with another sheet of paper towels and cover with the same sheet of paper towels while preparing the next batch. Repeat with the rest of the pasta, bringing the water to a rolling boil before each batch and changing the iced water as needed to keep it cold. If using dried lasagne noodles, cook them five pieces at a time in plenty of boiling salted water until al dente. Once cooked, handle the pasta as directed above.

4 Make the béchamel: In a heavy medium saucepan, melt 4½ tablespoons of the butter over medium-low heat. When the foam subsides, add the flour and whisk for 2 to 3 minutes. Slowly pour in the hot milk, whisking as you go. Cook, whisking constantly until the sauce is bubbly and thick, about 10 minutes. Stir in the nutmeg, salt to taste, and ¼ cup of the cheese. Put a piece of waxed paper directly on top of the sauce to prevent a crust from forming and set aside until ready to use.

5 Assemble the lasagne: preheat the oven to 475°F. Generously butter the sides and the bottom of a 14-inch lasagne pan or a 9 by 12 by 3-inch baking dish. Line the bottom of the dish with one layer of pasta sheets, making sure there are no gaps and no overlaps. You will have to trim the pasta accordingly and fill the gaps with bits of extra pasta. Stir the ragu well and spread one-third of it on the pasta. Sprinkle about ⅓ cup cheese evenly over it. Cover with another layer of pasta, spread one-third of the béchamel evenly on top, and sprinkle with another ⅓ cup of cheese. Continue layering the ingredients, alternating meat layers with béchamel layers and sprinkling each layer with cheese. You should end up with six layers: three of meat and three of béchamel, with béchamel on top. Sprinkle the top with the remaining cheese and bake the lasagne until the top is golden and bubbly, about 18 minutes. (If the top isn't browned after 18 minutes, pass the pan under a broiler for 2 or 3 minutes.) Cut the lasagne into large squares and serve, with additional cheese on the side.

Serves 8

egg pasta sheets (*pasta sfoglia*)

cook's notes The flour used in Italy is usually *doppio zero* (or "00") variety. Finer and softer than American all-purpose flour, it gives the dough great elasticity. Lately, I've been able to find "00" flour at good Italian bakeries and specialty stores. (Little Italy food shops in big cities might carry it.) Otherwise, you can use all-purpose flour or a combination of all-purpose and pastry flour.

4 large eggs, plus 1 egg yolk

2 to 2½ cups flour, preferably Italian "00" (see Cook's Notes) or half all-purpose and half pastry flour

1 In a large bowl, beat the eggs and egg yolk. Add 1¼ cups of flour ¼ cup at a time, beating well after each addition. By this stage, you should have a very soft dough. Now add ¾ cup flour all at once and begin kneading the dough in the bowl, incorporating the flour you have just added, until the dough comes together. It will be quite sticky. Turn the dough out onto a floured surface and knead, adding flour to the work surface 1 or 2 tablespoons at a time to incorporate, until the dough no longer sticks to your hands. The dough shouldn't be too hard. Knead the dough, pressing and folding, until smooth and elastic, at least 8 minutes. Wrap the dough tightly in plastic and let it relax for at least 30 minutes. (The dough can be made a day ahead and refrigerated, wrapped in plastic. Bring it to room temperature before rolling.)

2 Unwrap the dough, divide it into four parts, and flatten each part into a disk. Cover three of the disks with plastic.

3 Set the pasta machine on its widest setting and run the uncovered disk through the roller six times. After each roll, fold the pasta into thirds, with the two ends folded inward, like a letter. Make the setting one notch smaller and run the dough through again. Keep rolling the dough (this time without folding) until you reach the next to last (thinnest) setting. The rolled-out pieces of dough will be about 6 inches wide. Cut them into 6-inch segments.

4 Line a large baking tray with a clean towel lightly dusted with flour, place the sheets of dough on it, and cover with a sheet of plastic or a barely damp paper towel to prevent it from drying. Repeat with the other three pieces of dough, keeping the finished sheets covered.

Makes enough dough for 1 lasagne

With its cool confident loveliness, lemon tart is the Grace Kelly of sweets. You want zest? You want charm? You want classier than classy? No matter how much cream or butter are lurking inside, a lemon tart always appears light and virtuous. And it's equally swell to serve after a French, Indian, Thai, or Italian meal. If stuck with only one all-purpose dessert to grace my days, lemon tart would be it.

A smooth sophisticated custard inside an elegantly buttery *pâté sucre*, lemon tart has a nineteenth-century *haute-patisserie* aura. Yet tarts are way older than Carême and Escoffier. Ancient Romans, for instance, adored all kinds of egg custards and flans. Tarts and tartlets were already making lips smack back in the *Forme of Cury,* a landmark fourteenth-century recipe compendium. Tarts filled with meats, fruit, or egg custards—scented with saffron and rose water but otherwise not radically different from today's—were as common on Renaissance menus as they are today in the French countryside.

lemon tart

Contemporary lemon tarts come in many variations. One might stir ground almonds into the pastry or adorn the top with berries or fruit. The custard can be caramelized like crème brûlée or baked under a cloud of Italian meringue. Quivery lemon curd or a citrus-perfumed mascarpone could replace the more straight-ahead lemon custard. Still, most lemon tarts fall into two basic camps: those with a prebaked pastry shell filled with a cooked custard, and those with the filling actually baked in the pastry until just set.

The unbaked custard is sleek and professional, the stuff you get at fancy French pastry shops. But to me this is assembling rather than baking. My ideal is the rustic *tarte au citron* from the ovens of unassuming family bakeries and village restaurants in Provence: immensely buttery, caramelized at the top, with that mouthwatering citrus zing bursting out of a classic baked custard. It's hard to think of a more gracious sweet.

anya von bremzen

caramelized lemon tart

cook's notes This is my adaptation of Tamasin Day-Lewis's terrific recipe from *The Art of the Tart*, using my mom's delicious almond pastry. The top of this tart, you'll note, is caramelized with a blowtorch. For more on this method, see Crème Brûlée (page 76) and its Resources for a mail-order source for a blowtorch. You can caramelize the tart under a broiler, too, taking care not to burn the crust.

almond pastry

1½ cups all-purpose flour

⅓ cup granulated sugar

¼ cup finely ground blanched almonds

9 tablespoons unsalted butter, chilled and cut into small pieces

1 egg yolk, beaten with 2 tablespoons heavy cream

1 to 3 tablespoons ice water

filling

8 large egg yolks

1¼ cups granulated sugar

1 teaspoon pure vanilla extract

1¼ cups heavy cream

1 cup plus 2 tablespoons fresh lemon juice

Finely grated zest from 2 lemons

3 tablespoons dark brown sugar, for caramelizing the top

1 Make the almond pastry: In a food processor, combine the flour, sugar and almonds and pulse two or three times. Add the butter and pulse until the mixture resembles coarse meal. Transfer the mixture to a bowl and, using two forks, stir in the egg yolk mixture. Gather the dough into a ball, sprinkling on the ice water if it doesn't quite hold together. On a lightly floured surface, flatten the ball into a disk, wrap it in plastic, and refrigerate for at least 2 hours. (The pastry can be prepared up to 2 days ahead.)

2 On a floured surface, roll out the pastry to a 14-inch circle. Transfer it to an 11-inch tart pan with a removable bottom, press the dough into the sides of the pan, and trim the overhang. Refrigerate, covered with foil, for 20 minutes.

3 While the dough is chilling, preheat the oven to 375°F. Remove the pastry from the refrigerator and, without removing the foil, fill the bottom with pie weights or beans. Bake for 15 minutes. Remove the pie weights and the foil, and continue baking for another 10 minutes. Cool slightly on the rack before filling. (The crust can be made up to one day ahead.) Set the oven temperature to 300°F.

4 Make the filling: In a large bowl, whisk the egg yolks, sugar, and vanilla until light and fluffy. Gradually, whisk in the cream, lemon juice, and zest. Set the tart shell on a baking sheet and carefully pour in three-fourths of the custard mixture.

5 Very carefully, transfer the baking sheet with the tart to the oven. With a ladle pour in as much of the remaining custard as will fit without overflowing. Bake until the custard is just set but a little wobbly, as it will continue to set out of the oven. This should take 45 to 50 minutes. Remove from the oven and cool on a rack for about 1 hour. Tent the tart loosely with foil and refrigerate for 2 hours.

6 Just before serving, sift the brown sugar from a small strainer evenly onto the top of the tart. Caramelize the top with a blowtorch, working in circular motion. (If you don't have a blowtorch, cover the edges of the pastry carefully with foil and broil the tart about 4 inches from the source of heat until the top is bubbly and caramelized, about 1½ minutes.) The tart can be served warm or at room temperature.

Serves 8 to 10

Come summer I start dreaming of Maine—the Maine of spruce woods and blueberry barrens. The Maine of picnic benches out on the docks. The Maine of lobster salad wedged into a humble hot dog bun for that Rolls-Royce of American summer sandwiches: the lobster roll.

Like a classic New England lobster stew—a lobster per person, butter, milk, and a dash of paprika—a lobster roll is both indulgent and puritanical, down-home and deluxe. It is nothing more than a full 4 ounces of lobster meat on a bun, with minimal seasonings. If the lobster is fresh, if the pink meat has been pried from the shell just minutes ago, if the mayo is Hellmann's and the bun is toasted or griddled to a crusty tan—you can't really go wrong with a lobster roll. Which is not to say New Englanders don't argue forever about this classic.

lobster rolls

Should the crustacean be warm or cold? Lavished with lashings of mayo or just enough to bind the lobster nuggets together? Tail or claw meat? Some lobster-roll lovers cast off the mayo in favor of melted butter. Some (perversely!) hiss at the crisp bed of shredded lettuce. And you just wouldn't believe all the fuss about a teaspoon of minced onion and a few tiny celery bits.

Then, there is the matter of ambience.

"The only way to eat lobster roll is on a dock—the bait shack smelling up a storm, fishermen unloading bluefin in front of you, big hungry seagulls circling overhead," insisted Sam Hayward, lobster expert and owner of the extraordinary Fore Street restaurant in Portland, Maine. You wind up your feast with a wedge of blueberry or whoopie pie, and if you're still hungry, you circle around searching for a soft ice cream stand.

The lobster pot is an archetypal New England vision; the crustacean's claw-y likeness, after all, used to grace Maine's license plate (replaced recently by the chickadee). And to understand the lobster's deep-rooted Down East appeal, it helps to realize just how plentiful it once was on New England shores. When America was still young, lobsters were caught with bare hands on the beach at low tide, used as bait for cod (the money fish) and as fertilizer for fields.

Back in 1608, guys from the Poplam Colony were driven to strike by the unbearable tedium of lobster for breakfast, lunch, and dinner. And as all Maine schoolchildren learn, indentured servants famously demanded that their contracts clearly state: "No lobster more than three times a week." Even as late as the end of the nineteenth century, lobsters went for twenty-five cents. Per dozen. This utopia didn't quite last, and by the 1930s supplies had dwindled dramatically. Thanks, however, to strict conservation measures and improvements in gear and technology, the supply has since risen— and is rising still.

Nevertheless, buying and cooking a whole lobster for just one or two white bread sandwiches might seem like a crazy extravagance. But that, you see, is the point. You can always boil your crustacean and eat it with butter. But a lobster roll is more fun and not that much of a splurge compared, to say, the price of a room service club sandwich at a fancy hotel.

Now, the ultimate question: Can you really enjoy a Maine lobster roll away from foggy salt marshes, pine woods, and the briny tang of the ocean? Yes, because as you eat, you'll begin to imagine those foggy salt marshes, pine woods, and the briny tang of the ocean. Maybe even a bait shack or two.

Can't buy live lobster directly from a boat? Try a good Maine mail-order source (see Resources). The tastiest lobsters come November to January and you should select ones that are particularly frisky (tails kicking, antennas wiggling). To cook the beast, chef Sam Hayward endorses steaming over boiling, because boiling, to him, washes away the flavor. When testing for doneness, don't judge by the looks, Hayward cautions, as some older lobsters don't turn a uniform red. The lobster is cooked when the long antennae breaks easily.

new england lobster rolls

cook's notes Hayward's lobster salad recipe is simplicity itself; for a little crunch, you can add finely chopped celery and onion. Pepperidge Farm hot dog rolls are the tastiest.

Two 1¼-pound lobsters

Salt

3 tablespoons Hellmann's mayonnaise, or more to taste

A squirt of fresh lemon juice

Dash of Tabasco sauce

2 tablespoons finely minced onion (optional)

½ small celery rib, cut into small dice (optional)

2 or 3 teaspoons unsalted butter

2 or 3 good best-quality hot dog rolls, preferably top-split

¼ cup shredded romaine lettuce, or to taste

Potato chips and bread and butter pickles, as an accompaniment

1 In a 5- or 6-gallon stockpot set with a rack, bring 2 inches of seawater or salted water to a rolling boil. Wearing oven mitts, grab the lobsters, place them on their backs on the rack and cover tightly. After 4 minutes, turn the lobsters over with tongs, taking care not to burn yourself with the steam. Cook for another 3 or 4 minutes, until the antennas snap easily. Using tongs, remove the lobsters to a big pot filled with ice water and let cool.

2 Crack the lobsters with a cleaver in several places and remove the meat from the claws and tail. After being submerged in iced water, the meat should come out easily. Pick over the meat, removing the cartilage, tomalley, and the digestive vein behind the tail. If there is roe, reserve it for garnishing the salad.

3 Chop or tear the lobster meat into irregular nuggets about ½ inch. Gently toss with the mayonnaise, lemon juice, and Tabasco. Add the grated onion and celery, if desired. If you like, grate the lobster roe over the salad as a garnish.

4 In a griddle or heavy skillet, melt the butter over medium-low heat. Toast the roll for about 2 minutes on each side. Line the bottom of each roll with a little lettuce and loosely pile the salad onto the roll. Serve with potato chips and bread-and-butter pickles.

Makes 2 or 3 lobster rolls

resources Maine Lobster Direct (tel: 800-556-2783; or *www.mainelobsterdirect*) ships all over the United States.

lain Ducasse, Mr. Michelin All-Star, featured it on the menu at his Paris restaurant, Spoon. Diana Vreeland dished it out at her swank soirees. Ron and Nancy sent a recipe for it to their fans along with autographed glossies. And the man credited with bringing it to this country is none other than Thomas Jefferson. Did somebody say mac and cheese was plebeian?

Of course, Jefferson didn't *invent* mac and cheese, as some suggest. But in 1787 he did dispatch an envoy to Italy to buy a pasta machine, and later had Parmesan shipped to him in Virginia. We also know that an 1802 menu at Monticello featured "a pie called macaroni" and that in 1824 Jefferson's cousin, Mary Randolf, published a recipe for macaroni pudding, which consisted of boiled pasta steamed in a mold with cream, eggs, and bits of ham. The first recipe for

macaroni and cheese

baked macaroni layered with Parmesan cheese and white sauce appeared in *The Carolina Housewife* (1847) by Sarah Rutledge, and from here on the dish began to acquire its present form.

The idea of baked pasta bound with cheese and/or white sauce is, of course, hardly new. Every Italian cook knows *pasta al forno*. The Swiss have their awesome *Aelpelmagronen,* which is baked macaroni laced with apples and *speck* (ham). Macaroni gratins are a staple in France, every Greek taverna offers *pasticcio,* and the Brits have long relished macaroni puddings. Still, calling mac and cheese Italian or British is like calling burgers German.

Mac and cheese reached its zenith and became prodigiously American in the 1940s, thanks to the efforts of J. H. Kraft, the patentor of processed cheese. A combo of Tenderoni macaroni and Kraft's rather unpopular instant cheese powder, the dish was the bright idea of a St. Louis salesman for National Dairy Products. Kraft's instant macaroni dinner was launched in 1937 and never looked back. And though popularity waned somewhat in the 1960s, its appeal holds on. Even my mother, who after more than twenty years in this country still regards American cuisine as an oxymoron, took to the blue box with a vengeance.

These days macaroni and cheese recipes are legion, ranging from dotingly nostalgic back-of-the-box basics, to 24-karat affairs with black truffles or medleys of imported *fromages,* to elegantly minimalist propositions that eschew white sauce (big mistake!). To my mind, a great mac and cheese falls somewhere in between these styles: it should be classy and lush but still recognizable as a wallop of Americana. Boutique Italian pasta? Hand-crafted goat cheese? Nah.

The following recipe is just the right stuff, and I've come to swear by it. It came to me via an e-mail attachment containing a vicious virus, its accompanying note so scrambled that to this day I have no idea who sent it. Whoever it was, he or she deserves a gooey expression of gratitude (as well as a computer utility update).

classic macaroni and cheese

cook's notes This recipe, while luscious, is a little restrained; if you like your mac and cheese extra gooey and are not calorie-conscious, increase the amount of Cheddar by either adding it to the sauce or layering the cooked macaroni and sauce with extra shredded cheese in the baking dish (*really* gooey). Beer adds a savory note that goes well with the Cheddar; if it seems too unorthodox, substitute ⅓ extra cup of milk.

1⅔ cups milk

⅓ cup flat lager-style beer

3½ tablespoons unsalted butter

1 small onion, finely chopped

3 tablespoons all-purpose flour

8 to 10 ounces elbow macaroni

2½ cups shredded extra-sharp Cheddar cheese, or more to taste

6 tablespoons grated Parmesan cheese

1½ teaspoons Dijon mustard, or more to taste

Pinch of freshly ground white pepper

Pinch of grated nutmeg

Dash of Tabasco sauce, or more to taste

Salt

5 tablespoons fine white bread crumbs, sautéed in butter if desired

1 Preheat the oven to 450°F. and bring a large pot of salted water to a boil.

2 In a medium saucepan, heat the milk and beer until almost boiling and take off the heat. (Don't worry if the beer curdles the milk a little.)

3 In another saucepan, melt the butter over medium-low heat and sauté the onion until limp but not browned, about 5 minutes. Add the flour, and cook the roux for 2 minutes, stirring constantly. Add the milk-beer mixture and cook, whisking, until the sauce is thick, smooth, and bubbly, 5 to 7 minutes. While the sauce is cooking, add the pasta to the boiling water.

4 Remove the sauce from the heat and stir in the Cheddar, 2 tablespoons of the Parmesan, mustard, pepper, nutmeg, Tabasco, and salt to taste. Taste and adjust the seasonings as you wish.

5 When the pasta is cooked al dente, about 6 minutes, drain and transfer it to an ovenproof casserole or gratin dish. Immediately pour the cheese sauce over it, mixing it in gently with 2 forks. Do no overstir. Sprinkle evenly with the bread crumbs and the remaining 4 tablespoons of the Parmesan. Bake until the top is golden and bubbly, about 12 minutes.

Serves 4 to 6

the meatball question kept me awake many nights. Do they or don't they belong in the pantheon of the world's greatest dishes? In the mornings, I'd rub my eyes, gulp down some coffee, and make meatball columns: for and against.

Con: Ikea's Swedish meatballs (punishment for lusting after another $9.99 torchère). My Soviet childhood ruined by *bitki*—Ping-Pongs smothered in sour cream. Dutch *bitterballen* that sink in the stomach like cannonballs. Gloopy goodfella meatballs over spaghetti, the equivalent of eating a tomato-drenched floor mop. Isn't *meatball* a code word for meat not fit for anything else?

Pro: Indelibly delicious pistachio *köfte* from Istanbul. In Lecce, Puglia, the vision of tiny *polpette* scattered on a bed of braised wild greens. *Albóndigas* stuffed with eggs and smothered in a complex smoky black mole that sent me into swoons

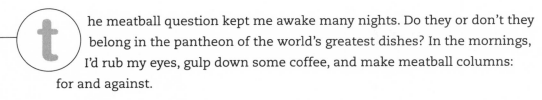

once in Oaxaca. Dime-size coins of minced lamb grilled inside a whole eggplant in Aleppo's old Armenian quarter. Not to mention mom's *yozhiki* (little hedgehogs) studded with rice. My "pro meatballs" column soon filled up a whole notebook, and I began to contemplate devoting the rest of my days to celebrating the delights of ground meat.

Take Vietnamese *nem luong*—walnut-sized grilled pork balls wrapped in rice paper along with a few sprigs of herbs and dipped into sweet-tangy *nuoc cham*. Take Greek *keftedes* touched up with ouzo and parsley, or the wealth of Turkish *köfte*. And how can we forget Persia, a culinary power that deserves most credit for turning the meatball into a masterpiece that transcends its humble origins as a way of using up inferior meat. Persian meatballs can be as simple as *gondi*—minced chicken balls fluffed up with chickpea flour and floated in broth—or as improbable as the legendary *koofteh Tabrizi*, a colossus made of lamb hand-pounded with rice and split peas, then stuffed with prunes, boiled egg, barberries, and sometimes a whole chicken. Meatballs don't get more grandiose. And it was Persia that lent most Arab, Indian, and Eastern

Mediterranean cooks both the dish and the term. Turkish *köfte*, Greek *keftedes*, Moroccan *kefte*, Bulgarian *kyufte*—they all stem from the Persian root *koft*, "to pound."

Still, if forced to choose among a million meatball recipes, I'd turn to China, for Shanghainese Lion's Head meatballs. Based on ground pork plumped with hand-chopped fat (or, today, tofu), these are golf-ball-sized balls braised in a soy-flavored sauce alongside napa cabbage (to the Chinese the cabbage resembles a lion's mane). Unlike showy Cantonese seafood creations or incendiary Sichuan street food, these meatballs are terrifically homey and mild—pure Shanghainese home cooking. Among the world's most soothing mood-lifting dishes, they are light and faintly exotic, and one of my absolute favorites for a casual winter meal. Welcome on any cold day, these are especially relished during Chinese New Year, their roundness being the symbol of family unity.

lion's head meatballs

cook's notes Ideally, this dish should be cooked and served in a Chinese clay pot, a wonderfully entertaining and inexpensive piece of cookware. But any snug casserole will do just fine. Some cooks add a 1.2- or 1.8-ounce package of cellophane noodles (softened in hot water and drained) toward the end for more texture.

meatballs

1¼ pounds coarsely ground pork butt

One 3-inch square soft tofu (about 4 ounces), mashed well

1½ tablespoons soy sauce

1½ teaspoons sugar

1 tablespoon oyster sauce (optional)

1 tablespoon Chinese rice wine (Shaoxing) or medium-dry sherry

1 tablespoon grated fresh ginger

1 tablespoon minced scallion

1½ teaspoons salt

Large pinch of freshly ground white pepper

Peanut oil, for frying the meatballs

1 tablespoon cornstarch, mixed with 2 tablespoons chicken broth or water, plus 2 or 3 tablespoons for dredging the meatballs

1 Make the meatballs: Place all the ingredients except the oil and cornstarch mixture in a large bowl. Blend until well combined, working in quick upward motions with the tips of your fingers. Do not overwork the mixture. Shape the mixture into eight meatballs by bouncing and throwing it gently between cupped hands five or six times, wetting your hands with cold water between each meatball.

2 In a large wok or skillet, heat 1 inch of oil over medium-high heat. Spread 2 or 3 tablespoons of the cornstarch on a plate and dust the meatballs very lightly. In two batches, brown the meatballs for about 3 minutes per side. Transfer to a plate lined with paper towels to drain.

3 Prepare the casserole: Bring a large pot of water to a boil. While the water is heating, remove the tough outer leaves from the cabbage and trim off about 1½ inches of the lower ends. Cut the tender inner leaves in half lengthwise, then crosswise into 2½-inch lengths. Measure 6 cups of the cabbage and save the rest for another use. Blanch the cut leaves in the boiling water for 30 seconds. Drain and refresh under cold running water.

4 In a small saucepan, bring the chicken stock, soy sauce, rice wine, and sugar to a simmer.

casserole

1 small head napa (Chinese) cabbage

2½ cups chicken stock or canned broth

2 tablespoons soy sauce, or more to taste

1 tablespoon Chinese rice wine (Shaoxing) or medium-dry sherry

2 teaspoons sugar

2 teaspoons cornstarch, mixed with 2 tablespoons water

Minced scallions, for garnish

Cooked white rice, as an accompaniment

5 Arrange half the cabbage on the bottom of a 4-quart Chinese clay pot or heavy casserole. Arrange the meatballs on top in one layer and cover with the remaining cabbage. Pour in the chicken stock mixture; it should barely cover the cabbage. Cook the meatballs at a bare simmer for 12 to 15 minutes, until the cabbage is just tender but not overcooked. Drizzle in the cornstarch mixture and simmer, stirring gently, until the sauce thickens, about 4 minutes. Serve directly from the clay pot or transfer to a serving dish and garnish with scallions. Serve with rice.

Serves 4

Cinzia and Roberto, a couple of robust zucchini vendors I befriended at Genova's bustling Mercato Orientale, had their respective theories about minestrone alla Genovese. "It was women—sailors' wives— who created Ligurian cooking," Cinzia proclaimed. "They cooked *stocafisso* [stockfish] and minestrone and meat sauce for ravioli—*lento*, slowly, for hours, as they waited for their husbands to come back from sea."

"Rubbish!" scoffed Roberto. "Minestrone's a man's dish! It was invented by Genovese galley cooks aboard ships, with dried beans, potatoes, and broken-up pasta. It's the soup of the *marinai*—served at the kind of places around port my wife would never set foot in. Sailors from Tunisia, Russia, America—they all know minestrone!"

minestrone

"You are both lying to the *giornalista Americana!*" the porcini lady next to us suddenly chimed in. "I'm from Lombardia, and if you want minestrone *buono,* come to us in the fall." "Fall?" Roberto grimaced. "Minestrone is a *piatto invernale,* a winter dish!" "Ha! Only an idiot would make it in winter when vegetables are so ugly!" countered Cinzia.

I visit Liguria often and I always eat *menestron,* as they call it. But this was the first argument I had ever witnessed over a soup so comforting and ubiquitous most Ligurians simply take it for granted. Aside from its having been served to sailors at "floating" *osterias* set up on small boats docked around Genova port, no one had much information to share about its history. Its preparation isn't by any means codified: its ingredients are spontaneous; its cooking time long but approximate. But while the first taste might seem modest, undistinguished even, with each spoonful life gets better and better. This isn't just a *minestra*—that Italian *cucina povera* staple that falls somewhere between pasta and soup—but a minestrone: a BIG soup, and serious nourishment in a region poor in meat and not that rich in fish, but blessed with Italy's most poetic cuisine.

Minestrone recipes given to me by Genovese cooks sometimes didn't even list each vegetable. To any local, the words *verdure di stagione* (seasonal vegetables) say enough. Almost any combination of vegetables can find its way into a minestrone: eggplant, cabbage, pumpkin, potatoes, borage, or chard—and always small pasta and beans. A Ligurian minestrone, as opposed to a Lombardian one, should contain no broth, no *sofrito* (sautéed onion and garlic), not a trace of pancetta or meat, and no elaborate seasonings aside from good olive oil added half way through cooking and a Parmesan rind. A little grated Parmesan and a dollop of pesto are stirred in at serving time. It's the cheese and the pesto that snap all the flavors into focus and lift the soup into another dimension. Pesto for minestrone is made without pine nuts and sometimes flavored with extra doses of the strong-tasting pecorino cheese.

"Usually people dump everything into the pot at once," noted the proprietress of restaurant Rina, a Genova institution by the old port that serves my favorite minestrone in town. "But my secret is to add each vegetable in its time." For instance, beans, potato, zucchini, or pumpkin must "melt" into the broth; whereas chard or green beans should be soft but retain some of their character. "Finish this," said the proprietress, plonking an enormous soup bowl in front of me, "and you'll understand Genova."

minestrone alla genovese

cook's notes Flavors meld even further when the minestrone is made a day ahead; I give a rather large quantity here, since this is a dish you can happily eat three days in a row. In Liguria, minestrone is never served piping hot, but rather warm or even at room temperature, which is surprisingly delicious.

15 cups water

1½ cups fresh borlotti or cranberry beans; or ½ cup dried beans soaked overnight; or 1½ cups canned cranberry beans, drained

1¼ cups chopped green or savoy cabbage

1 large celery rib, sliced

2 medium carrots, peeled and cut into large dice

2 medium boiling potatoes, cut into chunks

1½ cups diced pumpkin or yellow squash

2 medium zucchini, cut into large dice

2 leeks, white parts only, thickly sliced

Rind from Parmesan cheese, rinsed (optional)

Salt and freshly ground black pepper

1½ cups green beans, cut into 1½-inch lengths

3 loosely packed cups slivered borage, Swiss chard, or spinach

2 garlic cloves, crushed through a press

6 tablespoons delicate extra-virgin olive oil, preferably Ligurian (do not use strong, peppery oil)

¾ cup any dried pasta, broken into very small pieces

Freshly grated Parmesan cheese, preferably Parmigiano-Regianno

Pesto (page 198) made without pine nuts, or best-quality store-bought pesto

1 In a large stockpot, bring the water to a boil. Add all the ingredients (except canned beans, if using) through the green beans, season to taste with salt and pepper, and wait for the water to come back to the boil. Partially cover the pot and cook the vegetables over low heat for 1 hour, stirring and skimming from time to time. If using canned beans, add them now.

2 Add the green beans, borage, garlic, and 4 tablespoons of the olive oil and continue cooking, stirring occasionally, until the potatoes and pumpkin are half dissolved, and the soup is thick and creamy, about 30 minutes. Turn the heat up to medium-high, add the pasta, and cook until soft, about 20 minutes more, stirring to prevent the pasta from sticking to the bottom. Stir the soup vigorously to get a homogenous texture, adjust salt to taste, and let cool for 10 minutes. Stir in the remaining 2 tablespoons olive oil. Ladle the soup into bowls, and serve, passing the Parmigiano and pesto on the side. A teaspoon of each per portion is about right. Serve hot or warm. The soup tends to thicken on standing; thin it out with a little water if making ahead.

Serves 8 to 10

anya von bremzen

Like many lucky New Yorkers and Angelinos, I experienced my first miso-glazed cod epiphany courtesy of chef Nobu Matsuhisa, the emperor of New Wave Japanese cuisine. This was at the Tribeca Nobu some years ago, and if I close my eyes I can still revisit the taste: sweet, rich, subtly fermented glaze melting into the white buttery fish that dissolved in my mouth like whipped cream. A kind of piscine confection, the dish was decadent, unctuous, and completely ethereal all at once. Not even Matsuhisa's groovy sushi, not to mention Uma and Ethan at the next table, could compete with this cod.

Apparently I wasn't the only one so smitten. Quicker than you can say *arigato*, Matsuhisa's signature black cod—marinated forever in white Kyoto miso, sake, sugar, and mirin, the sweet Japanese rice wine—became the copycat Pacific Rim special of the nineties.

miso-glazed black cod

But while the Western world might tout it as a Nobu invention, miso-glazed grilled fish had been enjoyed in Japan centuries before Matsuhisa was born. Back in pre-refrigeration days, it was a popular homestyle staple, with cooks marinating fish in soybean paste to retard spoiling. Hiroko Shimbo, author of the delightful *Japanese Kitchen*, surmises that the dish might have originated in landlocked Kyoto, the epicenter of white miso. The journey from sea to the city took several days and the fish traveled to the capital preserved in miso.

The Japanese are a nation willing to ferment anything—let's not forget that sushi began as a way of preserving fish in fermented rice. They've been onto *miso-zuke*, a method of pickling in salted soybean paste, for nearly a millennium. Extending the idea to chicken, beef, grilled sweet Kyoto eggplant, and, of course, fish seemed pretty inevitable. Today, the Japanese buy raw miso-steeped fish from fish markets or the lavish food halls of department stores to turn into a quick, scrumptious meal at home.

Any oily fish—bluefish, salmon, Spanish mackerel—tastes amazing when marinated in sugary miso and broiled. But none takes better to the sweet-salty-earthy marinade than black cod. A silky-textured North Pacific fish, black cod with its gray-to-black skin and snowy flesh is a member of the little-known skilfish family. Devotees of traditional Jewish delis know it as sable, that buttery hot-smoked fish with a paprika glaze you put on bagels. To confuse matters, black cod is related neither to cod nor to butterfish, another one of its aliases. Much of it is caught in Alaska and a great deal ends up being frozen at sea and sent to Japan. There it's known as *tara* and deemed a great delicacy.

Having started out as a cheap "ethnic" fish usually sold smoked, fresh black cod has lately leapt from obscurity into the limelight of big city restaurants. And for that we have Nobu Matsuhisa and his miso-glazed cod to thank. The man might have not invented the dish, but without him, the Western world might have been deprived of this delicacy.

miso magic A protein-rich, earthy essence of Japanese cooking, miso arrived in Japan from China in the early eighth century. What gives miso life is *koji* (*Aspergillus oryzae*), a natural fermentation agent also used for soy sauces and sake. This mold is added to either soy beans alone (*mamemiso*), or to soy beans mixed with barley (*mugimiso*) or with rice (*komemiso*). The rice-and-soybean miso is the most common by far. Placed in large wooden tubs or kegs, miso is left to ferment anywhere from two months to three years. Each of the three miso types is further classified according to color and salt-content: *shiromiso* (white), *shinshumiso* (yellow), *akamiso* (red), and others.

The final flavor of miso reflects many factors: the base ingredients, length and temperature of aging, amount of salt, and the skill of the maker. Color ranges from creamy beige to muddy brown to brick red to chocolate; flavors include the winy sweetness of white *saiykyo* miso of Kyoto Prefecture and the nutty saltiness of *akamiso* (brown miso), with many shades of taste in between. Japanese palates are as attuned to the subtleties and variations of miso as Western ones are to the various nuances of cheese—with preference for a particular regional style being something of an identity statement. Though a crock of homemade miso no longer graces every household, there's hardly a Japanese fridge lacking a package of this healthful staple.

miso-glazed black cod

cook's notes In an ideal world, the dish would be made with fresh black cod and white *saikyo* miso, a lightly fermented, sweet Kyoto miso, available at better Asian groceries or by mail (see Resources). Fresh black cod can be found at fish markets in the Pacific Northwest or at gourmet fish shops in other regions from September to January.

Lacking these ingredients, the dish is still incredible (and shockingly easy) with regular white miso (shiromiso) and almost any buttery fish. If using *saikyo* miso, cut the sugar to 2 or 3 tablespoons.

⅓ cup sake

⅓ cup mirin (sweet Japanese rice wine)

1 cup *saikyo* miso or regular white miso paste (*shiromiso*)

½ cup sugar (see Cook's Note)

4 unskinned fresh black cod, salmon, or halibut filets, about 8 ounces each

Sea salt

1 tablespoon Asian (toasted) sesame oil

1 In a medium saucepan, bring the sake and mirin to a boil over medium heat and boil for 30 seconds to evaporate some of the alcohol. Turn the heat down to very low and add the miso, stirring constantly with a wooden spoon to prevent it from sticking. Add the sugar and stir until completely dissolved, about 2 minutes. Remove from the heat and cool to room temperature.

2 Pat-dry the fish with paper towels and rub lightly with salt. Place the miso marinade in a large nonreactive dish, add the fish, turn to coat with the marinade, and cover with plastic. The fish can be marinated anywhere from 6 hours to 3 days.

3 Preheat the oven to 400°F. Once the oven is hot, turn on the broiler. Place the fish skin side up on an oiled broiler pan, gently wiping off excess marinade. Brush the top lightly with the sesame oil and broil until the top is browned, about 5 minutes. Turn off the broiler, turn the oven back on, and bake the fish until it flakes easily when tested with a fork, about 10 more minutes. If you'd like to serve the marinade as a sauce, bring it to a simmer over medium-high heat while the fish is baking.

4 Divide the fish among 4 plates, adding a light drizzle of the marinade to each plate if you wish.

Serves 4

resources *Saikyo* miso can be mail-ordered from Katagiri & Co. in New York (tel: 212-755-3536 or *www.katagiri.com*).

Puebla, Mexico, some time in the 1680s. On a breezy day, Sister Andrea de la Asunción—a celebrated cook and Mother Superior of the Baroque Dominican convent of Santa Rosa—paces nervously around her vaulted tiled kitchen. The nuns, you see, are expecting a guest: his Excellency the Viceroy of New Spain, on whose generous funds the entire convent is counting. It is Sister Andrea's special duty to impress him with a dish like no other he tasted before, a creation that will truly symbolize New Spain with its blend of Aztec and Iberian cultures.

A gargantuan turkey fed for days on chestnuts and nuts has already been slaughtered and boiled. Now, Sister Andrea has to divine a sauce. She roasts some dried chiles—mulatos, pasillas, chipotles—over an open fire and fries them in lard to bring out the flavor. Next, from her spice chest, she plucks out

mole poblano

cinnamon, cloves, and anise—all precious commodities that have been arriving in wealthy Puebla from the Orient. Taking to her *metate* (the indigenous three-legged grinding stone) with a vengeance, Sister Andrea pulverizes some peanuts, almonds, and sesame seeds. As she grinds away, another sister looks in to cheer her on: "*Que bien mole, hermana*" (how well you grind, sister), she exclaims. "Watch your conjugations," Sister Andrea giggles, "it's *muele*—not mole."

But it's too late, the name *mole* sticks.

As the original mole contained more than a hundred ingredients, our Sister keeps grinding for hours, adding lard-fried tortilla for texture, raisins for sweetness, onions and garlic for pungency. Finally she gathers it all in a huge earthenware *olla*, adds the turkey broth, and begins to stir. She stirs and tastes and stirs some more—but clearly something is missing. At this very moment (so goes the tale), an errant wind blows some powdered chocolate through the window right into the pot. Now Sister Andrea has a masterpiece on her hands. The Viceroy tastes, the Viceroy swoons, and Andrea's mole becomes the pride of Puebla and Mexico's national dish.

The story of the creation of mole poblano—there are a dozen different versions circulating—is an enchanting blend of fiction and fact, with that requisite touch of magical realism. Certainly, some of the greatest Mexican dishes were conceived in convents, especially in the wealthy Puebla de los Angeles (*chiles en nogada* being another Poblano conventual classic). It is also true that for nuns, cooking was a way of currying financial favors from visiting Bishops and Viceroys. But the word *mole*, as no one disputes, is from the Nahuatl Indian *molli*, meaning a stew, sauce, or concoction. Such indigenous "stews" thick with pulverized chiles and nuts had been around long before the arrival of the Spanish. As for chocolate, it was for centuries a prized ingredient in the kitchens of Aztec nobility (though it probably wasn't stirred into stews until the seventeenth century, or even later).

Still, a dish as rich and ornate as mole poblano deserves a legend to match.

My recipe came from a posh suburb of Tijuana where society ladies often entertained themselves by holding cooking contests among their maids. The contest I attended was taken seriously. One señora brought her *domestica's* six Zapotec sisters straight from Oaxaca to prepare tamales. Another set up an elaborate carnitas tent in her garden, tended by a dynasty of carnita makers from Michoacán. The winner, however, was a modest elderly housekeeper from a village near Puebla. Her name was Irene, and her tour de force mole poblano was worthy of Andrea herself.

While she soaked the chiles and toasted the nuts, Irene told me that this was the mole she served for the weddings of every one of her 11 children, and for the baptisms of their children—all 49 of them. At the end of the session, I learned that Irene had been able to save enough money to buy *licuadoras* (the sought-after Osterizer blender) for each of her daughters, so as to keep the mole tradition alive.

This was the single best recipe I ever received. The top notes of this mole are sweet and surprisingly mild; the lower notes hint at smoke and gradually blossom into full heat on the back palate. The second mouthful is nutty, the third ties all the flavors together. It's a sauce to savor and marvel at, with the disciplined structure of a fine Burgundy and the elusive mystique of expensive perfume. I've been making this recipe for over a decade without changing so much as a peppercorn.

irene's mole poblano with turkey and vegetables

cook's notes Besides the intricacy of the sauce, I love Irene's presentation, which includes whole red new potatoes, green beans, lima beans, and spinach. However, for a more straightforward mole, you can omit these. Classically, mole poblano is made with a whole poached small turkey, but I suggest poached turkey breast or two chickens; Thanksgiving turkey leftovers and canned chicken broth will also do nicely. With rice, tortillas, and a big salad, this recipe makes a fiesta for twelve. For a smaller crowd, make the whole sauce recipe, use as much of it as you like (halve all the other accompaniments), and freeze the sauce for later. It makes an awesome dip for tortillas or a filling for tamales (see page 296).

turkey and stock

1 whole bone-in turkey breast (6 to 7 pounds) or two 4-pound chickens

14 cups water

2 medium onions, trimmed but unpeeled

2 large carrots, peeled and cut into large chunks

4 garlic cloves, peeled and smashed

8 black peppercorns

Salt

mole sauce

10 dried pasilla chiles (about 3 ounces)

7 dried ancho chiles (about 3 ounces)

2 large dried chipotle chiles

3 large garlic cloves

1 small onion, quartered

1 corn tortilla, cut in half and toasted

3 thin slices soft French bread, toasted

1 cup chopped tomatoes

¼ cup toasted peanuts (see Note)

¼ cup toasted unskinned almonds

½ cup toasted sesame seeds

¼ cup toasted pecans

⅓ cup dark raisins

1 Make the turkey: Place the turkey breast and water in a large stockpot, cover, and bring to a boil. Skim thoroughly, add the onions, carrots, garlic, peppercorns, and salt; cover and simmer until a thermometer inserted into the thickest part of the meat registers 155°F., about 1¼ hours or longer. Remove from the heat and let the turkey cool in the broth for 30 minutes. It will continue cooking as it stands. Strain the broth, measure out 8 cups, and save the rest for another use. Once the meat is completely cool, cut it against the grain into thick slices. (This step can be prepared ahead, with the turkey slices refrigerated in the liquid.) If using chickens, cook them in the same broth mixture until tender, about 1 hour; let cool, skin, and tear into large chunks.

2 Make the mole sauce: Wipe all the chiles clean with a damp cloth. Split them open and remove the seeds and ribs. In a griddle, or a large cast-iron skillet, toast the chiles in batches over medium heat until they turn several shades darker, about 20 seconds per side, pressing down with a spatula. Set aside. In the same skillet, dry-roast the garlic and onion, turning often, until slightly charred, about 4 minutes. Set aside.

3 Break the tortilla and the bread into pieces. Place the chiles in a large bowl, add hot water to cover, and soak for 20 minutes. Add the toasted tortilla and bread pieces and soak for another 5 to 10 minutes.

4 Toss the tomatoes, roasted onion and garlic, peanuts, almonds, sesame seeds, pecans, raisins, ground cinnamon, cloves, and pepper together in a large bowl. Working in two batches, puree all these ingredients thoroughly in a blender together with 4 cups of the stock. The puree should be completely smooth. Transfer the puree to a large bowl.

5 Working in batches, if necessary, puree the chiles with the bread and tortilla, together with their liquid and 2 more cups of the stock. Make sure the puree is completely smooth and no bits of chile skin remain.

6 In a large, heavy stockpot, heat the lard over medium heat. Add the blended nut mixture and cook, stirring and scraping the bottom of the pot for 5 minutes. Stir in the chile mixture and 2 more cups of the stock. Bring to a simmer, stirring, and add the chocolate. Cook, scraping the bottom of the pot, for 15 minutes. If the sauce seems too thick, add additional stock, up to 2 cups. (The mole sauce can be prepared up to 2 days ahead and refrigerated.)

7 Add the turkey slices and all the vegetables to the sauce, season with salt, and cook over medium-low heat until heated through, about 10 minutes. Serve with rice and tortillas.

Serves 10 to 12

Note To toast seeds and nuts, heat a small skillet over medium heat, add the nuts in small batches, and stir until darkened and aromatic, about 1 minute.

1 stick Mexican cinnamon, broken, toasted, and ground in a spice grinder

½ teaspoon ground cloves

½ teaspoon freshly ground black pepper

5 tablespoons lard or peanut oil

Half of a 3-ounce tablet Mexican chocolate (use regular semisweet chocolate only as a last resort), finely chopped

vegetables (optional)

12 very small red-skinned potatoes, boiled

1½ pounds spinach, cooked

3 cups cooked lima beans

½ pound cooked green beans

for serving

Cooked white rice

Steamed corn tortillas

moussaka

think of moussaka as the Parthenon of Mediterranean casseroles, an exalted Greek gratin that has sweetly spiced lamb sandwiched between strata of potatoes, eggplants, and sometimes zucchini, under a cap of cheesy béchamel sauce.

Moussaka is the urban cosmopolitan showpiece of lamb-and-eggplant combinations, a pairing as fundamental to Middle and Near Eastern cuisines as pasta and tomatoes are to Italy and potatoes and cream to the French. (Notwithstanding numerous warnings from medieval medics that eggplant causes melancholia, insanity—even freckles.) The word *moussaka* supposedly derives from the Arabic *musaqqa,* meaning "moistened."

A number of Turkish food writers argue that the classic béchamel-topped moussaka was the brainchild of some Westernized chef working at Istanbul's Topkapi Palace toward the end of the Ottoman empire. This opinion was shared by my friend, the Greek food writer Aglaia Kremezi, author of *Cooking from the Greek Islands* and other great books, whose magnificent moussaka recipe is offered below. Yet having dug deeper into historical sources without finding any moussaka recipes prior to the 1920s, Aglaia concluded the following: credit for the modern-day moussaka, replete with its creamy white hat, goes to one Nicholas Tselementes, author of a legendary 500-page Greek kitchen bible from the 1920s.

Tselementes was a curious character. A European-trained yet deeply nationalist chef, he went on a crusade to strip Greek cuisine of its Turkish Ottoman overtones. In his monumental tome he even goes so far as to cast off traditional olive oil, herbs, and spices in favor of French-style creamy white sauces—like béchamel—claiming that such thickened buttery sauces were an ancient Greek legacy usurped by the Gauls! Both Tselementes' Hellenic theories and his Gallicized dishes, like moussaka to which he devotes a whole chapter, struck a deep chord with aspiring Athenian upper classes. And eventually, moussaka came to represent Greek cuisine to the world, from Alabama to Zaragoza.

Baked in urban homes as a festive treat, homemade moussaka is far from the mundane square of mush we know from Greek dinerland. A cosmopolitan dish and a relatively young one at that, it doesn't boast dramatic regional variations; but cooks do have preferences. I, for one, love moussakas layered with zucchini and tomato slices in addition to eggplant. Some swear by potatoes. For sweetness and a touch of surprise, Aglaia adds sautéed peppers, while her eggplant is grilled rather than fried. For topping she devised a tangy light béchamel of yogurt and olive oil. Lucky moussaka.

molyvos moussaka with yogurt béchamel

cook's notes   At the haute-rustic Molyvos restaurant in New York, for which Aglaia created this moussaka, it is served in individual baking dishes. However, because it's such a knockout party dish, I went back to the communal one-pan version. The spicing here is rather restrained; if you're into sweet seasonings, add little pinches of cinnamon and allspice to the meat. All the layers can be prepared the day before and assembled before serving. The béchamel here is rather thin; you can make it thicker by using 8 tablespoons flour.

vegetables

2 large eggplants (about 1¾ pounds each), stemmed and sliced lengthwise ¼ inch thick

Salt

Olive oil, preferably Greek, for frying

1½ pounds russet (Idaho) potatoes, peeled and sliced ¼ inch thick

3 large green bell peppers, seeded, quartered lengthwise, and cut into 1-inch pieces

1¼ pounds lean ground lamb or beef or a combination

2 medium onions, chopped

1 teaspoon Aleppo pepper or pinch of red pepper flakes

½ cup dry red wine

½ cup dried Zante currants (optional)

2½ cups best-quality chopped canned tomatoes with ⅓ cup of their juice

Freshly ground black pepper

1 to 2 pinches of freshly ground nutmeg

1   Rub the eggplant slices generously with salt and place them in a colander. Let stand for at least 30 minutes. Rinse well and pat dry thoroughly with paper towels.

2   While the eggplants are standing, in a deep heavy skillet, heat about 1 inch of oil and fry the potato slices over medium heat until almost cooked, about 2 to 3 minutes per side. With a slotted spoon, transfer the potatoes to drain on paper towels.

3   In the same oil, sauté the peppers over medium-low heat, stirring often, until they soften and begin to color, about 10 minutes. With a slotted spoon, transfer the peppers to drain on paper towels. Blot off the excess oil with more paper towels if the peppers look oily and reserve the peppers and the potatoes.

4 Spoon off and reserve ¼ cup of the oil from the frying pan for broiling the eggplants. Heat the remaining oil in the pan over medium-high heat and sauté the ground lamb, stirring often and breaking it up thoroughly with a fork, 7 to 8 minutes. If there seems to be too much fat in the skillet, spoon off the excess. Add the onions and continue to cook, stirring, for another 8 minutes, or until the onions are soft. Add the Aleppo pepper, red wine, currants if using, and tomatoes. Bring to a boil, lower the heat, and simmer until the sauce thickens, about 15 minutes. Add salt, freshly ground black pepper, and nutmeg to taste, and remove from the heat.

5 While the meat is cooking, preheat the broiler. Place the eggplants on a large baking sheet (you might have to do this in two batches), brush both sides generously with the reserved oil, and sprinkle with salt. Broil, turning once, until golden on both sides, about 15 minutes.

6 Make the béchamel: In a heavy saucepan, whisk together the olive oil and flour over medium heat until foamy, about 2 minutes. Remove from the heat, whisk a bit longer, and add the milk and yogurt. Return to medium heat and cook, whisking constantly, until the mixture is thick and bubbly, about 6 minutes. Don't worry if it looks a little curdled; it will smooth out as it cooks. When the sauce starts to boil, remove from the heat and stir in the cheese and salt and pepper to taste.

7 Preheat the oven to 400°F. Place the potatoes in one slightly overlapping layer on the bottom of a rectangular 9 by 13-inch baking dish at least 2½ inches deep. Arrange half of the eggplant slices in one layer over the potatoes. Layer the sautéed peppers over the eggplant and top with an even layer of the lamb mixture. Top with a layer of eggplant. As you layer the ingredients, season them lightly with salt and pepper as needed. With a rubber spatula, spread the béchamel evenly over the moussaka. Bake until the top is browned and bubbly, about 30 minutes. If you'd like to further brown the top, place the moussaka under the broiler for 1 to 2 minutes. Serve hot or warm cut into squares.

Serves 6

béchamel

6 tablespoons olive oil

6 tablespoons all-purpose flour

2 cups whole milk

1 cup full-fat plain yogurt

1¼ cups grated aged white Cheddar or Gruyère cheese

Salt and freshly ground white or black pepper

it's deep, dark, and brooding. It's bread, cheese, and soup all in one bowl. It's the stalwart *soupe a l'oignon,* a classic that for all the *frisées aux lardons* and retro-chic andouillettes remains a symbol of ancien régime bistro cooking—a populist icon resonating with memories of the vanished Les Halles market. There, in Zola's proverbial belly of Paris, cauldrons of this high-octane potage used to warm and revive vendors in the early hours of dawn. And not just vendors. "Large white onions," mused Alexandre Dumas, "are very nourishing and therefore chosen to make soup for huntsmen and drunkards, two classes of people who require fast recuperation."

Like most classics, onion soup comes with a fable attached. The story—at least as told by Alexandre Dumas *père*—takes place in 1725 and involves

onion soup

a Polish ex-king with the operatic name of Stanislas, father-in-law to Louis XV and a gourmet credited with inventing *baba au rhum.* So smitten was this Polish royal with a humble onion soup presented to him at an inn in Chalons (his lunch stop en route to Versailles) that he appeared before the chef in his dressing gown, demanding a recipe demo. "Neither the smoke nor the smell of the onion, which brought great tears to his eyes," Dumas *père* writes, "was able to distract him from paying the closest attention." Nothing like a royal obsession to make a humble soup a sensation.

These days on these shores awash in neo-retro-quasi-Parisian brasseries, onion soup seems to have fallen out of favor as a cholesterol-laden 1950s cliché of Frenchness. But show me a militant food snob who doesn't fantasize, every once in a while, about inhaling those sweet vapors for a good minute or two, before—slowly—breaking into the gooey bouffant of *fromage* to submerge a spoon into the dark puddle of caramelized onions.

anya von bremzen

178

french onion soup

cook's notes Today, onion soup is often judged on the strength and intensity of its broth. Most people assume it should be beef, yet Dumas *père* actually admonishes against using strong bouillon, lest the soup's delicacy be overpowered. I happen to agree with Dumas and besides, a good beef broth made from roasted bones isn't something most cooks have on hand. Your best stock option here is a well-reduced homemade chicken stock or canned broth. For extra oomph, you can fortify chicken stock with a beef bouillon cube, or use 6 cups chicken stock and 1 cup canned beef broth. If you have excellent homemade beef broth, that's great too but do not use all canned beef broth: its taste is just too artificial.

4 tablespoons unsalted butter, plus more as needed

2 tablespoons mild olive oil

3½ pounds sweet white onions (Spanish, Vidalia, or Maui), halved and thinly sliced (about 12 cups)

Salt

1 teaspoon brown sugar

10 cups homemade chicken stock or canned broth (see Cook's Notes)

1 tablespoon all-purpose flour

¾ cup dry red wine

1 bay leaf

½ teaspoon dried thyme

Freshly ground black pepper

2 tablespoons Calvados or cognac

2 teaspoons red wine vinegar, or more to taste

3 cups shredded Gruyère or Emmentaler cheese

6 thick slices chewy dense French country bread, cut from a round loaf, lightly toasted

1 In a wide heavy-bottomed saucepan, preferably nonstick, melt 4 tablespoons of the butter in the oil. Add the onions and sauté over high heat, stirring often, until they begin to soften and brown, about 7 minutes. Stir in three pinches of salt and the brown sugar and continue to cook until the onions turn a light caramel color, lowering the heat if necessary and adding a little more butter if the onions look dry. This should take about 20 minutes. Don't worry if the bottom of the pan looks brown and caramelized.

2 While the onions are cooking, reduce the chicken stock over high heat to 7 cups, 12 to 15 minutes.

3 Sprinkle the onions evenly with the flour and stir well. Add the wine and 1 cup of the stock and bring to a boil over high heat, stirring to dissolve the flour and dislodge the brown bits in the bottom of the pan. Add the rest of the stock, the bay leaf, thyme, and salt and pepper to taste. Bring to a simmer and cook the soup over medium-low heat for 20 minutes. Stir in the Calvados and the vinegar. (The soup can be prepared a day ahead and refrigerated. When you take it out of the refrigerator, skim off the fat and reheat it before baking.)

4 Right before serving, preheat the oven to 475°F. Ladle the soup into six large ovenproof soup cups or bowls and stir ¼ cup of cheese into each cup. Trim the toasted bread slices to fit the cups, top each with a slice of bread, and sprinkle another ¼ cup of cheese evenly on each slice. Set the bowls on a large baking sheet and bake until the tops are golden brown and bubbly, about 8 minutes. Using oven mitts, carefully remove the bowls from the oven and serve. (The soup can also be baked and served in one large ovenproof soup tureen, in which case you will need less bread.)

Serves 6

While the soup's reputation would be forged indelibly in the cafés and bistros around Les Halles, other regions, such as Savoie, contest the capital's claim of propriety. So does Lyons. "In Lyons," writes the grand French chef Paul Bocuse, "we put onions in almost everything, and we claim a copyright on the celebrated onion soup that the Île-de-France and specifically Les Halles market in Paris adopted as their own." With its layering of bread slices and cheese, Bocuse's recipe for Gratinée Lyonnaise is actually less soup than a savory pudding. Delicious, but not exactly the taste we all crave.

no one has to be sold on the delights of Thailand's most famous noodle dish. Take *pad thai* off the menu and half the Thai restaurants outside Thailand would close instantaneously. So what is it about pad thai that makes it so attractive to the Western palate? The slightly guilty, sweet-sour appeal? That curious contrast of textures? The blend of the homey and the exotic? Whatever it is, I know how impossible it is to resist. Whenever I happen on that rare truly authentic Thai place abroad, I order a caustic shrimp paste dip called *naam prig gapi*, a complex massaman (Muslim-style) curry, frogs' legs, and preserved duck eggs, plus black rice with salty coconut milk for dessert. Then I turn to my friends and snobbishly taunt: "*You*, of course, want pad thai?" I always hope they'll say yes. They always do.

pad thai

Pad thai isn't chop suey or egg foo young, those Chinese-American dishes unknown in China. Thais do eat pad thai, even if they regard it as something of a *farang* (foreigner's) obsession. At street stalls and noodle carts all over the country pad thai is cheap, plentiful, and ever tasty. *Pad thai kuay tiaow*—as the dish is properly called—means, simply, "Thai stir-fried noodles." Both noodles and the technique of stir-frying were Chinese contributions to Thai cuisine. In her charming Thai cookbook *It Rains Fishes*, Kasma Loha-unchit says that after World War II, the Thai government tried to boost the country's ailing economy and relieve unemployment by aggressively promoting the production and consumption of rice noodles.

It might lack the multi-tiered complexity of Thai curries and salads, but a well-made pad thai has plenty of nuances: the silky chewiness of the noodles shot through with soft bits of tofu, omelet, and shrimp; the plush sweet-tart foil of tamarind and palm sugar; the crunchy counterpoints of fresh bean sprouts and peanuts. And that underlying layer of spicy heat. The recipe below, is the genuine article, a dish far more dignified and alluring than anything you'll find at most Thai restaurants in this country.

pad thai

cook's notes The plush sourness of the tamarind and the fudge-like sweetness of palm sugar are the authentic Thai flavorings (see Resources). Looking for a pad thai that resembles the one you love at your neighborhood Thai joint? Try flavoring the sauce with ketchup, white sugar, and rice vinegar. For an extra layer of salty flavor, use the dried shrimp. Different noodles will absorb various amounts of liquid, so keep a little water or chicken broth by the stove to moisten them.

1 Make the sauce: Soak the tamarind in the boiling water for 15 minutes. Stir well to dissolve and strain if the pulp has seeds. While the tamarind is soaking, place the chiles, garlic, and shallots in a mini food processor and process to a coarse paste, adding a little water to help the blending. Alternatively, the aromatics can be pounded with a large mortar and pestle. Reserve 2 teaspoons of the chile mixture and stir the rest into the tamarind liquid. Stir in the sugar, fish sauce, and lime juice, then taste and adjust the balance of sweet, sour and spicy. (The sauce can be prepared ahead.)

sauce

3 tablespoons tamarind pulp (do not use concentrate)

⅓ cup boiling water

5 small fresh 2-inch long red Thai chiles, chopped; or 2 or 3 large dried red chiles, about 4 inches long, crumbled

4 large garlic cloves, chopped

3 medium shallots, preferably purple, chopped

2½ tablespoons palm sugar, packed light brown sugar, or maple syrup

4½ tablespoons fish sauce (*nam pla*), or more to taste

1 tablespoon fresh lime juice, or more to taste

2 Prepare the noodles: Soften them in warm water to cover for 20 to 30 minutes. Drain well.

3 In a large wok, heat 1 tablespoon of the oil over high heat until almost smoking. Stir-fry the fresh shrimp and the tofu for 2 minutes. With a slotted spoon, remove them to a bowl. Add the dried shrimp, if using, and stir for 1 minute. Add 2 more tablespoons of the oil and the reserved 2 teaspoons of the chile mixture and stir for 30 seconds. Add the noodles and stir-fry for 1 minute. Sprinkle in 2 tablespoons of water or broth and stir-fry for another minute. The noodles should be soft and just slightly resilient. Add a little more liquid if they are too chewy.

4 Push the noodles to the side of the wok. Drizzle in the 2 remaining teaspoons of the oil and add the eggs, breaking them up with chopsticks as they cook. When the eggs are just set, stir them into the noodles. Stir in the reserved fresh shrimp and tofu and the bean sprouts, then drizzle in the sauce. Stir-fry everything together over high heat, tossing and stirring until well mixed, about 1 more minute. Taste and add a little more fish sauce or lime juice if you wish.

5 To serve, transfer the noodles to a platter and top with all the garnishes. Serve at once.

*Serves 3 or 4 as an entree,
6 with other dishes*

resources A good mail-order source for Thai ingredients is Adriana's Caravan (tel: 800-316-0820 or *www.adrianascaravan.com*).

noodles

½ pound dried wide rice noodles (*kway tiaw* or *pho*)

3 tablespoons plus 2 teaspoons peanut or canola oil

12 small fresh shrimp, peeled and deveined, with the tails left on

½ cup diced firm tofu

¼ cup small dried shrimp (optional)

2 large eggs, beaten

1½ cups fresh bean sprouts

¼ cup water or chicken broth, or more as needed

garnishes

⅓ cup coarsely ground roasted unsalted peanuts

½ to 1 teaspoon thinly sliced fresh red chiles

2 tablespoons thinly sliced scallions

¼ cup cilantro leaves

1 lime, cut into wedges

perfectly done for a weekend family ritual or at the right restaurant in its natural habitat—which is to say, the rice-producing Levante region of Spain—paella stands as one of life's defining gastronomic experiences. You inhale the smoky aromas of vine cuttings over which the paella is grilled; you scoop the rice straight from the pan marveling how each grain can be miraculously sticky, spongy, and firm all at once; you devour every last crunchy scrap of *socarrat,* the brown bottom crust, staring sadly at the empty pan before you.

Soldiers returning from Alexander the Great's expedition to India carried rice to the Mediterranean shores around 325 B.C. Yet for centuries it remained a rarefied grain, mostly ground into powder to thicken medicinal milks. The

paella

cultivation—and subsequent consumption—of rice became widespread and sophisticated only after the Arabs conquered most of the Mediterranean coast in the eighth century, perfecting the Roman irrigation system with a mind-boggling network of canals, dikes, and waterwheels. The ingenious Arab watercourses still irrigate Albufera, an otherworldly marshy wetlands surrounding a large freshwater lake south of Valencia. Albufera is the epicenter of paella art, the heart of Spain's rizoculture, and a place that still honors patron saints of rice with elaborate processions and masses.

"There is one and only paella, and that's paella Valenciana made with rabbit, chicken, duck, and land snails called *vaquetas,*" explained Pilar Castro, owner of restaurant La Riua in Valencia, creator of how-to paella videos and a sought-after judge at paella cookoffs. "Paella *must* be cooked outdoors," Pilar continued, "over a fire made of vine branches or orange tree shoots, with liquid flavored with a simple but delicious *sofrito* of tomatoes, garlic, saffron, and *pimenton.*" To her, the only permissible flourishes included broad beans, artichokes, and *garrofon,* or flat butter beans.

For Valencian traditionalists like Pilar, anything that isn't paella Valenciana with rabbit and chicken must be called simply *arroz con* (or "rice with"). However, the term is really more flexible than that, a kind of extended brand name that describes both a particular dish (the paella Valenciana with rabbit and chicken) and a family of some 200 rice dishes cooked in a paella pan by a specific method. And while Valencia province grabs all the attention, some truly spectacular rices dishes are found farther south in Alicante.

Paella is both defined by and named for the round, shallow, flat-bottomed two-handled pan in which it's cooked. Paella pans are relatively thin, made from carbon or stainless steel, which reacts quickly to fluctuations in temperature and allows the liquid to evaporate rapidly. Lourdes March, author of *Paellas and Arroces*, argues that Valencians got the name from *patela*, a Roman term originally describing ceremonial chalices, later coming to denote all manner of cooking vessels. The official birthdate of classic paella Valenciana, some say, is 1840, when the dish and its name were "inaugurated" in a local newspaper. "A liberal dish in which a grain is a grain, as each man is a vote," waxed one Valencian poet. Long before that, however, rural laborers in the rice fields and farms of the Levante were applying Moorish cooking techniques to their rice, flavoring it with whatever was hunted or gathered: eel, duck, rabbit, water rats, artichokes, beans.

Nineteenth-century paella Valenciana, devoured straight from the pan, was a celebratory feast, and it remains a grand regional institution. It's a centerpiece of Sunday family luncheons cooked outdoors by the patriarchs. It's an excuse for countryside restaurant outings. It's a reason for the whole village to gather around a giant communal paella pan.

paella valenciana with rabbit, chicken, and duck

cook's notes This fabulous recipe for classic paella Valenciana with rabbit, chicken, and duck, comes from an ancient chef at La Matandeta restaurant in Albufera. For a simpler version, use all chicken: four or five boneless skinless thighs. And feel free to add a few slices of sautéed pork sausage or chorizo.

For their paellas, cooks in the Levante region rely on local short-grain rice varieties. Among the best is Calasparra rice grown in the nitrogen-rich soil of Murcia; king of Calasparra rices is *arroz bomba,* an heirloom variety prized for its plumpness and absorption capacity (see Resources). Regular long-grain or Oriental short-grain rice isn't right for paella, but Italian risotto rice, especially *vialone nano,* works just fine. Goya medium-grain rice is a tasty and readily available option. Note: Calasparra rices soak up at least 3 cups liquid per one cup of rice. If using another kind of rice, use 1 to 1½ cups of liquid for each cup of rice.

2 boneless skinless chicken thighs, each cut into 2 pieces

¾ pound rabbit pieces

2 small duck legs, separated into drumsticks and thighs or 1 duck breast, cut into 4 pieces

Salt and freshly ground black pepper

1½ teaspoons smoky Spanish paprika, such as *pimenton de la Vera*

6 to 8 cups chicken stock or canned broth (see Cook's Notes)

½ teaspoon saffron, toasted and pulverized in a mortar

7 tablespoons good virgin olive oil, preferably Spanish

½ pound broad beans or green beans, trimmed and cut into 2-inch lengths

2 frozen quartered artichoke hearts, thawed

1 cup fresh or frozen and thawed lima beans

1 small onion, finely chopped

1 Rub the chicken, rabbit, and duck pieces generously with salt, pepper, and ½ teaspoon of the paprika and let stand until ready to use.

2 Place the stock in a medium saucepan and bring to a simmer. Add the saffron, reduce the heat to very low, and keep the liquid at a low simmer until ready to use.

3 In a 15- to 16-inch paella pan set over one burner, heat 4 tablespoons of the oil over medium heat until it starts to smoke. Add the chicken, rabbit, and duck (the oil might splatter) and sauté, turning once until golden and half-cooked, about 7 minutes. Add the broad beans, artichokes, and lima beans and stir for another 2 to 3 minutes. Push everything to the periphery of the pan where it is not as hot.

4 Add the remaining 3 tablespoons oil to the center of the pan and sauté the onion over medium-low heat until it softens, about 3 minutes. Add the garlic, cook for 1 minute, then stir in the grated tomatoes. Turn the heat to very low and cook, stirring several times, until the *sofrito* turns dark and thick, about 7 minutes. With two wooden spoons, push the meat pieces and the vegetables toward the center of the pan and mix them with the *sofrito*. Add the remaining 1 teaspoon paprika and toss everything for 30 seconds.

6 garlic cloves, crushed through a press

2 large, ripe tomatoes, grated on the large holes of a four-sided grater, skins discarded

2 cups Calasparra or bomba rice, risotto rice, or Goya medium-grain rice (see Cook's Notes)

1 sprig fresh rosemary

1 red bell pepper, broiled, peeled, and cut into strips, for garnish

Lemon wedges, if desired

5 Add the rice and stir gently to coat with the mixture. If using Calsparra or *bomba* rice, pour in 6 cups of the simmering broth (if using other rice, add 4 cups broth, keeping a little more for later). Set the pan over two burners, tuck in the rosemary sprig, shake the pan lightly to distribute the rice evenly, and cook over medium heat until the liquid is level with the rice, 8 to 10 minutes. Do not stir the rice, but periodically move and rotate the pan so that the liquid boils evenly.

6 Preheat the oven to 425°F. Reduce the heat to low and continue to cook the rice until the liquid is almost absorbed and the exterior of the grains soften but the center is still slightly hard to the bite, about 12 minutes. Keep rotating the pan as the rice cooks. If the liquid is absorbing too fast and the rice still seems raw, add more liquid, ½ cup at a time. Cover the top with foil and cook over very low heat for 3 to 4 minutes.

7 Remove the foil and taste the rice. If it doesn't seem right—either too wet or still slightly undercooked on top—place the paella, covered with foil in the oven, sprinkling it with a little more liquid beforehand if it seems dry and undercooked. After 5 minutes, remove the foil and bake for another 5 minutes. To create a *socarrat*—the crunchy burnt layer of rice on the bottom—set the pan, covered with foil, over high heat for 2 to 3 minutes, rotating the pan as you cook. Recover the paella with foil and let stand for at least 10 minutes (the rice gets better as it stands). Uncover and let stand for another 5 minutes before serving.

8 To serve, decorate the top of the paella with roasted pepper strips and lemon wedges, if desired. Serve it straight from the pan.

Serves 4 or 5

resources Tienda is an excellent source for Spanish rice, plus paella pans and accessories (tel: 888-472-1022 or *www.tienda.com*).

palov

Uzbek Lamb Pilaf

even the most adventurous and intrepid among you probably haven't had the pleasure of tasting *palov,* an extraordinary Central Asian incarnation of pilaf. What a shame. Along with paella and biryani, the flagship delicacy of the Silk Route region deserves pride of place in the pantheon of the world's rice masterpieces.

Uzbeks, who have perfected palov, like to repeat the following tale: While sweeping through the expanses of Central Asia, Alexander the Great—or Genghis Khan in some versions—summoned his wisest adviser and bid him to invent a dish that would provide proper nutrition to a soldier on horseback, possess a taste that inspires a fighter for battle, be easily transportable, and be prepared from entirely local ingredients. The adviser brought back a palov. While one-pot rice dishes might indeed have been created by soldiers of Alexander the Great—a man credited with bringing rice from the Indian subcontinent to the Mediterranean—no hard evidence links Central Asian palov to either Alexander or Genghis. Nevertheless, the anecdote bears testament to the high regard in which palov is held in this part of the world.

A feast of spiced lamb and rice steamed together until every spoonful is as eloquent as an Omar Khayyam quatrain, in Uzbekistan palov is considered a cultural force and a national treasure. It's the pièce de resistance at business banquets and wedding receptions. It's a treat shared by a group of men on their monthly *gap* (boy's cookoff) or savored languidly along with slow sips of green tea at a *chaikhana* (teahouse) in the shade of a mulberry tree. It's a token of hospitality *always* offered to guests and the cement that holds together the *muhallah* (neighborhood or community), a concept even more powerful in this part of the world than religion.

So how does one cook a palov? The soul of the dish is *zirvak,* a stew of lamb (preferably from a prized fat-tailed sheep) and masses of onions and carrots, which lend palov its unmistakable sweetness and yellow hue. Central Asian markets explode with spices, but palov seasonings are strictly codified: *zeera,* or wild cumin seeds (the defining perfume of the region); hot and mild pepper; and barberries, tiny dried berries with a sharp lemony taste. Once the *zirvak* is good and brown, in goes the rice: not the delicate long-grained variety favored by most pilaf-making cultures, but sturdy medium-grain rice that can sustain long steaming.

Like paella, a truly authentic palov is cooked outdoors over a charcoal or gas fire—mostly by men. And the actual business of cooking is treated with the sanctity of a religious ceremony, with the cook (*oshpaz*) regarded more as a magician than menial. The best of them are often part of a dynasty and achieve a celebrity status afforded to matadors in Spain.

The palov kettle is called *kazan* (spelled *kazgan* in Turkish). This huge cast-metal vessel that resembles a wok was an essential piece of cooking equipment for Turkic nomads—transported by tying it to a horse by the lugs on its rim. The shape remained unchanged for almost a millennium. Then again, as the Uzbeks say, the older the *kazan,* the better the palov.

palov

cook's notes Palov is a gift to a cook: inexpensive, unfussy, using simple ingredients, and always exotic enough to impress. The kazan has an ideal shape but any large, heavy, round-bottomed pot is fine. After the palov has steamed long enough, the rice is scooped out onto a huge blue and white ceramic platter, the zirvak is mounded on top, and the dish is served with a tangy salad of tomatoes, onions, and pepper. To prepare the salad, thinly slice 1 large white onion, 2 large green peppers, and 3 large ripe tomatoes, and layer them in a shallow bowl, seasoning the layers with salt and pepper and sprinkling them with mild olive oil and red wine vinegar. A tannic green tea is what they drink with palov in Uzbekistan.

2½ pounds shoulder lamb chops

Salt

1½ teaspoons sweet paprika

1 teaspoon hot paprika or cayenne

¼ cup mild olive oil

¼ cup peanut or canola oil

3 large onions, cut into ½-inch dice

2 large carrots, peeled and cut into strips 1 inch long and ⅛ inch wide

¼ teaspoon ground turmeric

1½ tablespoons cumin seeds

¾ cup canned chickpeas, well drained

⅓ cup raisins

3½ cups boiling water

2 cups medium-grain rice, rinsed in several changes of water and drained

1 whole head of garlic, outer layer of skin removed

1 Trim most but not all the fat from the lamb and cut it off the bone, into 1-inch chunks. Reserve a few of the meatier bones and discard the rest. Rub the meat with salt and ½ teaspoon each of the sweet and hot paprika.

2 In a large, heavy casserole, preferably with an oval bottom, heat the olive and canola oil over high heat until a light haze forms, about 2 minutes. In batches, cook the lamb until well browned on all sides, transferring the browned pieces to a bowl. Add the onions and carrots and cook, stirring, for 10 minutes. Stir in the remaining paprika, turmeric, cumin, and salt to taste and stir for 1 minute longer. Stir in the chickpeas and raisins, replace the lamb in the pot, and add ½ cup of the water. Reduce the heat to low, cover, and simmer for 15 minutes.

3   Flatten the surface of the meat mixture with a spatula. Pour the rice over the meat and bury the garlic head in it. Flatten the surface of the rice. Place a small lid or a heatproof plate directly on the surface of the rice and pour the boiling water in a steady stream. (Covering the rice with a lid ensures that the arrangement of meat and rice will not be disturbed by the pouring water.) Remove the plate, taking care not to burn yourself. Taste the liquid and add salt as necessary. Cook the rice, uncovered, over medium-low heat until the liquid is level with the rice and small bubbles appear on the surface, about 17 minutes.

4   Gather the rice into a mound and make five holes in it with the back of a long wooden spoon. Reduce the heat to very low, place a Flame Tamer under the pot, cover the pot tightly, and let the palov steam until the rice is tender, 25 to 30 minutes. Remove from the heat and let stand, without opening, for 20 to 30 minutes. (You can make the palov up to 1 hour ahead and keep it wam in a 200°F. oven.)

5   To serve, transfer all the rice with a slotted spoon to a large platter. Arrange the meat and vegetables in a mound over it, topping with the garlic head. Serve with the tomato, onion, and pepper salad (see Cook's Notes).

Serves 6

i was on my way to buy a bicycle pump. Now, I don't actually own a bike. What lured me to the bicycle store was my earnest desire to reproduce a real Peking duck at home. What does bicycle gear have to do with the queen of Chinese poultry dishes so beloved by Ming Dynasty emperors? A bike pump—or a blowpipe or even a straw—is used to inflate the duck's skin, so that it balloons away from the flesh and allows the fat to be released during roasting, yielding incredibly crispy results. The Chinese preoccupation with crackling skin doesn't end there. The bird is plunged in boiling water to make the skin taut, glazed with maltose to give it that gorgeous mahogany sheen, then hung up to dry in a cool dry place so no moisture can ruin the crisping.

Peking duck, they say, originally hailed from Nanjing. When the capital was moved to Peking, resettled Nanjing ducks were apparently thrilled with their new surroundings, growing fatter and fatter on tidbits from grain barges passing through the canals where they foraged. Royal cooks were even more

peking duck

thrilled. They plumped the ducks even further by force-feeding them, and devised sophisticated procedures for rearing, dressing, and roasting the birds. In the nineteenth century, Peking restaurants got their hands on these royal secrets, and the crispy duck has been the city's best-known edible emblem ever since.

The lack of a bicycle pump, I soon learned, wasn't the only obstacle that stood between me and a true Peking duck. In a perfect world, I'd have to incubate, hatch, and lovingly raise the bird somewhere on the outskirts of Beijing. I'd have to force-feed it until 35 percent of its weight was pure fat, kill it at seventy days old, pluck away all its feathers with utmost care, and cunningly eviscerate it through a tiny opening under its wing. Last but not least, to get the duck properly crisp, I'd need to roast it hung by the neck in a mud-lined fruitwood-fired kiln approximately the size of a Manhattan apartment. Oh, and performing all this with panache would require five years of learning and another dozen of mastering.

Clearly, a compromise had to be devised.

At this point I happened to meet David Gingrass, owner of Hawthorne Lane restaurant in San Francisco, famous for its magnificent, if slightly westernized, crispy duck. I listened attentively to David's thoughts on the subject—"Forget inflating the skin," he admonished—and dutifully took down his advice to add baking soda to the blanching liquid (he wasn't sure why but that's what the Chinese cooks in his kitchen did). Another breakthrough came from Clifford Chow, manager of San Francisco's Harbor Village restaurant, where Cantonese bigwigs feast on roast ducks in private banquet rooms. Clifford had just returned from a roast-duck research tour of Beijing and Canton convinced that the absolute best duck for the job was the Pekin variety, also known as Long Island Duckling and as common in this country as Oscar Mayer bologna.

With inflating ruled unnecessary and the perfect bird waiting at my neighborhood Chinese market, I started experimenting. The road to a supernally crisp duck wasn't smooth. Finding a safe, simple method for drying and a way to simulate vertical roasting took some ingenuity. But as I went through a not insignificant number of ducks, the perfect technique finally emerged. Would my skills earn me a job at Quanjude Roast Duck Restaurant, Beijing's Peking duck mecca? Maybe not. Did all the men invited to my Peking duck dinner propose to me instantaneously? That they did.

peking duck

cook's notes Chinese Peking duck masters roast the duck vertically hung by its neck. At home, the bird can be propped on a tall beer can filled with soy sauce, rice wine, and sweet spices—a fabulous trick resulting in moist flesh and brittle skin. Or you can use a vertical roaster. Buy the pancakes at a Chinese grocery and steam them to warm through right before serving, or microwave for 1 minute wrapped in a moist towel. The recipe is so amazing and so (relatively) simple, I recommend roasting two ducks to feed seven or eight.

1 Prepare the ducks: Remove the giblets, discarding the livers, and cut off the wing tips and the head and feet, if attached. Remove all the fat from the cavity and discard. Rub the ducks' cavities with five-spice powder, salt, and pepper.

2 Bring about 3 quarts of water to a boil in a tea kettle and add the baking soda. Tie a long piece of heavy kitchen string around the necks of the ducks. Place one duck in the sink on a rack or in a large metal colander. Pour some boiling water over it, making sure that all parts of the skin are moistened. Turn the duck over and repeat. Repeat with the other duck. Carefully pat the duck skin with paper towels. Hang the ducks from the handles of your top kitchen cabinet, with a pan placed under them to catch the drips. Point a small fan turned on high at the ducks. Let the ducks dry for 1 hour.

ducks

2 fresh Long Island ducklings (5½ to 6 pounds each), preferably from a Chinese grocery with heads still on

2 teaspoons five-spice powder

2 teaspoons salt

Two large pinches of freshly ground white pepper

1 tablespoon baking soda

3 tablespoons maltose or 4 tablespoons honey

½ cup water

1 tablespoon dark soy sauce

1 tablespoon Chinese rice wine (Shaoxing) or medium-dry sherry

3 While the ducks are drying, prepare the glaze. In a heavy saucepan, melt the maltose in the water; add the soy sauce and rice wine and stir to blend. With a large pastry brush, apply the glaze to the ducks, covering the entire surface and reaching under the wings. If your kitchen is cool, leave the ducks to dry on the kitchen cabinet for another 4 hours, with the fan pointing at them. If your kitchen is warm (over 50°F.), prop the ducks on beer cans or on two vertical roasters set over a large baking pan to catch the drips and place in the lowest shelf of the refrigerator. In the refrigerator, the ducks can dry for 24 hours and up to 2 days.

4 If the ducks were refrigerated, bring them to room temperature before roasting. Position an oven rack on the lowest level and remove the other racks. Preheat the oven to 375°F. Divide the water, soy sauce, ginger, garlic, star anise, and rice wine between the beer cans. Holding one duck with its legs facing down, push the can into its cavity. If the can is not tall enough, place a crumpled piece of foil in the cavity. Repeat with the other duck. Place the can with the duck on a small roasting or baking pan and stand it upright, shifting its weight until it is secure and solid. Repeat with the second duck. Carefully transfer the pans with the ducks to the oven. Add about 1½ cups of water to each pan so that the fat drips down into the water, reducing the smoke. Roast the ducks for 2 hours, or until a meat thermometer registers 170°F.

for roasting

2 cups water

½ cup dark soy sauce

4 thick slices fresh ginger, smashed

4 large garlic cloves, smashed

4 star anise

¼ cup rice wine or medium-dry sherry

2 empty 16-ounce beer cans, cleaned well

accompaniments

16 scallions

3 firm Kirby (pickling) cucumbers

Store-bought Mandarin pancakes (See Cook's Notes)

Hoisin sauce

5 While the ducks are roasting, prepare the garnishes. Trim the scallions, leaving 2 inches of the green tops. With a small sharp knife, make four vertical 1-inch-long cuts through the length of the scallions. Drop the scallions into a large bowl filled with ice water and refrigerate until they curl up into brushes. Cut the cucumbers in half lengthwise and scoop out the seeds. Cut each cucumber half into eight strips, then cut the strips in half crosswise on the diagonal. Refrigerate until ready to use. When the duck is almost ready, remove the scallion brushes from the refrigerator, pat them dry, and arrange on a small serving plate along with the cucumbers.

6 Remove the ducks from the oven and ask someone to help you get the ducks off the cans. With one person holding the top of the duck with both hands and being careful not to damage the skin, the other person (wearing oven mitts) should pull the can away from the cavity. Let the cans cool in the sink before emptying and discarding. Transfer the ducks to a carving board and let them rest for no more than 5 minutes. Hack the duck into smallish serving pieces and serve at once with all the trimmings. To eat, smear some hoisin sauce on a pancake, add a piece of duck, a sliver of cucumber and a scallion brush and eat it like a taco.

Serves 7 or 8

it's hard to disassociate pesto from the dinnertime din of upscale American trattorias. But sniff out its roots and you'll find yourself in Liguria, Italy's charmed crescent of Mediterranean coastline curving gently from Tuscany all the way to Provence. Visitors flock to Liguria for the poetic Riviera vistas and for Genova's raffish, salty allure. But pesto was the reason for my last pilgrimage to the region. "You'll be green as pesto by the time you finish your research!" laughed Pietro Uslengo, head of the Confraternita del Pesto, a fraternity of Pesto Chevaliers formed in 1992 to uphold the standards and defend the honor of pesto against imposters and dilettantes.

To eat pesto in Liguria—even in the humblest trattorias—is to discover it for the first time. I'll always remember my own introduction, at Balzi Rossi, a rather

pesto

staid Michelin-starred Ligurian restaurant on the Italo-French border. There was spumante and fancy *amuse-gueulles* and a view. Then I caught a whiff of my *lasagne con pesto.* So delicate was the aroma, and yet so pervasive, the whole place fell into a collective swoon. My lasagne shimmered in a sunny-green swath, as of just-sprouted grass. It was the most poignantly lyrical thing I'd ever eaten.

Ligurian scholars, poets, and gastronomes like to wax rhapsodic about their green gem, yet no one seems to have traced its history further back than the nineteenth century. There are fuzzy evocations of Africa and the Orient. There are suggestions that pesto belongs to a genre of pounded nut sauces— like the popular Ligurian walnut *salsa di noci*—that were borrowed by the seafaring Genovese traders from Black Sea cuisines. (This is not too convincing, considering that pine nuts are absent from historical pesto recipes.) There are suppositions that pesto descends from the popular *aggiada* (or *agliata*), a crushed garlic and olive-oil condiment that Ligurian food savants like to relate to the Roman *moretum,* a pounded mixture of coriander, garlic, parsley, and dried cheese.

Today, pesto without basil is completely unthinkable—at least in Liguria where mint or sesame pesto would provoke street riots. But, curiously, some early recipes and dictionary entries freely suggest substituting basil with marjoram or parsley. More curious still, the recipe for *battuta di aglio*—pesto— in the classic 1860 *La Cucinera Genovese* calls for *formaggio d'Olanda* (Dutch Gouda) instead of the now-common pecorino and Parmigiano.

The proper basil for pesto is the *basilico di Pra* grown just west of Genova. Pra basil has small concave leaves and an aroma that is described by Ligurians as "lemony" rather than "minty"—*mentolato* being a dirty word in any pesto cook's book. Otherwise, one can use young leaves from regular basil plants—preferably light green in color and no bigger than 1 inch by 1½ inches. Ligurians don't toss pesto idly into everything. Some of the favorite pastas for pesto include *troffie*, tiny thin gnocchi that look like bits of frayed rope; *trenette*, a long, thin pasta of the linguini family; *mandilli di saea* ("silk handkerchiefs"), which are floppy pasta sheets similar to lasagne; and *pansotti*, cousins of ravioli filled with wild greens and ricotta.

Pesto derives from the verb *pestare*, or "crush," a rite performed with an olive-wood pestle in a large marble *mortaio*, or mortar. The process starts with garlic reduced to a paste with coarse sea salt. Most cooks, especially in Western Liguria, religiously degerm the garlic for fear of bitterness, since the garlic taste shouldn't be pronounced. After the garlic, in go basil and nuts, and the whole is patiently crushed in a circular motion against the wall of the mortar until it's time to add cheese and oil. The nuts are usually pine nuts (though some regional variations use fresh walnuts). The oil, of course, is a Ligurian extra-virgin. Gouda aside, original pestos contained pecorino from Sardegna (another one of Genova's trade partners). Parmigiano came later, and today both are usually added in varying proportions. There are also regional variations mellowed with ricotta, or the yogurt-like local cheese, *prescinseua*. And some cooks cut the sharp flavors with butter or cream.

Many Americans entertain a romantic notion that all Ligurians dutifully make pesto by hand, which is like assuming that every Italian woman patiently makes her own pasta. This issue was summed up to me by Pierina Bruschi, the perfectionist cook who makes a magical pesto at the rustic Osteria dell' Acquasanta near Genova. "*Il mondo va avanti!*" (The world moves forward!) Pierina declared, thrusting her arm out. "Once we rode horses and carriages and made pesto by hand. Now, we have blenders."

As I said good-bye to Signor Uslengo, he presented me with a little white banner emblazoned with a crest of a mortar and pestle, given to new Cavalieri del Pesto upon their initiation into the Confraternita. It dangles proudly in my kitchen above my mortar and pestle. And my blender.

classic ligurian pesto

cook's notes This is a great all-purpose recipe, based on the one I got from Signor Uslengo. The proportion of Parmigiano to pecorino will depend on the pecorino. If you can find the sweet sheep's milk Sardinian pecorino, go fifty-fifty. With the sharper pecorino Romano, use only about 1 tablespoon and increase the amount of Parmigiano accordingly. You might also want to try adding a tablespoon of fresh ricotta mixed with a teaspoon of plain yogurt to simulate the taste of the Ligurian *prescinseua*. If serving the pesto right away, I recommend adding a tablespoon of heavy cream.

The best mortar is a large one made of marble; the pestle should ideally be as large as possible, flat-headed and made of wood. Look for them at good Italian cookware shops (Little Italies in large cities are a good bet) or order by mail (see Resources). Otherwise, make the blender version. For a simple, classic Ligurian pesto-pasta dish, see the trenette recipe below.

2 cups packed small basil leaves, no longer than 1½ inches

1 small garlic clove (firm and young), chopped

2 tablespoons pine nuts

6 to 7 tablespoons delicate extra-virgin olive oil, preferably Ligurian

3½ tablespoons grated Parmigiano-Reggiano cheese

2 tablespoons grated pecorino Sardo or 1 tablespoon pecorino Romano (increase the amount of Parmigiano to 4½ tablespoons)

One large pinch of coarse sea salt

1 Rinse the basil gently under cold running water and drain. Pat dry gently but thoroughly between two sheets of paper towels, being careful not to bruise the leaves. If the center "ribs" on the leaves look large, remove them with a small sharp knife. Tear the leaves gently into smallish pieces.

2 In a large mortar, pound the garlic with the salt to a smooth paste. Add the pine nuts and a few basil leaves and continue crushing. Keep adding more basil leaves, working in a circular motion and crushing and grinding the leaves against the wall and base of the mortar. Drizzle in a little oil as you work. Continue grinding until the mixture is fairly homogenous. (Mortar pesto won't be as smooth as the one made in the blender; for a smoother texture you can finish it in the blender.) Transfer the mixture to a bowl; stir in the cheeses and the rest of the oil. If planning to keep the pesto for longer than 3 days, do not add garlic and cheese until serving time. (To store the pesto, place it in a clean jar, cover the surface with a thin layer of oil, and seal tightly.)

Makes about ¾ cup pesto, enough to sauce 4 to 6 portions of pasta

anya von bremzen

variation **To make pesto in the blender:** Place the garlic, salt, and pine nuts in the blender with about 2 tablespoons of the oil and process in quick pulses. Add the basil all at once and pulse until the mixture is smooth. You'll have to push the mixture down with a rubber spatula several times. Scrape the mixture into a bowl and add the cheese and olive oil. Note: it is actually easier to make blender pesto in larger quantities, so consider doubling the recipe.

trenette al pesto, genova-style

cook's notes This is a classic Genovese pasta dish. Trenette is a pasta similar to linguine, with which it can be substituted.

2 medium-small waxy boiling potatoes (about ½ pound in total), peeled and cut into 1-inch chunks

1½ cups green beans, cut into 2-inch lengths

12 ounces dried trenette or linguini pasta

¾ cup Pesto (page 198)

1 tablespoon heavy cream

Freshly grated Parmesan cheese, preferably Parmigiano-Reggiano

1 In a medium saucepan, cover the potatoes with 3 inches of water and bring to a boil. Cook until they are almost done, about 8 minutes. Add the beans and cook until soft but still bright green, about 5 minutes. Drain the vegetables, reserving about ¼ cup of their cooking liquid.

2 Bring a large pot of salted water to a boil. Cook the pasta until al dente.

3 While the pasta is cooking, place the pesto in a small bowl and stir in the cream and 2 to 3 tablespoons of the vegetable cooking water.

4 Drain the pasta and transfer it back to the pot. Toss with the pesto, the potatoes, and the beans. Transfer to a serving bowl and serve with the Parmigiano.

Serves 4

resources Carara marble mortar with a large hardwood pestle is available from Sur La Table (tel: 800-243-0852 or *www.surlatable.com*).

prowl the clamorous streets of Hanoi in the wee hours of the morning, and you'll be walking through billowing clouds of sweet-smelling steam that rises from dozens of stockpots set over charcoal braziers. The whole town, it seems, is greeting the day by slurping down a vast bowl of *pho,* the pinnacle of Asian noodle soup cookery and quite possibly the best soup *ever.*

There are many things that combine to make the dish so spectacular. First, there's the broth, a rich long-simmered beef consommé scented with charred onion and ginger, the sweet notes of star anise and cinnamon, and a salty splash of fish sauce added at the end. Then, the noodles, those chewy slithery rice sticks called *banh pho*—made to be slurped with abandon. And, of course, the meat. The fun of being in a good pho shop is deciding between well-done brisket or shin, chewy tendon or tripe, paper-thin slices of raw beef round that cook in the heat of the broth, or Vietnamese sausage or meatballs, even chicken or shrimp.

pho

*Vietnamese Beef
and Noodle Soup*

But what makes the whole affair unique is the final blending of flavors. *Pho,* roughly, translates to "your own bowl," and no two people eat the soup the same way. Some squirt lime juice or hoisin, others prefer chiles and fish sauce. A generous dose of bean sprouts, sliced onion, basil, cilantro and scallion turns the soup into something of a salad.

Pho has become Vietnam's culinary calling card, but it isn't really an ancient or even indigenous dish. Since the Vietnamese consumed little red meat before the French arrived in the 1880s, some historians argue that beef pho was modeled on French *pot-au-feu,* even pointing to the similarity between the words *pho* and *feu.* Others contend that noodle soups, like pho, came from China, whose cuisine especially influenced northern Vietnam. Perhaps a little of both is true, but the Vietnamese made pho emphatically and uniquely their own.

While most everyone in Vietnam agrees that the best pho comes from the north, some find the beefy Hanoi version rather austere. As the pho craze spread beyond the northern capital, other regions contributed their own flavors and flourishes. In Hue—known for its elaborate royal cuisine—the broth is enlivened with lemongrass and dried shrimp. In Saigon, pho might feature chicken or pork; the lavish use of fragrant herbs is also a southern addition. But ultimately it's all in the broth.

a quick fix Admittedly, a proper long-simmered beef pho is pretty easy to make. But as the taste depends on the depth of the broth, it does take time. When I'm desperate for a bowl of pho, which is often, I make the following quick version with chicken. Reduce 10 cups of good chicken broth to about 6 or 7 cups with the charred ginger and onions, the rock sugar, and the spice bag from the beef pho recipe below. Add a whole bone-in chicken breast, plump side down, to the simmering broth, cover, and cook over low heat until the chicken is tender, about 20 minutes, adding fish sauce toward the end. While the chicken cooks, make the noodles. When the chicken is ready and cool enough to handle, tear it into pieces, discarding the bones, and add to soup bowls with the broth, the noodles, and some or all of the suggested garnishes. It's the kind of simple, satisfying meal I could cook every day.

pho bo

cook's notes Making pho at home is a leisurely affair. Plonk the bones, meat, and aromatics in a pot, and leave the broth to simmer for as long as possible. Ten minutes or so before serving, boil some noodles, arrange all the garnishes, and voilà. Leftover broth freezes beautifully, so you can defrost it, soak some dried rice noodles, and have an improvised meal almost at whim. You'll be doing it often.

Many Vietnamese cooks use oxtail as a base for the broth. I prefer leaner bones, such as neck, chuck and shin. With oxtails, you'll want to prepare the broth ahead and degrease. Some cooks also blanch the bones first for a clearer broth but I find that it washes away some of the flavor. For the meat, I prefer the cooked brisket over the thin raw slices of steak, mainly because the raw slices tend to cloud up the broth in your bowl as they cook in the hot liquid. But again, it's a matter of preference. Pho is good every which way.

stock

5 to 6 pounds meaty beef bones (shin, neck, chuck, oxtail, marrow bones)

5 quarts water

Two 2-inch pieces fresh ginger, unpeeled

2 medium onions, peeled and halved

One 3½-pound lean beef brisket, trimmed of all fat

2-inch piece Chinese rock sugar or 2 tablespoons white sugar, or more to taste

6 whole star anise, 1 cinnamon stick, and 6 whole cloves tied in a cheesecloth bag

3 tablespoons fish sauce (*nam pla*), plus more for serving

Salt

1 Make the stock: In a colander, rinse all the bones thoroughly, removing all traces of blood. Place the bones in a large stockpot, add the water, and bring to a boil over high heat. Skim the broth thoroughly as it comes to a boil. Reduce the heat to low, partially cover the pot, and cook at a mere simmer for 1 hour, skimming every once in a while.

2 While the broth cooks, skewer the ginger pieces onto a fork and hold directly over an open flame, turning, until lightly charred, about 3 minutes. Repeat this with the onion halves. Rinse the ginger and onions. Add the ginger, onions, brisket, sugar, spice bag, fish sauce, and salt (if needed) to the simmering broth. Bring the broth back to a simmer and skim as necessary. Reduce the heat to very low and continue cooking, partially covered, until the brisket is very tender, about 2 more hours.

3 With a slotted spoon, remove the brisket from the stock, cool, and refrigerate until ready to use. With a slotted spoon, fish out the onion, ginger, and spice bag and discard. If you'd like a deeper-tasting stock, cook uncovered over medium heat for another 30 minutes to an hour. If the stock looks cloudy, strain it through a double layer of cheesecloth into a clean pot. Add more fish sauce and sugar to taste, if necessary. Keep the stock at a simmer if using right away or cool and refrigerate until ready to use. (The stock can be prepared up to 2 days ahead and brought to a simmer before serving.)

4 Prepare the noodles: If using fresh noodles, bring about 4 quarts of water to a boil in a large pot. Separate the noodles with a fork to untangle. Plunge the noodles into the water for about 30 seconds, just until heated through, stirring with chopsticks. Do not overcook. If using dry noodles, soak them in warm water for 20 to 30 minutes and then cook as directed above. Drain the noodles in a colander, quickly divide among serving bowls, and moisten with a little simmering broth. This will keep them warm and prevent them from clumping.

5 Cut the reserved brisket across the grain into thin slices. Place some sliced brisket and raw beef slices, if using, into each serving bowl with the noodles. Ladle some piping-hot broth into each bowl and sprinkle with scallions. Arrange the rest of the garnish ingredients on individual plates and in bowls and pass around, along with extra fish sauce, chile sauce, and hoisin sauce.

Serves 8

noodles and garnishes

1 pound fresh ⅛-inch-wide rice noodles, or 12 ounces dried noodles

½ pound beef sirloin or filet, frozen for 30 minutes and cut into paper-thin slices (optional)

2 or 3 scallions, finely sliced

1 cup fresh bean sprouts

3 small red or green hot chiles, seeded and sliced

2 limes, cut into wedges

1 small purple onion, halved and sliced paper-thin

½ cup torn cilantro leaves

½ cup torn fresh basil leaves (preferably Vietnamese basil called *rau que*)

¼ cup torn fresh mint leaves

Sambal oelek or Chinese chile sauce

Hoisin sauce

antonio Pace and I were having dinner at his Naples restaurant, Ciro Santa Brigita, a well-worn bastion of classic Neapolitan cooking. There was a whole *mozzarella di buffala* the size of a baby's head. There were rigatoni with an ur-Neapolitan sauce called Genovese. But these faded into insignificance when the pizza arrived.

It's no surprise that Pace's pizza was easily the world's most rigorously authentic pie. Not only does this man hail from six generations of *pizzaioli,* he's also the president of Associazione Verace Pizza Napolitana, an association founded in 1984 to defend the status of pizza as a uniquely Neapolitan product and to preach respect for tradition to pizza makers around the world. The Associazione even lobbied to get Neapolitan pizza a DOC (controlled

pizza

denomination of origin), a battle lost, alas.

To anyone not truly passionate about pizza, the Association's rules might seem a little draconian. According to them, the only pie that deserves to be called *pizza Napolitana*

is made in Naples and subject to exact specifications outlined in the Pizza Discipline, a set of bylaws drafted by Pace and his colleagues. "Anyone can slop dough in the oven and call it pizza," Pace lamented. "But most of what passes for pizza around the world is flatbread with toppings." And don't get Pace started on the trendy pizzerias of Rome. "A few anchovies on a pie and they call it pizza Napolitana," he scoffed. "And that northern Italian crust . . . *Sottile* (thin)! *Croccante* (crispy)!" Not pizza. Not even close.

So what *is* pizza according to the Neapolitan pizza police?

Pace's margherita in front of me offered a textbook example. I was looking at a slightly jagged hand-shaped disk the size of a dinner plate. Its puffed-up edges ringed a core just thick enough to support the austere but articulate toppings. The crust was light golden and the dough had a suggestion of chewiness and the slightest intimation of crispness. Topping it was a discreet smear of hand-crushed San Marzano tomatoes, three thin pieces of buffalo mozzarella, a drizzle of extra-virgin olive oil, and two basil leaves. *Basta.* In a city consumed by perpetual chaos, oozing Baroque from every pavement crack, Pace's miraculously engineered pie seemed like the ultimate minimalist statement—a triumph of logic and elegance.

Pizza devoured, Pace took me downstairs to meet his oven. A beehive cranked up to 500 degrees centigrade (800°F.), it was built of red firebrick and fueled with oak. Before sliding the pizza paddle into this furnace, Pace quickly tossed in a few wood chips; they flared up furiously, sending a ball of fire and clouds of sweet smoke to the oven ceiling. The pizza was puffy and blistered in exactly 1 minute. Yes, this was the *vera pizza Napolitana.*

Or was it?

"Did Pace give you his spiel about extra-virgin olive oil, San Marzano tomatoes, and buffalo mozzarella?" asked Francesco Colonnesi, an amateur pizza scholar and a member of the Naples division of Slow Food. "Don't believe a word," Colonnesi implored. The olive oil is way too heavy for the thin dough, buffalo mozzarella oozes out too much fat, while the whole San Marzano tomato thing was, to Colonnesi, a ploy to promote a boutique regional product.

Ah, the politics of pizza.

If there's one thing that unites all Neapolitan pizza camps it's their belief that topping should never—but never!—take precedence over the crust. To purists, pizza is an *impasto poco condito:* scantly dressed dough.

Colonnesi believes that before the New World tomato was embraced by Neapolitan cooks in the eighteenth century, the Napolitani were already enjoying *pizza bianca,* white pizza garnished with pork cracklings, and, later, anchovies. Others hold that pre-*pomodoro,* pizza was simply another flatbread. The word *pizza* does appear in A.D. 997 in a southern Italian Latin *Codex Cajetanus,* yet what it describes is just a foccacia topped with garlic and pork fat.

By around the 1760s, Neapolitan streets were already teeming with iron-lunged roving pizza vendors. And around this time pizza marinara—tomatoes, garlic, oregano, olive oil—was conceived near Naples' port, providing breakfast for mariners returning from sea. More than a century later, Queen Margherita, a Piedmontese royal who summered in Naples became curious about pizza and a *pizzaiolo* named Raffaele Esposito was bidden to make a pizza delivery to her palace. For the occasion, Esposito devised a dramatic pie decorated with mozzarella, tomatoes, and basil—the colors of *tricolore,* the Italian flag. And he christened his creation in her majesty's honor. Today, you'll hear this tale proudly relayed by waiters at Pizzeria Brandi (originally Pizzeria di Pietro), where Esposito's descendants ply camera-toting tourists with utterly mediocre pies. The pizza police do not approve.

neapolitan pizza margherita

cook's notes Per the advice of Neapolitan *pizzaiolos*, I use less yeast than most recipes call for, make the dough rather loose, and add cake flour to all-purpose flour to simulate Italian "00" flour, which is softer than American all-purpose flour. The dough is best when left to "ripen" overnight in the refrigerator, so plan accordingly. This amount is enough for four 10-inch pies, but you can use half the dough and half the topping for a smaller number of people and save the rest of the dough for later. Placed in a zippered bag, the dough will keep in the refrigerator for several days; it also freezes well. For best results you will want a baker's peel and pizza stone. Unglazed quarry tiles work, too. Lacking these, use a heavy-duty baking sheet that doesn't warp at high temperatures and a smaller rimless cookie sheet instead of a paddle.

dough

1½ teaspoons active dry yeast

1½ cups bottled spring water, slightly warmed (115°F.)

½ teaspoon sugar

1½ teaspoons salt

1¼ cups cake flour (not self-rising), or Italian "00" flour, if available

2¾ to 3 cups all-purpose flour

topping

12 to 14 canned San Marzano tomatoes (from a 32-ounce can), drained and seeded

1 tablespoon virgin olive oil, preferably from Campania, plus more for drizzling

Salt

½ to 1 teaspoon red wine vinegar, if needed

Large pinch of sugar, if needed

Twelve ⅓-inch-thick slices fresh cow's milk mozzarella (about 1¼ pounds)

12 small basil leaves

1 Make the dough: In a large mixing bowl, stir together the yeast, water, and sugar and let stand until foamy, about 5 minutes. Stir in the salt and the cake flour, stirring until smooth, then stir in 2¾ cups of the all-purpose flour. Knead a few times in the bowl until the dough holds together.

2 On a floured surface with floured hands, knead the dough until smooth and elastic, about 8 minutes. Add all-purpose flour, 1 tablespoon at a time, if the dough feels too sticky. Resist the urge to add too much flour: the dough should feel soft and slightly tacky. Shape the dough into a ball, place in an oiled bowl, and turn to coat with the oil. Cover loosely with plastic, giving the dough room to expand, and let it rise in a warm place until almost doubled in bulk, 1½ hours. Punch the dough down, coat again with oil, re-cover loosely with plastic, and place the dough on the lowest shelf of a refrigerator for at least 6 hours or overnight. (The dough can be prepared up to 2 days ahead and wrapped in plastic.)

3 Preheat the oven to the highest temperature, 500 to 550°F. Twenty minutes before baking, place the pizza stone or a large, heavy-duty baking sheet on the lowest shelf of the oven.

4 Make the topping: In a food processor, pulse the tomatoes until just crushed but not pureed. Transfer them to a bowl and add 1 tablespoon of the olive oil and salt to taste. Taste the tomatoes: if they seem a bit flavorless, add ½ teaspoon or more wine vinegar and a pinch of sugar to heighten the flavor.

5 Divide the dough into four parts and gently shape each part into a ball. Keep the unused balls wrapped in plastic as you work. On a floured surface, gently flatten one ball into a 6-inch disk. Don't flatten too hard as the dough needs to retain some air bubbles. Coat your hands with flour and start pulling the edges of the dough outward to stretch, holding the center in place with the other hand and rotating the disk as you pull. Turn the disk over several times as you stretch, lifting the dough in the air and stretching the middle over the backs of both hands. As you work, keep a raised border around the periphery of the disk. You should end up with a 10-inch circle with a raised border about ½ inch thick. Cover the disk with a kitchen towel and let rest for 5 minutes.

6 Dust the baker's peel or a rimless cookie sheet generously with flour and transfer the dough to the peel. Smear one-fourth of the tomatoes evenly on top, leaving a ½-inch border. Put your thumb over the opening of the olive oil bottle so that only a thin stream comes out, and drizzle the oil over the pizza in a spiral shape. Arrange three mozzarella slices and three basil leaves on top.

7 Shake the peel lightly to make sure the pizza doesn't stick. Open the oven door, place the peel, slightly tilted downward on the stone or the baking sheet, and give it a forward thrust, pulling the peel quickly away. Bake the pizza until puffed up and light golden, 6 to 7 minutes. Transfer the pizza to a serving plate or a wooden board and tent with foil for 2 to 3 minutes to relax the dough.

8 Make the other three pizzas in the same fashion, shaping one pie as another one bakes.

Makes four 10-inch pizzas to serve 4 as a main course or 8 as a snack

a harvest moon in a large circle of mist," waxed the Italian literary great Alessando Manzoni, describing a circle of polenta. Arrigo Boito, Verdi's celebrated librettist, dedicated a poem in Venetian dialect to the glories of cornmeal. Over centuries Italians have paid homage to *la polentina* with songs, *sagras* (festivals), and secret societies. And with intimate family rites.

"Polenta was acclaimed, written and sung about, and altogether celebrated, more than any Italian food," says Italian writer Anna Del Conte says. Are you surprised?

In the early 1500s, the first maize made its way to Venice's Rialto market from the New World by way of Spain. Soon after, that stirringly delicious corn mush called polenta became not just a necessity for northern Italians but also a

polenta

source of inspiration and joy. Salvation, too. When the fortunes of the Venetian Republic flagged with the demise of its trade routes, a diet of mush made of maize (so cheap, so easy to cultivate) came as a godsend. True, there was the prerequisite huffing and puffing among Europeans when they encountered their first corn. (Initially it was used as animal fodder.) But compared to, say, potatoes, which fought for recognition for centuries, maize was an overnight hit. Especially in the form of polenta.

That *simpatico* taste aside, perhaps this was because prior to meeting corn, northern Italians already made other polentas from barley, chestnut flour, and buckwheat. Compared to these coarse dark gruels, cornmeal polenta was a definite upgrade—sweeter, creamier, sunnier. The word *polenta* harks back to the Roman *puls* or *potage,* which the ancients were concocting from millet, barley, or chickpea flour. The Greeks chomped on these porridges, too, fashioning them mostly from spelt (*farro*) and calling them *poltos.* Today polenta answers to names like *mamaliga* in Romania, *ghome* in the Caucasus, *la pouce* in the Perigord, or mush on our shores. In Italy, the pasta-polenta divide—between northern *polentoni,* or polenta eaters, and the southern *mangiamaccheroni*—falls squarely along the Po River.

A great deal of polenta's folkloric allure lies in the mystique of its cooking rites. The pouring of the grain in a thin golden stream into water gurgling in the *paiolo* (a bucket-like polenta pot made of unlined copper). *La nonna* forever complaining of her blistered hand as she moves the mass of cornmeal around in the pot. The spreading of the steaming fragrant mush on a wooden board. The letting it rest for a while, then cutting it with a cotton *spago* (thread) as the kids huddle around the pot waiting for bits of the crisp bottom crust. Italians just thrive on this sort of romance.

As a sponge for sauces and flavors, polenta outperforms even pasta. "Polenta can be stretched further to do more things than anything else you cook," says Marcella Hazan. In parts of Piedmont, its promiscuity at the table has even earned polenta the nickname of *la Traviata*. Layer polenta with other ingredients in a kind of lasagne, and you'll have *polenta pastizzata*. Mix it with beans, and you have *polenta infasola*. Near Mantua, you'll taste soft polenta topped with the famous *lucio in saor,* or pike in onion marinade. Polenta with long-braised horsemeat ragu awaits you in Verona, while in Venice don't even think of missing grilled polenta with the rich, fluffy *baccalà mantecata* (buttered salt cod).

But delicious as it is with sausage, salt cod, or a good unctuous *tocio* (a Veneto stew), more than anything else, polenta loves butter and cheese. Especially a good northern Italian cheese, like a wedge of rich, earthy Montasio from Friuli, nutty Fontina d'Aosta, or, best of all, creamy sharp crumbles of Gorgonzola. Melt some Gorgonzola cheese over a smooth slice of polenta and you, too, will be composing eulogies to the magnificent mush.

three-cheese polenta with mushrooms

cook's notes What separates a merely good polenta from a sublime one is the quality of the cornmeal. One of the best imported polentas comes from Molino Sorbino in Piedmont (see Resources). Made from heirloom "red" corn picked by hand, it packs oodles of earthy corn flavor. Otherwise look for a good domestic stone-ground cornmeal; cheaper imported varieties tend to be old and flavorless.

While nothing beats polenta stirred continuously for over an hour, when time is short, I often turn to the easy no-stir polenta method suggested by Michelle Anna Jordan in her book, *Polenta*. The incredibly delicious recipe below is for polenta pasticciata, or pastizzata (a kind of polenta bake) layered with mushrooms and enriched with three cheeses. It makes a hearty first course for a crowd or a vegetarian main dish. If you omit the mushroom layer, the polenta makes a great side dish with just about anything.

mushrooms

½ ounce dried porcini mushrooms

4 to 6 tablespoons unsalted butter

3 garlic cloves, minced

1 pound mixed portobello and cremini mushrooms, trimmed, wiped clean with a damp paper towel and chopped medium-fine

¼ cup dry white wine

¼ cup heavy cream

Salt and freshly ground black pepper

polenta

4 cups cold water

4 cups cold milk

1⅔ cups polenta, preferably stone-ground

2 tablespoons unsalted butter, cut into pieces

2 cups (about 8 ounces) shredded fontina cheese

1 cup grated Parmesan cheese, preferably Parmigiano-Reggiano

Salt and white pepper

6 to 7 ounces Gorgonzola cheese, crumbled

1 Make the mushrooms: Soak the porcini in ½ cup warm water for 30 minutes. Drain, reserving the soaking liquid, and chop the mushrooms fine. Pass the soaking liquid through a small sieve lined with a coffee filter or a piece of damp paper towel to remove the grit. Reserve.

2 In a large skillet, melt 4 tablespoons of the butter over medium-low heat. Add the dried porcini and garlic and sauté, stirring, for about 5 minutes, until the mixture is fragrant. Turn the heat up to medium-high, add the fresh mushrooms, and cook until they have thrown off and partially reabsorbed their liquid, about 10 minutes, adding more butter if the skillet looks dry. Add the wine and cook until it is almost evaporated, about 3 minutes. Add the mushroom soaking liquid and the cream, and cook until the sauce has thickened and partially reduced, 5 to 7 minutes. Season with salt and pepper to taste. (The mushrooms can be prepared up to 1 day ahead and refrigerated.)

4 Make the polenta: If using traditional method, bring the water and milk to a rolling boil in a wide, heavy pot. Place the polenta into a measuring cup with a spout. Whisk the water to create a whirlpool. Whisking with one hand, pour the cornmeal into the water by shaking the cup lightly over the pot so that the cornmeal falls in a thin steady trickle. Once all the cornmeal has been added, whisk steadily and vigorously as the polenta begins to bubble and sputter and thicken (watch out for that sputter). Now start stirring the polenta with a long wooden spoon, alternating circular with scooping motions to scrape the cornmeal up from the bottom of the pot. Keep stirring and turning the polenta until it is thick and smooth and comes away from the sides of the pot. (It's OK to leave the pot for a few minutes every once in a while.) This should take about 40 minutes, but the longer you cook and the more diligently you stir, the better.

If using the no-stir oven method (see Cook's Notes), preheat the oven to 350°F. In a heavy 5-quart pot, preferably with a round bottom, stir together the water, milk, cornmeal, and butter. The mixture won't be homogenous. Place it in the oven and bake, uncovered, until the polenta is soft and smooth and begins to pull away from the sides of the pot, about 1½ hours. Stir it once or twice after about 1 hour.

5 Five minutes before the polenta (made by either method) is ready, stir in the fontina, Parmigiano, salt, and white pepper. Cook either in the oven or on top of the stove for another 5 minutes. The polenta will be medium-soft.

6 Spoon half of the polenta evenly on the bottom of a 9 by 12 by 2-inch baking dish. Spread the mushroom mixture on top and top with the remaining polenta. Smooth the top of the dish with the back of a wet spoon. Let the polenta sit for about 20 minutes to set. (The dish can be assembled a few hours ahead.)

7 Preheat the oven to 450°F. Sprinkle the top of the polenta evenly with Gorgonzola and bake until the cheese is melted and bubbly, about 10 minutes. To brown the top, you can finish the polenta under a broiler. Cut the polenta into squares and serve.

Serves 8 to 10

resources Superior Italian cornmeal such as Molino Sorbino can be found at Formaggio Kitchen (tel: 888-212-3224 or *www.formaggiokitchen.com*). Note that better-quality polentas might take longer to cook than others.

Once I chatted about the greatest dishes of France with François Simon, the famously opinionated Parisian restaurant critic for *Le Figaro*. In his inimitably contrarian fashion, Simon dismissed cassoulet as a "museum monument" and wrote off chef Joël Robuchon's mythical mashed potatoes as a "regressive idea for snobs with no teeth." Ouch.

But for potato gratin he had the following tender words: "Potato gratin is a childhood dream: burnt on top, burnt on the bottom, creamy inside. It's the ultimate mama dish resistant to chef's egos—a treat meant for people with gentle naive appetites." Yes!

In fact, it's hard to imagine an authentic French country restaurant—lacy curtains, checkered oilcloths, chipped carafes of slightly coarse red—without a vast earthenware dish of potato gratin. The gratin makes its rounds from table to table, seducing customers with its browned lid and an oozing center of sliced potatoes that melt into a soft velvety mass. Just like the *restaurant du village,* the gratin is an ode to coziness, a monument to comfort. It's so good, you want to keep the pan to yourself to scrape every cheesy brown bit that hugs the bottom.

potato gratin

As it happens, scrape—*gratter* in French—is the word that gives gratin its name. Today *gratin* describes a baked dish mainly of vegetables, sometimes bound with cheese, butter, and eggs, sometimes with béchamel, other times simply with cream or broth. The point is to bake the vegetables in a shallow gratin pan until the top browns and the interior goes impossibly soft. French cooks fashion tasty gratins from anything: fennel, chard, endives, mushrooms. But it is for the *pomme de terre* that they reserve their tenderest thoughts.

Among the first regions in France to embrace the potato was the Dauphine, a rugged and mountainous wedge of southeastern France bordered by Provence, Languedoc, and Savoie. Potatoes arrived locally by way of Switzerland in the seventeenth century, and the region's pioneering penchant for the spud might be attributed to the Dauphine's dire fuel shortages, and to the inferior quality of its wheat. All this meant that bread wasn't a given, and this alternative source of carbohydrates must have come as God's gift.

The Dauphine and neighboring Savoie also happen to be France's great dairy meccas. And when milk and cream were joined with potatoes, France got its *pomme de terre* masterpiece: gratin dauphinois. According to legend the dish was cooked up less than a century ago, in 1910, by a lady named Philomene Revollet, the proprietress of Hotel Revollet.

French cooks can argue until the cows come home about potato gratins in general and dauphinois in particular. Some say the potatoes should be mealy, others waxy. Must the slices be washed? Thick or thin? Do eggs dry out the gratin or lend extra body? The most classic version of dauphinois seems to be the purest. Claude Muller, in his book about the traditions and folklore in the Dauphine, cautions: "*Pas d'ail, pas d'oeuf, et encore moins de fromage*"—no garlic, no eggs, and even less cheese. Truth be told though, it's pretty hard to ruin a potato gratin.

gratin dauphinois

cook's notes This gratin does contain a whiff of garlic and is finished with cream plus a sprinkling of Parmesan. In this classic form the gratin tastes plenty cheesy on account of the reduced milk, but not gooey. For extra goo, sprinkle some shredded Beaufort or Gruyère between potato layers, and more on top. Use half-and-half or milk depending on the richness desired and add a little crème fraîche for extra tang, if you wish.

3 pounds russet (Idaho) potatoes of uniform size

2 tablespoons unsalted butter, softened

1 medium garlic clove, crushed through a press

1½ to 2 cups half-and-half or milk

Salt and freshly ground black pepper to taste

Freshly grated nutmeg to taste

4 tablespoons crème fraîche (optional)

⅓ to ½ cup heavy cream

¼ cup Parmesan cheese

1 Peel and wash the potatoes and slice them into rounds ⅛ inch thick, using a mandoline, the slicing disk of a food processor, or a sharp knife.

2 Generously butter a 9 by 12-inch heavy shallow baking dish, preferably earthenware or cast-enamel, or an oval gratin dish of comparable size. (You can also use a 12-inch cast-iron skillet.) Rub the dish with half of the crushed garlic.

3 In a small saucepan, bring the half-and-half to a simmer with the remaining garlic and season generously with salt and pepper. Set aside.

4   Preheat the oven to 350°F. Arrange the potatoes in one overlapping layer on the bottom of the dish. Season the layer generously with salt, pepper, and nutmeg. Arrange two more layers on top, seasoning each layer liberally. You might not need all the potatoes. Press the layers down to compact them. Pour in enough half-and-half to come up just a little below the top layer of potatoes. Set the baking dish on a larger baking sheet, cover with foil, and bake until the potatoes feel tender when pierced with a knife, about 1 hour.

5   Raise the oven temperature to 425°F., remove the foil, and bake until the top begins to brown, about 10 minutes. Pour just enough cream to cover the top, dab it with crème fraîche, if using, and sprinkle evenly with the Parmesan. Bake until the top is brown and bubbly, 15 to 20 minutes more. Remove from the oven and let the potatoes stand for 10 minutes to absorb the cream. Cut into squares and serve.

Serves 6 to 8

Say the words "potato salad" and I flash back to the *kartoffelsalat* made by my landlady, Helga, during my days as a near-starving piano student in Freiburg in southern Germany. Helga wasn't your nurturing type. But I soon learned the way to her heart: my performance of a particular Brahms intermezzo was always followed by a half-grudging invitation to share her supper of cold beef and potato salad (to this day I associate Brahms with spuds). Helga's *kartoffelsalat* approached the Platonic ideal. The play of sharp onions and flecks of crisp speck against the perfect creaminess of potato slices. The impeccably sweet-sour balance of puckery white vinegar dressing. Helga never offered me coffee or plum cake, but I forgive her.

Flashing back lots further, to grade school, I recall learning that potatoes were "discovered" in the Peruvian highlands by Spanish explorers who mistook

potato salad

them for truffles. After reaching Spain around 1570, the tuber embarked on a long and bumpy route to acceptance in Europe, taking nearly three centuries to find its place among the world's indispensable staples. And while a crisp fry or a rustic gratin are among life's finer pleasures, potato salad is a kind of primal thing one could eat every day. Happily, there are recipes enough for a lifetime.

The oldest and most "authentic" potato salad has to be the stuff one still eats at *chicha* (indigenous corn beer) houses in Andean Peruvian villages. This is where Quechua Indians huddle over huge glasses of the fizzy strange brew, dousing wedges of fleshy Andean potatoes with various chile sauces (*ajies*) arrayed on tables. The world's most omnipresent potato salad is probably a concoction globally called "Russian salad" and known to us Russians as *salat olivier,* after a famous French chef. Diced cooked potatoes, carrots, pickles, and peas bound with mayonnaise, Russian salad has a way of showing up at Madrid tapas bars, at railway restaurants in Turkey, or as part of Korean *panchan* (a spread of small plates). The most lyrical potato salad is anything from the Mediterranean, splashed with good olive oil and laced with shallots, olives, capers, or tuna. And the prize for the most entertaining potato salad goes to the Indian *aloo chat:* diced potatoes revved up with a special *chat* masala and drizzled with thin yogurt and chutneys.

As for the American mayonnaise-laden potato salads, these were not enjoyed in this country before 1912, when Richard Hellmann, a German-born New York delicatesser launched his blue-ribbon white condiment. Before then American potato salad mostly meant German potato salad introduced by Teutonic immigrants. And for all the other potato salads we might know and love, the real German version still sets the gold standard.

Germans cook the potatoes with the most perfect pitch. They grow some of the world's most delicious waxy varieties, giving them poetic names like Gloria, Sieglinde, or Mauschen (little mice). And when German women shop for potatoes at farmers' markets, with all the prodding, sniffing, and haggling, you'd think they were buying truffles.

And these ladies *really* know how to make a potato salad.

potatoes and prussians   Like all European potato dishes, *kartoffelsalat* is fairly new to German cuisine. In 1774, when Frederick the Great sent wagonloads of potatoes to ease the famines in Kolberg, he got the following response: "The thing has neither smell nor taste, not even dogs will eat them, so what use are they to us?" A Prussian if there ever was one, Frederick remained unmoved. He ordered his subjects to plant potatoes under the supervision of dragoons—poor performance would earn a flogging—and dispatched soldiers to force the spud down his starving populace's throat. At gunpoint. But over the next hundred years, German feelings toward the potato evolved from contemptuous suspicion to grudging acceptance to deep, everlasting love.

german potato salad

cook's notes The classic German potato salad one encounters at *biergartens* or wood-paneled *Stuben* usually involves sliced waxy potatoes marinated while still warm in a simple vinaigrette composed of water or broth, oil, white wine vinegar, minced onions, and gratings of white pepper. Sometimes there are bits of bacon, sometimes slices of wurst. A touch of mustard or a discreet hint of herbs might enliven the dressing. Mayonnaise might be a go in the north, but Southerners frown upon it.

The recipe here draws on my memories of watching Helga doing it right. She used very yellow warm potato slices and layered them just so with the dressing so that each slice absorbed the right amount while remaining separate and intact. I remember how obsessive she was about not crushing her neat, almost paper-thin slices. Her dressing was warm, made in the same skillet she used for sautéing the tiny matchsticks of speck. And I can still see her grating the onions to squeeze out the juice.

Because the flavors here are pretty transparent, success depends on finding good butcher's bacon and the tastiest, waxiest farmers' market potatoes. My favorites are the incredibly buttery German Butterballs, but any yellow fingerling, such as Ratte would be fine. Vegetarians can skip the bacon and add chopped hard-boiled egg and/or diced cornichons.

3 pounds best-quality yellow waxy potatoes, about 2 inches in diameter, scrubbed

2 teaspoons salt, plus more to taste

6 ounces lean slab bacon, preferably double-smoked, cut into matchsticks or small dice

1¼ cups chicken stock or canned broth

¼ cup mild olive oil

⅓ cup white wine vinegar, or more to taste

4 teaspoons sugar

½ cup minced red or white shallots

About 1 tablespoon onion juice squeezed from grated onion

Freshly grated white pepper

2 to 3 tablespoons finely minced chives, dill, or parsley

1 Place the potatoes in a large pot, cover them with cold water by 2 inches, and bring to a boil. Reduce the heat to low, add 2 teaspoons of the salt, and simmer partially covered until the potatoes feel tender but not mushy when pierced with a skewer, 22 to 25 minutes. Do not overcook. Drain the potatoes and cool until just manageable.

2 While the potatoes are cooking and cooling, prepare the dressing. In a medium skillet, cook the bacon over medium-low heat until it renders its fat. Increase the heat to medium and cook until the bacon is crisp. Remove the bacon to drain on paper towels, then set aside until ready to use. Pour off all but 1 tablespoon of the bacon fat from the skillet and add the broth, olive oil, vinegar, sugar, shallots, onion juice, and salt and pepper to taste. Bring to a simmer and take off the heat.

3 Gently peel the skins off the potatoes, or leave unskinned if the skin is tender. Using a knife dipped in cold water, slice them as thin as you can without breaking. I do this directly over a wide, shallow bowl. When you have a full, even layer of potatoes, sprinkle them with salt to taste and drizzle evenly with the dressing. Repeat this until all the potatoes and dressing are used up. Marinate the salad at room temperature for at least 3 hours. Using two forks, carefully toss the potatoes every hour or so.

4 Gently transfer the potatoes to a serving bowl and toss with the reserved bacon and the chives. Adjust the amount of salt, vinegar, or pepper to taste. Serve slightly warm or at room temperature, but not cold.

Serves 4 to 6

Whenever I visit Paris in winter, I always find myself squeezing into line at a cozy cubbyhole called Le Roi du Pot-au-Feu, or The King of Boiled Dinner. Le Roi is a tattered old bistro straight out of Central Casting: walls plastered with yellowed letters from grateful customers, stubby glasses of cheap Gamay, and an illegible hand-scrawled menu. The *carte*, of course, is redundant. Maybe the place does a decent *steak frites*. But all these people patiently crowding the entrance are here for one thing: *pot-au-feu*, literally "pot on the fire" and France's premiere cold-weather indulgence.

The meal might kick off with a slab of rugged *pâté de maison* and a plate of leeks *en vinaigrette*. Then the pot-au-feu ritual begins, with the spreading of warm bone marrow onto grilled bread with a sprinkle of gray sea salt. Up next,

pot-au-feu

a bowl of amber beef consommé, fortifying and thoroughly skimmed of all fat, followed by a messy platter of various cow parts

and vegetables—carrots, leeks, parsnips—gently poached in the broth. Truth be told, Le Roi's pot-au-feu isn't all that spectacular (you'll make a better one at home with the recipe that follows). But it delivers all the reassuring warmth of a great winter meal. That, and the sense that classic *cuisine bourgeois* is alive and cozy and well.

The whole world, of course, loves a boiled dinner. There is Italian *bollito misto*, Austria's extraordinary beef-in-broth called *tafelspitz*; the *cocido* of Castille loaded with meats, chorizo, and chickpeas. But it's the Gauls who view their boiled dinner as something nearly sacred: a national dish, a symbol of family life, an earthy antidote to haute cuisine excess. One scholar finds it nothing less than a "mythical conjuncture of water, fire and flesh." Goethe, a Prussian who knew from myths, marveled at a pot-au-feu he ate while visiting Lorraine. Mirabeau called it a foundation of empires. And the French culinary lions— Carême, Escoffier, and Brillat-Savarin—all discuss pot-au-feu in their *oeuvre* as a pillar of French cuisine. Not coincidentally, *Le Pot-au-feu* was the title of a popular French cooking magazine published from 1893 to 1956 and geared to women of modest means.

As one travels through France, the boiled-dinner idea assumes different regional guises. The *potée* of Lorraine comes thick with cabbage, saltback, and white beans. In the southwest, *garbure* mixes vegetables and cured meats. There's the proverbial *poule-au-pot* (boiled chicken) in Bearne; and in Brittany one encounters *kig ha fars,* a boiled meatfest accompanied by a buckwheat pudding that has been poached in the broth bundled in cheesecloth. For all the sautéing, flambéing, and elaborate sauce making, it's the bouillon—broth, stock, consommé—that still powers France's *cuisine populaire.*

Classic beef pot-au-feu with full trimmings evolved fully as a dish in the nineteenth century, but rather flexibly. It can include anywhere from two to five cuts of beef—and depending on cook and region, may feature lamb shoulder, pork, bacon, sausages, hens, and a varying selection of vegetables. As recipes get more detailed and refined, French cookbooks begin to call for making the dish in two stages: bones and bouillon cuts started in cold water for a strong flavorful broth; choicer cuts cooked by plunging in boiling liquid to seal in their succulence. (That said, I know plenty of French cooks who happily dump everything together into one pot.) Prerequisite trimmings include bone marrow spread on toast, sea salt, mustards, cornichons, pickled onions, and pickled cherries, if you're lucky enough to find them. But at heart, pot-au-feu boils down to three things: comfort, coziness, conviviality.

beef pot-au-feu

cook's notes The meat tastes infinitely juicier when poached in hot liquid while the best broth results from starting the meats and bones in cold water—hence the dish here is made in two stages. Not to mess up the beautiful broth, I cook the vegetables separately; if you prefer to cook them in the soup broth, wrap them in cheesecloth. Of course you can make a decent pot-au-feu in one stage by dumping everything into the pot—as long as you make it a day ahead to degrease, and leave the beef in the broth overnight. But doesn't the "dish that makes France" deserve a little extra attention?

1 Make the broth one day before serving: Rinse the bones, oxtails, and veal shank thoroughly of any traces of blood. Place them in a large stockpot and add the water. Bring to a simmer over medium-high heat and skim the broth thoroughly. Reduce the heat to low and continue skimming without allowing the broth to boil. Add the rest of the broth ingredients except for salt. Cover and simmer the broth for 3 hours, skimming carefully every once in a while. Add salt in the last hour of cooking. The broth should be kept at a mere simmer, never boil.

2 Let the broth cool to room temperature, then ladle by ladle, strain it through a fine sieve trying not to disturb the bits that have sunk to the bottom. Remove the beef oxtails from the broth into a bowl, add enough broth to keep them moist, and refrigerate them. Discard the rest of the strained ingredients and chill the broth overnight.

broth

3 pounds meaty beef bones, preferably shin

2 pounds oxtails

1 to 1½ pounds veal knuckles or shank

5 quarts water

2 medium onions, studded with 4 or 5 whole cloves

2 large carrots

2 celery ribs

2 leeks, green part only, rinsed thoroughly

2 medium parsnips

4 sprigs thyme, 6 sprigs parsley, 2 bay leaves, and 1 teaspoon black peppercorns tied in a cheesecloth bag

Coarse sea salt to taste

3 Prepare the meat: Degrease the broth. Measure and reserve 10 cups to serve as a soup course. Place the remaining broth in a large stockpot and add enough water to make about 4 quarts. Bring this broth to a low boil over medium heat. Add the chuck and the short ribs, reduce the heat to very low, and simmer, partially covered, until the meats are very tender, 2½ to 3 hours. If the short ribs are done before the chuck, remove them to a bowl. In the last 30 minutes of cooking, tie the marrow bones in cheesecloth and add to the simmering liquid; 15 minutes before the meats are done, add the reserved oxtails and salt to taste. When the meats are very tender, turn off the heat and keep them in the warm liquid until ready to serve.

4   While the meats are cooking, prepare the vegetables. Cover the potatoes with cold salted water and cook until tender, about 25 minutes. Drain and keep warm. In a large shallow pot, cover the turnips with water, bring to a simmer, and simmer for 10 minutes. Add the carrots, simmer for 10 minutes, add the leeks and simmer until all the vegetables are tender, about 15 more minutes. With a slotted spoon, transfer the potatoes and vegetables to a deep dish and ladle over 2 cups of the beef cooking liquid to infuse them with the broth flavor. Cover with foil and keep warm.

5   Reheat the 10 cups of the reserved broth without the meats for serving as a soup. While the soup is heating, slice the chuck into medium slices and slice the short ribs if large. Arrange the oxtails, short ribs, chuck, and all the vegetables on a large serving platter; sprinkle generously with the broth, sprinkle with parsley, and keep covered with foil while serving the first course.

7   To serve, preheat the broiler, place 8 to 10 of the toasted bread slices on a baking sheet, sprinkle with cheese, and brown under the broiler. Reserve these for the soup. Begin the meal by serving the marrow bone, which should be spread on the other 8 to 10 toasted bread slices and sprinkled with sea salt. Proceed to serve the reserved heated broth as a soup course, afloat with the cheese toasts. Then bring out the meat and vegetables platter with the cornichons, pickled onions, mustards, horseradish, and a bowl of hot broth for sprinkling.

Serves 8 to 10

meats and vegetables

One 4-pound chuck roast (top blade, arm, or shoulder) or sirloin tip, tied

3 pounds meaty short ribs, trimmed of excess fat

Two 2-pound marrow bones, cut into 1-inch pieces (ask your butcher to do this)

8 to 10 small new potatoes, well scrubbed

5 medium white turnips, halved

3 large thick carrots, halved crosswise and quartered

8 to 10 medium leeks, white part and 1 inch of the green, thoroughly rinsed

for serving

Finely minced parsley, for garnish

16 to 20 thick slices of baguette (2 baguettes), lightly toasted

½ cup grated Gruyère or Parmesan cheese

Gray sea salt

Cornichons

Pickled baby onions

An assortment of mustards and horseradish

as long as there has been sugar and rice, the idea of stretching a handful of grains into a sweet, soothing porridge has been inevitable. Consequently, every rice-eating culture developed its own rice pudding recipe. Whether eaten for no particular reason or for important religious occasions, baked or cooked on the stove, stirred continuously or left completely alone, jazzed up with vanilla, *canela* (cinnamon), coconut, mastic, lemon, or cardamom, or eaten plain, rice puddings are beloved east to west and north to south.

No other dish basks in such universal devotion. In ancient Rome, where rice was exotic and pricey, a kind of liquidy proto rice pudding was consumed by the rich for medicinal purposes. Medieval Arabs and Persians created sweet

rice pudding

masterpieces by mixing rice with cow's milk or milk extracted from almonds, a practice still enjoyed in North Africa. In Britain, a recipe for baked rice enriched with egg yolks, oranges, and exotic spices was already in circulation in Elizabethan times. In the 1850s, the French honored the Spanish wife of Napoleon III with an haute version, *riz au imperatrice,* a rococo rice mold set with gelatin and studded with glacéed fruit. This was probably a Gallicized take on Spanish *arroz con leche,* the cold creamy rice sweet Iberians inherited from the Arabs. Today, Spanish-style *arroz con leche* is the best-loved dessert in Latin America.

Elsewhere, the Greeks relish their modest but disarmingly delicious *rizogalo,* cooked on the stove top and made creamy by constant stirring. The Far Eastern repertoire of sweet rice treats stretches from Chinese eight-treasure rice, to sticky Filipino *bibingkang malakkit,* to sweetened glutinous Thai black rice served drizzled with salted coconut cream (my vote for the funkiest rice pudding award). And have I mentioned Norwegian, Portuguese, or American contributions to rice-pudding culture?

anya von bremzen

I've never met a rice pudding I didn't like, but when I think of the ultimate marriage of rice and milk, my thoughts turn to India and the Middle East.

A rice pudding isn't supposed to be transporting; innocent, reassuring, and basic is more like it. But the Persian *sholleh zard,* and its Turkish offspring, *zerde,* and the Indian *kheer,* which is made with basmati rice and often enhanced with coconut, are the true aristocrats of the rice-pudding world, served for weddings, the birth of a son, or festivities ending Ramadan. Not too sweet, plump, or dense, they are cooling and elegant. With the exotic mystique of rose water, saffron, pistachios, and almonds, this is nursery food for worldly sophisticates.

proof of the pudding Savants claim that the earliest puddings were neither sweet, nor comforting, nor, of course, made of rice. In the fourteenth century, the word *pudding*—from the Latin *bottelus* (sausage)—described something more like a French boudin, meaning animal innards stuffed with minced meats and huge doses of fat and plumped out with some grain or crumbs. Over time, puddings got better and sweeter (though they still often contained meaty stuff, like suet). Wrapped in a doughy paste, they were baked in a slow hearth; boiled in a cloth bag invented specially for that purpose (a tradition that survived well into the nineteenth century); and subsequently composed of sweet batter and steamed in a mold.

Back in Elizabethan times, a rice pudding would be probably called a tart. "To Make a Tart of Ryse . . . boyle your rice, and put in the yolkes of two or three Egges into the Rice, and when it is boyled put it into a dish and season it with sugar, synamon and ginger, and butter, and the juice of two or three Orenges, and set it on the fire againe." So goes a rice pudding recipe in *The Good Huswifes Jewell* (1596) by Thomas Dawson. As we can see: not that radically different from what we eat today.

saffron rice pudding with pistachios

cook's notes Here is a blueprint for a tantalizing basmati rice pudding hued with saffron, flavored with a little coconut milk, and topped with pistachios. You can play with the recipe by adding a touch of orange-flower water or anise liqueur instead of the rose water, stirring in some plumped-up raisins or dried currants, or diced pineapple or mango, or by topping the pudding with toasted coconut instead of the nuts. If the pudding seems a little dense when you take it out of the oven, add some extra milk or coconut milk; or you can thin it out right before serving. For something more straightforward, make this recipe with regular long- or medium-grained rice.

¾ cup basmati rice, unwashed

2 cups boiling water

Pinch of salt

6 to 8 cardamom pods lightly smashed; two 3-inch-long strips of lemon rind; and 1 cinnamon stick, broken into 3 pieces, tied in a cheesecloth bag

7 tablespoons sugar, or more to taste

3½ cups milk, or a little more as needed

1½ cups canned coconut milk, well stirred

2 to 4 teaspoons rose water

¼ teaspoon saffron threads, toasted and pulverized in a mortar

4 to 5 tablespoons finely chopped unsalted skinned green pistachios, for garnish

Pomegranate seeds, for garnish

1 In a 5-quart ovenproof casserole, combine the rice, boiling water, salt, and the cheesecloth bag with the spices and bring to a boil. Cover and simmer over low heat until the rice is tender and all the liquid has been absorbed, 17 to 20 minutes.

2 While the rice is cooking, preheat the oven to 325°F.

3 Stir in 7 tablespoons of the sugar, 3½ cups of milk, and 1¼ cups of coconut milk, reserving the rest. Bring the mixture to a boil over medium heat, stirring gently. Transfer the casserole to the oven and bake, uncovered, until the mixture is thickened and the rice is very tender, about 30 minutes, stirring every 10 minutes.

4 Remove the pudding from the oven and remove and discard the cheesecloth bag. Taste the pudding and adjust the amount of sugar to taste. Stir in the remaining ¼ cup of the coconut milk and a little extra regular milk if the pudding seems dense. The pudding will thicken further as it cools. Let the pudding cool to warm, stirring every once in a while.

4 Steep the saffron in about 2 tablespoons hot water for 5 minutes. Stir in the saffron and the rose water to taste into the pudding and chill for at least 6 hours, placing a circle of waxed paper directly on top of the pudding to prevent a crust from forming.

5 Spoon the pudding into glass serving bowls and garnish with the pistachios and pomegranate seeds.

Serves 6 to 7

in the name of research, I've OD'ed on dough sampling pizza in Naples, tried more paella in Valencia than was altogether sane, and half-drowned in bouillabaisse in Marseilles. It was a thrill, but risotto was different.

Eating nothing but risotto for days put me in a meditative, almost Zen state of mind. The interior of each grain became a universe unto itself. I attuned my palate to the particular nuances of each rice variety, to the levels of creaminess teased out from the rice by each cook, to the degree of al dente bite at the core of each *chicco,* or kernel. When my week-long risotto-research binge in Italy's Veneto region finally ended, I suffered withdrawal symptoms.

For my risotto tutorials I could have chosen Lombardy or the Piedmont, Italy's other great rice centers. But if Piedmontese risotti tend to be rather dense,

risotto

in Veneto they make theirs *al'onda*—from the word "wave," meaning sublimely runny and soupy. That's what I wanted.

My research kicked off in Venice at Fiascchetteria Toscana, where I feasted on *schie,* the tiny sweet local shrimp with polenta, Veneto's other starch. And risotto. A resolutely Venetian risotto laced with sweet morsels of clams. The risotto startled me. While perfectly soupy and loose, it was hardly creamy, each grain defiantly clutching on to its character. The effect was aristocratic and slightly aloof—an endearing savory rice pudding this wasn't. The grains were gigantic. The secret? Aged organic carnaroli rice called Acquerello, from a small Piedmontese producer. Super-chef Alain Ducasse calls it the Rolls-Royce of rices.

Risotto, as we all know, is a singularly Italian way of approaching rice. Unlike pilafs and paellas where the liquid is added at once and allowed to absorb, for risotto the broth is fed to the grain ladle by ladle, accompanied by constant stirring, which teases out starch and creates a sauce. This time-honored method exploits the particular structure and proportion of starches of Italian risotto rice. Each kernel's interior is composed of amylose, a sturdy starch that remains firm despite vigorous stirring. Meanwhile, its pearlescent shell—consisting of amylopectin—"melts" into that ethereal soothing sauce. Many cooks whisk in butter and Parmesan at the end for extra lusciousness. This is called *manteccatura,* or "beating in."

Ultimately, risotto is less about flavors than it is about method and texture. And while the technique is encoded in the DNA of every Venetian, Piedmontese, or Lombardian cook, the Grail of dedicated modern risotto chefs is that little producer whose rice has what they consider the perfect union of these two starches. Choosing rice is a deeply personal thing. To Mara and Maurizio Martin of Venice's seafood temple, Da Fiore, that perfect rice is Riso Principe, from a seriously obscure *riseria* near Pavia. As I ate I was distracted by the immaculate little *crudo* (raw fish), but I did register that the Principe grains—threaded with slippery bits of scampi and chanterelles—were springier, less resilient than Acquerello.

Tradition dictates that the risotto be stirred nonstop, but some chefs are beginning to question this wisdom. To get to the grain of the matter I went to chat with Cesare Benelli, the risotto maestro of Al Covo restaurant. "Stirring *continuously?*" Benelli widened his eyes. "This will give you mashed potatoes instead of risotto!"

For risotto cooking, Cesare's relies on the following method. In a flavor base of olive oil and chopped onions, he sautés the rice until the grains scream "We're thirsty!" "You will hear it," he assured. "It's when the rice starts making funny hissing noises." The first addition of liquid "shocks" the rice and opens its pores. Cesare stirs the rice seriously only for the first 5 minutes or so—"when most of the starch is released"—thereafter only occasionally because from here on the starch oozes out by itself. Sturdier ingredients can flavor the rice from the start. More delicate stuff—seafood, tender peas, asparagus—goes in at the very end. For subtler ingredients, Cesare prefers smaller-grain rice grades like *fino* (see box). Larger-grained *superfino* rice (arborio, carnaroli) work with gutsier flavors. To finish, Cesare puts his one-handled risotto pot on a marble counter and gives it a vigorous shake.

Cesare concluded by waxing rhapsodic about Venetian risottos. Autumnal pumpkin risotto, as luscious and yellow as zabaglione. Unctuous *risotto di secoe*, flavored with those fatty delectable beef backbone trimmings butchers usually keep to themselves. Striking *risotto al hero di seppia con piselli,* which plays the dark marine taste of cuttlefish ink against bright sweetness of local peas.

"Just don't overstir," he shouted from across the room, waving good-bye.

autumnal pumpkin risotto

cook's notes A good risotto is simple and rather minimalist, deriving its expression from just one or two complimenting flavors. Texture is the name of the game. Al *dente* means that each grain of rice has a center that's firm and slightly chewy but not chalky or grainy. I love the runny Venetian-style runny *risotto al onda*, with a texture of a thick soup rather than mashed potatoes. To achieve this, add slightly more liquid toward the end, as the finished risotto will thicken further on its way from the pot to the table.

Inspired by a *risotto di zucca* I tasted all over Venice, this pumpkin risotto is comforting, creamy, and utterly wonderful. Northern Italian pumpkins are dense, intensely orange, and almost sweet enough for dessert. I substitute butternut squash and add a tiny dash of vanilla and nutmeg to coax out the sweetness. A good Parmigiano-Reggiano is a must.

1 In a medium saucepan, melt 1 tablespoon of the butter in 1 tablespoon of the oil over medium-low heat. Sauté the onion until softened but not browned, about 5 minutes. Add the squash and cook, stirring for 1 to 2 minutes. Add the vanilla, nutmeg, ⅓ cup of the wine, and ½ cup of the broth; cover tightly and cook until the pumpkin is tender, about 20 minutes, adding a little broth if the contents of the pan look dry.

2 In a heavy-bottomed sauté pan or another sturdy shallow pan, melt 1 tablespoon of the butter in the remaining 2 tablespoons of the oil over medium heat. Add the rice and cook, stirring constantly, without letting it burn, until it begins to hiss quietly, 2 to 3 minutes. Add the remaining ⅔ cup of the wine and stir until evaporated. Add 1 cup of the broth and cook, stirring vigorously with a wooden spoon in one direction, until the liquid is absorbed. Add the entire contents of the pumpkin pan to the rice. Continue cooking the rice, adding broth ¾ cup at a time as it gets absorbed, stirring for about 30 seconds after each addition, and then just often enough to prevent the rice from sticking to the bottom. The liquid should be simmering at a nice

- 2 tablespoons unsalted butter, plus 2 to 3 more tablespoons for finishing the rice
- 3 tablespoons mild olive oil
- 1 small onion, finely chopped
- 1 pound butternut squash, peeled and cut into 1½-inch cubes (about 3 cups)
- 2 to 3 drops pure vanilla extract
- 2 to 3 gratings of nutmeg
- 1 cup dry white wine
- 4½ to 5 cups light chicken stock or canned broth kept at a simmer
- 1½ cups carnaroli or good imported arborio rice
- Salt and freshly ground black pepper
- ⅓ cup Parmesan cheese, preferably Parmigiano-Reggiano, plus more for serving

steady bubble. When the rice begins to swell and soften, start adding less liquid, about ½ cup at a time, and lower the heat just a little. If midway through cooking, the rice doesn't seem creamy enough for you, give it a vigorous continuous stir for about 1 minute. Cook the rice in this fashion until al dente, 22 minutes or more depending on the rice. The center of the rice should feel firm but not grainy.

3 Once the rice is cooked to your liking, season the risotto with salt and pepper to taste. Stir in the remaining 2 to 3 tablespoons of the butter and the Parmigiano, cover the pan, and give it a vigorous shake, tossing and shaking the contents. Check the rice; if you'd like it creamier, stir it a little more with a wooden spoon. Serve immediately, with additional Parmigiano on the side.

Serves 4 as a first course

resources Acquerello, from the Rondolino family, Tenuta Columbara, is an organic huge-grained carnaroli rice "cured" for 12 months. Principato di Lucedio carnaroli is another fine pedigreed Piedmontese product. Both can be ordered from ChefSource (877-337-2491 or *www.chefsource.com*). Riseria Ferron carnaroli and vialone nano rices are a great Veneto find, carried by Formaggio Kitchen (Tel: 888-212-3224 or *www.formaggiokitchen.com*). Scotti and Gallo, while far less interesting than the above producers, both make perfectly acceptable and easily available risotto rices, especially carnaroli. Gallo has enlisted many of Italy's finest chefs to use their product, which they do with fine results. Both are found at good specialty markets. American arborio rice still has a long way to go.

perfect risotto rice Italians grade their rice according to size. *Commune,* the smallest, is usually used for soupy *menestre. Semifino* is a little larger, and includes the *vialone nano* strain popular in Veneto and Mantua and especially lovely with seafood. *Fino* grade is larger still, including the lesser-known *ribe* and St. Andrea varieties. Then, we have the huge-grained *superfino.* Best among *superfinos* are American-known arborio, with its roundish polished grains, and carnaroli, which has slightly elongated kernels and a supremely chewy interior thanks to a particularly high degree of amylose. Carnaroli is the rice preferred by the majority of good modern Italian chefs for most types of risotto.

Now that you're familiar with the basics, see the Resources for some outstanding producers to look for and for places to mail order from if these aren't yet available at the gourmet grocery near you. The more special the rice, the more magnificent the risotto.

n merrie eighteenth-century England, roast beef signified a lot more than lunch. The very essence of nationalism, it flourished as an edible flag of the Empire—personified by the meat-gobbling, ale-guzzling figure of John Bull. Eating beef—prodigious amounts of it—was an affirmation of prosperity and robust conservatism. (To this day beef is decidedly more Tory than Labor.) "Beef and Liberty" read the motto of an eighteenth-century dining club, The Sublime Society of Beefsteaks, whose members gathered together to attack rare beef and bellow anti-French songs. One of the club's most prominent members, William Hogarth—that most "hyperpatriotic" of British painters—portrayed in his *Gates of Calais* a group of effeminate undernourished French characters, all enviously ogling a huge hunk of good British beef. *O the Roast Beef of Old England* was the painting's subtitle, after a jingoistic tune composed by Hogarth's pal, Henry Fielding.

roast beef with yorkshire pudding

Chauvinism aside, a well-roasted "joint" did and does make a jolly good Sunday lunch. Especially with golden roasted potatoes, puffy-brown Yorkshire pudding suffused with beef drippings, and plum pie for dessert.

Gastronomically speaking, roast beef offered the one culinary accomplishment the British could properly flaunt at the Gauls, who had for centuries consumed their beef mostly boiled. In the eighteenth century, author Tobias Smollett observed from the John Bull side of the Channel that French beef was good mainly for soup. And even when the French did take up the rotisserie, many a British traveler reported that their beef was burnt. Even the great French gastronome Alexandre Dumas *père* conceded in mid-nineteenth century that for proper *bifteck à l'anglais,* one must travel to England.

The ur-British roast beef was cooked on a spit, with the grunt work of tending and turning given to unfortunate turnspit boys. (In Tudor days lads were replaced by dogs (!) harnessed to "dog wheels" attached to the spit.) Well before the seventeenth century apparently every cook knew something about roasting a joint; but the first detailed recipe appears in Gervase Markham's *The English Housewife* in 1615. Markham gives especially meticulous instructions for basting—with suet rendered with mace, cloves, and cinnamon—and for dredging with bread crumbs or oatmeal to protect against drying and charring.

In the best-selling *The Art of Cookery Made Plain and Easy* from 1741, British food maven Hannah Glasse starts her roast beef recipes with instructions on how to build a fire, a then-sensible approach. Those who didn't have an ample enough hearth, or means for the expense of fuel, deposited their joints at the communal baker's oven on their way to the Sunday mass.

Today such bastions of British beef as Simpson on the Strand are falling prey to trendy restaurant ways, and a Sunday lunch is more likely to revolve around a Moroccan tajine or a Keralan curry. With roast beef acquiring an aura of nostalgic quasi-exoticism, one is grateful for places that still dish out the real thing—a rare joint, artfully carved and served with all the classic accoutrements. Among these, the wood-paneled Grill Room at the Dorchester is my own Sunday lunch mecca whenever I am in London. And this recipe is inspired by its chef, Henry Brosi, and his awesome Aberdeenshire Black Angus roast with port gravy and herbed Yorkshire pudding. Hale and hearty. You don't have to be Hogarth to roar about it.

roast beef with port gravy and yorkshire pudding

cook's notes Twentieth-century British cookbooks justly devote as much attention to the meat itself as to cooking it. In America, a 3- to 5-rib roast—well-marbled, dry-aged USDA prime, of course—is the beef of dreams (see Resources). Not cheap, but how much more regal can a feast get, especially for Christmas or New Year's Eve?

yorkshire pudding

3 large eggs

1¼ cups whole milk

2 tablespoons finely chopped fresh sage or a combination of sage and thyme

¼ cup grated Parmesan cheese

½ teaspoon salt

1¼ cups all-purpose flour

beef and port gravy

One bone-in standing rib roast (5 ribs), 10 to 12 pounds, preferably from the loin end, chine bone removed

Coarse salt and coarsely ground black pepper

4 medium garlic cloves, crushed through a press, and 3 garlic cloves, smashed

2 tablespoons crumbled dried rosemary

2 tablespoons crumbled dried thyme

2 tablespoons olive oil

3 cups chicken stock or canned broth

3 cups canned beef broth

1 cup full-bodied red wine

2 teaspoons tomato paste

¾ teaspoon Dijon mustard

½ cup port wine

3 tablespoons unsalted butter, cut into pieces

If you prefer something tidier, go for the rolled rib roast, boned and trimly tied for you. Note that one rib will feed two to three people, so calculate accordingly.

If you never had Yorkshire pudding, a soufflé-like pancake that comes out of the oven all puffy and browned, you're in for a treat. Instead of individual muffin tins, you can bake the pudding in a 9 by 13 by 2-inch baking pan. You will need 4 tablespoons beef dripping for greasing the pan, and it should bake at 450°F. for about 20 minutes. It is served cut into squares.

1 Make the Yorkshire pudding: In a large bowl, beat together the eggs, milk, sage, cheese, and salt. Whisk in the flour in three batches, beating well after each addition. Place the batter in the lowest shelf of the refrigerator until ready to use.

2 Make the roast: Preheat the oven to 450°F. Rub the roast generously with salt and cracked pepper. In a small bowl, combine the crushed garlic, 1 tablespoon of the rosemary,

anya von bremzen

234

1 tablespoon of the thyme, and the oil and stir into a thick paste. Rub this paste all over the beef.

3 In a heavy skillet, sear the beef until well browned over high heat, beginning with the fatty side, about 10 minutes. When just cool enough to handle, set the beef in a large roasting pan fat side up. Set the roasting pan in the lower third of the oven and roast the beef for 25 minutes. Reduce the heat to 375°F. and continue roasting the meat until a meat thermometer inserted into the center registers 115 to 120°F. for rare beef. The roasting should take about 2 hours and 15 minutes total.

4 While the meat is roasting, make the gravy. In a large, heavy saucepan, combine the chicken stock and beef broth, red wine, smashed garlic, and the remaining 1 tablespoon each rosemary and thyme. Cook over high heat until reduced to 3½ cups, 35 to 40 minutes. In a small bowl, dilute the tomato paste and the mustard with a little broth and whisk it back into the saucepan. Add the port and reduce over high heat to about 2½ cups, about 15 more minutes. Strain into a bowl and whisk in the butter, which will make the sauce rich and glossy. Keep warm or reheat at serving time.

5 During the last 10 minutes of cooking the roast, place two 6-cup muffin trays on a large baking sheet and place them in the oven to heat. When the beef is ready, remove it from the oven, cover loosely with foil, and let stand while preparing the Yorkshire puddings. Reduce the oven temperature to 400°F. and reserve about ⅓ cup of the pan drippings for the puddings.

6 Remove the batter from the refrigerator and whisk again to blend. Remove the muffin trays from the oven, spoon equal amounts of the beef drippings into each cup, and return the muffin trays to the oven for another 5 minutes. Remove from the oven again, fill each muffin cup with the batter until about two-thirds full (you might not need all the batter), return to the oven, and bake until the puddings are golden and puffy, about 15 minutes.

7 While the puddings are baking, carve the beef into thick slices, removing the bones as you slice. Carefully remove the muffin trays from the oven. Using a large spoon, remove the puddings from the cups onto a serving platter or individual plates. (The puddings will sink a little, like a soufflé.) Serve the beef with the puddings and the port gravy.

Serves 12

resources One of the best mail-order sources for dry-aged beef is Lobel's Prime Meats (tel: 800-556-2357 or *www.lobels.com*).

unlike most people, I didn't experience the joys of eating roast chicken until later in life. Which is why I never take it for granted. During my Soviet childhood, our ovens barely functioned and the chicken was always a hen destined to be boiled to a fare-thee-well and reserved for the frail, the very young, and the aged. For an average *homo sovieticus,* the promise of chicken in every pot was a notion more elusive than freedom of speech. It was that chicken promise, both literal and metaphoric, that lured many of my fellow émigrés to America. "Pack your bags and come," my mother's friend wrote to us from Philadelphia, "the chickens here are as big as elephants and we eat them every day—every day!"

The leathery *Gallus sovieticus* of my childhood was likely as inedible as the *Gallus gallus* (aka red jungle fowl), the mother of all chickens, that was domesticated in India some 4,000 years ago. Tucked under the arm of merchants and soldiers, this chicken slowly migrated westward

roast chicken

along ancient trade roots to Persia, Mesopotamia, Egypt, and Asia Minor. These prototypical chickens weren't meant to function as food; rather, they were heroes of cockfights and objects of ritual sacrifice. But with slowly acquired wisdom about breeding and feeding, the gallus was finally ready for table by the first century B.C.

And yet it had to wait centuries to become omnipresent. Even as late as the seventeenth century, American colonists used chickens mainly for featherbedding. At the same time in France, chicken as food was enough of a luxury for Henry IV to utter his legendary coronation pledge of a chicken in every peasant's pot every Sunday—a pledge co-opted by Herbert Hoover for the 1928 American presidential campaign. The Depression notwithstanding, by mid–twentieth century, developed Western nations were indeed gorging on chickens while the not-so-developed ones watched in envy.

Which brings me back to roast chicken. The best restaurant roast chicken I've ever had is a toss-up among Zuni in San Francisco, Craft in New York, the Parisian stalwart L'Amie Louis, and a certain murky Peruvian chicken joint in Jackson Heights, Queens. The best home-roasted chicken? At almost every dinner party. After all, roast chicken is the most genial and forgiving of foods—which is why we're so attached to it.

In my long chicken-roasting career, I've baked the bird covered loosely with foil at 325°F., then uncovered to crisp the skin at a high temperature. Succulent. I've done the smoky blitz-roast at 500°F., setting off fire alarms in the entire neighborhood to have my guests licking their fingers. I've tried the steady 425°F., as well as every other conceivable temperature combination. I've put the chicken on the rack, in a Romertopf, in a cast-iron skillet.

Along the way, I have developed strong convictions. Trussing the bird is pretty but pointless, resulting in pallid undercooked inner thigh meat. Browning it in a skillet before baking—as practiced by many chefs—is fine, but who needs the fuss? Ditto for butterflying. And while basting might be an old wives' tale, for meddlers like me it's a happy excuse to peek, prod, and pick. For a big dinner party I unquestionably prefer two smaller birds to one oversized oven stuffer (more wings, more legs, more flavor). I've come to regard a steady 425°F. temperature as ideal and couldn't live without my vertical roaster. This gadget cooks the chicken evenly, yielding golden crispiness all around (you'd be surprised how much crackling skin there is on the back!); while the fat that drips into the small basin bastes the bird in the process.

My strongest feelings concern the chicken itself. Glowing accounts of big-bosomed hormone-pumped beasts might have been what brought Russian émigrés to America. But it didn't take long before we started pining for the scrawny hen with the true chickeny taste that we'd left behind. Besides, commercial chickens are fed on stuff you'd rather not know about and confined to poultry gulags for the duration of their short sorry lives. If that's okay with you, you can still make a tasty chicken dinner of a supermarket bird.

roast chicken with lemons and apples

cook's notes An organic bird from a reputable producer is the most delicious option. If you'd rather not splurge, I recommend an Empire kosher bird, which has the triple virtue of being easy to find, extremely moist because it is soaked in salt brine, and vividly flavorful, thanks again to the salt. Another excellent option is Chinese poultry, labeled "Buddhist style" chickens by the USDA, and found at most Chinese groceries. While a little lean, Chinese chickens tend to be very fresh and well-fed (often on soybeans and corn), with plenty of that good old-fashioned chicken taste.

I love this simple Mediterranean-style roast chicken with a flavorful garlic and herb rub and a panful of apples, onions, and lemon wedges baked alongside. For something exotic, you can substitute quince for apples. You will need a vertical roaster for this chicken; it is available at many cookware shops. The liquid underneath steams the chicken lightly as it roasts, producing a terrifically moist flesh. Lacking a vertical roaster, roast the chicken on a V-shaped rack set over a roasting pan. The recipe is easily doubled for a larger crowd.

One 3½-pound chicken, preferably certified organic, kosher, or Chinese, rinsed and patted dry

Kosher salt

14 garlic cloves, peeled

1 teaspoon sweet paprika

1½ teaspoons freshly ground black pepper

1 tablespoon crumbled dried rosemary, oregano, or mint, or a combination

1 tablespoon fruity olive oil, or more as needed

2 small thin-skinned lemons, scrubbed well and cut into 2-inch chunks

2 medium Granny Smith apples, peeled, cored, and cut into 2-inch chunks

1 large onion, cut into 2-inch chunks

1 to 2 cups chicken stock or canned broth, or more as needed

1 Place the chicken in a large glass bowl and rub it inside and out with 2 teaspoons of the salt. Cover loosely with plastic and refrigerate the chicken for 6 hours or overnight. (This light salt-curing imparts a great deal of flavor, but you can shorten the time to 1 hour if rushed.)

2 Preheat the oven to 425°F. Crush 3 cloves of garlic through a press. In a small bowl, combine the crushed garlic, paprika, pepper, and rosemary. Add enough oil to make a medium-thick paste. Reserve 1 teaspoon of this paste for the vegetables. With your hands, loosen the skin around the breast, thighs, and legs of the chicken. Slide your hand under the skin and rub some spice paste between the skin and the flesh. Rub the remaining paste evenly over the outside of the chicken.

3 Blanch the lemons in boiling water for 1 minute and drain. With the flat side of a knife, lightly smash eight of the remaining garlic cloves. In a small roasting pan, toss the garlic, apples, onion, and lemons with the reserved spice paste, adding a little olive oil and salt to taste. Use your hands to distribute the oil and the paste evenly among the vegetables.

4 Prop the chicken on a vertical roaster. Smash the remaining three garlic cloves. If the roaster has a basin underneath, fill the basin three-quarters full with water and add the smashed garlic cloves. If the roaster doesn't have a basin, set your roaster over a small baking pan half-filled with water and add the garlic.

5 Set the chicken and the roasting pan with the vegetables on a rack in the lower third of the oven and cook for 15 minutes. When the vegetables begin to brown, add 1 cup of the chicken stock. Roast the chickens until the skin is crisp and golden and the juices run clear when you pierce the thickest part of the thigh with a small knife, about 55 minutes total. Check periodically and replenish the chicken stock in the pan with the vegetables to keep them moist.

6 Remove the chicken and vegetables from the oven, and let the chicken stand for 5 minutes. Carefully remove the chicken from the vertical roaster, transfer to a cutting board, carve, and arrange on a serving platter. As you carve, pull the skin off the chicken back and scatter on top of the white meat. Transfer the vegetables with their liquid to a bowl to spoon over the meat.

Serves 3 to 4

Sometimes it seems that my entire career as an itinerant foodie can be summed up as a collage of sheep thrills.

In Iceland I once savored a lamb chop so pure and delicate I wanted to compare it to spring snow or a minty breath of fresh air. If Icelandic lamb is the world's greatest, it's because the local round-bellied sheep practically season themselves as they follow the snowline from mountains to coast, grazing on mosses and grasses that cushion Iceland's volcanic soil. So sweet is the milky-white flesh, local gourmets never even use salt.

On the parched plains of central Castille, earthenware *cazuelas* held whole quarters of the region's fabled *lechazo* (suckling lamb), roasted in wood-burning ovens by the growling, lisping maestros whose craft draws epicures from hundreds of miles around.

roast leg of lamb

My greatest memory of Uzbekistan is the wedding feast for twelve hundred for which dozens of kurdiuk sheep had been slaughtered and turned into epic kebabs. Among sheep connoisseurs, Central Asian fat-tailed sheep are legendary—as much for their fleece (used for Persian carpets) as for the huge deposits of deliciously creamy fat under their tails.

And how could I ever forget the whole spit-roasted sheep in the tiny Croatian town of Sinj? It was prepared in our honor by the lavishly mustachioed mayor, who showed his respect by cleaving the head with an ax, scooping the brain out right with his hands, and shoving the tremulous mass onto our plates. I ate it. Because I really really like lamb.

So do Romans, who can't imagine Easter without baby *abbacchio*. And the Greeks and Albanians, the Turks and Iranians, the Aussies and Kiwis. Only Americans have been treating lamb with suspicion, consuming a meager one pound per capita per year compared to around 60 times that of beef. But thankfully, this is changing.

For all the steakhouse lamb chops, fancy racks, and those omnipresent braised shanks, meat dishes don't get simpler and more rewarding than a roast leg. A leg of lamb is the perfect shape to carve into neat beautiful slices. A 7-pound joint cooks in just over an hour, and unlike turkey or pork loin, there is much less danger of drying thanks to the generous layer of fat basting the meat as it roasts. While leg of lamb is delicious rare, it is also terrific when slow-roasted to a melting well-done, which is how most of the world's lamb-loving nations prefer it.

Lamb also tends to be tender. That's because to be labeled lamb and not mutton, the animals must be brought to market up to a year old, five to seven months being standard in the United States and normally younger elsewhere. In the past, spring lamb was available only, well, in spring, the season's sacrificial rites indelibly tied to rituals of rebirth practiced by Christians, Muslims, and Jews alike. However, improved breeding now guarantees young lamb year-round, though to be properly classified as "spring lamb" by the USDA, it has to be sold from March to October.

Most domestic lamb is reared on grain and wheat. This renders American sheep big, tender, and tasty, but lacking that special savor of grass-fed sheep of southern Europe, the Middle East, and Down Under. But things are looking up here, too, with lamb from Sonoma, boutique Colorado farms, and such visionary producers as Summerfield Farm and Jamison Farm (see Resources) setting new standards. For lamb lovers out there, it's a brave new world.

mint-crusted roast leg of lamb with tart plum sauce

cook's notes If you like, scatter some parboiled halved small red potatoes in the pan, tossing them with a bit of olive oil and some of the mint crust mixture. Or bake a Gratin Dauphinois (page 214) alongside. My favorite sauce for roast lamb (as well as for grills) is this tart, lavishly spiced condiment from the Republic of Georgia.

Its name, *tkemali,* comes from the deliciously sour Caucasian plum, which is unavailable in this country. The best substitutes are underripe fresh prunes (Italian plums), but you can also use unripe black or red plums. Georgians also improvise with rhubarb or unripe blackberries.

tart plum sauce

3 cups (about 2 pounds) pitted chopped unripe fresh prunes, unripe black or red plums, or sliced rhubarb

1 cup water

1 to 2 teaspoons sugar (optional)

2 large garlic cloves, crushed through a press

1 teaspoon crushed or ground coriander seeds

Large pinch of fenugreek (available at Indian and Middle Eastern groceries)

1 teaspoon dried savory or mint

½ teaspoon Aleppo pepper, or ¼ teaspoon red pepper flakes (use more for spicier sauce)

½ cup finely chopped cilantro leaves

1 to 2 tablespoons chopped tarragon leaves, if available

Salt

lamb

12 garlic cloves, peeled

⅓ cup dried mint, crumbled

1½ tablespoons coarsely ground black pepper

1 tablespoon coarse salt

½ cup olive oil, or more as needed

1 shank-end leg of lamb, about 6 pounds

1 Make the tart plum sauce: Place the plums and water in a medium nonreactive pan and bring to a boil. Cover and simmer the plums over low heat until soft, 15 to 20 minutes. The plums and their cooking liquid should be very tart; however, if you would like the sauce a little sweeter, add sugar to taste. Cool the plums for 30 minutes.

2 In a blender or a food processor, process the plums with their cooking liquid to a coarse puree. Add the rest of the ingredients and process just to combine. Transfer to a bowl and let stand for at least 2 hours before serving. (The sauce will keep in the refrigerator for several days.)

3 Make the lamb: Crush 6 garlic cloves through a press. In a small bowl, combine the mint, garlic, pepper, and salt with enough oil to make a medium-coarse paste.

4 Sliver the 6 remaining garlic cloves. With a tip of a small knife, make ½-inch-deep slits in the lamb. Insert the garlic slivers into the lamb, coating them first with a little of the mint mixture. Rub the remaining mint paste evenly over the lamb.

5 Preheat the oven to 425°F. Place the lamb on a rack set over a roasting pan and roast for 25 minutes. Turn the lamb over and continue roasting until the meat thermometer inserted in the fleshiest part registers 130°F. for medium-rare meat, 30 to 35 minutes longer. Turn the lamb once more during roasting. Remove the lamb to a carving board, cover loosely with foil, and let stand for 10 minutes. Carve the lamb into thin slices and serve with the plum sauce on the side.

Serves 6

resources Jamison Farm (tel: 800-237-5262; or www.jamisonfarm.com) is your source of truly exceptional grass-fed organic lamb.

ackson Heights, New York, the intensely Latino barrio where I live, is probably the *sancocho* capital of the world. Our sancocho is Dominican, Colombian and Panamanian, Venezuelan and Puerto Rican. It's hen sancocho on Monday, pigeon pea sancocho Tuesday, oxtail sancocho Wednesday, and always a fish sancocho on Friday. There've been times in my life where I ate pretty much nothing but sancocho for days, and it never occurred to me to complain.

Sancocho is the epitome of Criollo cuisine, perhaps the ultimate post-Columbian pan-Latin stewpot. Protein, broth, and soft chunks of tropical tubers, all crowded into one hearty bowl, sancocho is to Latinos what pot-au-feu is to the French, borshch to Ukrainians, and *bollito misto* to Italians. The very essence

sancocho

of *comida casera* (home cooking), it inevitably also shows up at street fairs and restaurants. And while its roots are in Spain—perhaps even North Africa—its heart beats in the New World. Like salsa, the music, it transcends national boundaries, even if a number of countries claim sancocho as *their plato tipico.*

The word *sancocho*—from the verb *sancochar,* or "to boil lightly"—resonates with multiple meanings. You can have an aesthetic sancocho (a potpourri), a sancocho of sound, a sancocho of ideas. If it's hot and you swelter, you're sancocho, while a sancocho on the street denotes a disorganized crowd. Sancocho also happens to be a popular name for bands, songs, magazines, and volumes of poetry.

The dish has its origins in Iberian *cocidos* and *pucheros* (boiled dinners), as well as the proverbial medieval *olla podrida* (literally "rotten pot"), a clay vessel in which ingredients were left to simmer sometimes for weeks, with a this or that added at whim. The *olla* itself most likely derives from a Jewish dish called *adafina*—a North African Sephardic equivalent of cholent: a potage of beef, chicken, chickpeas, and eggs set on the stove on a Friday before sunset to stew overnight, so that no cooking was performed on Shabbat. The Iberians appropriated the *adafina* and transformed it into *cocido,* adding pork, bacon, and sausages to Catholicize it.

As *cocido* went on its New World adventures, it met and teamed up with similar indigenous concoctions—such as the Caribbean *ajiaco,* a liquidy stew of tropical tubers prepared by Taino Indians; and the Inca *locros,* porridges often based on corn. The classic *cocido* components of Iberian chickpeas and cabbage would be either replaced with or bolstered by indigenous corn, potatoes, yams, yuca, plantains, and squash.

No two sancochos, need I say, are ever alike. They range in scope from a modest Panamanian hen soup, to a Venezuelan *sancocho cruzado* that combines meats and fish, to a celebratory Dominican *sancocho de siete carnes* ("seven meats"), an extravaganza of smoked pork, longaniza sausage, chicken, beef—even goat. Still, there are shared traits. Sancocho is thicker than a *sopa* (soup) and brothier than a *guiso* (stew). It usually includes a whole repertoire of tropical tubers, plantains, and chunks of corn on the cob. Because these tubers are bland, sancocho is likely to be sparked with *sofrito*—the Latino flavor base consisting of garlic, chiles, tomatoes, and often cilantro. Eat it with rice. Pile on the sliced onion and avocado. And don't skimp on the hot sauce. ¡*Que rrrr-ico!*

beef and pork sancocho

cook's notes Sancocho is a great, rugged winter meal-in-a-bowl gone all zesty and tropical. Chicken, fish, oxtail: Latin sancochos are legion. I love them all, but none more than one prepared with short ribs and pork spareribs by my Colombian ex–cleaning lady, Pia. Her sancocho teemed with meats, yuca, plantain, and calabaza, zapped with a piquant *sofrito* of pureed cilantro, tomatoes, and chiles. If your meats are fatty, make the broth in advance and refrigerate for easy degreasing. With rice, sancocho makes a fabulous one-pot dish for a crowd.

If you're not familiar with tubers like yuca and green plantains, you will discover a whole new world of texture. These Latino staples are found at any Hispanic market and many regular grocery shops in urban areas. When you shop for yuca, buy an extra bark just in case, as it tends to be of uneven quality.

meat and broth

1 large onion, quartered

8 garlic cloves, smashed

1 large carrot, cut into chunks

2 pounds meaty beef short ribs, trimmed of excess fat

2 pounds meaty pork spareribs

4 quarts water

Salt and freshly ground black pepper

vegetables

1 pound yuca (see Cook's Notes)

2 small green plantains

3 medium boiling potatoes, peeled and quartered

1 large carrot, cut into chunks

1 pound calabaza or pumpkin, seeded, cleaned, and cut into 1½-inch chunks

2 ears corn on the cob, each hacked crosswise into 4 pieces

1 Make the broth: Tie the onion, garlic, and carrot in a cheesecloth bag for easy removal. Place the beef and pork in a large pot, add water and the cheesecloth bag with the vegetables, and bring to a boil over high heat. Skim the foam that rises to the surface. Season with salt and pepper, reduce the heat to low, cover, and cook, skimming periodically, until the meats are tender, about 2 hours. (Don't worry if the pork cooks faster than the short ribs.) If the stock is fatty and full of dregs, degrease it and strain it into a clean pot. Remove and discard the cheesecloth bag with the vegetables. With a slotted spoon, transfer the meat to a bowl. When cool enough to handle, remove the bones, gristle, and excess fat; cut the meat into large chunks and place back in the pot. (If preparing the broth ahead of time, cool the meats in the broth.) Adjust salt and pepper to taste.

2 Prepare the vegetables: Hack the yuca bark with a cleaver or heavy knife crosswise into 3-inch sections. Working lengthwise, slash off the skin from each section (including the pink part underneath) with a sturdy vegetable peeler or large sharp knife. Slice the ends of the plantains. With a small knife, make two continuous slits along the length of each plantain, one inside and one outside the curve. Cross-cut another continuous slit around the periphery of the plantains at the middle. Under cold running water, insert your thumbs under the skin and pry it away from the flesh. If there are bits of skin still stuck to the flesh, cut them out with a knife or they will discolor during cooking. Break the plantains into pieces with your fingers. Keep the yuca and the peeled plantains in a bowl of ice water until ready to use.

3 Bring the broth with the meat to a simmer over medium heat and add the yuca, plantains, potatoes, and carrot. When the broth returns to a simmer, reduce the heat to medium-low and cook, partially covered, for 15 minutes. Add the calabaza and corn, and cook until all the vegetables are just tender, 15 to 20 minutes longer.

4 While the soup is simmering, make the *sofrito*: Place all the ingredients in a blender, add 1 cup of the simmering stock, wait a few minutes for the stock to cool, and puree until smooth. Stir the *sofrito* into the soup and cook until all the vegetables are very soft and some are beginning to dissolve into the broth, about 10 minutes or more. Adjust the amount of salt and pepper to taste. Let the sancocho stand for 10 minutes before serving.

5 To serve, ladle the vegetables, meat, and broth into large bowls. Invite the diners to add about ½ cup of cooked rice, sliced avocado and red onion, cilantro, lime juice, and hot sauce to their sancocho.

Serves 8

sofrito

½ cup chopped onion

½ cup chopped green bell pepper

6 large garlic cloves, chopped

1 large jalapeño chile, seeded and chopped

1 teaspoon dried oregano

½ teaspoon ground cumin

1 teaspoon paprika

2 large underripe tomatoes, chopped

1 tablespoon distilled white vinegar

½ cup chopped cilantro leaves (or more if you like cilantro)

Salt and freshly ground black pepper

accompaniments

Cooked white rice

1 Hass avocado, thinly sliced

1 small red onion, quartered and thinly sliced

1 small bunch cilantro, minced

Hot sauce of your choice

2 limes, cut into wedges

decisions decisions. Just thinking about which saté (spelled *satay* in Malaysia) to choose I was beginning to panic. It probably wasn't going to be anything as exotic or endangered as turtle meat, which some Balinese prize above all other satés. Nor was I sharing my heirloom recipe for *saté padang* made from beef tripe, lungs, and heart. Beef *saté lalat?* Too tiny (*lalat* means "fly"). *Saté ayam* (chicken)? Too common. That narrowed it down somewhat, leaving me with at least four dozens saté ideas—and that's just from Indonesia. Then there are the multitudes of meats-on-a-stick from Malaysia, and the delicious pork satés with pineapple dip dispensed by Chinese hawkers in the back alleys of Singapore. Not to forget satés from Thailand: chicken or beef cosseted in a lush coconut and red curry marinade and dipped into a smooth-sweet peanut sauce.

saté

I smacked my lips as my thoughts turned to *saté lillit*. This delicacy I once tasted at a Balinese religious ceremony consists of exquisite skewers of seafood paste infused with kaffir lime and a complex curry paste, impaled on lemongrass sticks and grilled over coconut chips. Then my thoughts wandered from the unexpectedly wonderful rabbit saté I chanced upon at a murky Javanese joint in Rotterdam to the famous saté of Melaka, Malaysia. I recalled hailing a rickshaw that delivered me to a remote stall specializing in *saté celup*. This Melekan delicacy turned out to be a kind of fondue: sticks of raw meats, seafood, and fish balls that one cooked by dipping them in a bubbling, hissing caldron of spiced broth. After cooking the meat, you helped yourself to a whole smorgasbord of fiery sauces and condiments arrayed on the counter. I remember losing count after twenty-two skewers.

Believing that nothing is unsaté-able, Southeast Asians have over the centuries created a whole dollhouse universe of satés—Lilliputian morsels of meat or fish marinated in a thicket of spices with dark, sweet soy sauce (*ketcap manis*), lime, and sometimes coconut milk. These are threaded on wooden sticks, grilled over charcoal, and served with one or more dipping sauces. Throughout Southeast Asia satés are a street food more common than hot dogs at Fenway Park, offered by vendors who patiently fan their little braziers with bamboo fans. You can smell the sweet-smoky aromas from blocks away. Today, *saté* is the lingua franca of Southeast Asian cooking, but its spiritual birthplace is believed to be Indonesia where it most probably arrived—first as kebab—with the Arab spice traders who traveled to Sumatra in the twelfth century from Indian ports.

For all the dazzling diversity of Southeast Asian satés, the kind closest to my heart, I decided after much pondering, is the classic Malaysian version. Say saté, and I picture myself hovering over a vendor on a street corner in Kuala Lumpur, waiting hungrily for him to finish charring his skewers and to hand me a dozen of these without so much as a plate. The accompaniment is an incomparable peanut sauce spooned unceremoniously into a plastic bag. The sauce is rich and sweet with palm sugar and coconut, fiery from the rempeh chile paste, textured with the crunch of coarsely ground peanuts. It's so delicious I could just eat it on its own with a spoon. Another accompaniment to a Malaysian saté is a sprightly salad of cucumber and pineapple to offset the sugar. This is meat-on-a-stick raised to an art form.

malaysian chicken and lamb saté with peanut sauce

cook's notes

Undeniably, the tastiest satés are done on the grill, with its heat caramelizing the sugar in the marinade. But in winter the broiler will also do. Instead of lamb, this saté can be made with beef, such as skirt steak or sirloin cut into strips; and instead of strips, you can cut the meat into ¾-inch cubes.

1 Make the marinade: In a mini food processor or a blender, process all the marinade ingredients to a medium-fine paste. Divide the marinade between two bowls, add the chicken to one bowl and lamb to the other bowl, and toss the meats to coat with the marinade. Season lightly with salt, cover with plastic, and refrigerate for 2 to 6 hours. Bring the meat to room temperature before grilling.

2 While the meat is marinating, make the peanut sauce: In a heavy medium saucepan, heat the oil over low heat. Add the spice paste and stir until the paste is aromatic and the oil separates, about 5 minutes, adding a teaspoon of coconut milk if the paste sticks to the pan. Add the cumin, coriander, and curry powder and stir for 30 seconds. Add the remaining coconut milk and bring to a simmer. In a bowl, whisk the peanut butter with ¼ cup of the water until smooth and stir into the saucepan along with the remaining ¾ cup water. Stir until the sauce is smooth, bring the mixture to a simmer, and cook over medium-low heat until the sauce is lightly thickened and flavorful, about 7 minutes. Add the ground peanuts, soy sauce and 2 teaspoons of the sugar and taste, adding more sugar if you like the sauce sweeter. Season with salt, transfer to a serving bowl, and let the sauce stand while grilling the meat.

meat and marinade

3 tablespoons chopped shallots

2 tablespoons chopped fresh ginger

2 lemongrass stalks (3 inches of the lower stalk, tough outer leaves discarded)

1 tablespoon rempeh (spice paste; page 142) or store-bought Thai red curry paste

2 teaspoons rice vinegar

½ cup canned coconut milk, well shaken

1 tablespoon palm sugar, maple syrup, or light brown sugar

1 tablespoon soy sauce

2 teaspoons best-quality curry powder

1¼ pounds chicken breast or boneless thigh meat, cut into ½-inch-wide strips

1¼ pounds boneless lamb leg meat, cut into 3 by ½-inch strips

Salt

3 Prepare the coals for grilling (medium-high heat) or preheat the broiler. Remove the chicken and beef from the marinade and thread on separate skewers, using about two beef or chicken pieces per skewer. (If using long metal skewers, thread about four pieces on each skewer.) If using bamboo skewers, grill one skewer first to see if the ends burn. If they burn, snip off the ends not covered with meat. Brush the skewered meats with the oil-sugar mixture and grill or broil 3 inches from the source of heat until cooked through, about 3 minutes per side, turning the skewers with tongs and brushing the other side with the oil-sugar mixture.

4 To serve, line a platter with kale leaves and toss the pineapple and cucumber together in a bowl. Place the bowl with the sauce in the center and surround with the meat skewers. To eat, dip a saté in the sauce and follow by a bite of pineapple and cucumber mixture.

Serves 6 as a sit-down appetizer, 12 as an hors d'oeuvre

peanut sauce

2 tablespoons peanut or canola oil

1 tablespoon rempeh (spice paste; page 142) or store-bought Thai red curry paste

¾ cup canned coconut milk, well shaken

½ teaspoon ground cumin

½ teaspoon ground coriander

Large pinch of best-quality curry powder

½ cup smooth unsalted unsweetened peanut butter

1 cup water

½ cup coarsely ground dry-roasted peanuts

1 tablespoon dark soy sauce

2 to 3 teaspoons palm sugar, maple syrup, or light brown sugar

Salt

for serving

24 (8-inch) bamboo skewers, soaked in cold water for 1 hour, or 12 to 15 long metal skewers

3 tablespoons vegetable oil stirred with 2 tablespoons dark brown sugar, for brushing the meat

Decorative red kale or red leaf lettuce, for serving

1 cup diced slightly underripe pineapple

1 cup diced cucumber

China's noodles flourish as an edible life force, from wheaty and dense to slinky and almost transparent, from flat bands to thin slippery threads. They land in the bowl hand-cut or machine-made, shaved from big globs of dough into the boiling water, forced through a sieve, or swung, twisted, and pulled in the air into seemingly endless strands.

It's widely believed that large-scale production of noodles took off in Han Dynasty China around the first century A.D. The technique of milling wheat in large quantities had recently arrived here, probably from the Middle East, along the Silk Route. Prior to this, steamed millet was the staff of life in northern China, while wheat was consumed in the form of steamed berries, usually by the poor. Chewy and slightly bitter, these won no popularity contests.

sesame noodles

But *ping*—a Han word for noodles, dumplings, and buns made by blending flour and water—was another matter. *Ping* noodle foods flourished initially in China's north, where the climate was conducive to wheat cultivation. Here, *ping* provided cheap, filling food for cold months; and unlike bread, noodles didn't require rising or baking. While emperors reportedly indulged in noodles occasionally, learned fourth-century author Shu Hsi describes *ping* as "an invention of the common people."

Over time, noodles gradually began to acquire cachet, and by the 1660s, *ping* were positively "in," relished by both peasants and emperors. Around this time a Qing Dynasty poet, Li Yu, offered a very modern recipe for "Noodles Befitting a Gentleman." "Keep it simple," he counseled wisely. For fine noodles he prescribed a restrained elegant dressing of broth, soy, and vinegar, or a splash of sesame oil and a cool garnish of slivered bamboo shoots. Clearly, the man knew his noodles.

These days, the Chinese eat their noodles in soups under a shower of garnishes. They mold them into crisp pan-fried pillows for saucy stir-fries. They fashion them into dramatic deep-fried nests for nouvelle seafood creations. Noodles exist to be stir-fried, deep-fried, and braised in sandpots. And they are beautiful cold, infused with a spiced chile oil or laced with a piquant, creamy dressing.

Which finally brings us to the legendary Sichuan *don-don mian*—sesame or peanut noodles. Well made, this Sichuanese street food consists of delicate noodle strands dressed to order with a smooth sesame sauce that hums with ginger, chile, and garlic. Cool cucumber slivers contribute a lovely textural contrast. Every vendor has his or her sauce formula and *don-don mian* isn't always necessarily cold: in China I've had some outstanding hot versions consisting of thin wheat noodles floating in peanut broth drizzled with tongue-searing chile oil, or tossed with stir-fried pork and moistened with sauce before serving. As for the curious moniker—*don-don*—it's onomatopoeic for the banging that announces the noodle vendor's cart as he threads his way through the clamorous streets. Like the jingle of American ice cream trucks, it's the sort of sound that makes your mouth water.

sesame noodles

sesame sauce

½ cup Chinese roasted sesame paste at room temperature, well stirred (or use smooth all-natural peanut butter)

½ cup chicken stock, canned broth, or water

3½ tablespoons Chinese black vinegar, or equal parts Worcestershire sauce, rice vinegar, and thin balsamic vinegar

¼ cup soy sauce

2½ tablespoons Chinese rice wine (Shaoxing) or medium-dry sherry

2 tablespoons Asian (toasted) sesame oil

1½ teaspoons hot Asian chile paste, or more to taste

3 large garlic cloves, crushed through a press

1½ tablespoons minced or grated fresh ginger

2 tablespoons sugar, or more to taste

Good-quality Chinese chile oil to taste (optional)

1 Make the sesame sauce: In a bowl, whisk the sesame paste with the stock until completely smooth. Whisk in all the other ingredients until well blended. Let stand for 30 minutes for the flavors to develop. (You can also blend everything in a blender or food processor.)

2 Bring a large pot of salted water to a rolling boil. Untangle the noodles, add to the pot, swish with chopsticks a few times to untangle further, and cook until slightly al dente, about 1½ minutes for fresh Chinese noodles. (If using spaghetti or linguine, cook according to the instructions on the box.) Drain the noodles, transfer them to a bowl, toss with the sesame oil, and let cool to warm or to room temperature.

anya von bremzen

254

3 Blanch the carrots in boiling water for 30 seconds and refresh under cold running water. Pat dry with paper towels.

4 To serve, place the bowl of noodles in the middle and arrange bowls of shredded chicken, carrots, cucumber, scallions, cilantro, sesame seeds or crushed peanuts, and sauce around it. To eat, toss the noodles with the other ingredients on a plate and drizzle with the sauce.

Serves 4 as a light luncheon dish

12 ounces fresh thin Chinese wheat noodles (*sun mian*) or thin spaghetti or linguine

1½ tablespoons Asian (toasted) sesame oil

2 cups carrots cut into matchsticks or shredded

2 cups shredded cooked chicken breast meat (optional)

1½ cups matchstick-sliced seeded cucumber

¼ cup finely sliced scallions, white and green parts

½ cup torn cilantro leaves

¼ cup toasted sesame seeds or crushed dry-roasted peanuts

udon is stubby, wheaty, and earnest. Somen is elusive and slippery. Soba, however—with its dark stylish hues, long slender strands, and elegant grainy nuttiness—has all the transient beauty of a haiku. If soba inspires cultlike devotion, it's because good soba can seem purer than spring water, more restorative than grandmother's chicken soup, more spirit-lifting than St. John's wort.

"Buckwheat is sweet, contains no poison, relaxes the nerves, eases irritability and helps to clear out the stomach and intestines," a Japanese nutritional text from 1697 proclaims. Modern science confirms that soba noodles are loaded with vitamin P (bioflavonoids, the stuff that dissolves bad cholesterol); vitamin B_1, which just might calm your nerves; and enough fiber to keep your digestive system going like clockwork. The choline in buckwheat is also a panacea for alcohol-ravaged livers—which is why all those "festive" Japanese guys pack into soba parlors at the end of a night on the town.

soba

For centuries the Japanese relied on buckwheat for porridges, steamed cakes, and dumplings. But no written mention of buckwheat noodles—*sobakiri*—exists before the 1660s. Historians assume that these noodles (inspired by the udon and somen that the Japanese borrowed from China almost a millennium earlier) were conceived in the late 1500s in the Buddhist monasteries of northern Japan. Apparently the monks made a pretty penny selling soba to pilgrims.

From these sacred confines soba marched into the streets during the construction of Edo (Tokyo) in the early seventeenth century, when hordes of rural laborers descended on the newly founded imperial capital. They needed food, fast and cheap, and soba was just the fuel. Over the next several decades soba houses were edging out udon and somen parlors, and by the nineteenth century soba was Japan's national fast food. The aristocracy craved soba, too, indulging in it at deluxe establishments where exquisitely austere handcrafted noodles came with fine sake and rarefied atmosphere. Not much has changed since.

On the fast-food side, Japan boasts thousands of slurp-and-run soba counters and even more *insutanto* soba machines dispensing the noodles into Styrofoam cups. At the other end, you have the *te-uchi* (hand-crafted) connoisseur's soba. Fashioned from newly harvested freshly milled buckwheat, the dough is kneaded by hand, rolled out on cypress wood with special dowels, then artfully cut right before boiling. This is the boutique artisanal stuff one swoons over at haute-rustic noodle temples of Tokyo and Nagano (Japan's great soba mecca).

Buckwheat flour is low in gluten—the protein that makes pasta elastic—so the dough takes a highly specialized skill to work. To make the strands pliable, mass-produced soba noodles are stretched out with wheat flour, often anywhere from 60 to 90 percent. (There are sobas made with other starches, too, like yam, and in flavors like green tea, mugwort, or squid ink.) In contrast, *kiko-uchi,* the expensive, artisanal soba, is almost pure buckwheat. Unless handled by a true soba master, this fragile dough chaffs and breaks. What you're paying for at the high end is that aromatic, earthy pure buckwheat sensation.

Soba can be served in hot dashi-based broth (*kako soba*) or cold (*mori soba*), topped with anything from tempura to grated radish, slices of duck, sweet tofu, or a whipped mountain yam. It all depends on where you're eating it. A true test of a soba master, however, is *zaru soba*. Named for the slatted bamboo tray that holds the noodles, this is the purist's soba, served cold au naturel, save for a tiny flourish of nori and scallions, and a bit of *tsuki-jiru,* a dipping sauce composed of dashi, mirin, and shoyu. To heighten the taste you get a bowl of soba cooking water, *soba-yo,* to sip. Pure noodle nirvana.

chilled zaru soba
with dipping sauce

cook's notes When buying dried soba at Asian or health food stores, you may or may not be able to figure out the percentage of buckwheat to wheat flour from the package label. Sometimes the labels are only in Japanese, sometimes they just don't say. Unless you know a good Japanese grocery store, the best bet for high-quality 80 percent buckwheat soba (*hachiwari soba*) is to mail order it (see Resources).

The loveliest and the most authentic way to present soba is on a *zaru*, the Japanese bamboo tray sold at Japanese markets and craft stores. The trays are inexpensive and elegant to have around. If you like, add flavors like grated ginger or orange zest to the dipping sauce.

12 ounces dry soba noodles, preferably 80 percent buckwheat

Salt

1 cup instant dashi (kelp and bonito broth), prepared according to package instructions

½ cup plus 2 tablespoons shoyu soy sauce

1 tablespoon rice vinegar

¼ cup mirin (sweet Japanese wine)

3 tablespoons *katsuobushi* bonito flakes, if available

1 sheet nori seaweed, toasted lightly over a gas flame and julienned

¼ cup finely sliced scallions, for garnish

¼ cup finely grated daikon, for garnish

Wasabi

1 Bring a large pot of water to a boil over high heat. Add the soba and reduce the heat to medium. When the water comes back to a boil, stir the noodles with chopsticks and add about ¾ cup cold water. When the water returns to a boil, add more cold water and repeat this process one more time. Cook the noodles until slightly al dente, 6 to 8 minutes. (If using soba with a high percentage of wheat flour, cook it in boiling water without adding cold water for about 6 minutes.) Drain the soba and rinse under cold running water, running your fingers through the noodles to untangle.

2 Transfer the soba to a tray lined with paper towels and drain until dry. Place in a bowl and refrigerate, covered, until cool. If the noodles clump together, rinse and dry again.

3 In a small saucepan, combine the dashi, soy sauce, rice vinegar, and mirin and bring to a simmer. Add the bonito flakes and remove from the heat. After 5 minutes, strain the sauce into a serving bowl, cool, and chill.

4 To serve, divide the soba among Japanese bamboo baskets or rustic ceramic bowls, and sprinkle each portion with toasted nori. Serve the garnishes and individual small bowls of the dipping sauce on the side. To eat, either grab a tangle of soba with chopsticks and dunk it in the dipping sauce bowl, or spoon some dipping sauce over your portion.

Serves 4

resources Katagiri is a great source of high-quality soba and other Japanese ingredients (tel: 212-755-3566 or *www.katagiri.com*).

there was a time when I would never order soufflé at a restaurant, let alone cook it at home. For no good reason, I dismissed the soufflé as an old-school haute cuisine caricature, an inflated French myth that refused to collapse. The day I tasted eleven soufflés and was still craving more changed all that.

This happened at an old Paris restaurant off the posh rue Rivoli, called, fittingly, Le Soufflé. Its owner, the dapper, soft-spoken Claude Rigaud, seemed like a man on a mission: to guard the reputation of what he deems France's most majestic creation. Monsieur Rigaud has been at it for forty-plus years, serving 400 soufflés daily—eight sweet, eight savory—to packed houses.

No one knows when some smart cook whipped up the first batch of egg whites, mixed them with one thing or another, and realized that heat would

soufflé

expand them like little balloons in the oven. But we do know that by the late eighteenth century, soufflé—from the French word "to puff up"—was solidly tethered to the repertoire of most French patissiers. We can also infer from Antonin Carême's detailed and sympathetic instructions in *Patissier Royal Parisien* that, much like today, the possibility of deflation gave many cooks the jitters.

Nerves notwithstanding, the soufflé has remained for almost two centuries a haute cuisine warhorse, ordered well in advance and doted on by waiters as if it were the empress's jewels. Yet today in France the great soufflé tradition is being lost, M. Rigaud lamented. And the ones who care least about it are the French. "Maybe it's too precious and delicate for the young generation here," M. Rigaud wondered aloud. "Those kids . . . they just want steak."

As we tasted puffy clouds in timeless flavors such as foie gras, *fruits de mer*, and Roquefort, it struck me how different each one was from the next, how delicate and fleeting its nature, how each ingredient contributed subtle but significant variations in texture. Even when three of us ordered identical spinach soufflés, each one arrived with its own unique character, as if it were still breathing and living, a thing of the moment, impossible to clone even within a single kitchen.

Perhaps it's this ephemeral essence of the soufflé, its transience and fragility, that people confuse with complexity. Because, as my visit to M. Rigaud's kitchen proved, there's nothing difficult about making a soufflé—as long as you follow a few simple rules.

All soufflés are made up of two components, explained M. Rigaud. First, the base, prepared with béchamel and egg yolks, to which one adds individual flavorings. This base can also contain a dense fruit puree, be thickened with cornstarch, or be prepared with a pastry cream. Roux- and egg yolk–based soufflés are the least temperamental, which is why they are so loved by restaurants. Can you make white sauce? Then you can tackle a soufflé.

Into this sweet or savory base one folds beaten egg whites, which will puff up from contact with heat. Their consistency is important: the whites should be beaten vigorously until they form soft but solid peaks—about 2 minutes. Whisked until too glossy and grainy, they'll be too dry to support the weight of the base; overbeat, and the soufflé will crack.

Soufflé rates as the most anxiety-provoking of dishes; the fear of The Fall leads cooks not to blink, sneeze—let alone open the oven—while it's baking. This myth caved in as I watched Le Soufflé's oven door swing open and shut almost constantly to accommodate incoming orders. What prevents a soufflé from rising properly, Rigaud insisted, is a sloppily treated mold: it must be buttered and floured generously and evenly, or the cloud will stick to the sides and disaster is all but assured. For further security, sprinkle the mold with grated cheese, or with sugar if the soufflé is sweet.

When the moment came to judge M. Rigaud's creations, the magnificent Roquefort and walnut soufflé emerged as a winner. Its combination of lightness and strong personality was irresistible. Anyone who thinks soufflés are old hat is just full of hot air.

claude rigaud's roquefort and walnut soufflé

cook's notes You can play with the format here by making one large soufflé using one 1½-quart (6-cup) soufflé dish or eight smaller appetizer portions baked in ⅔-cup dishes. Serve the soufflé for lunch with a simple, lovely salad of peppery greens.

Once you master this Roquefort soufflé, the béchamel and egg yolk base in this recipe can become a blank canvas for experimentation. Instead of the Roquefort, try 1½ cups grated sharp Cheddar or 2 cups Gruyère, plus finely chopped scallions and crisp bacon bits; or 1½ cups flaked poached salmon or smoked white fish, lemon, and dill; or minced garlicky sautéed mushrooms and a little Parmesan; or 8 ounces crumbled goat cheese with tiny bits of roasted red pepper. For chocolate soufflés, add 8 ounces of grated good semisweet chocolate and ½ cup sugar to the flour-milk mixture and stir over low heat until the chocolate melts. Off the heat, whisk in the egg yolks as directed and sprinkle the buttered and floured ramekins with sugar instead of cheese.

3½ tablespoons unsalted butter, plus 4 teaspoons at room temperature for greasing the soufflé dishes

3½ tablespoons all-purpose flour, plus more for dusting the soufflé dishes

2 teaspoons grated Parmesan cheese

1¼ cups whole milk

Salt and freshly ground white pepper

Small pinch of freshly grated nutmeg

3 egg yolks, beaten

1¼ cups crumbled Roquefort or Gorgonzola cheese

5 large egg whites, at room temperature

Large pinch of cream of tartar

⅓ cup coarsely chopped toasted walnuts

1 Grease four 10-ounce (1½-cup) straight-sided soufflé dishes liberally and evenly with the 4 teaspoons of the butter. Sprinkle lightly with a few pinches of flour and Parmesan, tilting and rotating the dishes to coat them completely. Tap off the excess. Place the prepared dishes in the refrigerator until ready to use.

2 In a small, heavy saucepan, melt the 3½ tablespoons butter over low heat. When it foams, add the 3½ tablespoons flour and cook, whisking, for 1 minute without letting it brown. Turn the heat up to medium and slowly pour in the milk, whisking constantly to prevent lumps from forming. Simmer, whisking, until the mixture is thick and smooth, about 5 minutes. Season with salt, pepper, and nutmeg to taste. Off the heat, whisk in the beaten yolks, little by little. Whisk in the Roquefort, stirring until most of the cheese melts. Scrape this mixture into a large bowl and cool to room temperature. (The base can be prepared ahead and refrigerated for up to 1 day, with plastic wrap placed directly on the surface.)

3 Preheat the oven to 400°F. In a large bowl, beat the egg whites with a pinch of salt until frothy. Add the cream of tartar and continue beating until the whites form solid peaks but are not dry, about 2 minutes. With a rubber spatula, fold one-third of the beaten whites into the base, then gently fold in the remaining whites and the walnuts. Keep folding the mixture gently until no bits of white remain.

4 Using a large spoon, drop one-fourth of the mixture into each dish. Smooth the top with the back of a spoon. Run your pinky finger or the tip of a knife around the edge of each dish.

5 Place the dishes on a baking sheet, transfer the sheet to the lower third of the oven, and bake for 7 minutes. Reduce the oven temperature to 325°F. and continue baking until the tops are puffed up and golden and the interior is just set, 18 to 22 minutes. (The French like their soufflés runny, but I prefer them cooked until a toothpick inserted in the center comes out clean.) Serve the soufflés immediately.

Serves 4 as a substantial appetizer or a light luncheon course

geography is destiny when it comes to the pasta passions of Italians. Ask them to name their absolute favorite, and Apulians will rave about orecchiete with broccoli rabe, Sicilians insist on spaghetti with fresh sardines, Romans boost bucatini with that strong *guanciale*-enriched Amatriciana sauce, while Ligurians single out troffie with pesto. But ask an Italian—any Italian—to name his or her second favorite pasta, and the response will likely be a chorus: *spaghetti alle vongole*. Spaghetti with clams is the roast chicken of Italian cuisine—unfussy, direct, satisfying, and unanimously adored. Though I've had pretty sensational versions at restaurants far from the sea, the dish is the essence and the common denominator of Italy's coastal *cucina*, regarded as a regional specialty from Naples to Venice, from Livorno to Rimini, from Bari to Bordighera.

spaghetti alle vongole

Spaghetti with Clams

The very mention of *spaghetti alle vongole* transports me to old seafood trattorias at weather-beaten Italian ports. Like the precious place called Sottomarino that I once stumbled upon in a chaotic backstreet of Livorno in Tuscany. A kind of neo-realist red-checkered-tablecloth dive you thought disappeared with the films of de Sica, it was packed with large unruly families and sailors who strolled in with their "dates" for the night. The *cacciucco*, a Livornese seafood stew simmered until the fish becomes as melting as confit, was spectacular. But what sent the whole place into a communal swoon was the sublimely soupy spaghetti studded with tiny bivalves and accented with flecks of hot pepper. I recall, too, a salty old place called Il Pescatore—blue-checkered tablecloths this time—in the Apulian city of Bari. Grizzled wisecracking waiters patiently grilled whole octopi out on the sidewalk and the pasta came in huge communal bowls, brightened by mint and a handful of tiny *pomodorini* that burst with the concentrated sweetness of early fall. Sucking the small sweet clams out of their shells, I was almost delirious with joy.

One reason for the ubiquity of *spaghetti alle vongole* is its ease of preparation. In its simplest form it's nothing but thin pasta, good small clams, fragrant olive oil, garlic, and a flourish of parsley. In its most elaborate form, it's still pretty much the same—perhaps embellished with a splash of white wine, a teaspoon of cornstarch to thicken the sauce, some seafood broth, a few pepper flakes, or a handful of cherry tomatoes. *Pasta alle vongole* is prepared more often *bianco* than *rosso* (with tomatoes); some like it drier, some soupier; some leave the clams in their shells, others don't. And that's really about it. The essence remains immutable. It's the simplest thing in the world and it never fails to remind us why we are crazy about Italian food.

spaghetti alle vongole

cook's notes What makes this pasta so special when you sample it at good places in Italy are the clams: the twin-horned *vongole veraci*, translated as "carpet shells." A little bigger than a quarter with a brittle striped shell, they are sweet but strong tasting, imparting the briny perfume of the sea. My favorite substitute are cockles, the teensy clams found at Asian groceries or good fishmongers. Otherwise, use any clams—Mahogany, Manilas, steamers, Littlenecks—as long as they are *small*, preferably no more than 1½ inches in diameter (over 2 dozen per pound).

Kosher salt

2½ pounds cockles or other very small clams (see Cook's Notes), well scrubbed

½ cup fragrant good-quality extra-virgin olive oil

2 large garlic cloves, smashed, and 1 medium garlic clove, minced

Tiny pinch of red pepper flakes, or to taste

⅓ cup dry white wine

¼ cup bottled clam juice

12 ounces thin spaghetti or linguine

8 beautiful vine-ripened cherry tomatoes, quartered (optional)

¼ cup minced flat-leaf parsley, or more to taste

Salt and freshly ground black pepper

1 Place the clams in a bowl, cover with cold water, add 2 tablespoons Kosher salt, and let soak for 1 hour to remove any sand. Drain.

2 Bring a large pot of salted water to a boil for the pasta.

3 Meanwhile, in a heavy saucepan large enough to accommodate the cooked spaghetti later, heat ¼ cup of the oil over medium-low heat. Add the smashed garlic cloves and sauté until fragrant but not browned. With a slotted spoon, remove the garlic from the pot, add the minced garlic and red pepper flakes, and sauté for 30 seconds. Add the clams, the wine, and clam juice and cook over high heat until the liquids are slightly reduced, about 1 minute.

Cover the pan tightly, reduce the heat to medium high, and cook, shaking the pan occasionally, until all the clams open. Discard any unopened clams. If you don't like too many clam shells in your pasta, remove some clams from their shells, discard the shells, and toss the meats back into the pot. (You'll certainly want to get rid of some shells if using cockles.) Turn off the heat.

4 Add the spaghetti to the boiling water and cook until very al dente. Drain the pasta, reserving 1 cup of the cooking water.

5 Turn on the heat under the clams to medium, add the remaining ¼ cup of the oil and the tomatoes, and cook for 30 seconds. Add the pasta, toss gently with the clams, and add just enough of the pasta cooking water to make a moist sauce. Turn the heat down to low and cook the pasta with the clams, shaking the pot as you cook, until the pasta is done to your liking, about 1½ minutes for al dente. Add a little more of the cooking water if the pasta looks dry. Season with salt and pepper to taste, toss in the parsley and serve at once.

Serves 2 or 3 as a main course, or 4 or 5 as a pasta course

O f all my epicurean idylls, a week-long stay on Crete some years ago lingers in my memory as the sweetest. It was the height of the wine-making season. Then at its ripest, most benevolent stage, the fall brought finger-size squash, a profusion of *horta* (wild greens), and riots of apples and quince.

"Don't drive," locals warned. "The roads are slippery with fermented grape juice that leaks from the trucks."

But who could pass up roads slick with wine? So friends and I packed into a car with a food-obsessed local who claimed to know every taverna on Crete, and went roaming in search of great, simple meals. Everywhere we went, we found pies.

spanakopita
Spinach Pie

"Pitta (pie) is to the Greeks what pasta is to the Italians—food to warm the soul," says food writer Diane Kochilas. Truly protean things—simple, nourishing fillings between layers of dough—*pittes*, or *pitaki*, flourish on the islands and the Greek mainland in astounding profusion: the endless roster of *tyropitakia* (cheese pies); Cephalonian pies with a meat filling seasoned with sweet Byzantine spices; island pies stuffed with stewed octopus or salt cod and potatoes. Pies are offered to guests as a welcome, wrapped in foil and taken to work, turned out en masse for village festivities.

And *pittes* are the crowning glory of Cretan gastronomy: small pies, grand ones, pies fried or baked, thin as a pancake, or twisted in a coil and curled like a snail. One afternoon, we discovered a pie paradise under an old mulberry tree at a taverna in Vrahasi, a somnolent whitewashed village with a pair of Byzantine churches and an Ottoman fountain. As soon as we sat down, Eleni, the owner, mosaicked the table with plates of pies. There were *sarikopites*, or coiled pies bulging with myzithra, a ricotta-like whey cheese, eaten drizzled with honey. In the *kreatopita*, a lamb filling flavored with cumin and allspice spilled out of its sturdy bread-dough casing. There was a big, tall pie with a custardy center of minted cheese and zucchini—a Western Crete specialty, Eleni informed us. And there were little open cheese pies called *lichnarakia,* or oil lamps. But the best was a pie filled with spinach, wild fennel, esoteric field greens, and sharp cheese.

This was *hortopita,* the rugged country cousin of the *spanakopita* (spinach pie) we all know and love from Greek diners in the United States. In the spanakopita, the filling is tall and rich with eggs and cheese, reminiscent of Renaissance Italian pies like the Genovese *torta pasqualina* of chard and cheese. In the Cretan greens pie, the spinach is replaced or augmented with *horta*: wild field greens, from poppy leaves to mustard greens to purslane and edible chrysanthemum leaves. The effect is wonderfully aromatic.

Below I offer a Cretan variation on spinach pie inspired by a recipe from my friend Diana Farr Louis. A food writer living in Athens, Diana is the author of a wonderful book called *Feasting and Fasting on Crete,* in which she shares some pie epiphanies of her own. As I eat this pie, my Cretan sojourn and Eleni's *pitaki* under the mulberry tree come to mind.

spanakopita with wild greens

cook's notes If you prefer, you can use puff pastry or phyllo instead of the delightfully rugged village red wine pastry offered here. The wild greens used on Crete might include wild carrot, leek, wild fennel, beet tops, furry thistles, and edible chrysanthemum. At home, experiment with the likes of collard or turnip greens, chicory, dandelion, broccoli rabe, curly endive, beet greens, Swiss chard, or arugula— as long as you have a mixture of sweet and bitter greens. For a fluffier, more urban pie like those you know from Greek diners, you can add 1–2 beaten eggs to the filling.

1 Make the red wine pastry: In a large bowl, sift together the flour, salt, and baking powder. Gather the flour into a mound, make a well in the middle, and add the olive oil and wine. Swirl the flour in from the sides into the liquid ingredients, mixing in all the remaining flour. The dough will form in big, coarse crumbs. Knead in enough of the warm water to form a dough that sticks together. Turn the dough out onto a lightly floured surface and oil your hands. Knead the dough, adding a little more flour if it feels too sticky, until soft and smooth, about 7 minutes. Place the dough in an oiled bowl, cover with plastic, and let rest for at least 15 minutes. (The dough can be prepared the day before and refrigerated.)

2 Make the filling: Rinse the greens and the spinach well and squeeze out the water thoroughly with your hands. Chop them all finely and mix the greens and spinach in a bowl with the parsley, mint, scallions, and fennel fronds. In a large, deep skillet, heat the oil over medium-low heat and sauté the onion and fennel bulb until softened, about 5 minutes. Add the greens and cook, stirring until wilted, about 6 minutes. You might have to add the greens to the skillet in batches, letting the first batch wilt to allow for space. Season with sugar, salt, and pepper to taste. Transfer the greens to a colander and let drain for at least 15 minutes, pressing lightly to extract excess liquid and oil. Transfer to a bowl and stir in the feta and the eggs, if using. Adjust the seasoning as necessary. Let the filling cool completely. (The filling can be prepared up to a day ahead.)

red wine pastry

3½ cups all-purpose flour

¾ teaspoon salt

2 teaspoons baking powder

½ cup olive oil, plus more for greasing the pan

½ cup dry red wine

⅔ to ¾ cup warm water

OR 1 package frozen phyllo dough, thawed for 15 minutes; OR 1 (17½-ounce) package frozen puff pastry, thawed (see Variation)

anya von bremzen

3 Preheat the oven to 375°F. Divide the pastry into two balls, one slightly larger than the other. On a lightly floured surface, roll out the larger piece of dough into a rectangle about 12 by 15 inches.

4 Grease a 10 by 13-inch baking pan with the olive oil. Line it with the dough and spread the filling on top. Roll out the second piece of dough slightly smaller than the first and lay it over the filling. With scissors, trim off some of the bottom edge if necessary and fold the bottom edge over the top crust, pinching tightly to seal. With a sharp knife, lightly score the top into serving portions and make a few small slits in the top for steam vents. Brush the top with the egg wash. Bake until the top is golden, about 50 minutes to 1 hour. Cover with a kitchen towel and let rest for 10 minutes. The pie is best slightly warm or at room temperature and tastes even better the next day.

Serves 8 to 10

filling

1½ pounds assorted greens (see Cook's Notes), tough stalks removed

1½ pounds spinach, tough stalks removed

3 tablespoons finely chopped parsley

3 tablespoons finely chopped mint

1 bunch firm, young scallions, including 2 to 3 inches of green, finely chopped

3 tablespoons finely chopped fennel fronds or tender dill

½ cup olive oil, preferably Greek

1 medium onion, finely chopped

¾ cup finely chopped fennel bulb

1 teaspoon sugar

Salt and freshly ground pepper

7 ounces good Greek feta, finely crumbled

1 or 2 large eggs, beaten (optional)

1 large egg yolk beaten with 1 teaspoon milk

variation To make the pie with puff pastry, which some Greek cooks prefer to commercial phyllo, you will need two sheets from a 17½-ounce package, defrosted. Roll out the pastry and assemble the pie as directed in steps 3 and 4 of the main recipe. Brush the top with the egg wash and bake at 350°F. until golden brown, about 45 minutes.

If using phyllo, you will need 12 phyllo sheets, thawed in the package if frozen. To assemble the pie, oil a 10 by 13-inch baking pan and line it with four or five sheets of phyllo, brushing each sheet with a little olive oil. Spread the filling on top and cover with four or five more sheets of phyllo, folding over the bottom edges to form a rim. Brush the top with oil and bake at 350°F. until golden brown, about 45 minutes.

steak

good food is good food, but a steak is existential: thick as *War and Peace,* suavely charred and cholesterol-charged, a 2-inch-thick stomach-filling slab of protein to celebrate life's bounty. Even if the American steak of today is decidedly leaner than its predecessor thirty years ago, is there a more vital expression of feeling right with the world than declaring, "I feel like a steak!"?

The word *steak,* meaning beef cooked in strips on a stake or stick, goes far back to Middle English. Not indigenous to the Americas, beef cattle were exported to the West Indies by Columbus during his 1493 voyage, later making its way to Mexico with Hernán Cortés and to the American Southwest with the Spanish explorer Francisco Vasquez de Coronado. The hardy, primitive descendant of the Iberian cattle ran wild and multiplied famously in the shrublands of Texas. This was the Longhorn, that ur-American breed. (In the late nineteenth century, Longhorns were crossbred with fatter, more flavorful British breeds, such as the English Shorthorn, to create the tender beef we all crave today.) In the early 1800s Western ranchers began seriously herding livestock to market, a practice that culminated in the legendary cattle drives of the late 1800s, when great herds of livestock were "walked" north to midwestern and other markets along a series of mythical cattle trails, like the Shawnee, Chisholm, and Great Western.

The next great event in steak history was the introduction of refrigerated rail cars in 1871, allowing fresh corn-fattened beef to travel from the stockyards of Kansas to steak lovers in New York and Chicago. The archetypal New York style steakhouses—Keens Chop House, Old Homestead, Peter Luger—opened their doors in the 1880s, and this genre of restaurant continued to flourish, reaching its heyday during Prohibition (classics such as Palm and Gallagher's doubled as speakeasies). By the end of World War II, beef replaced pork as America's favorite meat.

In recent cholesterol-wary times, beef consumption has been decreasing, even with the resurgence of steakhouses. The amount of marbelized fat in fine beef has also been dropping alarmingly—and in spite of the claims of "leaner but just as tasty" beef, good old streaks of fat are what distinguish a great steak from a merely decent one. Prime, the highest of the three beef grades now used by the USDA, which are based mostly on marbling, applies to only 2 to 3 percent of all graded beef. And even among Prime beef, standards vary quite significantly. Almost all Prime goes to restaurants, mostly steakhouses, and to Japan. Your second-rank Choice steak in today's supermarket is usually a pretty wan piece of bounty, with Select not even worth mentioning.

Sadly, there's also the dying out of "dry aging," the controlled and formerly common process of hanging good beef for several weeks so that its enzymes break down the proteins, leaving the tissues softened and mellowed and the flavors intensified. Dry aging is expensive and time-consuming, so these days even some of the top steakhouses don't bother. One has to be grateful for great old beef bastions, like Peter Luger in Brooklyn, for keeping the practice alive.

Happily, these days you can partake in the pleasure of dry-aged USDA Prime steak in the clubby comfort of your own home. Instead of paying astronomical prices at a steakhouse, you can pay astronomical prices and mail-order it from one of the healthy number of boutique shippers (see Resources on page 275). Shelling out over $30 a pound for beef hurts, but it hurts so good. Nobody said existential pleasure comes cheap.

pan-seared rib-eye with argentinean parsley sauce

cook's notes There are many methods to tell if the steak is done to your liking: you can touch it (spongy for rare, springy for medium), you can time it, you can eye it. However, with a pricey steak, why leave things to chance? Get an instant-read meat thermometer.

Below I offer a recipe for what I consider to be an ideal at-home steak: a succulent, well-marbled boneless rib-eye (New York strip will also do nicely) pan-seared to a beautiful crustiness, finished with a little garlic butter, and served with a puckery parsley sauce. The sauce, called Chimichurri, is the national meat condiment of Argentina, a country where they know a thing or two about beef. Chimichurri is my all-time favorite sauce for just about any meat or chicken, seared or grilled.

argentinean parsley sauce (chimichurri)

1½ cups chopped flat-leaf parsley

6 large garlic cloves, chopped

¼ cup boiling water

2 teaspoons dried oregano

¼ to ½ teaspoon red pepper flakes

1 teaspoon freshly ground black pepper

1 teaspoon Goya adobo seasoning (optional)

Salt

¼ cup mild olive oil

⅔ cup red wine vinegar

1 Make the parsley sauce: In a mini food processor, process the parsley and garlic until finely minced but not pureed, adding a little vinegar, if necessary, to assist the blending. Scrape into a bowl. Add the boiling water and let stand for 10 minutes to wilt the parsley a little. Add the rest of the ingredients and mix well. Adjust the seasoning to taste and let the sauce stand for at least 30 minutes for the flavors to meld. (The sauce is best made ahead and will keep in the refrigerator in a clean jar for up to a week.)

anya von bremzen

2 Prepare the steak: Sprinkle the steak liberally with salt and pepper and brush on both sides with the oil. Let stand for 30 minutes or refrigerate, covered with plastic, for up to 6 hours, bringing it to room temperature before cooking.

3 Choose a cast-iron or a heavy nonstick skillet large enough to accommodate the steaks without crowding. If in doubt, use two skillets. Open your windows and turn off your smoke alarm. Heat the skillet over medium heat for 7 to 8 minutes. While the skillet is heating, stir the softened butter with the crushed garlic. Turn the heat up to high, add the steaks to the skillet, and cook for 4 minutes, until a nice crust forms. Flip the steaks and cook on the other side until a meat thermometer inserted into the thickest part registers 115°F. for rare or 125°F. for medium-rare, 3 to 4 minutes longer. Brush the steaks with the garlic butter and remove to a platter lined with paper towels. Tent with foil and let stand for 5 to 7 minutes. Serve whole or sliced with the Argentinean parsley sauce.

Serves 3 or 4

resources Among this country's best purveyors of dry-aged beef is Lobel's Prime Meats New York (tel: 800-556-2357 or *www.lobels.com*).

steak

2 boneless rib-eye or New York strip steaks (14 to 16 ounces each), about 1½ inches thick

Kosher salt and freshly ground black pepper

1 tablespoon olive oil, for brushing the meat

1 tablespoon unsalted butter, softened

1 large garlic clove, crushed through a press

a many-splendored thing is Chinese cuisine. There's poultry roasted until its skin is fine and brittle as spun sugar. There's gingered steamed fish with white, immaculate flesh. There are lavalike hotpots, cool silken tofu dishes, and dumplings that explode in the mouth with a deep-flavored broth. Yet for all the tea-smoked squab, red-braised pork, white-cooked chicken, and myriad noodle creations, no other Chinese dish makes me happier than a plate of beautifully stir-fried leafy greens. Kissed with the intense heat of the wok, bathed with a little soy sauce and broth, laced with garlic and ginger, these greens are so healthy and delicate some of us would happily eat them five times a day.

stir-fried greens

When I want to feel virtuous I eat Chinese greens with brown rice. (I detest brown rice, but the greens make it palatable.) When I sit down for a blow-out Cantonese banquet I get an order of greens—and then two more. When company comes, however, I prefer to cook broccoli rabe instead, since no wok is ever big enough to accommodate the demand. No matter how much stir-fried Chinese greens you serve them, guests will always leave the table craving more. Chinese greens may be a pleasure best kept to oneself.

A ramble through a Chinese market is all about the pleasure of greens, but making sense of them can be bewildering. Here's a quick field guide, in my order of preference.

Pea Shoots: Delicate curly tendrils of the pea plant that taste sweetly of spring. To cook, separate the leaves from the stems (because of shrinkage you'll need to start with 2 pounds for two to three servings) and stir-fry in a flash—no more than 30 seconds. Young leaves are also lovely raw in salads. If the stems look tough, remove them.

Gau Choi (Chinese chives): Long flat shoots with an addictive garlicky-oniony taste. Old ones can be woody, but the tender shoots are juicy and crunchy (nibble on one before buying). Trim the hard ends off the stalks, cut into 4-inch lengths, and stir-fry quickly in a very hot wok with a little chile and garlic. Even more delicious are the flowering chives: they're the ones with a little bud. Yellow chives are also wonderful, but are better added to stir-fried meats or fish.

Bok Choy (Chinese cabbage or Chinese kale): The first thing to know about bok choy is how astoundingly healthy it is—packed with calcium, folic acid, vitamin C, and just about everything else the nutritionist ordered. The second thing is that it's downright delectable. Last but not least, you can find bok choy at most supermarkets. To cook, separate the stalks and leaves from the cluster and rinse extremely well—or better, soak in cold water for 10 minutes. The fat juicy stalks take longer to cook than the leaves; cut them off, slice on the diagonal about ½ inch thick, and fry for about 1 minute before adding the leaves. Bok choy is also a joy simply steamed and drizzled with sizzling oil that has been heated with crushed garlic and chile.

Shanghai Bok Choy (baby bok choy): A big bok choy in miniature, it turns an iridescent emerald when cooked. The spoon-shaped white stems are the best part.

Ung Choy (water spinach or water convolvulus): Grown along swampy riverbanks, it has delicate stems that are crunchy and hollow, with elongated pointy leaves and a sweet subtle flavor. Best stir-fried with a little chile sauce.

Choy Sum (Chinese flowering cabbage): It's hard to miss with its small flowering heads that peep out among the leaves. The sturdy stems are actually more tender than they look; the leaves are deliciously peppery. Sliver and stir-fry the stems for about a minute before adding the leaves. *Choy sum* takes a little longer to cook than the more delicate greens.

Gai Choy (Chinese mustard greens, mustard cabbage): This is the big leafy bunch with curved stalks you first mistook for romaine lettuce. The flavor is assertive and a little astringent, making it a good candidate for Sichuan pickles. Usually eaten steamed or boiled in soups, it is also quite tasty when thinly sliced and stir-fried.

Once you bring your Chinese greens home, figuring out what to do with them is a no-brainer. While some, like *gai choy*, are best steamed, most beg to be stir-fried. All you need is a red-hot wok, a light hand with oil, a handful of seasoning, and a watchful eye for a minute or two while the greens cook.

chinese stir-fried greens

cook's notes Intense heat and a good wok are the secrets to perfectly stir-fried greens. As for flavorings, keep them simple to let the character of the greens come through. All greens, but especially bok choy, should be washed thoroughly or even soaked to get rid of grit. For greens with sturdy or juicy stems, add the stems to the wok first and cook for about 1 minute before adding the leaves.

2 pounds Chinese greens

1½ tablespoons peanut or canola oil

1 teaspoon Asian (toasted) sesame oil

6 medium garlic cloves, thinly sliced

½ tablespoon minced fresh ginger

¼ teaspoon Chinese chile paste or sambal oelek

3 tablespoons light chicken broth

2 tablespoons Chinese rice wine (Shaoxing) or medium-dry sherry

½ tablespoon soy sauce

Salt

1 Rinse the greens thoroughly under cold running water, pat dry lightly with a paper towel, and see text above for description and handling.

2 In a large wok, heat the peanut and sesame oils over the highest possible heat until almost smoking. Add the garlic, ginger, and chile paste and stir for 30 seconds. Add the greens and stir-fry for 1 minute, until they just wilt. (You might have to add them in two batches.) Add the broth, rice wine, and soy sauce; reduce the heat to very low, cover, and steam for 2 more minutes. With a slotted spoon, transfer the greens to a serving platter, shaking off the excess liquid. Serve at once.

Serves 3 or 4

from the very first bite, Vietnamese food enraptures you with its playful delicacy and effortless chic. The flavors are clean without being plain, virtuous without being austere, transparent without a trace of blandness. It's hard not to fall instantly for the minty, peppery crunch of the *rau* (aromatic herbs), the sweet-pungent grace notes of Vietnamese dipping sauces, the mahogany caramel sheen of the *kho* (those irresistible claypot dishes flavored with a caramel sauce called *nuoc mau*). Still, the best things are the rolls, either the dainty and crunchy fried *cha gio* (imperial rolls) or the intriguingly chewy uncooked rice paper wrappers rolled around cool salady things.

One of the glories of Vietnamese roll-ups is the wrapper itself. Called *banh trang,* this parchment-thin rice paper is a uniquely Vietnamese contribution to the world of food. Many low-lying provinces in Vietnam

summer rolls

produce *banh trang,* but the best come from Nam Trang, a city thirty miles south of Saigon also famed for its rice cakes. In this drowsy town, about a hundred families still eke out a living making rice paper by hand. This is backbreaking work. Women usually start pre-dawn by boiling water in a huge pot over fire powered with rice husks. Over this pot they steam paper-thin crepes made of rice flour, water, and salt. By noon, they might have gone through 20 pounds of rice flour.

The steamed crepes are spread out to dry in the sun—there's no production during the rainy season—and cut into squares or rounds. That characteristic crosshatched imprint is from the bamboo mats on which the *banh trang* dry. Perfectionist *banh trang* makers might dry them further in a special furnace, then spread them out again in the evening to absorb some nocturnal dew, for that extra resilience. The finished dried rice paper is a curious-looking thing, suggesting some translucent brittle plastic skin. A good one should be strong, shiny, and completely elastic when reconstituted with water. *Banh trang* is to the Vietnamese what the tortilla is to the Mexicans: an all-purpose envelope for stuffing with a whole universe of hot and cold foods, from a simple salad to the ingredients for an elaborate fondue feast called *bo bay mon,* or "beef seven ways."

For spring rolls—called *cha gio* in the south, *nem ran* in the north, and imperial rolls outside Vietnam—rice-paper rounds are packed with a filling of crab (or minced shrimp), grated taro, ground pork, tree ear mushrooms, and cellophane noodles, all bound with an egg. More charming still are the *coi gun.* The name translates roughly as "salad rolls," but Vietnamese restaurateurs call them, poetically, "summer rolls." For *coi gun,* uncooked moistened rice paper is rolled around slices of pork or chicken, pink shrimp halves, herbs, and perhaps a lettuce leaf, producing a lovely contrast of textures. Fancy East-West restaurants might stuff summer rolls with everything from roasted duck to prosciutto and figs. But in all honesty, it's hard to improve on a classic. Finger food doesn't get any sexier—or more Vietnamese.

summer rolls with mint, chicken, and shrimp

cook's notes This is a sort of salad to be eaten out of hand, perfect for serving at a summer fête. You can play with the filling, adding salmon, Chinese roast duck or pork, other herbs, shredded carrot or bean sprouts, even slivers of fruit. Or dab with some aioli instead of Hoisin.

The rolls must be rolled tightly and neatly; use all your fingers for best results, tugging and bunching as you roll. If you have a choice, I recommend the Kim Tar brand of rice paper rolls. Serve these with *nuoc cham* dipping sauce or the sesame sauce from the sesame noodles recipe on page 254, or both.

18 large shrimp, unpeeled

4 ounces rice vermicelli

12 round 8-inch rice paper wrappers

12 small leaves red leaf lettuce, ribs removed

Hoisin sauce, well stirred

12 ounces cooked chicken breast meat, coarsely shredded by hand

24 large mint leaves

12 sprigs of Chinese garlic chives or regular chives

Nuoc Cham Dipping Sauce (recipe follows) or Sesame Sauce (page 254)

1 Bring 3 quarts of salted water to a boil. Fill another bowl with ice water. Place the shrimp in a small sieve, lower the sieve into the water, and cook for exactly 2 minutes. Remove the shrimp to a bowl of ice water, reserving the cooking water, and cool for 5 minutes. Peel and devein the shrimp and pat dry with paper towels. Cut each shrimp in half lengthwise.

2 In a large bowl, soak the rice vermicelli in warm water to cover until soft and pliable, about 15 minutes. Bring the shrimp cooking water back to a boil. Place the vermicelli in a small sieve, lower the sieve into the boiling water, and cook the vermicelli for exactly 30 seconds. Drain the vermicelli, rinse under cold running water, and pat dry thoroughly with paper towels. Using scissors, cut them into 2-inch lengths, then divide into 12 portions.

3 Prepare 13 paper towels by moistening them with water and squeezing until just damp. Fill a very large bowl with hot (but not boiling) water and immerse one wrapper in water for about 10 seconds. Spread the moistened wrapper on a damp paper towel, dip your hand in the hot water, and with the palm of your hand, pat and smear some water evenly onto the wrapper. If a bit of wrapper feels dry under your hand, pat on a little more water. Cover the wrapper with another damp paper towel. Repeat this process with the remaining wrappers, stacking them between damp paper towels. Let the moistened wrappers stand for about 5 minutes.

4 Arrange all the filling ingredients around you. Remove the paper towel from the top wrapper. Trim one lettuce leaf to fit the wrapper and lay it across the bottom third of the wrapper. Dab the leaf lightly with Hoisin sauce. Arrange one portion of the vermicelli on the leaf about 1 inch from the bottom of the wrapper and pack it into a compact 4-inch cylinder. Arrange three shrimp halves cut sides up, with tails pointing down, across the top third of the wrapper, about 2½ inches from the top. The shrimp row should be parallel to the vermicelli cylinder. Lay a few pieces of chicken and two mint leaves across the vermicelli, keeping the log neat and compact. Fold the bottom edge of the wrapper over the vermicelli filling and roll it once as tightly as you can without breaking the wrapper. Fold in the sides to enclose the shrimp. Now lay a garlic chive across the wrapper so that it extends out from the roll on one side. Keep rolling tightly to the end (over the shrimp), pressing on the filling to keep it compact. The finished roll should have shrimp visible on one side and a chive extending from one end. As you work, place the finished rolls seam side down on a tray lined with damp paper towels. The finished rolls should be covered with damp paper towels until ready to serve.

5 To serve, cut the rolls in half on the diagonal and serve with the nuoc cham or sesame sauce.

Makes 12 rolls

nuoc cham dipping sauce

1 In a small saucepan, heat the sugar and water, stirring, until the sugar just dissolves, about 3 minutes. Let cool.

2 In a mixing bowl, combine the sugar mixture with all the remaining ingredients. Taste the sauce and adjust the balance of sweet, sour, and salty to taste. Let the sauce stand for about 30 minutes before serving.

Makes 1⅓ cups

- 5 tablespoons sugar
- ⅔ cup water
- ⅓ cup fresh lime juice
- 6 to 7 tablespoons fish sauce (*nam pla*), to taste
- 3 or 4 red bird's eye chiles, thinly sliced
- 1 large garlic clove, crushed through a press
- 2 to 3 tablespoons cilantro leaves

admittedly, to really understand sushi you have to prowl the narrow streets around Tokyo's Tsukiji fish market at 6 A.M., dodging the whizzing motorized carts and handtrucks of just-unloaded fish—and finally queuing outside the minuscule Daiwa-zushi. After what always seems like eternity, the waitress hustles you in and crams you against the short, narrow counter. There is nothing chic or designer here; just a battered smoky den where you're squashed in with fish-market workers well into their second bottle of sake and fellow bleary-eyed sushi fans. But, oh, the joys as the headbanded sushi *shokunin* (master) wields his knife and then passes down to you thumb-size morsels from heaven: deftly molded vinegared rice topped with sweet unctuous shrimp, petals of *tako* (octopus), or *ottoro* (extra-fatty tuna), its

sushi

flesh meltingly silky, astoundingly luxurious. Luxurious quite literally, being trimmings from fish that might have just auctioned off for $600 a pound to some fancy Ginza corporate men's club. And fresh beyond fresh—sushi *truly,* you

sigh, as you accept your last *tekka maki* roll in a sheet of toasty nori (dried seaweed), and quaff your simple *atsukan* hot sake with breakfast.

For a dish that's considered a celebration of freshness, sushi's origins are in fact the opposite. The raw fish itself is sashimi; *sushi* is a dish made with vinegared rice. *Tsukeba* ("pickling place") remains a term for a place where sushi is made because that's how sushi began: as a fish pickling method, probably in Southeast Asia's Mekong Delta. There, salted cleaned fish was layered with boiled rice and weighted down with a stone for some weeks, then lightly covered for months more. Lactic acid from the fermenting rice pickled and preserved the fish. When the dish was eaten, the mushy rice was discarded.

This method eventually crossed to Japan, where a 1,300-year-old version of "original" sushi survives to this day as *nare-zushi;* or *funa-zushi* (*sushi* takes on a z in these usages), a fermented tart delicacy featuring small carp from Lake Biwa in Shiba Prefecture. But the Japanese liked rice with their fish and did not like wasting precious grain and time. So they took to consuming the seafood still a little raw, tangy rice still intact. Hence, *nama-nare-zushi* (almost raw) was introduced in the fifteenth century. From here on, sushi began its evolution from a means of preserving to a style of cuisine.

In the seventeenth century, the notoriously impatient locals of Edo (as Tokyo was then known) got the taste, without all the labor, when vinegar was added to boiled rice to simulate the delicious tang of fermentation. Sushi as most of us know it today was born in the 1820s, thanks to one Hanaya Yohei, who hit on the idea at his outdoor Edo sushi stall of pairing sashimi with sushi—raw fish slices on thumbs of vinegar-tart rice. Prepared in the style called *nigiri-zushi* (squeezed), his morsels were a great hit. Portable sushi stalls began to proliferate in this era, and remained on city streets until post–World War II American occupation, later replaced with proper *sushi-ya* (restaurants) both humble and fancy.

Styles of sushi eventually settled into three major types, besides deluxe *nigiri-zushi* which is king. There's *oshi-zushi* (pressed sushi: rice and ingredients in a mold); *chirashi-zushi* (scattered sushi: seafood, cooked or uncooked, and vegetables strewn over a bowl of rice); and *maki-zushi* (a layer of rice topped with ingredients on a sheet of nori and rolled up). Rolled into a cone and uncut, it's *temaki-zushi,* or handroll, while *futomaki* denotes a fatter roll.

From utilitarian beginnings, sushi has rainbowed into the giddy postmodern worldwide thing it is today, limited only by chefs' skills and imagination, and the customer's wallet. After that unforgettable Tsukiji den, my second favorite Tokyo sushi place is Tokyo Shokudo Central Mikuni's, a swank neo-deco parlor where sushi dreams glide past you on a conveyer belt (that's called *kaiten-zushi*). Here, you'll taste sushi fancies they never dreamed of in old Edo: sushi with *neta* (toppings) like foie gras, paella handrolls with sea urchin, even a croissant sushi, as improbable as it is delicious. And not a pickling tub in sight.

sushi for a party

cook's notes My favorite (if lazy) way of making sushi is to turn the whole thing into a party, laying out the rice, nori sheets, and various filling ingredients buffet-style and having the guests roll their own. The only rice suitable for sushi is Japanese short-grain or California medium-grain varieties, such as Nishiki or Calrose brands. Before cooking, the rice is scrupulously rinsed to remove extra starch; a process known as *togu*, which has the nuance of polishing rather than just washing. To mix the rice with the vinegar, the Japanese use a cypress wood tub (*hangiri*) and a wooden paddle, but any shallow bowl and two wooden spatulas would do. For rolling sushi, there are bamboo mats called *maki-su* or *sudare*, but you'll be fine with a cloth napkin or simply without.

You can also use the ingredients below to prepare the simple *chirashi* sushi, which means rice placed in bowls and scattered with toppings. For chirashi sushi, the fish should be cut into slices rather than strips, the toppings arranged decoratively on the rice, and the whole sprinkled with toasted white sesame seeds or julienned nori. If your nori sheets taste listless and chewy, pass them very briefly over a low flame to toast. See Resources for ingredients and utensils.

rice

3 cups short or medium-grain Japanese or California sushi rice

½ cup rice vinegar

3 tablespoons sugar

2 teaspoons salt

A 2-inch square piece of *konbu* (dried kelp), wiped clean, if available

4 cups spring water

rolls

12 to 14 sheets nori (dried laver)

10 to 12 ounces sashimi-grade tuna or salmon, cut into ½-inch strips, or a combination

8 to 10 extra-large poached shrimp, butterflied

2 to 3 ounces *tobiko* (flying fish) roe or salmon roe

1 small bunch *shiso* or arugula leaves or both, cut into strips

1 Hass avocado, cut into ½-inch strips

2 firm Japanese cucumbers, peeled, seeded, and cut into ½-inch strips

Wasabi paste

Toasted white sesame seeds (optional)

Shuyu soy sauce, for serving

Gari (pickled ginger), for serving

1 Make the rice: Put a fine sieve over a large mixing bowl, place the rice in it, and add cold water to cover. Swish the rice in the water, pressing and rubbing it gently against the bottom of the sieve. Lift the sieve, drain the water from the bowl, add fresh water, and repeat the procedure. Do this once or twice more until the water in the bowl is almost clear. Cover the rice with water one final time and let it soak for 15 minutes. Lift out the sieve, rinse the rice, and leave it to dry for 30 minutes.

2 While the rice is standing, in a small nonreactive pan, mix the vinegar, sugar, and salt and heat, stirring, until the sugar dissolves, about 1 minute. Pour the seasoned vinegar into a cold mixing bowl (to stop it from cooking) and set aside.

3 Place the rice in a pot with a tight-fitting lid, add the kelp and the spring water, and bring to a boil over medium-high heat. Remove and discard the kelp, cover, and cook over low heat until all the water is absorbed and the rice is just tender, about 15 minutes. Remove the rice from the heat and let stand, covered, for 15 minutes.

4 While the rice is still hot, transfer it to a wooden tub or another large, shallow wooden or glass dish. Reserve 3 tablespoons of the seasoned vinegar for shaping the rolls. Using a rice paddle or two flat wooden spatulas, gradually mix in the seasoned vinegar by cutting and folding it thoroughly but very gently into the rice. Be careful not to stir or overwork the rice or else it becomes mushy. Cover the top of the rice with a damp towel and let it cool to slightly above room temperature. (Some Japanese cooks cool the rice by pointing a fan at it to get rid of excess moisture.) The rice is best fresh, but it can be prepared 2 to 3 hours ahead of time and kept at room temperature.

5 To make the *maki* rolls: Place a sheet of nori shiny side down on a bamboo mat or a cloth napkin with the long side facing you. Fill a small bowl with cold water and add the reserved 3 tablespoons of the seasoned vinegar. Wet your hands with this mixture and spread a thin, even layer of rice (about ¾ cup) on the nori sheet, leaving a ½-inch border on the long sides. Dip a spoon in the vinegar mixture and run the back of the spoon over the rice to smooth. Lay strips of tuna or salmon, a few shrimp halves, or some roe horizontally across the middle of the rice, dab with a little wasabi if you wish, and top with a shiso or arugula leaf and avocado or cucumber strips. The fish and vegetable strips should be arranged in a row end to end along the length of the nori sheet. Roll the sheet tightly away from you to enclose the filling, pressing down on the mat but holding on to the end of it so the mat doesn't get into the roll. Just before you reach the end, moisten the edge of the nori sheet not covered with rice with a little water and press to adhere. Press the roll down with your fingers to compact and give it one more full roll to give it a round shape. With a sharp, long knife, cut the roll into eight even slices.

6 To make handrolls: Place a nori sheet on a work surface with the long side facing you. Spread the rice on the left half of the sheet, place strips of desired fillings diagonally across the rice, and roll it up like a cone.

7 Invite your guests to roll more rolls, using different combinations of fish, shrimp, roe, vegetables, and leaves. To make inside-out rolls, spread the nori with the rice on a piece of plastic wrap, cover with the bamboo mat, and invert so that the nori sheet is on top. Inside-out rolls are nice sprinkled on the outside with sesame seeds or *tobiko*. Eat the rolls dipped into shoyu mixed with a little wasabi, followed by a little ginger.

Serves 6 as a light meal

resources Sushi Foods Co. (tel: 888-817-8744 or *www.sushifoods.com*) is a good source for sushi rice and rice vinegar; they also sell sushi starter kits with all the utensils.

When I lived in San Diego, every jaunt to Tijuana ended with a stop at a legendary *taquería* called El Gordo. Even at five in the morning the crowd was five-deep: Oaxacan women with braids, lovers from TJ high society, partygoers with every imaginable rhythm still flickering through their knees—plus a few exhausted mariachis. Everything you need to know about the taco unfolded in front of you in the few square feet inside the stand at the pace of a Bond movie's opening credits. The *tortilleros* rolled out thin corn tortillas; their quick-fingered assistants softened them with steam from the meat cauldrons; the *taqueros* sliced the meat on a wooden block—the *tronco*—and filled the tortillas with the precision of plastic surgeons. It was an assembly line of tastes: every motion perfectly synchronized, no part of the cow wasted. Bauhaus-meets-the-border.

tacos

After some *carne asada* (broiled beef), and *carnitas* (crisp pork chunks), we'd ease our way into local favorites: tripe, tongue, head—all ordered *con todo*, meaning the works: guacamole, chiles, cilantro, plus a dozen smoky-charred scallions. For last, you saved a few quesadillas. Sheer bliss and double-bliss.

Taco means anything wrapped, folded, or filled in a tortilla. "Wad" or "plug" is how it translates from Spanish (perhaps after the cotton scrap used for ramming old-time firearms). The exact origins are unclear, but we know that *taco* is a robustly loose word, democratic and regionally inflected, with profound Mesoamerican roots. We also know that tacos belong to the family of little dishes called *atonjitos* or "little whims." In Mexico proper, they are snacks involving *masa* corn dough from which the classic tortilla, that jack of every trade, that Swiss Army knife of Mexican cuisine, is created.

While now pretty much everyone takes it for granted, corn *masa* (Spanish for "dough") represents an extraordinary culinary evolution over thousands of years. Maize or field corn (not the sweet corn of summer picnics) was the staple of Mesoamerican cultures even before the empire of the Aztecs. Hard and starchy, a product entirely of human cultivation and the stuff of worship and creation myths, it happened to supply the least nutrition of any major food staple. Until, that is, pre-Columbian Mexicans had the inspiration to soak and boil dried maize kernels in water made alkaline with either mineral lime or ash. This simple alchemy dissolves away the hardly digestible outer hull—and chemically unlocks the nutrient value of the corn. (Today, calcium hydroxide replaces lime and ash.)

This transformed maize, or *nixtamal,* could be further boiled to yield *pozole* (hominy), or ground on a volcanic stone *metate* with a *mano* roller to make masa. Fine-ground masa became tortillas, traditionally shaped by hand (more and more so by machine). Of course, tortillas are made from wheat flour, too. This is a *norteno,* north-of-the-border Tex-Mex and Cal-Mex style. Tex-Mex might have its own hoard of culinary riches, but Mexico's *corazón* remains corn.

The full range of what tacos can hold is a savory marvel, from crumbly white cheese and lard-silkened *refritos,* to batter-fried fish in Baja and luscious *cochinito pibil* pork from the Yucatán—to cactus paddles, to the *charales* (small lake fish), Maguey worms, or even ant roe or crispy fried grasshoppers. All to be garnished from an arsenal of add-ons: chopped raw onions mixed with cilantro, licks of hot red and green sauces, chunky salsas with their fierce bits of chiles, wedges of lime, and fresh radishes. Plus a certain unctuous garnish that also traces impressively to pre-Columbian times, a sauce of mashed indigenous avocados the Aztecs called *ahuaca-mulli:* guacamole.

carnitas tacos with tomatillo salsa

cook's notes Deciding what to put on a taco is a question one usually ponders while perched on a stool at a *taquería* or lingering by a *puesto*, or taco truck. However, there is no reason a taco feast can't take place at home. One of my favorite taco fillings is pork *carnitas*, the joy of any good Mexican *taquería*. Now popular throughout the Republic but originally from the south-central city of Michoacán, these are traditionally prepared by frying pork chunks in bubbling cauldrons of lard until moist, crisp, and sinful. But since *frying in lard* are not words most of you want to hear, here is a braised alternative, crisped at the end in a hot oven. To offset the richness of the meat I offer a green, tart salsa of charred tomatillos. You can also whip up some guacamole and a simple colorful salsa Mexicana made from 4 large diced tomatoes, finely chopped white onion, cilantro, serrano chiles to taste, and a tablespoon or so of fresh lime juice.

carnitas

4 to 5 pounds well-marbled boneless pork shoulder or butt, in one piece, tied

1½ teaspoons dried oregano, preferably Mexican

1 teaspoon coarse salt

½ teaspoon crushed pequin chiles or other smoky ground chiles

3 tablespoons olive oil

4 to 5 cups chicken broth or water

¼ cup fresh lime juice

¼ cup Coca-Cola

1 medium onion, cut into chunks

4 large garlic cloves, crushed through a press

2 bay leaves

1 long strip orange rind, white pith removed

1 Make the carnitas: In a large bowl, rub the pork with oregano, salt, and ground chile. Heat the oil in a heavy 6-quart braising pot and sear the meat on all sides. Add enough broth to come halfway up the sides of the meat, add the lime juice and Coca-Cola, and bring to a simmer. Add the onion, garlic, bay leaves, orange rind, and more salt if needed; reduce the heat to low and simmer, turning the meat several times until it feels extremely tender when pierced with a tip of a knife, about 3 hours.

tomatillo salsa

1 pound fresh tomatillos (about 12 large), husked, rinsed, dried, and quartered

2 to 4 whole serrano chiles, cut in half crosswise

2 medium garlic cloves

Half a small onion, cut into wedges

1 small Hass avocado, pitted and chopped

⅓ cup packed chopped cilantro leaves, or more to taste

Salt

for serving

18 corn tortillas

1 medium red onion, quartered and thinly sliced

⅓ cup packed torn cilantro leaves

2 limes, cut into wedges

2 While the meat is cooking, make the tomatillo salsa: On an ungreased *comal,* griddle, or cast-iron skillet, sear the tomatillos, chiles, garlic, and onion until gently charred all over, about 5 minutes. You will have to do this in two batches. Transfer to a bowl and let cool.

3 In two batches, puree the tomatillos, chiles, onion, garlic, and the avocado in a blender until medium-smooth, adding about 2 tablespoons of water to each batch. Transfer to a serving bowl and add the cilantro and salt to taste. Let stand for 30 minutes.

4 Preheat the oven to 475°F. With a slotted spoon, transfer the pork to a 9 by 13-inch roasting pan. Discard the string, and use two forks to pull meat into bite-size chunks. Pour 1 cup of the braising liquid over the meat and bake until the juices have evaporated and the meat is browned, about 15 minutes. Take care not to dry out the meat. Remove the meat from the oven and cover with foil while preparing the tortillas.

5 Warm the tortillas by steaming them in stacks of six in a large, wide steamer set over boiling water and lined with a clean cloth napkin or kitchen towel. (Alternatively, the tortillas can be microwaved for about 1 minute, in stacks of six, wrapped in a damp cloth napkin or a small kitchen towel.) Transfer the meat to a platter and toss with the red onion and cilantro leaves. Serve surrounded by lime wedges, with the tortillas and tomatillo salsa alongside.

Serves 6

fish tacos When I'm not eating meat tacos, I daydream about the piscine tacos of Ensenada, the fishing town south of Tijuana in Baja California. Here, you roam the stalls of the fish market, sizing up the day's catch. Finally staking a perch at the counter, you order a couple plugs of lightly battered white fish on soft corn tortillas, which you sprinkle with crisp shredded cabbage and drizzles of tartar-sauce–like *crema*—the white stuff among the battery of sauce bottles and bowls. With the tang of the nearby sea in the air and an icy Tecate in hand, it's a snack to make the heart sing.

Sea breezes aside, fish tacos are just as delicious prepared at home as they are at the Ensenada Mercado Negro fish market. Just use 1½ pounds firm white-fleshed fish fillets, such as mako shark, halibut, or marlin, cut into 2-inch strips, and the batter recipe and frying directions from Fish and Chips (page 96). Serve with finely shredded cabbage or iceberg lettuce, salsas of your choice, and a sauce made by whisking together ⅔ cup mayonnaise, ⅓ cup water, and ¼ cup fresh lime juice and salt to taste.

taking a Sunday afternoon stroll in Jackson Heights, my neighborhood, I thread along jammed sidewalks past Indian sari stores, gold jewelers, and DVD shops flaunting the latest loopiness from Bombay Bollywood. Now come the Uruguayan and Colombian bakeries, the trim Ecuadorian restaurant with its pig marquee for *hornata,* the rowdy Colombian bar with flag draped for the afternoon's soccer match. Men in *futbol* shirts gulp hasty cheese-sprinkled *arepas* and grilled chorizos from sizzling sidewalk carts. Cars bobbing with Dominican kids slide by blasting *bachata* music, while the immigrant's subway line, the no. 7, screeches and snakes overhead.

And there they are, finally, up at a corner by the subway staircases—the Mexican tamale ladies, hovering over their stockpots. My *paseo* had a purpose.

tamales

"*¿Verde o rojo?*" my Pueblan señora amiably demands: with red mole inside or hotter green? One of each, please. She leans into the steaming depths and brings out my party favors, at least that's what they look like. I move off in slow motion, savoring the childish pleasure of unfurling the steamy cornhusk wrappers—and then pause to fork up a hunk of silky-smooth masa corn dough with its fiery core. This is snacking as one of life's little glories. Fast food with an ancient and unbroken history, back to long before Columbus.

Versions of tamales have flourished forever throughout Latin America. Peru, Bolivia, Argentina, and Chile have their *humitas,* as the Incas called them. Venezuela has its Christmas *hallacas;* Puerto Rico, *pasteles* fashioned from starchy tropical tubers. But to a Mexican, the corn *tamal* (singular) is an icon, the very emblem of the national soul. Though daily fare, too, tamales are a dish specially associated with Mexican revelries—in particular *fiestas diciembrinas,* beginning with honoring the Virgin of Guadalupe on December 3, leading up to a week of Christmas parties (*posadas*), and on until Three Kings Day in early January (not to slight the Day of the Dead, Cinco de Mayo, baptisms, and weddings).

anya von bremzen

The first Spanish found the corn-worshiping Aztecs making what they called *tamallis,* in the original Nahuatl, for their festivals, too. Fray Bernardino de Sahagún, a Spanish friar and a great sixteenth-century chronicler of Aztec customs, admired the fare of a tamale seller at market: "tamales with beans forming a seashell on top . . . spotted tamales, red fruit tamales, turkey egg tamales . . . tamales of green maize, adobe-shaped tamales . . . gourd tamales. . . ." To this fanfare the Spanish brought something new: pigs—that is, lard. Before that, the Aztecs used oil from sesame or avocado seeds for flavoring; about animal fats or frying, in fact, they knew *nada.* The addition of animal broth and lard made masa smoother, lighter, and fluffier, changing tamales forever. Vegetable shortening can be substituted, but you won't find many *abuelas* taking this seriously.

The gamut of tamale types today runs into the dozens. The wrapping makes for a major division: banana leaves mainly in coastal and tropical Mexico, corn husks north and central. Tamales come small as a thumb (*tamalitos*), big as a child and twice as heavy (like the 150-pound Yucatecan whoppers called *zacahuiles*). Pork, chicken, and turkey are the top three fillings. But the range, region to region, is almost magically prodigious. Shark, shellfish, dried shrimp— you'll also find tamales with frogs and tadpoles, with iguanas and squirrels, even aquatic flies and ant roe (though many of these are now disappearing). Tamales also come sweet and reassuring, like Mexico City's traditional breakfast *tamales de dulce,* with dried pineapple. Southernmost Chiapas is generally tipped as the number one tamale state in Mexico. *Tamales untados*—pork with a light *dulce* mole, wrapped in banana leaves—are sold here on Saturday nights at houses showing a red lantern. Neighboring Oaxaca features a filling with its celebrated black mole and a wrapping of banana leaves.

But note: nowhere in Mexico will you ever find a tamale with goat meat. Goat is simply taboo. What's not taboo is singing. The *tamalada,* the kitchen hours of tamale making, traditionally require song and music. Without these, the tamales will suffer.

green chicken tamales

cook's notes Reducing the wealth of tamales to a single recipe was a maddening task. That said, the ones I love most are the central-Mexican variety, made with fluffy corn masa and a sharp tomatillo-based chicken filling that contrasts deliciously with the mild dough. Any leftover chicken, either roasted or poached, is fine here, as is leftover cooked pork or beef. Leftover mole poblano also makes a fabulous, authentic filling.

filling

¾ pound fresh tomatillos (about 9 large), husked, rinsed, dried, and quartered

2 fresh poblano chiles, cored, seeded, and coarsely chopped

2 or 3 jalapeño chiles, cored, seeded, and coarsely chopped

2 large garlic cloves, chopped

1 small white onion, coarsely chopped

⅓ cup chopped cilantro leaves, or more if you like cilantro

1 teaspoon dried oregano leaves

1 teaspoon dried epazote leaves, if available

¼ teaspoon ground cumin

½ cup chicken stock or canned broth

1½ tablespoons peanut or canola oil

2 cups skinless cooked chicken or pork, torn into bite-size pieces

1 large boiled potato, diced

Salt

OR 2½ cups Mole Sauce (page 172) with 2 cups turkey or chicken meat torn into bite-size pieces

1 or 2 (5-ounce) packages dried corn husks (see Cook's Notes)

Undoubtedly, the best tamale dough is made with fresh masa of ground nixtamalized corn, which may be found at some Mexican groceries or tortilla factories. While it does taste somewhat "instant," dried *masa harina* for tortillas and tamales is a perfectly adequate and simple option. If you have a choice, get Maseca rather than Quaker brand, especially Maseca's coarser, instant corn masa mix specifically for tamales. Dried corn husks vary in size and quality; as they are inexpensive, get an extra package to pick out the largest husks. For steaming, I swear by my large, wide Chinese dumpling steamer, but almost any big steamer will do. See Resources for mail-order sources for tamale ingredients and utensils.

1 Make the filling: On an ungreased comal, griddle, or cast-iron skillet, sear the tomatillos, poblano and jalapeño chiles, and garlic until gently charred all over, about 5 minutes. You will have to do this in two batches. Transfer to a bowl and let cool.

2 In two batches, puree the tomatillos, chiles, garlic, onion, cilantro, oregano, epazote, and cumin in a blender, adding ¼ cup of stock to each batch.

3 In a wide, heavy pot, heat the oil until almost smoking. Add the tomatillo puree and cook over medium-low heat, stirring occasionally, for 15 minutes. The mixture will be darkened and reduced. Fold in the chicken and potato, stir gently to coat with the sauce, and season with salt to taste. Cool the filling completely before filling the tamales. (The filling can be prepared a day ahead and refrigerated. If using mole sauce, omit steps 1 to 3.)

dough

1½ pounds fresh masa or 2 cups dried masa harina (see Cook's Notes)

1¼ cups plus 2 tablespoons very hot water, if using masa harina

¼ to ¾ cup good butcher's lard or vegetable shortening, at room temperature

⅔ cup cold chicken stock or canned broth

1 teaspoon baking powder

1½ teaspoons salt

1 teaspoon sugar

4 Choose 12 to 14 of the largest and cleanest husks, each ideally about 8 inches long and 5 inches wide. If your husks are small, you will have to use two for each tamal, so choose 24 to 28, plus 8 for lining the steamer. Place the husks in a large bowl, add hot water to cover, weigh them down with a lid or a plate, and soak until the husks are pliable, 1 to 2 hours. Right before using, remove the husks from the water, drain, and pat dry with paper towels.

5 Make the dough: Place the masa harina in a large bowl and gradually add the hot water, mixing it in with a fork. Knead the dough until it just holds together. Wrap in plastic and refrigerate until cold, about 1 hour. (If using fresh masa, omit this step.)

6 While the dough is cooling, in another bowl, beat the lard or shortening with an electric mixer until it resembles cake frosting, 2 to 3 minutes. In a small bowl, stir together the cold stock, baking powder, salt, and sugar.

7 Place the prepared masa dough (or the fresh masa) in a large bowl, gradually stir in the stock mixture and knead to incorporate. With an electric mixer, beat the lard into the dough until incorporated. Beat at high speed for about 5 minutes longer, until the dough is light and fluffy. The masa is ready when a small piece of dough floats when you drop it in a glass of chilled water. If it doesn't float, beat it for a few more minutes and test again.

8 Lay one large corn husk on a work surface or lay two smaller husks side by side lengthwise, overlapping by about 1 inch. With lightly moistened hands or the back of a spoon, spread about ¼ cup of the dough down the center of the husk (or the overlapping husks) in a thin even layer. You should leave bare about 2 inches at the top and bottom ends and 1 inch on each long side. Spread about 1½ tablespoons of the filling in a row down the center of the dough. Using the long sides of the husk, bring the long sides of the dough up to enclose the filling. Fold both long sides of the husk toward the center, then fold the top and bottom sides toward the center, forming a package. Secure the ends by tying a cotton string around the *tamal*. (Alternatively, instead of folding the top and bottom ends, you can twist them and tie them with a string like a party favor.) Don't tie too tight, as the tamales need room to expand during cooking, but make sure the tamales are properly sealed.

9 Pour about 4 inches of water into the bottom of a large, wide steamer, line the steamer rack with a few corn husks, and bring the water to a boil. Arrange the tamales on their sides on the steamer rack without overcrowding and cover with another layer of corn husks. Wrap the steamer lid in a clean kitchen towel, tying the ends together over the top of the lid. Steam the tamales for 50 minutes to 1½ hours, depending on the freshness and the consistency of the dough. To test for doneness, remove and unwrap one *tamal* and break it open with a fork; it is done when the dough is firm throughout and the husk separates easily from the dough. As the tamales cook, check and replenish the water in the bottom of the steamer as necessary. For the best texture, cool the tamales and re-steam for about 25 minutes before serving. (Tamales steamed once can be cooled completely, frozen in airtight plastic bags, and steamed for about 40 minutes to heat through.) Let the tamales cool for about 10 minutes before eating.

Makes 12 to 14 medium tamales to serve 6 as a main course and 12 as an appetizer

resources MexGrocer sells a wide range of Mexican products, including Maseca masa harina, dried cornhusks, and tamale kits (*www.MexGrocer.com;* no phone).

there are times when I contemplate flying all the way to New Delhi just to have a tandoori lunch at Dastarkhwan e-Karim, a restaurant buried in the back streets of the city's intensely Muslim neighborhood of Nizzamudin. Inside, in the dim, shabby-plush room, a mood of slightly dour dignity hangs in the air. Patrons eat a lot and say very little—the sign of a great restaurant.

Fitting for a place located steps away from Humayun Tomb, the city's great Moghul landmark, Karim's menu is a showcase of royal-style Mughlai dishes. But the soul of the kitchen is the white-hot tandoori oven. From its smoldering depths emerge flaky multilayered *parathas* and billowy *roghni* naan breads with a glossy sheen of saffron-bright butter. Intricately spiced minced mutton kebabs

tandoori chicken

come neatly bundled in a handkerchief-thin bread called *rumali* roti. The *burra* kebab—hunks of lamb shoulder cosseted in a tangy lush yogurt marinade—ranks among this world's greatest barbecue treats. And the same goes for the famous tandoori chicken, tasting of smoke, hot clay, and mild spices. Karim is the Taj Mahal of tandoori cooking.

Unlike the city's posh hotel restaurants, Karim doesn't have a display kitchen where costumed cooks theatrically slap naan breads against the tandoor walls. Karim is discreet. But if I beg, they sometimes allow me backstage to observe the tandoori *wallahs* at work. I can stay here endlessly watching the beturbaned Punjabi guys thread well-tenderized hunks of meat onto saber-size skewers. The skewers are lowered upright into the tandoor, which is blackened and patinated from years of nonstop use. Every few minutes the meats are brushed with ghee; and as the fat drips down it bastes the flesh, imparting a smokiness a thousand times more complex than the tang of a Texas barbecue pit.

Tandoori describes a genre of dishes cooked in a tandoor, the staggeringly hot jug-shaped clay oven fired up well in advance until it reaches something like 800°F. The combination of radiant and convection heat—heat from the smoldering embers and the intense heat retained by the tandoor's clay walls—cooks food in minutes, leaving it succulent and irresistibly charred. To protect larger cuts of meat, Indian cooks marinate them in a tenderizing slurry of aromatics, spices, and yogurt.

The tandoor has been around for a while. According to food historian Charles Perry, its origins are in ancient Babylon; the word comes from Babylonian *tinuru,* which is the etymological root for Egyptian *tarur* and Hebrew and Arabic *tanur.* Even today these ovens are omnipresent. In Central Asia I've encountered them as *tandir,* in Caucasus as *tone,* and in Iran as *tanoor.* It is from Persia and Central Asia that India inherited its tandoori tradition.

While today the tandoor might stand as a symbol of Indian cooking (at least abroad), its popularity throughout India is rather recent. Associated with the rugged romance and the macho meat-fueled cuisine of India's former northwestern frontier of Lahore and Peshawar (present-day Pakistan), tandoori cooking became a fixture in northern India's restaurants only after 1947, when India and Pakistan split. At that time, waves of Pakistan's Punjabi refugees settled in northern cities like Delhi, and many of them made their name in the restaurant business. The place that started India's tandoori chicken craze was Moti Mahal in New Delhi, run by a transplanted Peshawari. Apparently the place still exists, though Delhites don't talk of it much.

Originally the tandoor functioned as a bread oven, but today the word instantly evokes chicken: either tandoori *murgh,* whole small chicken baked swaddled in a complex yogurt marinade; or *murgh tikka,* a chicken kebab eaten with a sprightly mint chutney. Unless you construct a tandoor in your garden—and there are several Web sites that will help you with this—there's no way of replicating that unique tang and aroma at home. The good news is that you might not even miss it that much if you marinate the bird properly, bake it, or simply grill it. Curiously, even Delhites are abandoning the tandoor in favor of backyard grills, broilers, and newly fashionable rotisseries. But if you're still craving that incomparable smoky taste, I support your pilgrimage to Dastarkhwan e-Karim in New Delhi.

grilled tandoori chicken

Tandoori Murgh

cook's notes This is the recipe for the legendary *tandoori murgh,* in this case done on the grill. To make the chicken in the oven, roast it at 500°F. on the rack in a shallow baking pan, turning occasionally, until cooked through, about forty minutes.

2 young chickens (about 3 pounds each), skinned and quartered

Salt

½ teaspoon chili powder, preferably Indian

Two large pinches of turmeric

⅓ cup fresh lemon juice

yogurt marinade

1 tablespoon ground coriander

2 teaspoons ground cumin

2 teaspoons purchased garam masala

1 teaspoon chili powder, preferably Indian

Large pinch of freshly grated nutmeg

Large pinch of ground cinnamon

1½ cups plain whole-milk yogurt

½ cup chopped onion

2 tablespoons chopped fresh ginger

5 large garlic cloves, chopped

A few drops red Tandoori coloring, available at Indian groceries (optional)

to cook and serve

2 to 3 tablespoons melted ghee or butter, for brushing the chickens

Mint Chutney (recipe follows)

Lemon wedges

Thickly sliced red onion

Just before serving, pass it under a broiler for one to two minutes. To make chicken tikka, or kebabs, use the same marinade for two pounds of boneless skinless chicken thighs, cut into 1¼-inch chunks. Thread them on skewers, brush lightly with ghee or peanut oil, and grill on a very hot grill for about five minutes per side. The red tandoori food coloring is garish and rather unnecessary, but it does trigger a kind of Pavlovian response: "Tandoori chicken!" Use it or not as you wish, or substitute with one tablespoon sweet paprika. The longer the chicken marinates, the more flavorful it becomes, so start ahead.

1 Make several ½-inch-deep diagonal slits in the thighs and breasts of each chicken. Place the chickens in a large nonreactive dish and rub them thoroughly with salt, chili powder, turmeric, and lemon juice. Cover with plastic and refrigerate for at least 2 hours.

2 In a small skillet, over low heat, stir all the dry ground spices until fragrant and a few shades darker, 15 to 20 seconds. In a food processor or a blender, process the yogurt with the onion, ginger, and garlic to a paste. Stir in the toasted dry spices and the food coloring, if using. Pour this marinade over the chickens, toss to coat, cover with plastic, and refrigerate for at least 4 hours. Bring the chickens to room temperature before grilling.

3 Light a grill. Set an oiled rack 4 to 6 inches over glowing coals and brush the chicken pieces with ghee. Grill, in batches if necessary, until the juices run clear when you insert a skewer into the thickest part of the thigh, 10 to 15 minutes per side. Grill the chicken covered for smokier taste.

4 Using tongs, transfer the cooked chicken pieces to a platter and serve with the mint chutney, if desired, lemon wedges, and sliced red onion.

Serves 4 to 6

mint chutney
Puree all the ingredients in a blender until fairly smooth. Scrape into a bowl, taste, and adjust the seasonings. Let the chutney stand for 30 minutes for the flavors to meld.

Makes about 1 cup

1½ cups tightly packed fresh mint leaves

½ cup tightly packed cilantro leaves

1 long mild green chile, such as Anaheim, seeded and chopped

1 tablespoon grated fresh ginger

¼ cup chopped white onion

Small pinch of ground cumin

2 tablespoons fresh lemon juice, or more to taste

2 teaspoons distilled white vinegar

½ teaspoon sugar, or more to taste

2 to 3 tablespoons plain yogurt

One day, on a road trip across France, I stopped for coffee in the perfectly nondescript Loire Valley town of Lamotte-Beuvron, and discovered that I had accidentally stumbled on a tarte Tatin paradise. I strolled around, wondering why every bakery in this town displayed a glistening upside down apple tart, until Hôtel-Terminus Tatin announced itself with a huge sign. After tasting my way around town, I'd decided that the Hôtel Tatin version of this famous sweet actually wasn't the best in town. But, they say that France's simple and sensational apple cake owes its birth to a felicitous mistake that happened at this very hostelry at the turn of the nineteenth century.

Run by two local sisters, Stephanie and Caroline Tatin, the hotel that sits familiarly across from the train station once played host to large parties of hunters and travelers on their way from Orléans to Vierzon. One busy day with guests streaming back from their hunt, Caroline—or was it Stephanie?—rushed to put a hastily concocted caramel apple tart in the oven. As she went about her numerous chores, she suddenly realized she'd forgotten to line the tart tin with pastry. *Quel horreur!* She opened the oven and was pleased with the sight of the lovely caramelized apples. Quickly she draped some pastry over them, put the dish back in the oven, and prayed for the best.

tarte tatin

As we know, God listened. Her inverted tart mistake proved a triumph and there was no looking back. Curnonsky, acclaimed as *Prince des Gastronomes,* made a special train trip to this drowsy town for a taste. And *la tarte des Demoiselles Tatin* even made its way to the menu of the celebrated Maxim's in the capital.

That *tartes renversée* (upside-down tarts) were known in Sologne long before the Tatin sisters were born doesn't make the tale any less sweet.

Tarte Tatin is equal measures simplicity and ingenuity. Butter and sugar are caramelized to a deep brown in a pan either on top of the stove or in the oven. Large chunks of apples are snugly layered on top, and the whole is baked under a thin sheet of puff pastry or *pâte sucrée.* The tarte is inverted while it's still hot—and voilà! Of course, each baker has his or her little *trucs,* and any discussion of a perfectly turned-out tarte Tatin usually involves an extended discourse on apples.

The official tarte Tatin apple is the crunchy pink Loire variety called Reine des Reinettes. In America, the chances of finding such apples are slim, and even in France the short growing season leads cooks to consider different options. I continued asking around for less esoteric suggestions, until it became clear that almost any apple (as long as it was crisp and not overly sweet) had its loyal champions.

One of my great tarte Tatin insights came at La Poule au Pot, a vintage Les Halles bistro famed for onion soup and poached chicken dinners. The chicken was fine and forgettable, but the tarte Tatin was a thing of beauty: a wonderfully flaky pastry disk holding burnished mahogany apple halves that arrived to the table perfectly intact, but melted at the mere touch of a fork; and the apple had enough flavor to cut through the butter and sugar. The secret? The ubiquitous Gala.

The following recipe is loosely based on the "official" rendition published by La Confrérie des Lichonneaux de Tarte Tatin. The mission of this tarte Tatin confraternity is to safeguard the town's precious patrimony from careless renderings and such cheap *contrefaçons* as Onion Tatin, or Mango Tatin.

You won't find such a lovely tarte Tatin at Hôtel Tatin. That much is certain.

tarte tatin

cook's notes If you *really* love tarte Tatin, you might want to invest in a pricey copper tarte Tatin pan, available at better kitchen shops. You should know, however, that a 10- to 11-inch cast-iron skillet works just as well. Tarte Tatin can be prepared ahead of time, left in the pan, and reheated in a 400°F. oven for 10 minutes before inverting.

1 Spread the butter evenly on the bottom and sides of a tarte Tatin mold or a 10-inch cast-iron skillet. Sprinkle the sugar evenly on the bottom and up the sides of the mold. Arrange as many apple quarters as will fit in the pan, placing them vertically in concentric circles. The apples should all face the same direction and be as close together as possible. Cut the apples that don't fit in the pan into slices and chunks, and place them in the gaps. (It's important to have the apples fit as snugly as possible; otherwise you are left with spaces when the apples cook down.)

4 tablespoons unsalted butter, at room
    temperature

⅔ cup sugar

7 or 8 Gala apples (about 3 pounds), peeled,
    cored, and quartered

1 sheet frozen puff pastry (from a 17¼-ounce
    package), thawed

Light corn syrup

Crème fraîche, for serving

2 Cook the apples over high heat until the sugar begins to melt, about 5 minutes. Turn the heat down to medium-high and cook without disturbing until the pan juices are a deep caramel color, about 30 minutes longer.

3 While the apples are cooking, preheat the oven to 350°F. Roll out the pastry to a circle 1 inch larger than the diameter of the skillet. Brush one side of the circle lightly with corn syrup. Turn off the heat under the apples. Being careful not to burn yourself, top the apples with the pastry round, placing it syrup side down and tucking in bits of dough around the edges. Prick the pastry with a fork in several places.

4 Bake until the apples are soft and the pastry is golden brown, about 35 minutes. Remove the tarte from the oven and let it rest for 5 to 10 minutes. Place a large serving plate over the pan, grip the pan with potholders, and quickly invert the tarte onto a plate. Rearrange the apples neatly on the crust if they've shifted during baking and serve the tarte with crème fraîche, if desired.

Serves 8

a uthentic Thai food is the most thrillingly multidimensional of world cuisines, with flavors that practically leap out at you, leaving your taste buds on full alert: perplexed, teased, sometimes challenged, charmed, and seduced by turns.

Thai cooking inherited many of its technical elements from Chinese cuisine. But the most significant legacy of the Chinese is the philosophy of the five flavors: salty, sweet, sour, bitter, and hot. This melding and juxtaposing of contrasting sensations is the cornerstone of Thai tastes—Chinese in origin, Thai in execution, and at its best performed with inimitable brilliance and originality. The Thai genius for layering, balancing, and punctuating is especially apparent in the *gaeng,* a family of soupy dishes often flavored with coconut milk and eaten spooned over rice. (*Nota bene:* Though in English, *gaeng,* or *kaeng,* is translated as "curry," Thai curries are different from their Indian counterparts.)

thai red curry

Thai curries tend to be democratic in regard to their main ingredient, usually named after the color or type of the curry paste on which they're based: red or green, yellow or orange. You may have also tasted the rich peanut-thickened southern Thai Penang curry, related to Malaysian and Indonesian *rendang* dishes; and the complex toasty *massaman,* or Muslim, curry inherited from Indian spice traders. Red and green curries, however, are the most classic, versatile, and beloved.

In an Indian or Malay curry, all the spices and aromatics are painstakingly blended and tamed to produce a unified whole. In a Thai curry, the spice base is mellowed by the creamy sweetness of coconut milk, only to be disrupted again at the last minute by the addition of crunchy, slightly bitter Thai eggplants; fragrant flourishes of shredded kaffir lime and Thai basil; and the salty grace notes of fish sauce. The effect is bewitching.

Key to Thai green and red curries are the aromatic pastes that mix chiles, lemongrass, galangal, shallots, garlic, kaffir lime zest, shrimp paste, and a host of dried spices. These are pounded or pureed until completely smooth, then cooked in thick oily coconut milk until the aromatics lose their harsh pungency, their flavors deepen and mellow, and their fragrant potential is fully realized and released.

The difference between red and green curry pastes is the color of chiles they include; the techniques for preparing them are almost identical. Because curries can be made with anything from roast duck to seafood to strips of beef, one good curry recipe opens the door to many options. Once you've prepared the aromatic paste—which can be done way ahead of time—the curries cook in a flash.

In old-fashioned Thai kitchens, curry pastes are pounded by hand in a mortar with a heavy pestle. As with pesto, this produces a superior flavor because the process opens the "pores" of the aromatics and releases their oils. But unless you have loads of kitchen help (or want to develop arm muscles), use a food processor or a blender—like any modern Thai cook. Some commercial brands can be okay, especially red curry. But homemade pastes will produce dishes infinitely brighter, more intricate and authentic than anything you ever experienced in your neighborhood Thai joint.

red curry of roast duck and pineapple

cook's notes This extravagant dish crowns the repertoire of Thai curries and is best prepared with purchased Chinese roast duck. (For those without access to a Chinese store, I include directions for roasting a whole duck.) You can use this as a master recipe for virtually any red curry dish, which can include strips of dark chicken meat, shrimp, or shellfish, such as mussels or clams. To make this curry with chicken, cut the meat into strips, as if for stir-frying, and cook in the curry mixture until just done. If using fish or seafood, cook until just cooked through, about 3 minutes. I also love this recipe with leftover roast pork or turkey.

½ large Chinese roast duck, hacked into dainty serving pieces; or 1 duckling (about 5 pounds), excess fat removed, well rinsed, and patted dry

Salt

3 (13½-ounce) cans coconut milk, chilled upright

9 tablespoons Red Curry Paste (recipe follows), or 7 tablespoons commercial red curry paste

4¼ tablespoons fish sauce (*nam pla*)

1½ tablespoons palm sugar or firmly packed light brown sugar

½ tablespoon fresh lime juice

10 cherry tomatoes, halved

10 Thai pea eggplants, or ½ cup fresh or frozen green peas

1 red bell pepper, cored, seeded, and thinly sliced

1¼ cups firm pineapple wedges

1 cup torn fresh Thai or Italian basil leaves

6 kaffir lime leaves, cut into very fine shreds

Cooked rice (preferably jasmine), for serving

Make the red curry paste before proceeding with the recipe. If you opt for commercial paste, I recommend the brands that come in small cans rather than plastic containers or jars. If you don't have access to a Thai grocery, see Resources. For a complete Thai meal, serve this with Tom Yum Kung (page 312) and Pad Thai (page 182).

1 If using fresh duck, preheat the oven to 400°F. Rub the duck inside and out with salt. Prick the skin with a fork. Place on a rack of a roasting pan breast side up and roast for 20 minutes. Reduce the oven temperature to 350°F. Pour off the accumulated fat and continue roasting the duck for 1¼ hours. Remove from the oven, cover loosely with foil, and let rest for 10 minutes. Gently pat with a paper towel to remove excess fat. With a sharp large knife, or a cleaver, cut the duck into bite-size pieces. Set aside.

2 Open the three cans of chilled coconut milk. Spoon out and reserve 2 cups of the cream that has risen to the top. Stir all the remaining coconut milk together, then measure out and reserve 2¾ cups, saving the rest for another use. Add 1 cup of water to the reserved 2¾ cups coconut milk to make thin coconut milk.

3 In a large, heavy casserole, boil the thick coconut cream over medium-high heat until it thickens and oil begins to separate from white solids, about 8 minutes. (Use a screen if the cream splatters.) Add the curry paste and stir-fry until the mixture looks cracked and no longer tastes raw, 6 to 8 minutes. (Add a little thin coconut milk, 1 tablespoon at a time, if paste begins to stick.) Add the thin coconut milk and bring to a simmer over medium heat. Add the duck and cook until heated through. Add the remaining ingredients and cook for 3 minutes. Serve with rice.

Serves 4 on its own or 8 with other dishes

red curry paste

cook's notes Curry pastes actually process more smoothly when you make them in larger quantities. The recipe below will make about 1 cup. The paste will keep in the refrigerator for up to two weeks and in a freezer for up to two months. If toasting and grinding the spices is too much of an undertaking, use pre-ground spices; stir them in a dry skillet over low heat for about 30 seconds to intensify their flavor. To make a green curry, follow the recipe for the red curry paste, substituting ¼ to ⅓ cup chopped fresh green cayenne or serrano chiles for the red, plus 5 chopped fresh Anaheim chiles.

24 to 26 dried medium-size red chiles

2 teaspoons Thai dried shrimp paste (*gapi*)

½ cup chopped red shallots or onion

½ cup chopped garlic

¼ cup thinly sliced fresh lemongrass (3 inches of the lower stalk, tough outer leaves discarded)

1 tablespoon peeled chopped fresh or frozen galangal or fresh ginger

3 tablespoons chopped well-washed coriander roots and/or stems

2 teaspoons finely grated kaffir or regular lime zest

2 teaspoon white peppercorns, toasted and ground

1 teaspoon cumin seeds, toasted and ground

2 teaspoons coriander seeds, toasted and ground

1 teaspoon freshly grated nutmeg

1½ tablespoons peanut oil

1 Cut the stems off the chiles and shake out the seeds. Using scissors, cut the chiles into 1½-inch lengths. Place in a bowl, cover with warm water, and soak for 20 minutes. Drain well, reserving 1 tablespoon of the soaking liquid.

2 While the chiles are soaking, flatten the shrimp paste, wrap it in a double layer of foil, and toast on a dry hot skillet until fragrant, about 2 minutes per side.

3 In a small bowl, combine the chiles and the reserved cooking liquid, shrimp paste, and all the other ingredients. Working in batches if necessary, process to a smooth paste, adding the oil to assist the blending. Scrape into a container with a tight-fitting lid. Reserve 9 tablespoons of the curry paste for the duck curry and save the rest for another use.

Makes about 1 cup

resources   A good source for Thai ingredients is Adriana's Caravan (tel: 800-316-0820 or *www.adrianascaravan.com*).

i n the late nineties, when the Thai currency, the *baht,* took a nosedive, dragging the Far Eastern economy with it, the Asian press was quick to dub this economic affliction "*tom yum kung* disease." While this particular reference to the soup was unflattering, it affirmed the status of this hot-sour-salty *potage* as the country's best-known export—a dish as Thai as Thailand itself. In the year 2000, tom yum kung made headlines again, this time in nutrition and medical columns, when a joint Japanese-Thai study concluded that a bowl of tom yang kung a day keeps cancer at bay. (Substances in galangal, lemongrass, and kaffir lime leaves were found to be 100 times more effective in inhibiting tumors than other antioxidants.) The Thais rejoiced and pronounced these findings so portentous that they even began to worry foreigners might patent the recipe and rob Thailand of its culinary property.

tom yum kung

Thai Hot and Sour Soup with Shrimp

Tom means "to boil" and *yum* refers to that quintessentially Thai mixing and blending of flavors and textures (as in Thai *yums,* or salads). *Kung* means "shrimp"—though in Thailand *tom yum* connotes a whole group of clear soups that can be flavored with anything from smoked fish to wild boar. A royal-style dish associated with central Thailand, tom yum kung is usually presented together with other dishes—often in dramatic copper charcoal-fueled pots—and sipped between bites to revive the palate.

Present on every menu at every Thai restaurant all over the globe, tom yum kung is why we fell in love with Thai food in the first place. It's that citrusy zing, the fresh explosions of chiles, lemongrass, and cilantro, the unbearably exotic perfume of kaffir lime. And above all, it's that inimitably Thai combination of clarity, intensity, and complexity. So wildly popular is the soup in its homeland that it's spawned a whole industry: countless soup mixes and cans, tom yum–flavored Munchos, tom yum ramen—even tom yum–flavored candy! And the tom yum kung pizza I once tasted in Bangkok is one of Pizza Hut's greater inventions.

tom yum kung

cook's notes For the home cook, the beauty of tom yum kung is its simplicity and transparency; the only challenge is locating fresh aromatics. Some cooks finish the soup with an extra boost of *nam phrik pao*, a mild red chile paste that adds an extra layer of flavor. I prefer adding a fresh jolt of the chile-lemongrass mixture at the end. You can also prepare this soup with cooked shredded white chicken meat and a very light chicken broth, or add sliced scallops to the shrimp in this version.

18 extra-large shrimp in their shells

8 cups water

2 stalks fresh lemongrass, smashed, plus 3 tablespoons chopped (3 inches of the lower stalk, tough outer leaves discarded)

4 kaffir limes, 1 whole and 3 torn

1 teaspoon white peppercorns

2 garlic cloves, chopped

2½ tablespoons cilantro roots and/or stems, washed thoroughly and chopped

4 to 6 green bird's eye chiles (if unavailable, use cayenne or serrano), seeded and sliced

3 slices fresh or frozen peeled galangal, smashed

12 small cherry tomatoes

1 cup fresh oyster mushrooms, halved if large, or canned straw mushrooms, drained

¼ cup fresh lime juice

3 tablespoons fish sauce (*nam pla*), or more to taste

2 teaspoons sugar

¼ cup fresh cilantro leaves, for garnish

1 Shell and devein the shrimp, reserving the shells. In a stockpot, combine the shrimp shells with the water, 2 smashed lemongrass stalks, and 1 whole kaffir lime leaf, smashed and bruised. Bring to a boil over medium-high heat. Cook, uncovered, until the liquid is reduced to about 6 cups, about 10 minutes. Strain into a clean pot and discard the shrimp shells and aromatics.

2 Using a mortar and pestle or a mini food processor, grind the peppercorns, garlic, cilantro roots, 3 tablespoons chopped lemongrass, and chiles to a paste. (If using a processor, add about 2 tablespoons of the shrimp stock to assist the blending.) Reserve 1 tablespoon of this mixture.

3 Bring the shrimp broth to a simmer. Add the peppercorn mixture except for 1 tablespoon, the galangal, and the 3 torn kaffir lime leaves, and simmer for 10 minutes. (In Thailand, it is customary to have bits of aromatics floating in the soup, but you can strain the soup at this point if you wish.)

4 Add the shrimp, the tomatoes, and mushrooms and cook for 1 minute. Stir in the lime juice, fish sauce, sugar, and the reserved 1 tablespoon of the peppercorn mixture and simmer for 2 more minutes. Taste the soup and adjust the amounts of lime juice and fish sauce to taste. (You may also add a little more sugar, but the taste should be tart rather than sweet-sour.) Serve in pretty bowls, garnished with cilantro.

Serves 6

he marriage of three elemental ingredients—potatoes, eggs, and olive oil—gave birth to the most omnipresent and totemic creation of the Spanish kitchen: *tortilla de patata,* the plump moonlike potato omelet without which most tapas bars would instantly go out of business. (The tortilla of the New World is, of course, a different item all together.) A testament to Spain's love affair with the egg, this tortilla is eaten for breakfast, lunch, dinner, supper, and anytime in between. It might not be particularly glamorous, but to the Spanish this is comfort food par excellence.

tortilla de patata

Spanish Potato Omelet

Of the tortilla's origins, Spanish gastronomes can say very little. They know that the potato arrived from Peru, that olive oil was a gift from the Arabs, that the tortilla itself was probably born in Navarra. And that the first mention of the dish didn't appear until the late nineteenth century. They also take great umbrage at Alexandre Dumas (Paris's Dumas *père*), who lovingly described the tortilla in accounts of his journey to Spain but failed to include it in his *Dictionnaire de Cuisine.*

Common it may be. But in Spain tortilla de patata is never taken for granted. One of the country's great annual gastronomic events is the Tortilla de Patata contest held in Spain's food capital, San Sebastián, and organized by the famously fickle food critic Rafael García Santos, who includes a section on Spain's best tortillas in his influential annual restaurant guide *Lo Mejor de la Gastronomía.* At this competition, the tortillas are judged and dissected with a seriousness usually reserved for the sublime creations of Spain's super-chef Ferran Adriá. Quality and cut of the potatoes, the acidity level of the olive oil, the succulence and creaminess of the eggs—all are scrutinized.

In Spain, bad cooks, even militant anti-cooks, can make a decent tortilla. And while the dish is eaten daily from Almería to Zaragoza, everyone concurs that the best of the best is made in the agriculturally minded Galicia, where you find the very finest potatoes and eggs. Each cook will swear by his or her particular technique, but the qualities demanded of a great tortilla are that it be *jugosa* (juicy), *gorda* (fat), and *sponjosa* (spongy). In Spain, tortillas come in a whole rainbow of flavors, including spinach, salt cod, or the famous Andalusian *tortilla sacramonte* that contains brains. But the potato tortilla is classic. After all, there's nothing like that delectably elemental union of spud, egg, and olive oil.

tortilla variations The pure potato tortilla is iconic—which isn't to say that dozens of riffs on it don't exist throughout Spain. When cooking potatoes, you can add to the recipe on the next page julienned red pepper; a couple of cups of chopped spinach or greens; some diced Serrano ham, prosciutto, chorizo or bacon; leeks or mushrooms, or quartered artichoke hearts.

tortilla de patata

cook's notes Making a perfect tortilla is a tiny bit tricky, but once you get the gist you'll be doing it all the time. Most Spanish cooks favor medium-starch Kennebec potatoes. However, in this country I've had much better result with russets. The potatoes have to be sliced extremely thin and "poached" in plenty of olive oil—never pre-boiled, even though that saves time. Draining off all the oil is important, too, and the famous *vuelta*—the flip—takes a little practice. As for the results, with a salad of ripe tomatoes bathed in good oil and aged sherry vinegar, and a glass of Rioja, it's one of life's great humble pleasures.

3 medium russet (Idaho) potatoes (about 1½ pounds), peeled and quartered lengthwise into long wedges

Kosher salt

⅔ cup fruity virgin olive oil, preferably Spanish

1 small onion, quartered and thinly sliced

6 large very fresh eggs, preferably organic

2 tablespoons chicken stock or canned broth

Freshly ground black pepper

1 Slice the potato quarters thinly in a food processor and pat dry thoroughly with paper towels to remove excess moisture. Rub them with 1 teaspoon of the salt.

2 In a large, heavy skillet, heat the oil for 3 minutes over medium-high heat. Reduce the heat to medium-low and add the potatoes in even layers. Cook, stirring occasionally, to prevent the potatoes from sticking and browning, until they are half-cooked, about 7 minutes. Add the onion and more salt to taste, if needed, and continue cooking over low heat until all the potatoes are soft, about 15 more minutes. With a slotted spoon remove the potatoes and onion to a colander set over a bowl and let the mixture drain thoroughly. Reserve 2 tablespoons of the cooking oil and strain the rest for another use. Pat onion and potatoes dry with paper towels.

3 Place the eggs, a few pinches of salt, pepper, and the broth in a large mixing bowl and beat vigorously until frothy. Gently stir in the potato mixture. Mash and stir the mixture gently with a fork to crush the potatoes just a little and mix them well with the eggs. Let stand for 10 minutes.

4 In a heavy 8-inch skillet, heat 1½ tablespoons of the reserved oil over high heat until it is just beginning to smoke. Pour the egg mixture into the skillet and flatten the potatoes with a spatula until the top is fairly even. Reduce the heat to medium-low. Cook, constantly moving and shaking the skillet in a clockwise motion, and running a flat knife around the edges and sliding it in the middle so that some of the eggs run under. Cook in this fashion until the top is a little wet but not liquid, about 6 minutes. Slide a spatula under the omelet to loosen it from the skillet. Top the skillet with a plate slightly larger than the skillet, and, using oven mitts, quickly invert the tortilla onto a plate. If the pan looks dry, add a little olive oil, and carefully slide the tortilla back into the skillet, uncooked side down. Shake the skillet to straighten the tortilla. Reduce the heat to very low and cook the tortilla for another 5 minutes. Invert again as before and cook on the first side for another minute.

5 Invert the tortilla onto a serving plate, cool, cut into wedges, and serve. The tortilla can be served slightly warm or at room temperature. To serve as a tapa, cut the tortilla into squares and serve with toothpicks.

Serves 4 as a light entree or 8 as a tapa

he most wonderful object of domestic art called trifle . . . with its charming confusion of cream and cake and almonds and jam and jelley and cinnamon and froth."

—Oliver Wendell Holmes, 1861

Trifle. "A thing of only slight value or importance," the dictionaries would have us believe. A paltry affair, a jot, a small amount. The word is from the Old French *trufe,* meaning "mockery." Trifle. Something inconsequential.

Well, to the British or to anyone else who has tasted and fallen for this layered extravaganza of the three C's—cake, custard, and cream—a trifle is anything but.

When I met my first trifle at the home of an old English Presbyterian minister in Virginia, it was love at first bite. The boiled meat and three-veg dinner bordered on a boardinghouse nightmare. Then out came a footed glass bowl exposing strata of cake, fruit, custard, and jelly. I sank my spoon in with abandon. My extravagant praises must have embarrassed the minister's wife. She blushed and explained that the custard came from Bird's powder, the sponge cake from a corner grocer, and the berries—well—those were just defrosted. Well, so what? Can you really go wrong with booze-drenched cake drowned under a silky, creamy, fruity, custardy cloud? Trifle is nursery food gone all frilly and tipsy.

Before there was tiramisù, before there was zuppa inglese, there was trifle. (What's tiramisù but coffee-flavored trifle with mascarpone instead of custard?) And while a proper British trifle conjures up visions of tea parties and lacy Victoriana, its origins go back to rowdier Elizabethan times. The first recipe with the moniker "trifle" appeared in *The Good Husewife's Jewell* (1596). It went like this: "Take a pinte of thicke Creame, and season it with Sugar and Ginger, and Rosewater, so stirre it as you would then have it, and make it luke warme in a dish on a Chafingdishe and coals . . . and after put it into a silver piece or bowle, and so serve it to the boorde." (The *boorde* must have liked it a lot.) Some half a century later, a recipe for a Foole—the terms *trifle* and *fool* were used interchangeably until much later—becomes more recognizable: bread soaked with sack, layered with cream and eggs, and perfumed with rose water and mace.

In the mid 1700s the British domestic guru of her times, Hannah Glasse, finally indulged Britain's sweet tooth with a properly fanciful trifle. Hers is a construction of Naples biscuits (twice-cooked hard sponge cakes), ratafia biscuits (something like amaretti), and macaroons, all moistened with sack and topped with a "good boiled custard." The whole is crowned with a syllabub (that's cream whipped with sweet wine), then garnished with flowers and currant jelly, and strewn "with different coloured nonpareils."

These days British trifles have gone all upmarket and multiculti. But I'm still a fancier of those remember-granny affairs: a footed glass bowl, red jelly on the bottom, Swiss roll (jelly roll) soaked in sweet sherry, instant custard, canned fruit, and glacé cherries on top. The thing is impossibly endearing and much more than the sum of its parts. Forget about granny, however, and variations on the theme of cake, custard, cream, fruit, and alcohol border on the infinite.

In Britain, ratafia biscuits (or macaroons), Madeira cake, and Victoria jam sandwiches are all classic trifle bases—as are trifle sponges from the corner store. But you can't go wrong with pound cake or sponge cake, ginger bread, or brioche crumbs. Sherry may be replaced with Madeira, port wine, or any sweet booze, the vanilla custard with lemon curd, yogurt cream, or crème anglaise. Mascarpone, syllabub, and crème fraîche can all go on top instead of the whipped cream. As for decorations, the sky's the limit.

In my research, I've made a tropical trifle, an Arabian trifle with pomegranates and rose water, and an Italian trifle with espresso and zabaglione. While nothing quite matched the gorgeous confection below from my friend Elisabeth Luard, my efforts ranged from good to sublime. Because even a bad trifle is a good trifle. Because all you really need is a pretty glass bowl and a little patience while the layers meld into a heavenly soupy mess. That and a conviction that trifle is a sweet nothing of major importance.

elisabeth luard's scottish raspberry and peach trifle

cook's notes This breathtakingly delicious trifle is from my friend Elisabeth Luard, an erudite, an adventuress, a brilliant cook, and the author of *Sacred Food* and *The Old World Kitchen,* among other books. Her recipe came with the following note: "Here's my Edinburgh-born granny's recipe for her sherry-sodden, Drambuie-soaked, custard-bathed, cream-crowned, thoroughly-raspberried, peachy, almond-sprinkled bottom-broadening, thoroughly grown-up trifle. Make it in the raspberry season (Scottish raspberries are the best in the world—I used to pick them on the golf course at St. Andrews) and don't be mean with the hard stuff."

custard

1½ cups half-and-half

3 large egg yolks

5 tablespoons sugar

1½ tablespoons all-purpose flour

2 tablespoons unsalted butter, softened

Seeds from 1 vanilla pod, or ½ teaspoon pure vanilla extract

layers

1 pound fresh raspberries

3 to 4 tablespoons sugar

1 purchased sponge cake, about 1 pound

3 to 4 tablespoons good raspberry jam

½ to ⅔ cup medium-dry sherry, such as Amontillado

6 to 8 macaroons or amaretti-type almond cookies, roughly crushed

About ⅓ cups Drambuie or whisky, or to taste

3 to 4 ripe peaches, skinned, pitted, and sliced

Happiness comes in a cut-glass bowl, Elizabeth added. And if that glass bowl is shallow, no deeper than 5 inches, so much the better. Before you set off, size up your bowl and adjust the amount of ingredients to fit. A good purchased sponge cake is just peachy, and make sure to give the trifle enough time to soak up all the flavors and booze. Can't find candied flowers for decoration? Use your imagination.

1 Make the custard ahead to give it time to cool. Combine all the ingredients in a blender and process to a smooth cream. Transfer the custard to the top part of a double boiler or a stainless bowl set over simmering water. Whisk over low heat until the custard is thick enough to coat the back of a spoon, 3 to 5 minutes, without letting it boil. (If it scrambles, add a little cold milk and give it another quick whizz in the blender.) The custard will thicken more as it cools; it should be quite thick. Transfer the custard to a bowl, place plastic wrap directly on the top to prevent skin from forming, cool to room temperature, and chill until ready to use.

to finish

1 cup heavy cream, whipped with a little Drambuie, if you like

About 12 blanched almonds

About 12 crystallized rose petals

About 12 crystallized violets

2 Place the raspberries in a bowl, sprinkle with the sugar, and let stand until they throw off some juice, about 30 minutes.

3 Split the sponge cake in half lengthwise. Spread one half with the raspberry jam, and sandwich the other layer on top. Press the layers together lightly. Cut this "sandwich" into ½-inch-thick slices.

4 Layer the bottom and part of the sides of a glass bowl with the sponge cake slices. Sprinkle the sponge cake layer generously with the sherry. Place a layer of raspberries and their juice on top and top with a layer of macaroons. Sprinkle the macaroons generously with the Drambuie (if using amaretti cookies, sprinkle on even more). Add a layer of sliced peaches, and top with a layer of custard. Place a sheet of plastic wrap directly on the custard to prevent a crust from forming and refrigerate for a few hours or overnight for the flavors to blend.

5 To finish, spread the top with a thick layer of whipped cream or pipe it out decoratively from a pastry bag. Decorate the top with the blanched almonds and crystallized rose and violet petals. Serve in glass dessert bowls or large martini glasses.

Serves 6 to 8

Write off Wiener schnitzel as a faded postcard from Mittel Europa and you will cheat yourself out of one of the loveliest meals on this planet. Otherwise, waltz over to your butcher for a pound of nice veal, whip up some fresh bread crumbs, and get out your frying pan. Your reward will be a thin disk of white meat enrobed in a beautiful brittle cloak of fine nutty crumbs. With a side of potato salad and a frosty glass of good Pils, if you please.

Wiener schnitzel—literally, Viennese cutlet—was dreamed up in the Austrian capital, most people assume. Wrongly. The official anecdote goes something like this. In the 1840s, the great field marshall Radetzky (the man in charge of thwarting nationalist revolts in Hapsburg-ruled Lombardy) paused to present his Kaiser Ferdinand I with a mouthwatering tale. It involved a

wiener schnitzel

Lombardian specialty called *cotoletta alla Milanese:* a breaded thin veal escalope fried to a marvelous golden crunch.

The hungry Hapsburg swooned, smacked his imperial lips, and commanded his *chef de cuisine* to replicate this temptation at once. A hit. Having caused a stir in Vienna's haute circles, the dish soon was flourishing at Europe's fine restaurants, redubbed *Wiener schnitzel.* The rebellious Lombardians were irate.

This account, quoted in numerous Austrian sources, also cites a young aide-de-camp called Attems as the first to relay the story, as well as a letter written by Radetzky himself, describing the recipe in painstaking detail. That Attems was a semifictional character, that the said letter never materialized, and that military leaders aren't normally given to swapping recipes with their Kaisers in the middle of war—all this didn't prevent the anecdote from sticking to the dish like breading to egg wash.

A great schnitzel has a touch of paradox, a compromise between heft and weightlessness. Admittedly, the thing has to be pretty gigantic—big enough to drape over the edges of a dinner plate, as it does at Viennese schnitzel shrines like Figlmuller or Zum Weissen Rauchfangkehrer. At the same time, a good schnitzel is delicate as a whisper, and should be fried so bone-dry that when a gentleman sits on it, it won't stain his trousers. As for color, the Austrian journalist-fiddler-gourmet Joseph Wechsberg likened it to a Brueghel painting and a Stradivarius violin.

The *echte* schnitzel, according to most Austrian sources, comes from milk-fed veal cut from the leg. Many of my Austrian and Hungarian friends, however, swear that pork is juicer. Meanwhile, chicken (or turkey) schnitzel is something of an Israeli national dish, while the Argentines prepare their schnitzels with thin sheets of beef round, calling the dish *Milanesa*.

Watching Austrian, German, and Swiss *schnitzelmeisters*, I've come to believe that speed and efficiency are key to success. The meat is never pre-breaded lest the crust split away when it's fried. The escalopes, pounded gently to ⅛-inch thickness, pass from flour to egg to fine crumbs (traditionally made from Viennese white rolls) with lightning swiftness. The frying—either in the more traditional lard or a more contemporary mixture of butter and oil—takes mere minutes. And the correct temperature of the fat, about 350°F., assures that the crumbs are neither greasy nor burned.

Schnitzel accoutrements are spare and to the point: a wedge of lemon, a little salad of potatoes and/or cucumber, a flourish of fried parsley, perhaps. The next day nothing beats a cold schnitzel dabbed with a bit of lemony mayo and mounted on a slice of aromatic dense rye. Kind of makes you long for the return of the Hapsburgs.

wiener schnitzel

cook's notes Mario Lohninger is the Franz Schubert of schnitzelers. *Chef de cuisine* at David Bouley's haute Viennese Danube restaurant in New York, he's hip, young, and adorable—not your average vision of Mittel Europa. But say schnitzel, and Mario's eyes practically mist up. This is Mario's formidable recipe adapted from *East of Paris*. At Danube, besides the fried parsley garnish, the presentation features pickled ramps, a potato salad, lingonberry compote, and a small heap of greens dressed with dark Austrian pumpkin seed oil. At home, it is delicious with a simple dilled cucumber salad dressed with a mixture of sour cream and crème fraîche with a dash of vinegar and horseradish, or/and with potato salad.

⅔ cup flat-leaf parsley leaves washed and dried thoroughly

Canola oil, for deep-frying

Salt

1 baguette, dried overnight in an extremely low oven, or for a few days in the open air

4 large eggs

1½ cups all-purpose flour

8 thin pieces veal medallions cut from veal eye loin (1.5 to 2 ounces each), or leg scaloppini

Freshly ground black pepper

2 lemons, cut into wedges

German Potato Salad (page 218) made with diced cornichons instead of bacon, if desired

1 In a deep saucepan, heat one inch of oil over high heat until a parsley leaf dropped in the oil sizzles on contact. Fry the parsley until crisp and dark green but not brown. With a small mesh strainer, remove the parsley to drain on paper towels and sprinkle with salt. Set aside while making the schnitzel.

2 For the bread crumbs, break the bread into manageable chunks and grind until fine in a food processor. Shake the crumbs through a fine-mesh wire strainer. Measure about 3½ cups and reserve the rest for another use.

3 Place the eggs in a shallow bowl and beat well; place the flour in another large shallow bowl and the bread crumbs in another similar bowl. Set up a breading station by placing the flour, eggs, and breadcrumbs in that order from left to right.

4 Place the veal in a heavy-duty plastic bag and pound it to a ⅛-inch thickness. Season with salt and pepper on both sides. Repeat with the rest of the veal.

5 Dip one piece of veal in the flour on both sides and shake off the excess. Dip it into the egg and let the excess drip off the bottom. Lay the veal on the bread crumbs and pile more crumbs on the top, patting them very lightly. Scooping under the schnitzel and under the layer of bread crumbs on the plate, turn it over and repeat the process. Holding the schnitzel by the top, shake off the excess crumbs. Avoid overhandling the meat. Lay the breaded piece flat on a cookie sheet. Repeat with all the pieces.

6 Preheat the oven to 325°F. In a 12-inch, high-sided sauté pan or skillet, heat ¼ inch of oil over high heat for about 1 minute. Gently lay two pieces of schnitzel in the oil. Immediately begin to shake the pan backward and forward on the burner, bathing the veal in oil; this is necessary for the breading to puff. Turn down the heat just a little bit. The schnitzel should begin to puff up. When the schnitzel is golden brown on the bottom, about 4 minutes, turn it over and fry, continuing to shake the pan, until the underside is golden brown, about 3 minutes. With a slotted spoon, remove the schnitzel from the pan and drain on paper towels. Repeat with the rest of the meat, keeping the finished schnitzels warm in the oven.

7 Serve the schnitzels immediately, garnished with fried parsley and accompanied by lemon wedges and cucumber or potato salad.

Serves 4

appendix

anya's address book   Once you've made some of these great dishes at home, here are a few of my favorite places to taste them. *Bon Voyage.*

BEST BOUILLABAISSE IN MARSEILLES

Miramar (12 quai du Port; tel: 04-91-91-10-40), run by the ebullient Minguella brothers might seem a little touristic and down at the heels. Never mind: the bouillabaisse is so intense, it's almost unreal. **Michel** (6 rue des Catalans; tel: 04-91-52-64-22) has the most pristine and elegant bouillabaisse in town, while **L'Escale** (2 BD Alexandre-Delabre, les Goudes; tel: 04-91-73-16-78) offers the best overall experience: great fish, perfectly balanced broth, delicious rouille, all served up with glorious Mediterranean vistas. Well worth the cab ride.

BEST CASSOULET

Paris

Le Trou Gascon (40 rue Taine; tel: 01-43-44-34-26). Chef Alain Dutournier's version with perfectly cooked tarbais beans justly ranks among the best in the capital. **Le Regalade** (49 Ave. Jean-Moulin; tel: 01-45-45-68-58). I love everything about this out-of-the-way neo-bistro in the 14th. Chef Yves Comdeborde's cassoulet with fresh beans and seven meats is my personal Holy Grail; it's not always on the menu, so call ahead.

Languedoc

Chez Emile (13 place St-Georges, Toulouse; tel: 05-61-21-05-56) is the great regional cassoulet mecca where the heroic casserole bakes for seven long hours. **Auberge Aux deux Acacias** (23, route nationale 113, Villepinte; tel: 04-68-94-24-67). By the antique stove here, you'll find glorious Castelnaudary-style cassoulet with pork or duck confit. **Restaurant l'Amphitryon** (Chemin de Gramont, Colomiers; tel: 05-61-15-55-55) is where the young Michelin-starred chef Yannick Delpech takes the Languedoc classic into the 21st century.

BEST COUSCOUS

Mansouria (11 rue Faidherbe, Paris; tel: 01-43-71-00-16) is my favorite Moroccan restaurant in the world, thanks to the passion and expertise of its owner, Fatéma Hal. Their couscous is actually better than anything I had in Morocco, outside of private homes.

BEST FISH AND CHIPS

London

Rock & Sole Plaice (47 Endell Street; tel: 020-7836-3785) claims to have been in business since 1871 and delivers everything you want from a chippie, throngs of tourists notwithstanding. Ditto for the **Two Brothers' Fish Restaurant** (297-303 Regent's Park Road; tel: 020-8346-0469), whose exemplary crisp haddock, fat chips, and mushy peas justify the long wait.

BEST FRIED CHICKEN

Watershed (406 W Ponce de Leon Ave., Decatur, GA; tel: 404-378-4900). Scott Peacock's recipe, featured in this book, is perfection. **Willie Mae's Scotch House** (2401 St. Ann St., New Orleans; tel: 504-822-9503). Other soul food places in New Orleans might have more buzz, but for the crispiest chicken look no further.

BEST PAELLAS

Madrid

Casa Benigna (Benigno Soto, 9; tel: 91-413-33-56). The proprietor's mother is from Alicante and this is the *only* place in the Spanish capital to savor a truly authentic paella.

Valencia

La Matandeta (Carretera Alfafar-El Saler, Albufera; tel: 962-11-21-84). In the heart of the rice-producing Albufera, paella cooked by a robust septuagenarian over a wood fire.

Alicante (If you're serious about paellas, this is your mecca)

El Poblet (Las Marinas, km 3; Denia; tel: 965-78-76-62). The best modern restaurant in the whole Levante region; with intensely Mediterranean flavors and seafood rices that are simply unsurpassed. **Piripi** (Avenida Oscar Espla, 301 Alicante; tel: 96-522-7940). The venerable Castello family offers more than a dozen rice dishes daily, each one terrific.

Best Pesto in Liguria

Paola e Barbara (Via Roma, 47; San Remo; tel: 0184-531-653). Liguria's best restaurant offers an incomparable rendition of chestnut flour *troffie* (tiny gnocchi) with mortar-made pesto. **Ca'Peo** (Via dei Caduti 80, Leivi; tel: 0185-319-696). In this elegant dining room in the hills above Chiavari, Melly Solari's hand-made pesto is legendary. **La Brinca** (Localita Campo di Ne, 58; Ne in Valgravegila; tel: 0185 337-480) offers rare regional inland specialties and immensely aromatic pesto.

Best Pizza

Naples

Pizzeria Da Michele (Via Cesare Sersale, 1-3-5-7; tel: 081-553-9204). If you had time for only one pizza in Naples, this is where you'd go. The toppings are margherita and marinara only. **Da Matteo** (Via Tribunale, 94; tel: 081-455-262) is another classic featuring pizza fritta and a sublime pizza topped with arugula, besides the classic pies. **Ciro Santa Brigita** (Via S. Brigita, 71-74; tel: 081-552-4072). Owner Antonio Pace, the president of Neapolitan Pizzamakers Association, delivers a letter-perfect rendition of the Neapolitan pie. A good restaurant, too.

Best Pie, USA

Pizzeria Bianco (623 E. Adams St; Phoenix, AZ; tel: 602-258-8300). Here it is, folks: the greatest pizza this side of Naples, made by Chris Bianco, the Michelangelo of American *pizzaiolos*.

Best Risotto in Venice

Fiaschetteria Toscana (San Giovani Crisostomo, Cannaregio; tel: 041-528-5281). The risotto here is usually laced with seafood and made with special Acquerello rice. **Da Fiore** (San Polo, Calle del Scaleter; tel: 041-721-343) is the city's haute seafood temple, with a spectacular black risotto. **Al Covo** (Campiello della Pescaria; tel: 041-522-3812). The owner, Cesare Benelli, is justly considered one of Italy's great rice maestros.

Outside Venice

Riseria Ferron (Via Saccovener 6, Pilavecia; Isola della Scala; tel: 045-730-1022), a short drive south of Verona, is a traditional rice mill with a rice-focused restaurant, guided tours, and occasional recipe demos.

BEST STEAK IN AMERICA

Peter Luger (178 Broadway, Brooklyn, NY; tel: 718-387-7400). You'll forgive the gruff service and a tomato salad that seems like someone's idea of a practical joke for the glorious dry-aged porterhouse. **Bern's Steak House** (1208 South Howard Ave, Tampa, FL; tel: 813-251-2421). Pilgrims of the beef faith flock to this tacky, sprawling Tampa institution for the incredible dry-aged beef. **Gene & Georgetti** (500 N. Franklin St., Chicago, IL; tel: 312/527-5718). An old Chicago beef and booze bastion if there ever was one. Don't miss the "garbage" salad and don't listen to people who prefer Gibsons.

BEST TANDOORI CHICKEN IN NEW DEHLI

Dastarkhwan e-Karim (168/2, Hzt. Nizamuddin West; tel: 11-469-8300) is considered by Dehlites as the Taj Mahal of tandoori cooking.

BEST SOBA

Tokyo

Yabu Soba (2-10 Kanda-Awajicho, Minato-ku; tel: 03-3258-0684) is Tokyo's most venerable noodle shop, with soba treated as a religion. **Matsugen** (Ginza Green 4F, 7-8-7 Ginza, Chuoku; tel: 03-5568-8989) might seem hyper-trendy but the soba is pure and classic.

New York

Honmura An (170 Mercer St.; tel: 212-334-5253) is the only place in America to savor real artisanal soba.

BEST SUSHI

Tokyo

The humble **Daiwa-zushi** (Chuo Shijo Bldg. No. 6, 5-2-1 Tsukiji, Chuo-ku; tel: 03-3547-6807) in the Tsukiji fish market offers my favorite Tokyo sushi experience. Best at 7 A.M. **Tokyo Shokudo Central Mikuni's** (Tokyo Station Marunouchi South Gate, B1F; tel: 03-5218-5123) is the home of the post-modern *kaiten* (conveyer belt) sushi, as delicious as it is entertaining.

New York

Sushi Yasuda (204 E. 43rd St; tel: 212-972-1001) is a sushi purist's paradise with astonishing fish and even better rice.

selected bibliography

Achaya, K.T. Indian Food: A Historical Companion. Delhi: OUP, 1994.

Aidells, Bruce, and Kelly, Denis. The Complete Meat Cookbook. New York: Houghton Mifflin, 1998.

Alarcon, Claudia. "Tamales in Mesoamerica," in Petits Propos Culinaires 63. Totnes: Prospect Books, 2000.

Anderson, E. N. The Food of China. New Haven: Yale University Press, 1988.

Anderson, Jean. The American Century Cookbook. New York: Clarkson N. Potter, 1997.

Andoh, Elizabeth. An American Taste of Japan. New York: William Morrow, 1985.

———. An Ocean of Flavor. New York: William Morrow, 1988.

André, Jean-Louis. Cuisines des pays de France. Paris: Éditions du Chene, 2001.

Andrews, Colman. Flavors of the Riviera. New York: Bantam Books, 1996.

Ayrton, Elizabeth. The Cookery of England. London: Purwell Book Services, 1975.

Bailey, Adrian. The Cooking of the British Isles. New York: Time-Life Books, 1969.

Bayless, Rick and Bayless, Deann Groen. Authentic Mexican. New York: William Morrow, 1987.

Bayless, Rick et al. Rick Bayless's Mexican Kitchen. New York: Scribners, 1996.

Beard, James. James Beard's American Cookery. Boston: Little, Brown and Company, 1972.

———. James Beard's Simple Foods. New York: Macmillan, 1993.

———. On Cookery. Boston: Little, Brown and Company, 1972.

Belleme, John et al. Culinary Treasures of Japan. New York: Avery Penguin Putnam, 1992.

Benincasa, Gabriele. La pizza napoletana: mito, storia e poesia. Naples: Alfredo Guida Editore, 1992.

Benning, Lee Edwards. *The Cook's Tales: Origins of Famous Foods and Recipes*. Old Saybrook, Connecticut: The Globe Pequot Press, 1992.

Bhumichitr, Vatcharin. *The Taste of Thai Food*. New York: Atheneum, 1988.

Bini, Bruno, and Lingua, Paolo. *Colombo invita a tavola*. Milan: GGallery s.r.l., 1992.

Bocuse, Paul. *Regional French Cooking*. Paris: Flammarion, 1991.

Briz, José. *Libro del gazpacho y los gazpachos*. Madrid: Editorial Grupo Libro 88, 1993.

Brothwell, Patricia and Don. *Food in Antiquity*. New York: Frederick A. Praeger, 1969.

Burning Stevens, Patricia. *Rare Bits: Unusual Origins of Popular Recipes*. Ohio: Ohio University Press, 1998.

Chang, K. C., ed. *Food in Chinese Culture*. New Haven: Yale University Press, 1977.

Chaslin, Pierre et al. *Discover Thai Cooking*. Singapore: Times Editions, 1987.

Child, Julia. *Mastering the Art of French Cooking*. Volumes I and II. New York: Random House Trade Paperbacks, 1983.

Coe, Sophie, and Coe, Michael. *The True Story of Chocolate*. New York: Thames and Hudson, 1996.

Coe, Sophie. *America's First Cuisines*. Austin: University of Texas Press, 1994.

Cost, Bruce. *Asian Ingredients*. New York: William Morrow and Company Inc., 1988.

Courtine, Robert. *The Hundred Glories of French Cooking*. New York: Farrar, Straus and Giroux, 1971.

Csergo, Julia, ed. *Pot-au-feu: Convivial, Familial: Histoires d'un mythe*. Paris: Éditions Autrement, 1999.

Dalby, Andrew, and Grainger, Sally. *Classical Cookbook*. London: British Museum Press, 1996.

David, Elizabeth. *Elizabeth David Classics: Mediterranean Food, French Country Cooking, Summer Cooking*. New York: Alfred A. Knopf, 1980.

Davidson, Alan. *North Atlantic Seafood*. New York: The Viking Press, 1979.

———. *The Oxford Companion to Food*. New York: Oxford University Press, Inc. 1999.

Day-Lewis, Tamasin. *The Art of the Tart*. New York: Random House, 2000.

Del Conte, Anna. "Polenta—An Italian Staple," in *Petit Propos Culinaires 75*. London: Prospect Books, 1989.

———. *Gastronomy of Italy*. London: Pavilion Books, 2001.

———. *The Classic Food of Northern Italy*. London: Pavilion Books, 1995.

Dickson, Paul. *The Great American Ice Cream Book*. New York: Atheneum, 1972.

Domine, André, ed. *Culinaria France*. Cologne: Könemann, 1999.

Donaldson, Enid. *The Real Taste of Jamaica*. Toronto: Warwick Publishing, 2000.

Du Plessix Gray, Francine. *At Home with Marquis de Sade*. New York: Simon & Schuster, 1998.

Dumas, Alexandre (Davidson, Alan and Jane, transl.). *Dumas on Food*. Oxford: Oxford University Press, 1987.

Editors of *Saveur* magazine. *Saveur Cooks Authentic French*. San Francisco: Chronicle Books, 1999.

Editors of *Cook's Illustrated* magazine. *The Best Recipe*. Brookline: Boston Common Press, 1999.

Edwards, John. *The Roman Cookery of Apicius*. Washington: Hartley & Marks, 1984.

Egerton, John. *Southern Food*. New York: Alfred A. Knopf, 1987.

Elbert, Virginia and George. *Down-Island Caribbean Cookery*. New York: Simon & Schuster, 1991.

Ellis, Merle. *The Great American Meat Cookbook*. New York: Alfred A. Knopf, 1996.

Escoffier, Auguste. *Ma Cuisine*. London: Paul Hamlyn, 1934.

Falcou, Francis. *Le Cassoulet de Castelnaudary*. Toulouse: Editions Loubatiéres, 1986.

Farmer, Fannie Merritt. *Original 1896 Boston Cooking-School Cook Book* New York: Unabridged Dover, 1997.

Farr Louis, Diana. *Feasting and Fasting in Crete*. Athens: Kedros Publishers, 2001.

Flandrin, Jean-Louis, ed. *Food: A Culinary History*. New York: Penguin Books, 2000.

Fochesato, Walter, et al. *Il Basilico: Pesto e salse da mortaio*. Genoa: Feguagiskia Studio Edizione, 1999.

Fowler, Damon Lee. *Classical Southern Cooking*. New York: Crown Publishers, Inc., 1995.

Friedland, Susan R. *Shabbat Shalom*. New York: Little, Brown and Company, 1999.

Fussel, Betty. *The Story of Corn*. New York: Alfred A. Knopf, 1994.

García Santos, Rafael. *Lo mejor de la gastronomia 2003*. Madrid: Ediciones Destino, 2002.

Glasse, Hannah. *Art of Cookery Made Plain and Easy*. Bedford: Applewood Books, 1998.

Glenn, Camille. *The Heritage of Southern Cooking*. New York: Workman Publishing, 1986.

Godard, Misette, and Dupuy, Jacques. "Bouillabaisse," in *Slow: The International Herald of Taste 21*. Bra: Slow Food Editore, 2000.

Gonzales de la Vara, Fernan. *La cocina Mexicana a traves de los siglos*. Vol II. Mexico City: Editorial Clio, 1996.

Graulich, David. *The Hamburger Companion*. New York: Lebhar-Friedman Books, 1999.

Guinaudeau, Zette. *Traditional Moroccan Cooking*. London: Serif, 1958.

Haber, Barbara. *From Hardtack to Home Fries: An Uncommon History of American Cooks and Meals*. New York: The Free Press, 2002.

Hahn, Emily. *The Cooking of China*. New York: Time-Life Books, 1968.

Hal, Fatéma. *Le livre du couscous*. Paris: Editions Stock, 2000.

Hanger, Catherine. *Lonely Planet World Food Morocco*. Victoria, Australia: Lonely Planet, 2000.

Hazan, Marcella. *Marcella Cucina*. New York: HarperCollins, 1997.

———. *Marcella's Italian Kitchen*. New York: Alfred. A. Knopf, 1987.

Hearon, Reed, and Knickerbocker, Peggy. *The Rose Pistola Cookbook*. New York: Broadway Books, 1999.

Ibrahim, Jabbar. *Hawkers Delight*. Kuala Lumpur: S. Abdul Majeed & Co., 1992.

Iturriaga, Jose N. *La cultura de antojito*. Mexico City: Editorial Diana, 1994.

Jaffrey, Madhur. *An Invitation to Indian Cooking*. New York: Vintage, 1975.

Jamison, Cheryl Alters, and Jamison, Bill. *American Home Cooking*. New York: Broadway Books, 1999.

Johnston, Mireille. *The French Family Feast*. New York: Simon & Schuster, 1988.

Jones, Evan. *American Food*. New York: Vintage Books, 2nd ed., 1981.

Kahrs, Kurt. *Thai Cooking*. Bangkok: Asia Books, 1990.

Kennedy, Diana. *My Mexico*. New York: Clarkson N. Potter, 1998.

———. *The Art of Mexican Cooking*. New York: Bantam Books, 1989.

———. *The Essential Cuisines of Mexico*. New York: Clarkson N. Potter, 2000.

Kochilas, Diane. *The Food and Wines of Greece*. New York: St. Martin's Press, 1990.

———. *The Glorious Food of Greece*. New York: William Morrow, 2001.

Kovalyov, N.I. *Rasskazi o russkoy kukhnye*. Moscow: Ekonomika, 1984.

Kremezi, Aglaia. *The Food of the Greek Islands*. Boston: Houghton Mifflin Company, 2000.

Kyle Leopold, Allison. *Victorian Frozen Dainties*. New York: Clarkson N. Potter, 1993.

Lallemand, Roger. *Les pot-au-feu*. France: Jeanne Lafitte, 1984.

Lewis, Edna, and Peacock, Scott. *The Gift of Southern Cooking: Recipes and Revelations from Two Great American Cooks*. New York: Alfred A. Knopf, 2003.

Acame, Franco. *Mandilli de Sœ*. Genoa: De Ferrari, 1990.

Lin, Hsiang-Ju. *Chinese Gastronomy*. New York: Harcourt Brace Jovanovich, 1969.

Lo, Eileen Yin-Fei. *New Cantonese Cooking*. New York: Viking Penguin, 1988.

———. *The Chinese Kitchen*. New York: William Morrow, 1999.

Lo, Kenneth. *Chinese Regional Cooking*. New York: Pantheon Books, 1979.

Loha-Unchit, Kasma. *It Rains Fishes*. San Francisco: Pomegranate Artbooks, 1994.

Luján, Néstor. *Historia de la gastronomía*. Madrid: Plaza & Janés Editores, S.A., 1988.

March, Lourdes. *El libro de la paella y de los arroces*. Madrid: Alianza Editorial, Libro de Bolsillo, 1985.

Mariani, John F. *The Encyclopedia of American Food & Drink*. New York: Lebhar-Friedman Books, 1999.

Marks, Gil. *The World of Jewish Cooking*. New York: Simon & Schuster, 1996.

Matsuhisa, Nobuyuki. *Nobu: The Cookbook*. Tokyo and New York: Kodansha International, 2001.

McGee, Harold. *On Food and Cooking: The Science and Lore of the Kitchen*. New York: Fireside, 1984.

McLaughlin, Michael. *Back of the Box Gourmet*. New York: Simon & Schuster, 1990.

———. *The New American Kitchen*. New York: Simon & Schuster, 1990.

Montagne, Prosper. *Larousse Gastronomique*. New York: Clarkson N. Potter; Revised edition, 2001.

Morse, Kitty. *Cooking at the Kasbah*. San Francisco: Chronicle Books, 1998.

———. *Couscous: Fresh and Flavorful Contemporary Recipes*. San Francisco: Chronicle Books, 2000.

Pilcher, Jeffrey M. *Que Vivan los Tamales! Food and the Making of Mexican Identity*. Albuquerque: University of New Mexico Press, 1998.

Muller, Claude. *Coutumes et traditions du Dauphiné*. Grenoble: Édition de Bellande, 1978.

Nathan, Joan. *Jewish Cooking in America*. New York: Random House, 1998.

Nekrylova, A.F. *Russkiye narodniye gorodskiye prazdniki*. Leningrad: Isskustvo, 1988.

Olney, Richard. *The French Menu Cookbook*. San Francisco: Ten Speed Press, 2002.

Omae, Hinjiro, and Tachibana, Yuzuru. *The Book of Sushi*. Tokyo, New York, San Francisco: Kodansha International, 1981.

Parker, Dorian Leigh. *Doughnuts*. New York: Clarkson N. Potter, 1994.

Peterson, James. *Fish and Shellfish*. New York: William Morrow, 1996.

Pham, Mai. *Pleasures of the Vietnamese Table*. New York: HarperCollins, 2001.

Plachutta, Ewald, and Wagner, Christoph. *Die Gute Kuche*. Vienna: Verlag Orac, 1993.

Plotkin, Fred. *Recipes from Paradise: Life and Food on the Italian Riviera*. New York: Little, Brown and Company, 1997.

Randolph, Mary. *The Virginia Housewife*. Columbia: University of South Carolina Press, 1984.

Ratto, G.B., and Ratto, Gio. *La cucinera genovese*. Genoa: Pagano, 1863.

Rice, William. *Steak Lover's Cookbook*. New York: Workman Publishing, 1997.

Richie, Donald. *A Taste of Japan*. Tokyo and New York: Kodansha International, 1985.

Roden, Claudia. *The Book of Jewish Food*. New York: Alfred A. Knopf, 1996.

———. *The New Book of Middle Eastern Food*. New York: Alfred. A. Knopf, 2000.

Root, Waverly, and de Rochemont, Richard. *Eating in America*. New Jersey: The Ecco Press, 1981.

Root, Waverly. *Food: An Authoritative Visual History and Dictionary of Food of the World*. New York: Simon & Schuster, 1980.

———. *The Food of France*. New York: Vintage, 1966.

Rosen, Diana. *The Ice Cream Lover's Companion*. New York: Citadel Press, 2000.

Rosetto-Kasper, Lynne. *The Splendid Table*. New York: William Morrow, 1992.

Routhier, Nicole. *The Foods of Vietnam*. New York: Stewart, Tabori & Chang, 1989.

Rozin, Elizabeth. *The Primal Cheeseburger*. New York: Penguin Books, 1994.

Rubin, Emmanuel. *Paris des Envies gourmandes 2002*. Paris: Flammarion, 2001.

Saberi, Helen, and Davidson, Alan. *Trifle (The English Kitchen)*. Totnes: Prospect Books, 2001.

Sahni, Julie. *Classic Indian Cooking*. New York: William Morrow, 1980.

Salloum, Habeeb, and Peters, James. *From the Land of Figs and Olives*. New York: Interlink Books, 1995.

Sax, Richard. *Classic Home Desserts.* Shelbourne, Vermont: Chapters, 1994.

Scharfenberg, Horst. *The Cuisines of Germany.* New York: Poseidon Books, 1989.

Schulz, Phillip. *As American as Apple Pie.* New York: Random House, 1990.

Schwartz, Arthur. *Naples at Table.* New York: HarperCollins, 1998.

Sheraton, Mimi. *Whole World Loves Chicken Soup.* New York: Warner Books, Inc., 2000.

Shimbo, Hiroko. *The Japanese Kitchen.* Boston: Harvard Common Press, 2000.

Silorata, Ettore Bernabo. *La pizza napoletana: storia, aneddoti, ricette.* Naples: M.P.S.r.l. Edizioni, 2000.

Simmons, Amelia. *American Cookery 1796.* Boston: Rowan Tree Press, 1982.

Simonds, Nina. *Classic Chinese Cuisine.* Boston: Houghton Mifflin Co., 1999.

Simoons, Frederick J. *Food in China.* Boca Raton, Florida: CRC Press, 1994.

Solomon, Charmaine. *Charmaine Solomon's Encyclopaedia of Asian Food.* Port Melbourne: William Heinemann, 1996.

Spurling, Hillary. *Elinor Fettiplace's Recipe Book: Elizabethan Country House Cooking.* London: Viking Salamander, 1986.

Grigson, Jane. *British Cookery.* New York: Atheneum, 1985.

Steinberg, Sally Levitt. *The Donut Book.* New York: Alfred A. Knopf, 1987.

Steingarten, Jeffrey. *The Man Who Ate Everything.* New York: Alfred A. Knopf, 1997.

Stern, Jane and Michael. *Roadfood.* New York: Broadway Books, 2002.

Tennyson, Jeffrey. *Hamburger Heaven: The Illustrated History of the Hamburger.* New York: Warner Books, 1995.

Thompson, David. *Thai Food.* San Francisco: Ten Speed Press, 2002.

Thorne, John, and Thorne, Matt Lewis. *Serious Pig.* New York: North Point Press, Farrar, Straus and Giroux, 1996.

Toussaint-Samat, Maguelonne. *History of Food.* Cambridge, Massachussets: Blackwell Publishers, 1992.

Trager, James. *The Food Chronology.* New York: Henry Holt and Co., 1995.

Tropp, Barbara. *The Modern Art of Chinese Cooking.* New York: William Morrow, 1982.

Tsuda, Nobuko. *Sushi Made Easy.* New York: Weatherhill, 1982.

Tsuji, Shizuo. *Japanese Cooking, A Simple Art*. Tokyo and New York: Kodansha International, 1980.

Udesky, James. *The Book of Soba*. Tokyo and New York: Kodansha International, 1988.

Valderrama, Mariano. *El libro de oro de las comidas Peruanas*. Lima: Peru Reporting E.I.R.I, 1996.

Villas, James. *American Taste*. New York: Arbor House, 1982.

Volokh, Anne. *The Art of Russian Cuisine*. New York: Macmillan Publishing Company, 1983.

Von Bremzen, Anya. *Fiesta: A Celebration of Latin Hospitality*. New York: Doubleday, 1997.

Von Bremzen, Anya, and Welchman, John. *Please to the Table: The Russian Cookbook*. New York: Workman Publishing, 1990.

———. *Terrific Pacific Cookbook*. New York: Workman Publishing, 1996.

Wechsberg, Joseph, et al. *The Cooking of Vienna's Empire*. New York: Time Life Books, 1968.

Wells, Patricia. *The Food Lover's Guide to France*. New York: Workman Publishing, 1987.

Westrip, Joyce. *Moghul Cooking*. London: Serif, 1997.

White, Florence. *Good Things in England*. London: Jonathan Cape, 1932.

White, Jasper. *50 Chowders*. New York: Scribner, 2000.

Willinsky, Helen. *Jerk Barbecue from Jamaica*. California: The Crossing Press, 1990.

Wilson, Ann. *Food and Drink in Britain*. New York: Harper & Row, 1974.

Wolfert, Paula. *Couscous and Other Good Food from Morocco*. New York: Harper & Row, 1973.

———. *The Cooking of South-West France*. New York: HarperCollins (paper); Reprint edition, 1994.

Wright, Clifford A. *A Mediterranean Feast*. New York: William Morrow, 1999.

Zuckerman, Larry. *The Potato: How the Humble Spud Rescued the Western World*. New York: North Point Press, 1999.

index

Adriá, Ferran, 314
Akin, Engin, 127
Al Covo restaurant, Venice, Italy, 229
almond(s)
    duck bastilla, 12–13
    pastry, 151–52
Alonso, Juan Carlos, 102
American Cookery (Simmons), 65
Anderson, J. Walter, 115
appetizers
    blini, 22–23
    Claude Rigaud's Roquefort and walnut
        soufflé, 262–63
    green chicken tamales, 296–98
    Malaysian chicken and lamb saté with
        peanut sauce, 250–51
    perfect hummus, 120–21
    Peruvian fish ceviche, 45
    spiced orange shrimp ceviche, 46–47
    summer rolls with mint, chicken, and
        shrimp, 282–83
    tortilla de patata (Spanish potato omelet),
        316–17
apple(s)
    Armenian summer dolma, 80–81
    pie, 45
    roast chicken with lemons and, 238–39
    tarte Tatin, 305
apple pie, xiv–xv, 2–5
    American-style, 4–5
    cook's notes, 4
    history, 2–3
arepas, 6–9
    cook's notes, 8
    history, 6
    masarepa (precooked arepa flour), 6, 8
    variations, 6
Argentinean parsley sauce (*chimichurri*), 274
Armenian dolma (stuffed vegetables), 78–81
Arte de Reposteria (Mata), 102
Art of Cookery (Glasse), 130, 233, 319
Art of Tart, The (Day-Lewis), 151
Asian Noodles (Simonds), 254

avocado
    sushi for a party, 286–88
    tomatillo salsa, 292
Austria
    Weiner schnitzel, 322–25

Baker, James, 60
Balzi Rossi restaurant, Liguria, Italy, 196
barbecue
    jerk pork, 136
    Korean, short ribs (Kalbi), xiii, 139–39
    marinades, 136, 138
basil: classic Ligurian pesto, 198–99
bastilla, 10–11
    cook's notes, 12
    duck bastilla, 12–13
    filling variations, 11, 12
    history, 10
    pastry for, 12
    warka (traditional dough), 10–11
beans
    cassoulet, 40–43
    Irene's mole poblano with turkey and
        vegetables, 172–73
    minestrone alla Genovese, 166
    paella Valenciana with rabbit, chicken, and
        duck, 186–87
    trenette al pesto, Genova-style, 199
béchamel, 147–48, 177
beef
    Armenian summer dolma, 80–81
    classic Bolognese lasagne al forno, 146–49
    feijoada completa, 92–93
    hamburger, 116–17
    Molyvos moussaka with yogurt béchamel,
        176–77
    pan-seared rib eye with Argentinean parsley
        sauce, 274–75
    pho bo, 202–3
    and pork sancocho, 246–47
    pot-au-feu, 222–23
    roast, with Port gravy and Yorkshire pudding,
        234–35

Russian winter borshch with, and pork, 26–27
beets
    Russian winter borshch with beef and pork, 26–27
Benedict, LeGrande, 86
Benedict, Lemuel, 86
Benelli, Cesare, 229
Bini, Anna, 110
biryani (Indian layered rice), 14–19
    chef, 15
    cook's notes, 16
    dum pukht (cooking method), 15
    garam masala, 16
    history, 14
    Hyderabadi lamb biryani, 16–19
    resources for rice, 19
    variation with chicken, 19
Bladen, Thomas, 123
blini, 20–23
    cook's notes, 22
    garnishes, 22
    history, 20–21
borshch, 24–27
    cook's notes, 26
    history, 24–25
    Russian winter, with beef and pork, 26–27
    various forms, 24
bouillabaisse, xiii, xiv–xv, 28–33
    cook's notes, 30
    fish species in, 29
    history, 28–29
    Marseillaise, 30–33
    rouille (mayonnaise) and croutons, 29, 31, 32
Bouley, David, 324
Brazil
    caiperinhas, 91
    feijoada, 90–93
breakfast
    arepas, 6–9
    buttermilk doughnuts, 84–85
    perfect hummus, 120–21
Brillat-Savarin, Anthelme, 34
Britain
    fish and chips, 96–97
    roast beef with Yorkshire pudding, 232–35
    trifle, 318–21
Brosi, Henry, 233
Bruschi, Pierina, 197
buttermilk doughnuts, 84–85

cabbage, napa (Chinese), 277
    lion's head meatballs, 162–63
    See also Chinese greens
cabbage, Savoy

minestrone alla Genovese, 166
Caesar salad, xii, 34–37
    cook's notes, 36
    history, 34–35
Café des Orient, Beirut, Lebanon, 118
cake
    cheesecake, 50–51
    Rose Pistola chocolate budino, 62–63
Canadian bacon
    eggs Benedict, 88–89
Cardini, Caesar, xii, 34
Carême, Antonin, 260
carnitas tacos with tomatillo salsa, xiii, 291–92
carrots
    beef pot-au-feu, 222–23
    couscous with seven vegetables, 70–73
    palov (Uzbek lamb pilaf), 188–91
    sesame noodles, 254–55
    Susan Friedland's double-strength chicken soup, 58
    traditional Russian Jewish gefilte fish, 108–9
cashews
    Hyderabadi lamb biryani, 16–19
cassoulet, xvi–xv, 40–43, 212
    chef, 40
    cook's notes, 40
    history, 38–39
    resources, 43
    Tarbais or Lingot beans, 39, 40
Castro, Pilar, 184–85
Cato, 48
cauliflower
    potato gnocchi with, -gorgonzola sauce, 112–13
celery
    couscous with seven vegetables, 70–73
ceviche, 44–47
    chef for, 46
    cook's notes, 46
    history, 44–45
    Peruvian fish, 45
    spiced orange shrimp, 46–47
Chapman, Johnny "Johnny Appleseed," 3
cheese
    arepas, 6–9
    béchamel, 147–48, 177
    Caesar salad, 36–37
    cheeseburger, 116–17
    cheesecake, 50–51
    classic Bolognese lasagne al forno, 146–49
    classic Ligurian pesto, 198–99
    classic macaroni and, 158–59
    Claude Rigaud's Roquefort and walnut soufflé, 262–63
    French onion soup, 179–80

cheese (cont.)
    gratin Dauphinois, 214–15
    Neapolitan pizza Margherita, 206–7
    potato gnocchi with cauliflower-gorgonzola
      sauce, 112–13
    spanakopita with wild greens, 270–71
    three-, polenta with mushrooms, 210–11
cheeseburger, 116–17
cheesecake, 48–51
    cook's notes, 50
    history, 48–49
Chekhov, Anton, 20
chelo (Persian steamed rice with a crust), 52–55
    accompaniments for, 53
    basmati rice for, 54
    cook's notes, 54
    darbari and domsiah rice for, 52
    history, 52–53
    resources, 55
    tah dig ("the bottom of the pot"), 53, 54
chicken
    couscous with seven vegetables, 70–73
    green, tamales, 296–98
    grilled tandoori, 301–2
    Hyderabadi biryani variation, 16–19
    laksa, 140–43
    Malaysian, and lamb saté with peanut sauce,
      250–51
    paella Valenciana with rabbit, and duck,
      186–87
    pho, quick version, 201
    roast, with lemons and apples, 238–39
    schmaltz, 59
    Scott Peacock's fried, with tomato gravy,
      100–101
    sesame noodles, 254–55
    summer rolls with mint, and shrimp, 282–83
    Susan Friedland's double-strength, soup,
      58–59
chicken soup, 56–59
    author's childhood and, 56
    chef, 58, 59
    cook's notes, 58
    matzo balls, 59
    restorative powers, 56–57
    schmaltz, 59
    Susan Friedland's double-strength, 58–59
chickpeas
    Armenian summer dolma, 80–81
    couscous with seven vegetables, 70–73
    hummus, 120–21
Child, Julia, 34
chiles
    carnitas tacos with tomatillo salsa, xiii,
      291–92

    green chicken tamales, 296–98
    mole poblano with turkey and vegetables,
      172–73
    Nuoc Cham dipping sauce, 283
    pad thai sauce, 182–83
    Thai red curry paste, 308–10
    tomatillo salsa, 292
    tom yum kung, 311–13
China
    lion's head meatballs, 162–63
    Peking duck, 192–95
    sesame noodles, 252–55
    stir-fried greens, 276–79
Chinese greens (list), 276–78
chocolate
    Baker's, 60
    cheesecake, 50–51
    Irene's mole poblano with turkey and
      vegetables, 172–73
    Rose Pistola, budino cake, 62–63
chocolate cake, 60–63
    brands of chocolate recommended, 62
    chef, 61
    cook's notes, 62
    German, 60
    history, 60–61
    Rose Pistola, budino cake, 62–63
Chow, Clifford, 193
chowder, 64–67
    chef, 66
    cook's notes, 66
    history, 64–65
    New England fish, 66–67
Churchill, Winston, 95
Ciro Santa Brigita restaurant, Naples, Italy,
    204–5
clams
    spaghetti alle vongole, 264–67
Clark, Melissa, 124
cocktails, *caiperinhas* or *caiperoska*, 91
coconut milk
    laksa, 140–43
    red curry of roast duck and pineapple, 308–10
Coe, Sophie, 60
Collins, S., 20
Colombia
    arepas, 6–9
    beef and pork sancocho, xiii, 246–47
Colonnesi, Francesco, 205
Cooking from the Greek Islands (Kremezi), 174
Cooks Illustrated magazine, 98
cornmeal
    resources for Molino Sorbino, 211
    three-cheese polenta with mushrooms,
      210–11

couscous, 68–73
   chef, 68
   cook's notes, 70
   history, 68–69
   with seven vegetables, 70–73
   variations, 73
Craft restaurant, NYC, 237
cream (heavy)
   best vanilla ice cream, 124–25
   caramelized lemon tart, 151–52
   classic crème brûlée, 76–77
   Elisabeth Luard's Scottish raspberry and
     peach trifle, 320–21
crème brûlée, 74–77
   chef, 75
   classic, 76–77
   history, 74–75
   resources, 77
   vanilla beans for, xvii, 76
Cretan spanakopita (spinach pie), 268–71
croutons, 31, 32
   garlic, 36
cucumbers
   classic Andalusian gazpacho, 104–5
   sesame noodles, 254–55
curry, 130–31
   Hyderabadi lamb biryani, 16–19
   Malabar shrimp, 132–33
   Thai red, 309

Da Fiore, Venice, Italy, 229
Danube restaurant, Vienna, Austria, 324
Dastarkhwa e-Karim restaurant, New Delhi,
   299, 300
Davis, Fletcher "Old Dave," 114
Day-Lewis, Tamasin, 151
Del Conte, Anna, 208
Delmonico's restaurant, NYC, 86
Delouvrier, Christian, 40
desserts
   apple pie, 2–5
   best vanilla ice cream, 124–25
   buttermilk doughnuts, 84–85
   caramelized lemon tart, 151–52
   cheesecake, 50–51
   classic crème brûlée, 74–77
   Elisabeth Luard's Scottish raspberry and
     peach trifle, 320–21
   Rose Pistola chocolate budino cake, 62–63
   saffron rice pudding with pistachios, 226–27
   tarte Tatin, 305
Diana restaurant, Bologna, Italy, 145
Dictionary of American Food and Drink (Mariani),
   98
dolma (stuffed vegetables), 78–81

Armenian summer, 80–81
   chef, 78–79
   cook's notes, 80
   history, 78–79
Dorchester Hotel, London, 233
doughnuts, 82–85
   buttermilk, 84–85
   cook's notes, 84
   glaze, 84
   history, 82–83
   lore, 83
Ducasse, Alain, 156, 228
duck
   bastilla, 12–13
   confit for cassoulet, 40–43
   paella Valenciana with rabbit, chicken, and,
     186–87
   Pekin (Long Island Ducking) variety, 193
   Peking, 192–95
   red curry of roast, and pineapple, 308–10
Dumas, Alexandre, père, 178, 179, 314
Dupuy, Jacques, 28–29

Ecuador
   spiced orange shrimp ceviche, 44–47
eggplant, 126
   Armenian summer dolma, 80–81
   imam bayildi (Turkish braised), 128–29
   Molyvos moussaka with yogurt béchamel,
     176–77
eggs
   best vanilla ice cream, 124–25
   classic crème brûlée, 76–77
   Claude Rigaud's Roquefort and walnut
     soufflé, 262–63
   duck bastilla, 12–13
   hollandaise sauce, 87, 88–89
   lemon tart, 151–52
   pasta dough (sfoglia, egg pasta sheets),
     148–49
   rouille (mayonnaise), 29, 31, 32
   tortilla de patata (Spanish potato omelet),
     316–17
eggs Benedict, 86–89
   cook's notes, 88–89
   history, 86–87
   hollandaise sauce, 87, 88–89
El Gordo, Tijuana, Mexico, 289
English Housewife, The (Markham), 233
entrees
   Armenian summer dolma, 80–81
   beef and pork sancocho, 246–47
   beef pot-au-feu, 222–23
   blini, 22–23
   bouillabaisse Marseillaise, 30–33

index

entrees (*cont.*)
  carnitas tacos with tomatillo salsa, xiii, 291–92
  cassoulet, 40–43
  chilled zaru soba with dipping sauce, 258–59
  classic Bolognese lasagne al forno, 146–49
  couscous with seven vegetables, 70–73
  duck bastila, 12–13
  feijoada completa, 92–93
  fish and chips, 96–97
  green chicken tamales, 296–98
  hamburger, 116–17
  Hyderabadi lamb biryani, 16–19
  laksa, 140–43
  lion's head meatballs, 162–63
  Malaysian chicken and lamb saté with peanut sauce, 250–51
  mint-crusted roast leg of lamb with tart plum sauce, 242–43
  miso-glazed black cod, 169
  Molyvos moussaka with yogurt béchamel, 176–77
  Neapolitan pizza Margherita, 206–7
  New England fish chowder, 66–67
  pad thai, 182–83
  palov (Uzbek lamb pilaf), 188–91
  pan-seared rib eye with Argentinean parsley sauce, 274–75
  Peking duck, 192–95
  potato gnocchi with cauliflower-gorgonzola sauce, 112–13
  red curry of roast duck and pineapple, 308–10
  roast beef with Port gravy and Yorkshire pudding, 234–35
  roast chicken with lemons and apples, 238–39
  Scott Peacock's fried chicken with tomato gravy, 100–101
  spaghetti alle vongole, 264–67
  tortilla de patata (Spanish potato omelet), 316–17
  trenette al pesto, Genova-style, 199
  Weiner schnitzel, 322–25
equipment
  couscousière, 70
  Flame Tamer, 191
  kazan, 189, 190
  mini blowtorch, 77
  mortar and pestle, 199
  paella pans, 185, 187
  tarte Tatin pan, 305
  vertical roaster, 238
  zaru, 258
Escudera restaurant, Ronda, Spain, 103
Esposito, Raffaele, 205

Fazal, Abul, 14
Feasting and Fasting on Crete (Louis), 269
feijoada (Brazilian black bean and mixed meats casserole), 90–93
  completa, 92–93
  cook's notes, 92
  history, 90–91
  stir-fried shredded kale with, 93
Fiascchetteria Toscana, Venice, Italy, 228
50 Chowders (White), 64
first course
  autumnal pumpkin risotto, 230–31
  potato gnocchi with cauliflower-gorgonzola sauce, 112–13
  spaghetti alle vongole, 264–67
  traditional Russian Jewish gefilte fish, 108–9
fish
  bouillabaisse Marseillaise, 30–33
  and chips, 96–97
  miso-glazed black cod, 169
  New England, chowder, 66–67
  Peruvian, ceviche, 45
  sushi for a party, 286–88
  tacos, 293
  traditional Russian Jewish gefilte, 108–9
fish and chips, 94–97
  cook's notes, 96
  history, 94–95
Food & Wine magazine, 136
Ford Street Restaurant, Portland, ME, 153
Forme of Cury, 48, 150
France
  bouillabaisse, xiii, 28–33
  caramelized lemon tart, 150–52
  cassoulet, 38–43
  crème brûlée, 74–77
  onion soup, 179–80
  potato gratin, 212–15
  pot-au-feu, 222–23
  soufflé, 260–63
  tarte Tatin, 305
fried chicken, 98–101
  chef, 99
  cook's notes, 100
  history, 98–99
  Scott Peacock's, with tomato gravy, 100–101
Friedland, Susan, 58

García Santos, Rafael, 314
garlic
  croutons, 36
  palov (Uzbek lamb pilaf), 188–91
gazpacho, 102–5
  chef, 103
  classic Andalusian, 104–5

cook's notes, 104
history, 102–3
resource for Spanish olive oil, 105
variations, 103
gefilte fish, 106–9
cook's notes, 108
history, 106–7
traditional Russian Jewish, 108–9
German, Samuel, 60
German potato salad, 218–19
Gift of Southern Cooking, The (Lewis), 99
Gingrass, David, 193
Glasse, Hannah, 130, 233, 319
Glenn, Camille, 98
gnocchi, 110–13
chef, 111
cook's notes, 112
history, 110–11
potato, with cauliflower-gorgonzola sauce,
112–13
Godard, Misette, 28–29
Goethe, Johann Wolfgang von, 220
Greece
Molyvos moussaka with yogurt béchamel,
176–77
spanakopita (spinach pie), 268–71
Greene, Robert, 2
Gregory, Hanson, 82
Grigson, Jane, 74
Guinaudeau, Zette, 10
Gutierrez, Francisco, 75

Hal, Fatéma, 68, 69
hamburger, xiv–xv, 114–17
cheeseburger, 115, 116
cook's notes, 116
global variations, 117
history, 114–15
Harbor Village restaurant, San Francisco, CA, 193
Hawthorne Lane restaurant, San Francisco, CA,
193
Hayward, Sam, 153, 154, 155
Hazan, Marcella, 209
Hellmann, Richard, 217
Helou, Anissa, 119
Herme, Pierre, 61
Heron, Reed, 61
Hogarth, William, 232, 233
hollandaise sauce, 87, 88–89
Holmes, Oliver Wendell, 318
hummus, 118–21
cook's notes, 120
history, 118–19
perfect hummus, 120–21
Hyderabadi lamb biryani, 16–19

ice cream, 122–25
best vanilla, 124–25
history, 122–23
Ice Cream Machine Cookbook (Clark), 124
Il Pescatore restaurant, Bari, Italy, 264
imam bayildi (Turkish braised eggplant), 126–29
chef, 127
cook's notes, 128
history, 126–27
Engin's imam bayilda, 128–29
India
biryani, 14–19
curry, 130–33
dum pukht (cooking method), 15
garam masala, 16
tandoori chicken, 299–302
Indian curry
cook's notes, 132
history, 130–31
Malabar shrimp curry, 132–33
ingredients, specialty. *See* resources
Iran
chelo (Persian steamed rice with a crust),
54–55
Irving, Washington, 83
Italy
autumnal pumpkin risotto, 230–31
classic Bolognese lasagne al forno, 146–49
classic Ligurian pesto, 198–99
flour, *doppio zero*, 148
gnocchi, 110–13
minestrone alla Genovese, 166
Neapolitan pizza Margherita, 206–7
spaghetti alle vongole, 264–67
three-cheese polenta with mushrooms,
210–11
trenette al pesto, Genova-style, 199
It Happened One Night (film), 83
It Rains Fishes (Loha-unchit), 181

Jackson Heights, Queens, NY, xiii, 7, 244, 294
Jamaica
jerk pork, 134–36
Japan
miso-glazed black cod, 167–69
soba, 256–59
sushi, 284–87
Japanese Kitchen (Shimbo), 167
jerk pork, 134–36
chef, 136
cook's notes, 136
history, 134–35
marinade, 136
Jones, Evan, 3
Jordan, Michelle Anna, 210

kale, stir-fried shredded, 93
Kennedy, Diana, 35
Khan, Durru and Fauzia, 15
Kochilas, Diane, 268
Korean barbecued short ribs (Kalbi Kui), xiii,
   138–39
   cook's notes, 138
   history, 137–38
   marinade, 138
   scallion salad, 139
Kremezi, Aglaia, 174, 175, 176
Kroc, Ray, 115
Kuprin, Aleksandr, 20

La Cucinera Genovese, 196
laksa (Malaysian noodles, chicken, and shrimp
   in spiced coconut broth), 140–43
   cook's notes, 152
   history, 140–41
   rempeh (spice paste), 142
La Matandeta restaurant, Albufera, Spain, 186
lamb
   Armenian summer dolma, 80–81
   cassoulet, 40–43
   couscous with seven vegetables, 70–73
   Hyderabadi, biryani, 16–19
   Malaysian chicken and, saté with peanut
      sauce, 250–51
   mint-crusted roast leg of, with tart plum
      sauce, 242–43
   Molyvos moussaka with yogurt béchamel,
      176–77
   palov (Uzbek pilaf), 188–91
L'Amie Louis restaurant, Paris, 237
Langhella, Michele, 111, 112
La Poule au Pot bistro, France, 304
La Riua restaurant, Valencia, Spain, 184
Larousse Gastronomique (Montagné), 38
lasagne, 144–49
   béchamel, 147–48
   classic Bolognese lasagne al forno, 146–49
   cook's notes, 146, 148
   egg pasta sheets (pasta sfoglia), 148–49
   history, 144–45
   ragu bolognese, 146–49
Latin America
   sancocho, xiii, 244–47
   tamales, versions of, 294–98
   See also specific countries
Le Cirque restaurant, NYC, 75
leeks
   beef pot-au-feu, 222–23
Le Miramar restaurant, Marseilles, France, 28
lemongrass
   tom yum kung, 311–13

L'Escale restaurant, Le Goudes, France, 39
lemon, roast chicken with, and apples, 238–39
lemon tart, 140–52
   caramelized, 151–52
   chef, 151
   cook's notes, 151
   history, 150
Le Soufflé restaurant, Paris, 260
Levitt, Adolph, 82
Lewis, Edna, 99
Lincoln, Abraham, 123
Li Yu, 252
lobster rolls, 153–55
   cook's notes, 155
   history, 153–54
   New England, 155
   resources, 155
Locanda del Borgo, Pistoia, Italy, 111
Loha-unchit, Kasma, 181
Lohninger, Mario, 324
Lopez, Serio, 103
Louis, Diana Farr, 269
Luard, Elisabeth, 319, 320
luncheon entrees
   Claude Rigaud's Roquefort and walnut
      soufflé, 262–63
   Engin's imam bayilda, 128–29
   sesame noodles, 254–55

macaroni and cheese, 156–59
   classic, 158–59
   cook's notes, 158
   history, 156–57
Maccioni, Sirio, 75
Malaysia
   chicken and lamb saté with peanut sauce,
      248–51
   kari laksa lemak, 140–43
Malin, Joseph, 94
Malabar shrimp curry, 132–33
Mansouria restaurant, Paris, 68
Man Who Ate Everything, The (Steingarten), 96
Manzoni, Alessando, 208
March, Lourdes, 185
Mariani, John, 98
marinades, 136, 138, 250, 301–2
Markham, Gervase, 233
Martin, Mara and Maurizio, 229
Mata, Juan de la, 102
Matsuhisa, Nobu, 167
matzo balls, 59
mayonnaise
   rouille, 29, 31, 32
McDonald's, 115
McGee, Harold, 87

meatballs, 160–63
   global variations, 160–61
   history, 160–61
   lion's head, 162–63
meat marinades, 136, 138, 250, 301
Mediterranean Feast, A (Wright), 144
Mediterranean Street Food (Helou), 119
Melville, Herman, 65
Mexico
   carnitas tacos with tomatillo salsa, xiii,
     291–92
   Caesar salad, 36–37
   mole poblano with turkey and vegetables,
     172–73
   tacos, 289–93
   tamales, 294–98
   tortillas, styles of, 290
Middle East
   hummus, 120–21
   imam bayildi (Turkish braised eggplant),
     126–29
   saffron rice pudding with pistachios, 226–27
   See also specific countries
minestrone, 164–66
   alla Genovese, 166
   cook's notes, 166
   history, 164–65
mint
   chutney, 302
   -crusted roast leg of lamb with tart plum
     sauce, 242–43
   summer rolls with chicken, and shrimp,
     282–83
miso-glazed black cod, 167–69
   cook's notes, 169
   history, 167–68
   miso varieties, 168
   resources, 169
mole poblano, 170–73
   chef, 171
   cook's notes, 172
   history, 170–71
   Irene's, with turkey and vegetables, 172–73
Molyvos restaurant, NYC, 176
Montagné, Prosper, 38
Morocco
   bastilla, 10–13
   couscous, 68–73
moussaka, 174–77
   chef, 174
   cook's notes, 176
   history, 174–75
   Molyvos, with yogurt béchamel, 176–77
Muller, Claude, 213
Murray, Mae, 83

mushrooms
   three-cheese polenta with, 210–11
   tom yum kung, 311–13

Nagreen, "Hamburger" Charlie, 114–15
New England fish chowder, 66–67
New England lobster rolls, 155
New Taste of Chocolate, The (Presilla), 60
nuts, toasting, 173. *See also specific varieties*

Old World Kitchen, The (Luard), 320
olive oil
   rouille (mayonnaise), 31, 32
   Spanish, resources, 105
"On Agriculture" (Cato), 48
"On Human Frailty: An Object Lesson for the
   Butter Festival" (Chekhov), 20
onion
   Engin's imam bayildi, 128–29
   Hyderabadi lamb biryani, 16–19
   palov (Uzbek lamb pilaf), 188–91
   Susan Friedland's double-strength chicken
     soup, 58
   tomatoes, pepper, and, salad, 190
   traditional Russian Jewish gefilte fish,
     108–9
onion soup, 178–80
   cook's notes, 179
   French, 179–80
   history, 178
Osteria dell'Acquasanta restaurant, Genova,
   Italy, 197

Pace, Antonio, 204–5
pad thai, 181–83
   cook's notes, 182
   history, 181
   resources, 183
paella, xiii, xiv–xv, 184–87
   cook's notes, 186
   history, 184–85
   pan, 185, 187
   resources, 186
   rice for, 186
   Valenciana with rabbit, chicken, and duck,
     186–87
Paellas and Arroces (March), 185
Panza, Sancho, 102
parsley sauce, Argentinean (*chimichurri*), 274
pasta
   classic Bolognese lasagne al forno, 146–49
   cook's notes, 148
   dough (*sfoglia*, egg pasta sheets), 148–49
   macaroni and cheese, 158–59
   minestrone alla Genovese, 166

pasta *(cont.)*
    spaghetti alle vongole (spaghetti with clams), 264–67
    trenette al pesto, Genova-style, 199
palov (Uzbek lamb pilaf), 188–91
    cook's notes, 190
    history, 188–89
    kettle (*kazan*), 189
Patissier Royal Parisien (Carême), 260
peach, Elisabeth Luard's Scottish raspberry and, trifle, 320–21
Peacock, Scott, 99
peanut sauce, 250–51
Peking duck, 192–95
    adaptation of, 193
    cook's notes, 194
    history, 192
    Long Island duckling, variety, 193
peppers, bell
    classic Andalusian gazpacho, 104–5
    Molyvos moussaka with yogurt béchamel, 176–77
    tomatoes, onion, and, salad, 190
Perry, Charles, 300
Peru
    fish ceviche, 44–45
pesto, 196–99
    basilico di Pra (basil variety), 197
    classic Ligurian, 198–99
    cook's notes, 198
    history, 196–97
    pastas for, 197
    trenette al pesto, Genova-style, 199
Peter Luger steakhouse, Brooklyn, NY, 272, 273
pho (Vietnamese beef and noodle soup), 200–203
    bo, 202–3
    cook's notes, 202
    history, 200–201
    quick version with chicken, 201
pie
    apple, 2–5
    crust recipe, 4–5
    duck bastilla, 12–13
    history of, 2
    red wine pastry, 270–71
    spanakopita with wild greens, 270–71
    term, 2
    warka, 10–11
    world's grandest, 10
    see also lemon tart; tarte Tatin
pine nuts
    classic Ligurian pesto, 198–99
pistachios, saffron rice pudding with, 226–27
pizza, 204–7

cook's notes, 206
    dough, 206–7
    history, 204–5
    Neapolitan, Margherita, 206–7
Pizzeria Brandi, Naples, Italy, 205
plantains
    beef and pork sancocho, 246–47
Please to the Table: The Russian Cookbook (Von Bremzen), 25, 107
plum
    mint-crusted roast leg of lamb with tart, sauce, 242–43
polenta, 208–11
    best imported, 210
    chef, 210
    cook's notes, 210
    global variations, 208
    history, 208–9
    resources, 211
    three-cheese, with mushrooms, 210–11
Polenta (Jordan), 210
pork
    beef and, sancocho, 246–47
    carnitas tacos with tomatillo salsa, xiii, 291–92
    cassoulet, 40–43
    classic Bolognese lasagne al forno, 146–49
    feijoada completa, 92–93
    jerk, 134–36
    lion's head meatballs, 162–63
    New England fish chowder, 66–67
    Russian winter borshch with beef and, 26–27
potato(es)
    beef and pork sancocho, 246–47
    beef pot-au-feu, 222–23
    bouillabaisse Marseillaise, 30–33
    couscous with seven vegetables, 70–73
    fish and chips, 96–97
    German potato salad, 218–19
    gratin Dauphinois, 214–15
    Irene's mole poblano with turkey and vegetables, 172–73
    Molyvos moussaka with yogurt béchamel, 176–77
    New England fish chowder, 66–67
    Prussians and, 217
    tortilla de patata (Spanish potato omelet), 316–17
    trenette al pesto, Genova-style, 199
potato gratin, 212–15
    cook's notes, 214
    history, 212–13
    gratin Dauphinois, 214–15
potato salad, xiv–xv, 216–19
    cook's notes, 218

German, 218–19
history, 216–17
potato varietal suggested, 218
pot-au-feu, 220–23
beef, 222–23
boiled dinner, global variations, 220
cook's notes, 222
history, 220–21
poultry. *See* chicken; duck; turkey
Presilla, Maricel, 60
puddings
history, 225
saffron rice, with pistachios, 226–27
Yorkshire, 234–35
See also crème brûlée; lemon tart
pumpkin
autumnal, risotto, 230–31

Quanjude Roast Duck restaurant, Beijing, 193

rabbit, paella Valenciana with chicken, and
duck, 186–87
raspberry, Elisabeth Luard's Scottish, and peach
trifle, 320–21
rempeh (spice paste), 142
resources
Adriana's Caravan, Thai ingredients, 183, 310
Altaibat, for exotic rice, 19, 55
ChefSource, Italian boutique rice, 231
D'Artagnan, for duck confit, 43
Formaggio Kitchen, for Tarbais beans, Molino
Sorbino polenta, Italian rice, 43, 211, 231
French Feast, for Tarbais beans, 43
Jamison Farm, organic lamb, 244
Kalustyans, for imported basmati, 55
Katagiri & Co, *saikyo* miso, soba, and other
Japanese ingredients, 169, 259
Lobel's Prime Meats, dry-aged beef, 235, 275
Maine Lobster Direct, 155
MexGrocer, Mexican products, 298
rockfish, cheap, 30
The Spice House, for vanilla beans, 77
Sur La Table, mortar and pestle, 199
Sushi Foods Co., sushi rice, rice vinegar, and
utensils, 288
Tienda, for Spanish olive oils, vinegars, rice,
paella pans, and accessories, 105, 187
Williams-Sonoma, for blowtorch, 77
Revollet, Philomene, 213
rice
basmati, 16
chelo (Persian steamed rice with a crust),
54–55
darbari and domsiah, 52
grading of Italian, 231

Hyderabadi lamb biryani, 16–19
paella Valenciana with rabbit, chicken, and
duck, 186–87
palov (Uzbek lamb pilaf), 188–91
resources for exotic, 19, 231
risotto, 228–31
sushi for a party, 286–88
rice noodles, 142
kari laksa lemak, 142–43
pho bo, 202–3
rice pudding, 224–27
cook's notes, 226
history, 224–25
Middle Eastern, 225
saffron rice, with pistachios, 226–27
Rigaud, Claude, 260–61, 262
Rina restaurant, Genova, Italy, 165
risotto, 228–31
autumnal pumpkin risotto, 230–31
boutique northern Italian rice for, xvii, 228,
229
cook's notes, 230
grading of rice, 231
history, 228–29
resources, 231
roast beef with Yorkshire pudding, 232–35
chef, 233
cook's notes, 234
history, 232–33
with Port gravy and, 234–35
resources, 235
roast chicken, 236–39
cook's notes, 238
history, 236–37
with lemons and apples, 238–39
recommended brand, 238
vertical roaster for, 238
roast leg of lamb, 240–43
boutique sheep farms, 241
cook's notes, 242
history, 240–41
mint-crusted, with tart plum sauce, 242–43
resources, 243
Robuchon, Joël, 60, 96, 212
Rorer, Sara, 3
Rose Pistola chocolate budino cake, 62–63
Rose Pistola Cookbook (Heron), 62
Rose Pistola restaurant, San Francisco, CA, 61
rouille (mayonnaise) and croutons, 29, 31, 32
Russia
blini, 20–23
borshch, 24–27
Maslenitsa (Butterweek), 20–21
mint-crusted roast leg of lamb with tart
plum sauce, 242–43

Russia (cont.)
    traditional, Jewish gefilte fish, 108–9
Russian winter borshch with beef and pork,
    26–27

Sacher, Franz, 60
Sacred Food (Luard), 320
Sade, Marquis de, 60
saffron rice pudding with pistachios, 226–27
salad
    Caesar, 36–37
    scallion, 139
    tomatoes, onion, pepper, 190
sancocho, xiii, 244–47
    beef and pork, 246–47
    cook's notes, 246
    history, 244–45
    sofrito, 247
Santich, Barbara, 57
saté, 248–51
    chicken and lamb, with peanut sauce, 250–51
    cook's notes, 250
    history, 248–49
sauces
    Argentinean parsley (chimichurri), 274
    béchamels, 147–48, 177
    dipping, for soba, 258–59
    hollandaise, 87, 88–89
    mint chutney, 302
    Nuoc Cham dipping, 283
    for pad thai, 182–83
    peanut, 250–51
    ragu Bolognese, 146–49
    sesame, 254
    tart plum, 242–43
    tomatillo salsa, 292
scallion salad, 139
schmaltz, 59
Schorner, Dieter, 75
Scott Peacock's fried chicken with tomato
    gravy, 100–101
seafood
    bouillabaisse Marseillaise, 30–33
    See also clams; lobster; shrimp
Serious Pig (Thorne), 64
sesame
    hummus, 120–21
sesame noodles, 252–55
    chef, 254
    cook's notes, 254
    history, 252–53
    sesame sauce, 254
Shabbat Shalom (Friedland), 58
Shimo, Hiroko, 167
shrimp

laksa (Malaysian noodles, chicken, and, in
    spiced coconut broth), 140–43
Malabar, curry, 132–33
pad thai, 182–83
spiced orange, ceviche, 46–47
summer rolls with mint, chicken, and,
    282–83
sushi for a party, 286–88
tom yum kung (Thai hot and sour soup
    with), 311–13
Simmons, Amelia, 65
Simon, François, 212
Simonds, Nina, 254
Smollett, Tobias, 232
snacks
    arepas, 6–9
    buttermilk doughnuts, 84–85
    Neapolitan pizza Margherita, 206–7
    perfect hummus, 120–21
soba, 256–59
    chilled zaru, with dipping sauce, 258–59
    cook's notes, 258
    history, 256–57
    resources, 259
sofrito, 247
Sottomarino restaurant, Livorno, Italy, 264
soufflé, 260–63
    chef, 260–61
    Claude Rigaud's Roquefort and walnut,
        262–63
    cook's notes, 262
    history, 260–61
    variations, 262
soup
    bouillabaisse Marseillaise, 30–33
    classic Andalusian gazpacho, 104–5
    fish stock, 66–67
    French onion, 179–80
    minestrone alla Genovese, 166
    New England fish chowder, 66–67
    pho bo, 202–3
    Russian winter borshch with beef and pork,
        26–27
    Susan Friedland's double-strength chicken,
        58–59
    tom yum kung (Thai hot and sour soup with
        shrimp), 311–13
spaghetti alle vongole (spaghetti with clams),
    264–67
    cook's notes, 266
    history, 264–65
    Italian vongole veraci variety and substitution,
        266
Spain
    gazpacho, 103–5

Levante region, xiii
paella, xiii, xiv, 184–87
tortilla de patata (potato omelet), 314–17
spanakopita (spinach pie), 268–71
chef, 269
cook's notes, 270
history, 268–69
red wine pastry, 270–71
with wild greens, 270–71
spinach
Irene's mole poblano with turkey and
vegetables, 172–73
spanakopita with wild greens, 270–71
Spoonful of Ginger (Simonds), 254
squash (winter)
couscous with seven vegetables, 70–73
steak, 272–75
boutique shippers, 273, 275
cook's notes, 274
dry-aging, 273, 275
history, 272–73
pan-seared rib eye with Argentinean parsley
sauce, 274–75
steakhouses, 272, 273
Steingarten, Jeffrey, 96
Stendhal, 122
Sternburger, Lionel, 115
stir-fried greens, 276–79
Chinese greens, 277–79
cook's notes, 279
history, 276
summer rolls (*cha gio* and *coi gun*), 280–83
cook's notes, 282
history, 280–81
with mint, chicken, and shrimp, 282–83
Nuoc Cham dipping sauce, 283
wrapper (*banh trang*), 280
sushi, 284–87
history, 284–85
maki rolls, 286–88
for a party, 286–88
resources, 288
rice, 286
styles of, 285
Suwon Kalbi Factory, Korea, xiii, 138
Syria
hummus, 120–21

tacos, 289–93
cook's notes, 291
fish, 293
history, 289–90
carnitas, with tomatillo salsa, xiii, 291–92
tortillas, styles of, 290
tamales, 294–98

brands of masa, 296
cook's notes, 296
dough, 297
green chicken, 296–98
history, 294–85
wrapping, 295
tamarind
pad thai, 182–83
tandoori chicken, xiv–xv, 299–302
cook's notes, 301
grilled (tandoori murgh), 301–2
history, 299–300
mint chutney, 302
yogurt marinade, 301–2
tarte Tatin, 303–5
apple variety for, 304
cook's notes, 305
history, 303–4
Thailand
pad thai, 182–83
red curry, 306–10
tom yum kung, 311–13
Thai red curry, 306–10
cook's notes, 308
history, 306–7
resources, 310
of roast duck and pineapple, 308–10
Thorne, John, 64
Toklas, Alice B., 102
Tokyo Shokudo Central Mikuni restaurant,
Japan, 285
tomatillo
green chicken tamales, 296–98
salsa, 292
tomato(es)
Armenian summer dolma, 80–81
classic Andalusian gazpacho, 104–5
Engin's imam bayilda, 128–29
Molyvos moussaka with yogurt béchamel,
176–77
Neapolitan pizza Margherita, 206–7
onion, pepper, and, salad, 190
Scott Peacock's fried chicken with, gravy,
100–101
tom yum kung (Thai hot and sour soup with
shrimp), 311–13
cook's notes, 312
history, 311
tortilla de patata (Spanish potato omelet),
314–17
cook's notes, 316
history, 314–15
potato varietal used, 316
variations, 315
Traditional Moroccan Cooking (Guinaudeau), 10

index

Tragabuche restaurant, Ronda, Spain, 103
trifle, 318–21
    cook's notes, 320
    Elisabeth Luard's Scottish raspberry and
        peach, 320–21
    history, 318–19
Trillin, Calvin, 122
True Story of Chocolate, The (Coe), 60
Tschirky, Oscar, 86
Tselementes, Nicholas, 174–75
turkey
    imam bayildi (braised eggplant), 126–29
    Irene's mole poblano with, and vegetables,
        172–73
turnips
    beef pot-au-feu, 222–23
Twain, Mark, 3

Ujlaki, Tina, 136
United States
    apple pie, 4–5
    cheesecake, 50–51
    doughnuts, 84–85
    eggs Benedict, 88–89
    hamburger, 116–17
    macaroni and cheese, 158–59
    New England fish chowder, 66–67
    New England lobster rolls, 155
    Rose Pistola chocolate budino cake, 62–63
    Scott Peacock's fried chicken with tomato
        gravy, 100–101
    steak, 272–75
    Susan Friedland's double-strength chicken
        soup, 58–59
    vanilla ice cream, 124–25
Uslengo, Pietro, 196, 197
Uzbekistan, 240
    palov (lamb pilaf), 188–91

veal
    couscous with seven vegetables, 70–73
    Weiner schnitzel, 322–25
vegetables
    Armenian summer dolma, 80–81
    classic Andalusian gazpacho, 104–5

couscous with seven, 70–73
Engin's imam bayilda, 128–29
German potato salad, 218–19
gratin Dauphinois, 214–15
Irene's mole poblano with turkey and,
    172–73
minestrone alla Genovese, 166
spanakopita with wild greens, 270–71
stir-fried greens, 276–79
Venezuela
    arepas, 6–9
Veyrat, Marc, 75
Vietnam
    pho (beef and noodle soup), 200–203
    summer rolls with mint, chicken, and
        shrimp, 280–83
Villas, James, 99
Vongerichten, Jean-George, 60

Waldorf-Astoria, NYC, 86
walnut, Claude Rigaud's Roquefort and, soufflé,
    262–63
Warner, Galan, 61
Watershed restaurant, Decatur, GA, 99
Weiner schnitzel, 322–25
    chef, 324
    cook's notes, 324
    history, 322–23
White, Jasper, 64, 66
Wright, Clifford, 11, 144

yogurt
    Armenian summer dolma, 80–81
    marinade, 301–2
    Molyvos moussaka with, béchamel, 176–77
yuca
    beef and pork sancocho, 246–47

Zarikian, Terry, 46
zucchini
    Armenian summer dolma, 80–81
    couscous with seven vegetables, 70–73
    minestrone alla Genovese, 166
Zitoune restaurant, NYC, 12
Zuni restaurant, San Francisco, CA, 237

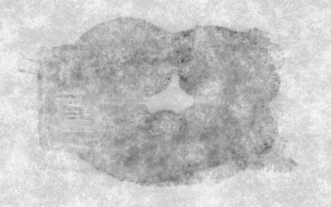